LESSONS FROM THOUGHT LEADERS

To

From

I wish for you a life of wealth, health, and happiness; a life in which you give to yourself the gift of patience, the virtue of reason, the value of knowledge, and the influence of faith in your own ability to dream about and to achieve worthy rewards.

– Jim Rohn

LESSONS FROM THOUGHT LEADERS

Receive Special Bonuses When Buying the *Lessons From Thought Leaders* Book

To access bonus gifts and to send us your testimonials and comments, please send an email to

gifts@lessonsfromthoughtleaders.com

Published by
Kyle Wilson International
KyleWilson.com

Distributed by
Kyle Wilson International
info@kylewilson.com

Lessons From Thought Leaders
ISBN: 978-1-7357428-6-1

Printed in the United States of America

EXCERPTS FROM
LESSONS FROM THOUGHT LEADERS

One of the most important things I teach over and over again is action. Action! It's not enough to have good ideas or the best information. There are a lot of average people who are self-made millionaires.

— Brian Tracy, Iconic Speaker, Author, Trainer

I was told to trust my intuition and expect miracles because they are everywhere—that everything has already happened and we just need to claim it. I took that to heart. I felt it meant if you want something, ask for it because if it's a strong desire, it is fate. But be careful what you wish for.

— Lisa Haisha, Speaker, Author, TV Host, Founder of SoulBlazing

Through travel, I've learned that life is the ultimate adventure. And the more I explore, the more I understand that the journey is never about the destination—it's about coming home to yourself.

— Leslie Vera, Retreat Leader, Casa Kallpa Healing Center

I learned what you put into something you will get out. Work hard and never take what is not yours.

— David Kafka, Broker, Syndicator, Investor

Your Crowning Achievement Is Our Crowning Achievement

— Dan McCarthy, Co-CEO, Artist, Coronate Productions

…to feel appreciated, people need to be seen, heard, and understood. People want to know three things before doing business with you: 1. Can I trust you? 2. Are you good at what you do? 3. Do you care about me? "Do you care about me?" was where I had failed in the past.

— Kelly Cort, Nationwide Lender, Team Leader, Connector

Everything you do today, tomorrow, and every day to come, happens first in your brain, period. To get better, you must think better, and to think better, you have to break your addiction to approval, and Brain Talk will do that.

— Sean G. Murphy, Mental Toughness Mentor, Founder NESS Program

Learning a system that's based on relationships changed me and my business. I just talk to my friend. I let them know I want to do such a good job for them, or whoever they refer to me, because that's the only way I'm going to get business.

— Earl Endrich, Realtor, Team Leader

Throughout our lives, a deep calling often arises—a whisper urging us to seek more, to understand ourselves on deeper levels, and to grow. This calling awakens a desire to explore the unknown depths of our hearts and minds, uncovering potential yet to be seen. My journey began with this intention—to create a life resonating with my true self.

— Christina Rendon, Therapist, Author, Meditation Guide

I realized a decade ago, I'm not paid to speak. I'm paid to think.

— Simon T. Bailey, Top Global Speaker, 10x Author

Resilience has become one of the most important things in my life. To be resilient, you have to be optimistic that you can handle anything God throws at you. Resilience has kept me going.
— Denis Waitley, Iconic Speaker, Author of Seeds of Greatness

A group of us were sitting around the lunch table griping, when out of my mouth came: "This is JUST a job, not a career." At that moment, I realized I wanted something bigger. Years later, I realized that a career wasn't enough. What I really wanted was a calling. A God-given, God-sized, God-inspired, God-energized purpose.
— Dale Young, Kingdom Business Power, Aligning Faith and Business

I didn't want to be a wealthy surgeon who was afraid of the stock market. I wanted to know how to build my wealth, protect it, and pass it on to future generations.
— Eberhard Samlowski, Former Surgeon, Real Estate Investor, Infinite Banking Coach

I realized, to be truly recession resilient, the wealthy know they need to allocate their wealth into alternative investments—those that won't rise and fall and that are non-correlated to the cycles of stock market and real estate investments.
— Patrick Grimes, Passive Investing Mastery, Founder, Speaker, Author

People ask how we like retirement. The reality is, yes, we are retired in that we live on our terms and can do what we want, when we want, living a life of abundance and adventure, but our destiny does not end there. We followed our "why" from the start, teaching to make a positive impact, and are now helping others learn how to leave a lasting legacy that will live long after we're gone.
— Randy Hubbs, Real Estate Broker, Investor, Professor Emeritus

I started my first business out of the trunk of my car and built it into a multi-million dollar business because I was able to build systems.
— Howard Partridge, International Business Coach

Regret and second-guessing don't honor the fact that we're where we're meant to be. Adding value and making a difference doesn't require a special degree or a trouble-free past. It does require the courage to fail forward, the tenacity to keep trying, and the attention to recognize clues pointing to your passion.
— Cheri Perry, Leadership Expert, Author, Speaker

You may be good. You may be very good. You may be a star, but you may not be aware of it. As I say, "If you are not aware, you are nowhere!" It takes a genuine mentor to uncover your potential and unleash it to the world.
— Ravin S. Papiah, Global Leadership Strategist, Legacy Architect

The number one lesson I learned from my dad was, control your input. When we intentionally choose the right input—what we read, what we listen to, and who we associate with—that changes our thinking.
— Tom Ziglar, Speaker, Author, CEO Ziglar.com

Live your best life, living fully and gratefully, building relationships, and inspiring and encouraging others. Show Up, Suit Up, and Get in the Game of your own life!
— Tim Cole, Colonel, USMC Retired, Veteran Honoring Expert

The true alchemy of Philotimo lies in its ability to transform us from the inside out. Living Philotimo is about the adventurous path of finding the courage to face our fears, to embrace our vulnerability, to serve others, and to live our truth.

— Sophia Stavron, Living Philotimo™, Speaker, Facilitator

Protecting our Republic and the American dream comes down to people having the ability to, first, focus on what they're uniquely good at or interested in and, second, prosper from that. I help people build a personal economy where they've got control over how they use their resources and what they choose to do in life.

— Gary Pinkerton, Former Navy Submarine Captain, Entrepreneur, Wealth Strategist

Without the right mindset, achieving anything of significance is incredibly difficult. Life and business are full of obstacles, but the ability to maintain a positive attitude, step out in faith, and believe in your ability to achieve great things makes all the difference.

— Bobby Adkins, Venture Capitalist, Oil & Gas, Technology

I believe that gratitude, attitude, and courage to do the hard things are critical in the pursuit of success, happiness, and fulfillment in life.

— Suzy Pendergraft, Business Owner, Broker, Residential Realtor

Rather than work toward a specific result, look around the entire landscape to see all sides of the issues. Remove the predetermined outcome and the idea of the adversarial relationship between their department and the others. When one takes out the melodrama and the "I must be right and win," a reasonable solution can be found.

— Howard Pierpont, Solutionist, Speaker, Confidant, Author

I believe with every inch of my soul that character contributes more to one's success than superior intelligence and that persistence beats talent every single time! The ability to persevere on a given path despite adversity and unexpected events is the key to achieving the desired results.

— Morkos Aziz, Real Estate Developer, Economist, Investment Banker

We're currently working on a global vision to release The World's Greatest Motivational Album Collection, a project that will be featured in the Guinness Book of World Records. Through this journey, I've learned that the secret to mastering your business brand is about making strategic connections, providing massive value, and creating big wins for clients.

— Roy Smoothe, The Music-Cool Branding Genius

"Go for no" is not a new concept. Where I like to shift the narrative with my leaders is, the goal is not a "no," the goal is "who do you have to be to change it into a 'yes.'" So my mentor always asks me—who do you need to be during that moment for them to say yes? We place so many standards and expectations on other people while we are the ones holding the power of "yes."

— Olenka Cullinan, Global C-Suite Coach, 2x Sold Founder, Speaker

I learned a lot about how the world really works, which diverged significantly from the Ivy League case studies I had read years earlier. I lost everything, including my marriage. Three things helped me get through this chapter and rebuild even stronger.

— Stefan Whitwell, Wealth Advisor, Speaker, Entrepreneur

More than 2,400 US Military died in the War in Afghanistan. As a Veteran and American, this deeply affects me. I've memorized the rank, first name, and last name of each of the fallen. Those 2,400 names were made of over 7,000 words, and I memorized each of them using the mind palace.

— Ron White, Speaker, 2x USA Memory Champion

Dyslexia has been a unique challenge, yet it has honed my listening skills and compelled me to develop strong coping mechanisms. These experiences have not only shaped my character but also strengthened my leadership abilities, teaching me the value of perseverance and adaptability. By the time I was 24, my deep-seated entrepreneurial spirit had fully emerged.

— Ron Jones, Entrepreneur, Author, Coach, Trainer

Life looked perfect: a beautiful family, a championship title, and a thriving business. Yet, beneath the surface, we struggled—financially, emotionally, and as parents. Facing these challenges taught me that true success is living with purpose and creating a legacy of love and strength.

— Dominic Lagrange, Expert Advisor, Coach of Visionary Leaders

I love health and fitness and always will, but to me, fitness means so much more than just the physical. We need to be fit in our minds, bodies, and souls for true health and wellness to occur. I knew I was here to help people heal emotionally, spiritually, and on a soul level, but first, it had to start with me.

— Jeanette Ortega, Celebrity Fitness Trainer, Creator of Bootoga

I could easily have quit at any time, and no one would have blamed me. After all, the company had been dormant for nearly 40 years. But, I hung in there. I knew I had something and just needed to study, learn, take my time, and most of all, NEVER GIVE UP!

— James Blakemore, Serial Entrepreneur, Chief Excitement Officer

Most investors base their perception of risk more on narrative than facts. I enjoy walking investors through facts with real-world examples to help them challenge what are often dangerous assumptions. My greatest satisfaction is seeing investors make better choices and not feel dependent upon their advisors.

— Andrew Rosenberg, Entrepreneur, Investor

Frank Sinatra was the greatest singer of the day, so going backstage and meeting him was not only improbable but also something most normal people would find intimidating. But not my dad! He wanted to show me something: "The greatest limitations in life are not external, but internal."

— Bob Beaudine, Sports Executive, Speaker, Author

It's amazing when you think of the big picture—when you're gone and still helping the people you love, even just a little bit. That's the undercurrent of what I do. People are not only getting a house, I'm helping their families for generations to come.

— Rita Gamil Kechejian, Real Estate Broker, Business Owner

Many people who started businesses outside of technology are now realizing that technology is deeply intertwined with both their business and daily lives. Knowledge of cybersecurity provides the peace of knowing that you are part of the solution rather than compounding a problem.

— Bill Malchisky, Project Rescue, Business Growth Enabler, Speaker

A legacy is built one conversation, one touch, one word, one person at a time. To me, a legacy is about listening. A legacy is about sharing. A legacy is about depth... staying a little longer in conversations with people. Legacy starts with the person in front of you.

— Kevin Eastman, NBA Championship Coach, Speaker, Author

When I share a message, I want to convey that hope is alive. It's not a strategy. It is something you've got to believe. Things can get better. I'm trying to be the antithesis of the news, which draws eyeballs because they highlight the negative. I'm trying to consistently share good information to help people improve their lives.

— Jim Johnson, Retired Basketball Coach, Inspirational Speaker

Adversity makes me stronger: it has been and will always be an opportunity to grow for me. I have also learned to enjoy the process. Each of us has a great responsibility above ourselves: we need to prosper to help our family, country, and humanity.

— Mai Duong, Real Estate Investor, CPA, Global Trade Coordinator, Manna Capital Group

After five years of passive and active investing outside of Wall Street assets, my wife and I were able to retire from our W-2 jobs. We achieved this by learning from others, joining mastermind groups, paying for advice from other professionals, reading relevant books, and listening to relevant podcasts.

— Jeff McKee, Alternative Asset Sponsor, Avid Traveler

Your true worth is determined by how much more you give in value than you take in payment. This is really the foundational principle. It sounds counterintuitive at first. 'Give more in value than I take in payment? Isn't that a recipe for bankruptcy?'

— Bob Burg, Speaker, Coauthor of The Go-Giver

"To whom much is given, much is expected." I am a true believer that the more you give and the more you pay it forward, the more you will be blessed and rewarded, both personally and in business.

— Kent Rodahaver, Real Estate Entrepreneur, Speaker, Author, Coach

Life looked perfect: a beautiful family, a championship title, and a thriving business. Yet, beneath the surface, we struggled—financially, emotionally, and as parents. Facing these challenges taught me that true success is living with purpose and creating a legacy of love and strength.

— Aaron Chapman, Author, Breaker of Molds

Sometimes it is so hard to find the good in certain experiences. Sometimes it just takes time. You aren't failing unless you give up, so I urge you to keep going! Find your tribe, and remember, the only thing holding you back is YOU!

— Courtney Moeller, US Navy Veteran, Speaker, Entrepreneur

Never underestimate your ability to redefine the limits of your comfort zone and accomplish something remarkable. By looking for opportunities to help others, you can solve problems, experience incredible personal growth, and change lives.

— Dr. Lee Newton, Optometrist, Value Engineer, Real Estate Developer

The power of the whole is greater than the sum of the parts. And that's exactly what the SEAL Teams live. We are completely synergistic, which is how we are able to do outrageous things with so few assets and so little resources.

— TC Cummings, Former Navy SEAL, Leadership Training

One of the easiest ways to make an emotionally-regulated investment is to have a long time horizon. And one of the safest ways to sustain a long time horizon is to have a portfolio that yields cash flow.

— Kunal Dewan, Immigrant Entrepreneur, Passive Income Expert

When I focus on taking care of my residents as well as my investors, my two main customers, great things happen.

— Sandhya Seshadri, Investor, Speaker, Founder Engineered Capital

In my journey, I had come to understand that all my "ouch" times I made worse when I held onto the emotion and the story that fueled it. What if, when a difficult emotion shows up, I ask, What is important to me? What really matters?

— Greg Zlevor, Global Leadership Expert, Founder of HopeMakers

I was an avid sports fan. We were stationed in Savannah, Georgia when I was called to participate in a mock newscast in my fifth grade class. It was Mr. McDuffie's class, to be exact. I played the sportscaster role, and I loved it. I had found my calling.

— Newy Scruggs, 15x Emmy-Winning Sportscaster

When faced with major decisions, imagine the worst-case scenario and plan for it. As soon as we can deal with the worst, the rest is upside! I believe this frees one to focus on achieving the upside and true financial freedom.

— Erik Mikkelson, Wealth Accumulation & Cash Flow Strategist

The shame of thinking that you're "other than" is dark. But when you tell the truth... you're truly in the light. From that moment on, my mantra became, "Where I live, you can't touch me." I had already taken the biggest risk I could take. What could anyone possibly do to me now? I was free.

— Carole Souza, Real Estate Broker, Entrepreneur, Coach

I realized the right mission for me was to find the most efficient way of building rental townhouses for these forever renters. Townhomes are as close to a single-family home as you can get. You've got a backyard, a garage, and no one living above you. And townhomes are significantly cheaper to build. I felt the townhome was the missing solution for America.

— Neal Bawa, Real Estate Developer, The Data Scientist of Multifamily

Live everyday with more intention and commitment. When time is spent, it is gone forever. I like to say, "God's not finished with me yet." I am dedicated to stewarding today's leaders through difficult decisions with business acumen based on biblical principles.

— Brett Binkley, Business Mentor, Transformed Life Enthusiast

When you prepare, you will be ready versus nervous. You can't play fast unless you know what you're doing.

— Chris Gronkowski, NFL Player, Shark Tank, Founder of Ice Shaker

How people live their lives is a result of the story they believe about themselves. When we speak, we distract, dispute, and inspire. We distract people from their current story through the presentation of our knowledge, which we gained from what we've experienced.

– Les Brown, Iconic Speaker, Author

Even an overachiever can only achieve to the level of their mindset.

– Linda Grizely, Financial Planner, Motivational Speaker

I dove into insane production, even through the COVID-19 pandemic and having my youngest still at home. I built a solid management team, implemented better job descriptions, and grew the fleet. In a little over three years, I increased my annual sales by $2.4 million.

– Craig Moody, Business Coach, Author, Speaker, Entrepreneur

Have you ever felt like you were worthless? Have you had life experience that kept you from living your life to its fullest potential? Well, that was me. Life's journey is full of obstacles and fears that hinder our goals, yet every day has potential for greatness.

– Teon Singletary, TSLE WLI Podcast, Motivator of Excellence

If you are willing to participate in the game of life, the opportunities that open up for you are boundless. The limits we perceive in our minds are created by us. The universe is flowing with abundance. You just have to believe it and take action.

– Carlos Delherra, Real Estate Investor, Entrepreneur

Discipline is the catalyst for confidence. Establishing consistent habits, building resilience, and pushing beyond what is comfortable fosters an unwavering sense of self-worth.

– Mary Hauptman, Entrepreneur, Real Estate Investor

Becoming comfortable outside your comfort zone sounds simple but is very difficult in practice. You must evolve and grow. YOU get to decide what you want your life to look like. Just remember, great rewards do not come unless there is great suffering and effort put in. It's not what you are capable of, it's what you DO that matters.

– Rick Gray, Real Estate Coach, Leader

The Special Forces has a motto: "Quiet Professional." Leaders must balance confidence with humility without becoming either conceited or insecure. We must see ourselves as more so that we can become more, for ourselves and for others. Don't downplay who you are or the skills, training, experience, and attributes you possess.

– Sam Robins, Army Green Beret, Security Ninja

If fear of failure is holding you back, redefine it. Every time you don't achieve your immediate goal, rejoice, because just the act of trying means that you've become a bigger person, you've increased your talent stack, and you've become more ready to take on the next challenge.

– Mitzi Perdue, Family Business Expert, Speaker, Humanitarian

In scarcity, I found abundance. Every small achievement was a triumph, teaching me to appreciate the simplest joys and to cultivate resilience. Life is an unpredictable journey, and today, where I stand was once beyond my wildest dreams.

– Dr. Raj Venkatramani, Physician, Entrepreneur

Consistency is so important. It's so easy to fall off, and when you do, you have to get back into it, and that's a lot harder. If you maintain whatever you're doing and are regularly inspired by it, you achieve more.

– Phil Collen, Lead Guitarist of Def Leppard

If you have been fortunate enough to make it to the top floor in your endeavors, your next greatest responsibility is to send the elevator back down. I am passionate about encouraging others to live the best lives they can live as the best version of themselves because I have been blessed.

– Clair Hoover, Investor, Entrepreneur, Speaker

We all have something special within us, uniquely formed from our experiences, passions, and successes, which give us the wisdom and heart to give exactly what someone else needs to receive. When we design our lives, investments, and businesses to serve a greater purpose than our own self-satisfaction, we discover the joy that comes from helping others and leave a far greater impact on this world.

– Anna Kelley, Impact Investor, Speaker, Wealth Coach

Everything starts with your mindset; it's all you can control. Think big, think abundantly and you will live with abundance. Be what others are afraid to be. Stand up for and do what is right, especially during times of adversity. Be your authentic self and let others be attracted to who you are.

– Alan Stewart, Real Estate Investor, Leader, Entrepreneur

In preparing for US Military Special Operations tryouts, I made up my mind that I was going to make it, and that I'd "Never Quit!" This commitment meant I would do whatever it took to succeed, which came at a significant personal cost.

– Ben Buzek, Servant Leader, Special Operations Veteran

One day, history may show that I kneecapped the career I worked so hard to build by following this riskier path. I am confident it will not show that I blew it where my life and sense of purpose were concerned.

– Jennifer Marchetti, Chief Marketing Officer, Speaker, and Coach

If I fail, even if I fail in front of the whole world, I'll be okay. They can say what they want. At least I'll know that I went all-in on my dream and did what I believed was right.

– Todd Stottlemyre, 3x World Series Winning Pitcher

If I didn't have the ability to speak up in the room that day and communicate my desire, I could have missed my once-in-a-lifetime opportunity. I could have been sitting in the movie theater watching Jersey Boys instead of on the screen IN Jersey Boys, never knowing that Clint Eastwood was waiting for me to walk through that door!

– Renée Marino, Keynote Speaker, Actress, Bestselling Author

Whoever your mentors are, realize that at one time, they were beginners. Everyone starts at zero. Everyone was a beginner. The key is to get started and to not compare. Run your race and you too will one day arrive.

– Kyle Wilson, Publisher, Marketer, Founder of KyleWilson.com and Jim Rohn International

Dedication

To all the mentors and influences that have shaped the lives of each of our authors.

To our families and loved ones who fan our flames.

To the lifelong learners and dreamers who dare to step into their next chapter with courage and wisdom.

Acknowledgments

A big thank you—

To Takara Sights, our writing coach, editor, and project manager extraordinaire, for your endless hours of work and passion in this book! Despite the complexities involved with a project like this, you keep the process a pleasure and always provide first-class results. A thousand praises! You are a rockstar!

To Joe Potter and Anne-Sophie Gomez who have put countless hours into designing this book. Technology and thoughtful design allow readers to receive the powerful wisdom of these authors. We are grateful!

To Tammy Hane, Brett Binkley, Sam Robins, Roxanne Bocyck, Aaron Nannini, Adrian Shepherd, Jo Hausman, Ethel Rucker, John Obenchain, James Blakemore, Mark Hartley, Dale Young, and Alan Neely for being our second eyes and proofreading the manuscript. We so appreciate it!

And to ALL the amazing mentors and world-class thought leaders for their contributions, wisdom, and insights to make this such a powerful book we're so proud of—thank you!

TABLE OF CONTENTS

ADDITIONAL RESOURCES

Order in Quantity and SAVE

Mix and Match

Order online KyleWilson.com/books

DISCLAIMER

The information in this book is not meant to replace the advice of a certified professional. Please consult a licensed advisor in matters relating to your personal and professional well-being including your mental, emotional and physical health, finances, business, legal matters, family planning, education, and spiritual practices. The views and opinions expressed throughout this book are those of the authors and do not necessarily reflect the views or opinions of all the authors or position of any other agency, organization, employer, publisher, or company.

Since we are critically-thinking human beings, the views of each of the authors are always subject to change or revision at any time. Please do not hold them or the publisher to them in perpetuity. Any references to past performance may not be indicative of future results. No warranties or guarantees are expressed or implied by the publisher's choice to include any of the content in this volume.

If you choose to attempt any of the methods mentioned in this book, the authors and publisher advise you to take full responsibility for your safety and know your limits. The authors and publisher are not liable for any damages or negative consequences from any treatment, action, application, or preparation to any person reading or following the information in this book.

This book is a collaboration between a number of authors and reflects their experiences, beliefs, opinions, and advice. The authors and publisher make no representations as to accuracy, completeness, correctness, suitability, or validity of any information in the book, and neither the publisher nor the individual authors shall be liable for any physical, psychological, emotional, financial, or commercial damages, including, but not limited to, special, incidental, consequential, or other damages to the readers of this book.

INTRODUCTION

Jim Rohn, my 18-year mentor, friend, and business partner would often say there are two ways to learn: your own experiences and other people's experiences. And, when it comes to the experiences of others, he would say to make sure you learn not just from their successes but also their failures.

I've always been a fan of biographies and documentaries about successful people. There are almost always many parallels in their journeys: challenges, defeats, and hardships along with perseverance, breakthroughs, synchronistic encounters, mentors, and just-in-time answers to prayers.

As the publisher, this is one of the things I love the most about *Lessons From Thought Leaders*! We get to learn from successful entrepreneurs, professionals, coaches, athletes, and experts—and not only from their successes but also their challenges and failures.

It's an honor for us to have some of the biggest names out there, including Brian Tracy, Les Brown, Phil Collen, Renée Marino, Tom Ziglar, Denis Waitley, Kevin Eastman, Chris Gronkowski, Bob Burg, Mitzi Perdue, Todd Stottlemyre, Simon T. Bailey, Ron White, Bob Beaudine, and more, share their wisdom on a variety of topics, including wealth, health, communication, relationships, investing, leadership, building companies, marketing and sales, lifestyle, mindset, creativity, spirituality, and so much more.

Creating this book was a BIG idea and undertaking, and it was a BIG responsibility to steward and share the stories and lessons from each interview. Editor Takara Sights and I ambitiously took it on, with the expectation of what the potential result could be.

We are excited and honored to introduce you to the authors of this book. Each one of them has made a difference in my life. Many are good friends and people I get to work with, hang out with, and learn from.

Whether you start at the beginning (or the end), I encourage you to read this book cover to cover or go to the table of contents to choose a name or title that jumps out to you. Also, feel free to share key lessons and quotes on social media with your audience and spheres of influence.

And tag the authors! We encourage you to let the authors and I know when a story, lesson, or idea impacts you! You will find contact info at the end of each story.

Enjoy!

Kyle Wilson
Publisher, Speaker, Author, Founder of KyleWilson.com and Jim Rohn International

"Learning is the beginning of wealth. Learning is the beginning of health. Learning is the beginning of spirituality. Searching and learning is where the miracle process all begins."

— JIM ROHN

KYLE WILSON

Sharing the Messages of Jim Rohn and Other Legends with the World

Kyle Wilson is a marketer, strategist, publisher, speaker, and host of the Success Habits podcast and the Kyle Wilson Inner Circle Mastermind. In addition to his 18-year business partner, friend, and mentor, Jim Rohn, Kyle has worked closely with Brian Tracy, Les Brown, Darren Hardy, Denis Waitley, Robin Sharma, Jeffrey Gitomer, and more.

Early Years

I grew up in a small town, Vernon, Texas. I was fortunate to be raised in a loving and supportive family. As a kid, I was always industrious and would go around the neighborhood selling different things. I got my first job at age 14, and I've been working ever since.

Unfortunately, as a teenager, I got into drugs for a few years. But, at age 19, I had a significant emotional experience that radically changed my life.

That led me to start my first business at age 19. It was a detail shop washing and cleaning cars. Then, I added oil changes and eventually took over running a service station. That led to opening Wilson's Texaco, a full service station located on a high-traffic freeway. I had 10 employees and was open 24/7.

Things were going well. But, by age 26, I really wanted something different. I felt compelled, a God Whisper, to sell my house and business and move away from the town I was born and raised in. I didn't have much of a plan, I just strongly felt the desire to move to a new and bigger place.

Plant a Tree

While making the decision to move, a friend shared with me a quote by Martin Luther. In response to the question, "If you were going to die today, what would you do?" Martin Luther said, "Even if I knew that tomorrow the world would end, I would still plant a tree today."

That hit me hard. So, I bought a peach tree, and I planted it in the front yard of the house I was selling. At the time, I had almost a fatalistic outlook. I felt our world was in some turbulent times. And, at times, I thought, What's the use?

Planting that tree symbolically helped lead me to a more long-term mindset that I still have today.

Getting into the Seminar Business

I moved to Dallas, and after several serendipitous events over the course of two years, I got a job working for a seminar company. The job entailed making 50-100 prospecting phone calls a day to book myself to speak at a company's weekly or monthly sales meeting. The presentation was designed to bring value to both salespeople and managers, and at the end of the talk, I invited those in the audience to buy a ticket to an upcoming seminar.

The thought of getting up and speaking in front of a group was terrifying to me, but I really felt I was supposed to give it a shot. I did everything I was taught to do. I made the phone calls. I followed up. I learned the presentation. I learned the close. And I went to work and gave it 100%!

After just one year, I became the company's top guy, but I was hardly making any money. The model was broken. So, I decided to go out on my own. I convinced Heidi, my wife at the time, to leave her job, and we began to travel the country putting on events. After a few years, we got really good at it, eventually getting 2,000-plus people in each city. We would hire Jim Rohn, Brian Tracy, and Og Mandino to speak at our events. We also enjoyed an amazing lifestyle traveling and exploring new places.

Launching and Growing Jim Rohn International

In 1993, Jim Rohn and his business partner split up. I told Jim I really believed he was the best speaker in the world and that I was a pretty good promoter, and I asked him for exclusive rights to promote and market him and his products. In two of Jim's previous partnerships, he had lost over a million dollars combined, so when considering another partner, he was reluctant. So I proposed the idea of it being my company. I would cover all the expenses and overhead, pay Jim's speaking fee off the top like a speakers bureau, plus give him a royalty on all the products I would create and sell. That way it was all profit for Jim with zero overhead and no risk of losing money.

Jim said yes. We did a handshake agreement which lasted for over 10 years until we finally put our agreement in writing in 2003. In the beginning, Jim did not have a customer list and had only a handful of products to offer. I knew I needed to go to work on both.

I now had exclusive rights to book Jim to speak and create new products. Within the first 12 months, I took Jim from 20 speaking dates a year to over 110 dates a year while tripling his fee.

Also, I wanted to create new products to take to the marketplace. The first was a viral quote booklet that went on to sell over six million copies.

My focus was to build the product line and a customer list using what I call The Wheel. Within two years of launching and building Jim Rohn International, business was booming, and I had grown a team of 20 people. I found that Jim was the gateway to personal development for so many people.

With my focus on list and customer building, I decided to also launch Your Success Store where I could market other speakers' products and book them to speak at the companies where I was booking Jim. The speakers included Brian Tracy, Les Brown, Mark Victor Hansen, Bob Burg, Jeffrey Gitomer, and many more.

I found each speaker and product would attract new people onto the overall marketing wheel. Then in 1999, I dove headfirst into the internet and was one of the first people to build a 1,000,000-plus email list. By 2002, I had multiple publications and over 300 different products (including digital) by Jim Rohn and other authors and speakers I was working with.

Working with my mentor, friend, and business partner, Jim Rohn, for 18 years (he passed away in 2009) as well as Brian Tracy, Denis Waitley, Mark Victor Hansen, Les Brown, Darren Hardy, Tom Ziglar, Robin Sharma, Bob Burg, and many more, going on 30 years now has been one of my life's greatest honors.

They have been the catalyst for much of the success I've had.

Selling It All in 2007

In 2006, one of the few companies that I felt could steward Jim's message and also take the other speakers and authors I managed to the next level wanted to buy me. They were also in the process of buying SUCCESS magazine.

I had over 20 employees, plus I was representing several speakers. Things were going well, but I was tired and burnt out, and my kids were growing up fast. I felt maybe the timing was right to hand it all off. I was able to negotiate a great deal for my team to stay on plus pay them profit sharing on the sale of the company. It felt like it was a win/win for my team, the speakers, and the company wanting to buy me. So, in late 2007, I sold the companies. I stayed on to help them transition up until the unexpected passing of Jim Rohn in December 2009.

Coming Back Out of Retirement

In 2013, I started getting the itch. I tested the waters a bit and knew it was time to get back into the industry that had changed my life. Being the promoter and marketer for others was my comfort zone. I didn't want to be the talent. But I found it necessary to come out from behind the curtain and start to share my knowledge and experience with others.

Today, I focus on three core things.

The first is my Kyle Wilson Inner Circle Mastermind, which is something I love. I started the group for me. Jim said who you spend time with matters. We have the best members who travel to Dallas, SoCal, and Philly from all over the country. It's an incredible community of heart-centered entrepreneurs, small business owners, investors, and speakers.

Second is publishing books like this one, *Lessons From Thought Leaders*, where Takara Sights and I get to connect amazing thought leaders with the marketplace.

And third is coaching, consulting, speaking, and my podcast.

I still get to be the promoter and shine the light on others and their talent through my Inner Circle, books, and podcast. But I'm now also the face (reluctantly at first) of the platforms.

I've learned that we all have a message of value to share. And I'm blessed I get to share others' valuable messages with the world!

KYLE'S THOUGHT LEADER LESSONS

Opportunity Precedes Personal Development

I believe that opportunity often precedes personal development. Sometimes we have to have something that gets us so excited that we decide to do all the things that will change our lives—that gets us up early, keeps us up late, motivates us to read the books, attend the seminars, have conversations, set goals, keep a journal, etc.

That's what happened to me when I found the seminar business and first heard Jim Rohn. I was inspired to become better. If I didn't have those opportunities, I wouldn't have made the changes and begun the new habits that forever changed my life.

Everyone Starts at Zero

Whoever your mentors are, realize that at one time, they were beginners. Everyone starts at zero. Everyone was a beginner. The key is to get started and to not compare. Run your race and you too will one day arrive.

Learn By Doing

I've always learned by doing. The more we can laser-focus all our learning on the exact thing we need to learn and find the best sources to help us, the quicker we can grow.

You can't learn it all at once. You learn it one step at a time. I got into the seminar business and I had to learn to cold call, sell, and present. I became Jim Rohn's agent, and I had to learn how to book him 100-plus times a year. I had to then learn to create and market products, to negotiate and write contracts, to build and manage a team, to publish books, to build an online business, and eventually to sell a business. You learn it over time as it unfolds.

What Do You Want to Be Known for in 3-5 Years?

A common exercise I often do (and take coaching clients and Inner Circle members through) is a very powerful centering question:

"Who do you want to be in three years and what do you want to be known and/or famous for?"

I truly believe everyone has unique gifts and the potential to be world-class in specific areas of their lives. But it requires clarity, focus, and commitment.

When you are clear on what you should and should not do, it will impact everything, from your daily to-do list to the books and seminars you decide to invest in and the people and mentors you choose to get around.

Q&A WITH KYLE

Favorite Quotes

In addition to curating and publishing The Treasury of Quotes by Jim Rohn as well as quote booklets for Brian Tracy, Zig Ziglar, Mark Victor Hansen, and Denis Waitley, I also had a daily email to 250,000 people: "Quotes From the Masters." So, I do love quotes!

Here are a few from Jim Rohn that changed my life.

"The major key to your better future is you." This was so powerful when I realized that the biggest influences in our lives are the things I can control. My health, my finances, my attitude, my work ethic, and who I spend time with, I get to control! Not the government, the economy, my job or boss, negative friends, or family!

"Be a student not a follower. Take advice, but not orders. Make sure everything you do is the product of your own conclusion." This gave me permission to take it all in, find what was valuable and applied to me, and leave the rest. There is no cookie-cutter. Get the principle that applies to you and personalize it to your unique gifts, skillset, and calling.

"If you want to be successful, learn to bring value to the marketplace. And if you want to be wealthy, learn to be valuable to valuable people." I caught that pass. And I realized for me to become wealthy, I had to be valuable. This dramatically changed my life. I became good at putting on events that connected talent with the marketplace. That made me valuable to both sides. I now build platforms to do this including podcasts, events, books, and more, connecting talent with an audience where both sides win. In everything I do, I want to always answer first, "How will this provide value?"

And one more that I'm not sure where I heard but I've always loved it. "Speed bumps keep out the tourists." It's just a reminder that everything in life that is valuable will have some obstacles along the way to make sure only those that are serious and committed keep going.

What is your favorite movie?

By far, the movie that impacted me the most going back to when I saw it on my birthday in 1993 and many times since is Groundhog Day. When Phil tried to get everything he wanted by beating the system or shortcuts, he only ended up frustrated, depressed, and hopeless. But when he started serving others and working on himself, he then became the person who attracted all that he wanted, including getting the girl at the end.

How do you recharge?

Alone time. Meditation and prayer. Nature. Playing sports and music.

Who are your mentors and greatest influences?

Over the past 30 years, I've had the incredible good fortune of knowing and working intimately with Jim Rohn as well as Brian Tracy, Darren Hardy, Les Brown, Mark Victor Hanson, Denis Waitley, Phil Collen, Paul J. Meyer, Bob Burg, Tom Ziglar, and so many more amazing thought leaders and humans. I'm beyond blessed.

Have you had any past challenges that turned out to be blessings?

All of them!

What hobbies do you enjoy?

Tennis, pickleball, basketball, guitar, hiking in nature, concerts and sporting events, and travel.

What books do you often recommend?

I've given away thousands of books by Jim Rohn and so many authors in this book. Giving away books has the power to change someone's life.

What would you tell your 18-year-old self?

That self-care is different from self-indulgence. Have health and spiritual routines while growing your business and being there for those in your life.

To learn more about Kyle Wilson's Inner Circle Mastermind, the #1 Bestseller Book Program, and The Strategic Marketing Wheel and to access over 100 blog posts and podcast episodes, go to KyleWilson.com. To receive over a dozen interviews by Kyle with Darren Hardy, Les Brown, Brian Tracy, Phil Collen, and more, email info@kylewilson.com with Interviews in the subject.
Follow Kyle on Instagram @kylewilsonjimrohn.

 Kyle Wilson Inner Circle

RENÉE MARINO

The Power of Authentic Communication
Broadway, International Speaking, and the Audition that Almost Wasn't

Renée Marino is an international keynote speaker, connection expert, and bestselling author who can be seen as Mary Delgado, in the movie Jersey Boys, directed by Clint Eastwood. She helps business owners and entrepreneurs communicate effectively to create genuine connections that lead to opportunities. Renée has shared the stage with Lewis Howes, Alex Rodriguez, Martha Stewart, David Goggins, Codie Sanchez, Mark Cuban, and more.

I'm a Jersey Girl

Growing up in New Jersey, you could often find me around the kitchen table with my family, eating, laughing, sometimes arguing, but nonetheless, communicating and connecting. In hindsight, I realize those moments are why I've always been so in love with people, with communicating and creating real bonds.

As early as three years old, I was a dancer. I loved performing, and I would sing and dance for my family, so I started taking dance lessons and from there began doing community theater. Once I stepped onto stage for my first vocal solo, I was hooked. I knew that performing was what I wanted to do for the rest of my life, and making it to Broadway became my goal.

Broadway, Rejection, and My First Break

Broadway is not an easy industry. So much is based on your "type," as they call it. I could be the best singer and best dancer in the room, but if the casting department is looking for a girl who is 5'9", I'm not getting the job if I'm 5'2". When someone says, "You look too Italian," or "You're not ethnic enough," it can be challenging not to take it personally, but to make it in the industry, you must develop the ability to move past the rejections. I've faced thousands and thousands of rejections throughout my life, but thanks to my father and mother who instilled in me a strong sense of self and the understanding that I am bigger than any rejection, I was able to move through them!

And then, in 2010, I reached my dream.

After touring the world for three and a half years on tour with musicals like *Cats, Disney's High School Musical,* and *Jersey Boys,* I returned to New York. I said, *"Renée, you still haven't gotten your Broadway dream. Even though these shows are amazing, you haven't reached Broadway."* So, I began auditioning, and *West Side Story* was my Broadway debut! From there, I would go on to do a total of five Broadway shows!

The Story Behind Getting Cast by Clint Eastwood

I then had the honor of doing my first major film, Jersey Boys directed by Clint Eastwood, and the story of how that happened is a true testament to the importance of authentic communication.

One Sunday afternoon in 2013, while playing Mary Delgado, Frankie Valli's wife in the Broadway musical *Jersey Boys*, I was on stage singing "My Boyfriend's Back" with my castmates. And who was looking back at me from the 10th row? The legend himself, Clint Eastwood. Clint was going around to all the different casts of *Jersey Boys* because he was going to be directing the film version.

At this point, I had never done TV or film before, so I didn't even see this as an opportunity. I assumed they would hire A-list celebrities out of Los Angeles and Marisa Tomei would play my role! That was... until they started calling people from our cast in to audition. And, they were looking for someone to play the role of Mary Delgado. At that point, I thought it'd be great to just get an audition to be seen, so I called my agent.

Weeks went by before my agent called me back: "Renée, I'm so sorry. I don't know what the problem is. They won't give you an audition for Mary, but they'll give you an audition for one of the Angels who sings, "My Boyfriend's Back." I hung up the phone so confused and disappointed because I was playing the role at the highest level I could be, yet every girl I knew on Broadway was getting an audition for Mary Delgado... but me.

After a little while of communicating with myself and feeling my feelings, I threw my hands up and decided to let it go. I'd still go in and audition for the smaller role.

The morning of the audition, the casting director asked me, "Would you like to sing 'My Boyfriend's Back' or read the scene first?"

At that moment, I heard this quiet, little voice within me say, *"You have to do this. It feels too right."*

I looked the casting director in the eyes and said, "You know, I was really hoping to read for the role of Mary Delgado."

I had no idea what he was going to say! He looked at me and said, "I was just thinking the same thing."

I did the audition, and I left there feeling so happy because I got the chance. That's all I wanted.

I went back to eight shows a week on Broadway, and two weeks later, my agent called again. This time she said, "You're Mary Delgado in the movie! Clint Eastwood loves you." It was one of the most surreal moments of my life!

The first day of filming was like jumping off of a cliff. I'd never been on a TV or film set before, but I heard that quiet voice within me say, *"Renée, you know what you're doing. Clint Eastwood hired you. Trust in your talent and leap."*

Every day I was on set, I would eat lunch with Clint Eastwood, ask him every question I could, and listen in a complete way. I am like a sponge, and I like to absorb every opportunity I can to learn and to grow. A month into the film, I was eating with Clint and one of the producers when they began talking about how the day Clint saw me on Broadway, he knew he wanted me for the role.

I put my fork down and said, "Do you guys want to hear a funny story? I never got an audition for Mary Delgado. The only reason I got to read the scenes is because I opened up my big mouth and asked!"

They looked at each other and said, "What do you mean? We requested you specifically." We later discovered that there was a middle-person, a casting associate, juggling a few films at once, who dropped the ball on calling me in to audition.

If I didn't have the ability to speak up in the room that day and communicate my desire, I could have missed my once-in-a-lifetime opportunity. I could have been sitting in the movie theater watching *Jersey Boys* instead of on the screen IN *Jersey Boys*, never knowing that Clint Eastwood was waiting for me to walk through that door!

That's why I love effective and clear communication so much. The confidence to speak up and ask for what I wanted allowed me to gain one of the greatest experiences of my life. Even if the casting director had said no, I would have been disappointed, but I still would have walked away with a sense of peace because I would have done everything I could have done.

After that, it's surrender, and knowing that what's meant for you will not miss you!

Writing My Book and Speaking

I love writing and have written personalized children's books for my nieces and nephews, because one of my other big dreams was always to have a published book.

So many of us who have dreams find ourselves talking about those dreams without taking action, and I was doing that. I got to a point where I said to myself, *"Renée, enough of talking about wanting to write a book. Sit down and write the first line."* On Thanksgiving Eve in 2017, with *A Charlie Brown Thanksgiving* playing on the TV, I sat down and began writing.

I knew I wanted to write a book about communication, but I wasn't sure exactly what part of communication and I had very little time doing eight shows a week on Broadway. One night, I was out to dinner with a friend, and as we were catching up, I noticed a family of five next to us: two parents, a teenage son, and two young kids under six. During the entire meal, no one spoke because everyone had their heads down on a digital device. I thought back to my upbringing, sitting around the kitchen table with my family, and my heart broke for this family missing out on beautiful moments of connection. That's when the light bulb went off. My book would be about authentically communicating in a world of digital technology! So I'd walk off the Broadway stage every night, sweating, with a full face of makeup on, and write in the offices of our crew members!

In 2019, that Broadway show ended, and I knew I was ready to activate my gifts of speaking, teaching, and wanted to continue writing my book. During the COVID-19 shutdown, I immersed myself in a course by Tony Robbins and Dean Graziosi on starting a business and I took action every day. I first began coaching people for free, and then created a course called "Connecting on Camera" to help business owners and entrepreneurs be themselves when speaking on video. That's how it started, and when I got my first book publishing deal and *Becoming a Master Communicator* became a bestseller, the business took off from there.

I'm so grateful because in my business I get to walk my walk. Right now, as a speaker, I don't have a speaker's agent, because up until this point I've been able to build a speaking business purely on referrals, which goes back to what I teach—connecting with people. Through my "C.O.N.N.E.C.T Method" program, I help people create genuine connections that lead to opportunities, which is exactly what I've done to go from the stages of Broadway, and screens of TV/film, to becoming a bestselling author, connection expert, and speaker!

I say it all the time. Do I think I reached Broadway because I was the world's best singer, dancer, or actor? No. But I believe where I excel is in connecting with people in a real way. It was an honor to have directors say, "Renée, we just love your energy and want you in the room with us."

My 2024 has been very exciting. I'm so grateful for all of the opportunities and to be amongst so many people I admire. Tony Robbins and Dean Graziosi launched a new program called the Mastermind Business System, and Dean interviewed me live on the launch so I could give my testimonial about how four years ago, taking one of their courses helped me start my business. It was a beautiful full circle moment. I'm also one of the speakers on the Aspire Tour and get to share the stage with some of the biggest names in business, personal development, and beyond. I was ecstatic to be back onstage in New York City, this time as the opening speaker for the Aspire Tour at Madison Square Garden. Grateful is an understatement!

RENÉE'S THOUGHT LEADER LESSONS

Connecting with Yourself—Mind, Body & Spirit

In "The C.O.N.N.E.C.T Method," I teach that step one is communication with self because that sets the foundation for all of your external communication. For me, it means time praying, meditating, journaling, grounding, and moving my body. Movement energizes and transforms my stale energy into fuel to allow me to focus, align, and connect with others in a real way.

Journaling is a simple but powerful practice. When you wake up in the morning, instead of rolling over to grab your smartphone, ask yourself, *"How am I feeling?"* Then, take five minutes and write the answer. Research shows writing, as opposed to typing, helps you activate more parts of the brain and gives you a deeper understanding of the information. Writing about how you're feeling connects you with yourself and gives you insight into what's going on within, so when you communicate with others, you're doing so from a more aligned and connected place.

We are a whole being. In the past, we thought of ourselves as having mental, spiritual, and physical parts. But really, they're all connected. That is why you get butterflies in your stomach when you get nervous. That's a thought affecting you physically, and that connection is always there.

Effective Communication

As human beings, all we want is to feel seen, heard, and understood. The world we live in can feel really complex. We have so many outlets for communication: text, email, video, Instagram, the news, blogs... We are inundated with information. Are digital technology and artificial intelligence gifts? Absolutely. But artificial intelligence can never replace human connection.

One of my purposes in life is to help people get back to authentic connection because I believe that no matter how smart, beautiful, talented, or rich you are, if you don't know how to connect with people in a real way, none of that matters—because it all starts with that human connection.

If you sit with someone and allow them to share their story, make eye contact, and let them know they're heard, you better believe you will positively affect that person because you are connecting with them in a real way.

Say Yes

It's so easy to hold yourself back from great opportunities because stepping outside of your comfort zone can feel scary. But outside your comfort zone is where the beauty of life resides.

Too often, I see people missing out on opportunities because instead of listening to their gut instincts, they listen to the loud chatter of the inner critic, that part of ourselves that's trying to protect us.

Do you think negative thoughts didn't go through my head in the audition room for the *Jersey Boys* film? *"Renée, who are you to ask for an audition? You've never even stepped on a film set before... They didn't give you an audition because you're not good enough."* I'm human. Of course they did, and they still do! But because I tune in and communicate with myself daily, I'm tapped into that quiet voice that's the truest part of ourselves. It always guides us in the right direction and reminds us that we can do whatever we want to do and that we ARE good enough!

Q&A WITH RENÉE

Would you share about your one woman show?

My show, *I Am Me Because of Three*, is based on the three people who raised me: my mom, my dad, and my grandmother. It tells a beautiful story about the lessons I learned from them with songs weaved throughout. My friend Dante Russo, a fantastic writer, co-wrote the show with me. Ron Melrose, an incredible talent and friend who wrote all of the musical arrangements for *Jersey Boys* on Broadway, also made the arrangements for my songs, which made the show a musical experience. We sold out the show in Los Angeles twice and once in New York City, and I'm so proud of it! The show is a fun, honest, and touching showcase of who I truly am!

Do you have a favorite quote?

"People will forget what you said. People will forget what you did. But people will never forget the way you made them feel." – Maya Angelou

Who are your mentors and greatest influences?

My father Frank, who passed away in 2019, was my greatest teacher. He always said to me, "People are always going to try to change you and try to knock you down, but you just always stay true to who you are and be confident in that person. The rest will fall into place."

He always told me that I had to speak up when I needed to, and every single day of my life, I'm full of gratitude that he taught me that from a young age. That guidance has helped me become who I am, and now, I get to help others speak up as well.

What would you tell your 18-year-old self?

There's no need to beat yourself up. Love yourself and know that the mistakes are where the juice is. The juice is in the journey, so stop being so hard on yourself and enjoy it more.

Have you had any past challenges that turned out to be blessings?

Being a perfectionist became a way of life. Beating myself up seemed like the only way to get better, so I was constantly taking myself down.

I got a C+ in reading comprehension in third grade and cried for two weeks! If I upset or disappointed somebody, I would feel horrible. As a performer, during rehearsals, or while onstage, if I messed up, it was torture! But I also think I wouldn't have had my successes without that quality.

I love and honor that inner child, that little girl who was beating herself up because she was just doing what she thought she had to do to help me, and it did help me in so many ways. But I'm now at a point in my life where that doesn't serve me anymore. I'm finding new ways to practice "Imperfect Action," and I like to say I'm now a "Reformed Perfectionist!"

I continually show up, even when I'm scared or doubtful and that's what "Imperfect Action" is all about and what I teach—to take action on things even when all the conditions are not yet the way you want them to be. Even when it's not easy, you are scared, or you lack confidence, keep showing up, and what's meant to be will be!

How do you define success?

Success is waking up in the morning and looking forward to your day. Success is having work/life harmony, where the work you do supports the life you want to lead.

"Everything starts with communication, and when we learn to master this skill, we become limitless!"

Speaker, connection expert, author, and actress Renée Marino's bestselling book, *"Becoming a Master Communicator,"* is a powerful guide for clear and honest communication in a world driven by digital technology. Access Renée's "The Secrets to Create Million Dollar Opportunities" on www.ReneeMarino.com or right below.
IG: @IamReneeMarino | LinkedIn: @RenéeMarino |
Facebook: @IAmReneeMarino | X: @ReneeMarino

 https://bit.ly/47vvCoz

TODD STOTTLEMYRE

Lessons From My Dad, Mentors, and Baseball

Todd Stottlemyre was a Major League Baseball player for 15 years, and he won three World Series championships. Today, he is a successful entrepreneur, speaker, and bestselling author.

Growing Up in the Shadows of Greatness

I grew up with baseball royalty. My dad was Mel Stottlemyre, who played and coached with the New York Yankees and was part of some of their great teams. He was surrounded by many future Hall of Fame players and coaches.

I'm so grateful that my brothers and I got to go to work with my father every day during his pitching career with the Yankees. We got to go to the stadium, put our Yankee uniforms on, be in clubhouses, dugouts, and outfield, and roam the field during batting practice. Monument Park was like our monkey bars.

Inheriting my father's environment, associations, and teammates like Whitey Ford, Yogi Berra, Mickey Mantle, Thurman Munson, and Bobby Murcer, and further, the way they went about the game, how they acted when they won, and more importantly, the way they acted when they lost, was a very special opportunity I treasure to this day.

My father meant so much to our family and was a true legend, not just in the sport, but also as a father and man. Dad constantly told us, "You need to be you. Don't worry about who I am and what I've done. You be you." I have now transferred that message to my kids. My father allowed us to spread our wings and dream and was always very helpful while we were dancing in his shadow. I am forever grateful to him.

The Decision to Go All-In

In 1989, my second year in the big leagues, I almost walked away. I was sent back down to the Minor Leagues the second time consecutively, and I was frustrated. At 23 years old, I had given my life—put in all the hours and made all the sacrifices, but I was still being told I wasn't good enough.

I remember driving back to the Minor Leagues from Toronto, Canada, to Syracuse, New York, by myself in silence—no radio. I had all my belongings with me, and many times, I pulled over, asking myself what I was doing. Even if I got back to the Major Leagues, was I ever going to be good enough to stay? Or was I just wasting my time?

I called my father, and he listened.

He was a pitching coach for the New York Mets, and he said, "Listen, I would love for you to be a starting pitcher here in New York with me, but not the way you're pitching today."

Then he said, "Man, you have so much more!"

He had belief in me when I had lost my belief.

I drove through the rest of the night and remember pulling into MacArthur Stadium around six in the morning. The sun was coming up, and I was the only one in the parking lot. I started dozing off then came to and thought, *I'm going to go all in.... I'm going to be the first one at the stadium and the last one to leave. I'm going to do everything I can to get better every single day. If I fail, even if I fail in front of the whole world, I'll be okay. They can say what they want. At least I'll know that I went all-in on my dream and did what I believed was right. If I succeed, I get to succeed in front of all those people who were telling me I'm not like my father and I'm not good enough!*

And, I went all in.

If I Would Have Quit

That was the only time during my amateur, professional, and Minor League Baseball career that I had self-doubt. I didn't have the vision that I would get called back to the big leagues, play for 15 years, or play on three World Championship teams and get paid tens of millions of dollars. I didn't know I was going to play for a Hall of Fame manager or that many of my teammates were going to go to the Hall of Fame.

I couldn't see any of that because I was where most people quit, not just in sports, but in life, from a marriage, job, or situation. It's a wall you run into where you decide you're just not good enough. You get over or around the wall or it becomes your limit forever.

If I had walked away, I wouldn't have come to believe that everything is possible. I wouldn't believe that I can create my own destiny. My mindset today is, if I'm not good enough, I need to grow to fit the dream.

My Greatest Loss in Life Was My Greatest Win

My little brother was 11 and on his third bout with leukemia when they said his only chance for survival was a bone marrow transplant. In 1981, our whole family got tested to see if any of us was a match. I was the closest match.

I remember the needles they used to pull the marrow from my hips, then how they put it through an IV into my brother. A couple of weeks later, he was bouncing around the hospital and doing great. They were even talking about allowing him to go home with a follow-up plan. Two days later, he went into a coma that he never came out of. Because his body rejected my marrow, I felt like the killer.

My brother had served others who had the disease every chance he had. He didn't have one ounce of quit, and he fought to the end.

I carried guilt and sadness for a long time. It became a problem because the feelings that didn't heal showed up in every aspect of my life. The darkness I was holding inside would come out when I was performing and competing. When that hate and guilt came out, I would turn into an animal. When something wasn't going my way, watch out. I was spiraling into black-out anger and going back later to apologize for what I had done.

The Toronto Blue Jays had just won back-to-back World Championships. I was 28 years old and a two-time World Champion. On paper, I had everything. But when I looked in the mirror, I couldn't stand the person looking back at me. If I didn't heal, this was going to control my life.

The Day My Healing Started

Harvey Dorfman, author of *The Mental Game of Baseball*, was a big deal in my life. He was a well-known sports psychologist and the go-to guy for Major League players. In 1993, Harvey taught me about the thoughts we have, how powerful they are, and how your brain and heart are connected. We spent 12 hours together that first day. My healing started when he asked if we could go back to 1981.

He asked me, "Would you do it all over again?"

I told him I would have.

Then he said, "Let it go, champ. If you would lay down all over again, then it's time you let it go. If you would have said no, then my answer to you would have been to fix it today and start changing the way you live your life. Start glorifying your little brother instead of crucifying yourself and everyone around you because of that situation."

In 1993, I started journaling and studying the way I thought. Harvey had me do a seven-day challenge of journaling every emotion. When I started to get to the point of intense anger, I had to write what I was feeling. Then we went through what I had written together. I don't think I would have turned the corner in my career if I had not done this work.

Retiring from Baseball

After retiring from baseball in 2002, I decided to take a year off. My family had never been on a summer vacation, and we traveled to many places.

In 2003, my neighbor, a director at Merrill Lynch, invited me to his office, and I walked out with a job. I decided I would give it a shot and learn new things.

I knew that teams win, and I had always accomplished a lot as an individual because I was a part of a team. So I built a team to talk to Major and Minor League players and agents, raise capital, and manage assets, and we did extraordinarily well.

In my fifth year in the position, I woke up, looked at my wife, and said, "This will be my last day." I couldn't see myself working in an office for the rest of my life. I went to the director that day, quit, and stayed 30 more days to meet with every client to help the team retain everyone.

Not long after, I got inspired and co-founded a hedge fund. I raised capital and ran the fund for eight months. I participated in and built a network marketing group and loved it because I was building a team and helping others dream. I was also involved in a lot of businesses from Wall Street firms to network marketing and owned a lot of companies. I was going from industry to industry, looking for my next Major League Baseball.

The Call That Led to the Book

My mother called and told me I needed to get to Sammamish outside of Seattle, Washington—now. My father wasn't well. I went straight to the cancer hospital. He was running a fever of over 105 and wasn't sure who I was.

The doctors didn't know what was going on, but three days later, my father led our family out of the hospital, refusing a wheelchair or a cane.

He said he wanted to take a drive through the mountains. As we drove through Snoqualmie, Washington, he said, "Someday I might buy a cabin up here."

That night, I couldn't sleep. All I could think about was how he could possibly see himself owning a cabin in the mountains when we just wanted him to get through the day.

Then, I realized that he was giving no power to his circumstances. Instead, he continued to be optimistic, fight the fight, live with zest, and see the good.

The next morning, I said, "Dad, I'm going to write a book."

For the first 50 years of my life, I used every example and lesson I came across for my benefit to become the best version of me. But I had never allowed those lessons to pass through me to someone else. I decided to dedicate my life to other people and helping them live their dreams.

I wanted the book to be relatable and about something I've lived through, overcame, and learned from. That's how I developed the nine steps, each was a lesson and trampoline to the next level of my life.

My Father's Passing

I was at my father's side when he died. He went to heaven with not one regret. My father did everything in his life he wanted to do. He lived out his dreams. This feeling came over me—the opposite of the hate, sadness, and guilt that entered my body with my little brother. For my father, I felt sadness and gratitude.

I decided I was going to test drive the word gratefulness—study it, intentionally be in it, and see what happens. Since then, that word has shown up everywhere because of my personal development from people like Jim Rohn and Kyle Wilson.

The night my father passed, I took out my journal in the guest bedroom of his home. I titled the page "Lessons," and started writing everything that I could think of, every situation I could capture, every lesson he taught me, every moment we had. I wrote until I had to stop. About a week later, I wrote a blog about my father and how he truly lived a legendary life and left a legacy. I captured part of that legacy in my journal because I was grateful.

TODD'S THOUGHT LEADER LESSONS

Opinions of Others

Sometimes we hold ourselves back more for fear of others' opinions than for fear of failing. Failing is scary, but the fear of failing in front of a friend who gave a different opinion can crush. I had to overcome the opinions of other people in baseball and in business. I had to remind myself that if I did not overcome that fear, I would not get there.

Never Give Up

In times of difficulty, we are given the opportunity to choose perseverance. Success is derived from continued progress through the lessons failure teaches.

When dreams face their darkest hour and there's no view around the corner, that's when many give up. If you get to your darkest hour, just remember you are getting close. That's the time to persevere. EVERYTHING IS POSSIBLE FOR THOSE THAT NEVER QUIT!

Creating an Entrepreneurial and Growth Culture

Our culture is very entrepreneurial. So, even though we're driving a company, each and every person who plays on the team needs an entrepreneurial mindset. It's like sports. In sports, you have to be great at overcoming failure. When you fail and then show up the next day as if you're the best in the world, you're ready to play the game. Same thing in business. In all of our companies, we aggressively tell our people to fail. Do not get bogged down by failure. Fix it and overcome it. Each failure will lead us to becoming the best company we can be.

Q&A WITH TODD

What is your favorite movie?

I love *The Greatest Showman* because it mirrors life. The protagonist starts with vision, makes progress, develops, and eventually succeeds. Then he ventures off and loses it all only to rebuild bigger and better. A lot of times when I'm struggling, I put on the soundtrack and find inspiration and strength.

How do you recharge?

Recharging is really a success principle. I'm a huge believer in it going back to my athletic career. In my schedule, I block series of weeks when I'm going to work really, really hard, and at the end of each of those blocks, I block time to get away and rest. I have to rejuvenate. It's also great time to think, dream, and create more clarity and awareness.

How do you define success?

When you're willing to prepare with every ounce of effort and persistence that you have in your body for a performance and then you're willing to go all-in on that performance, that's the day that you discover your greatness.

Todd Stottlemyre is a former professional Major League Baseball player, winner of three World Series championships, author, and speaker. More information about his book *Relentless Success: 9-Point System for Major League Achievement*, his online program, and his contact information can be found at toddofficial.com.

 Ready to find out where your dreams can take you?

JENNIFER MARCHETTI
The Thrill of a Second Act

Jennifer Marchetti is a chief marketing officer who helps companies grow through branding, marketing, and competitive positioning. She is an author, coach, and speaker on topics including women in leadership, career and life transitions, the importance of branding, and winning growth strategies.

The Push

I was forty-six years old and unemployed. When the company I had been with for twelve years reorganized to adapt to the changing real estate market, I lost my job as a chief marketing officer.

I was supposed to feel upset, lost, and maybe even angry. Strangely, I felt exhilarated.

I would miss—and forever be grateful to—the leaders, colleagues, and clients who changed my career. Deep down, however, I knew it was time. I needed this external force to push me toward my future.

Musical Chairs

My job as chief marketing officer (CMO) was to help entrepreneurs grow their businesses by delivering marketing, technology, and services as part of their investment in our brand franchise networks. Although the pressures of that responsibility felt constant, the exceptional people I worked with and for made staying in my role for as long as I did the better calculus.

In the earlier phases of my career, I was hungry for new knowledge and experiences. Once I hit a certain level, my professional development leveled off. I became too comfortable. In the blink of an eye, twelve years of my career (and life) had flown by.

As the first phase of the reorganization took shape early in 2022, it was clear that the strategy made sense for the company, but I would most certainly lose my chair. I didn't know how long it would take.

The corporate chess pieces were moving in a way that I had seen more than a decade prior at a previous company. Those changes had forced me to jump ship to my current job. At that earlier point in my career, I couldn't afford to be standing when the music stopped. I had to find a new job to replace the one I was going to lose.

This time, I had more flexibility.

The transition took several months. Thankfully, it gave me time to prepare: emotionally, strategically, and financially. I was ready.

The Unexpected Path

With that chapter closing, I had a unique opportunity. I had been working steadily for nearly twenty-five years. That effort brought bigger roles, more senior titles, and opportunities that surpassed my original career goals. In that time, I had become a wife and a mother. I had been fortunate to keep my dearest friends and to make many new ones.

I had begun a new phase of my life. My children needed me differently than they did when they were young. My parents were aging. It was important to me to spend as much time with them as possible and to be available to them should they need me. I wanted to devote time to the hobbies, creative pursuits, and volunteerism that had given my younger life so much dimension.

When I lost my job, I was in my prime earning years. The rational move would have been to find a new job and not miss a beat.

Instead, I decided to take meaningful time to reset. I needed to start over, but I had no idea what I wanted to do.

This decision was out of character for a person who had consistently followed the expected path. I went to a top university. I worked hard throughout my career and enhanced my professional standing as a result. I was supposed to keep achieving, earning, and pushing. I was not supposed to exit the race at my peak performance.

Reset

To make this opportunity count, I committed to architecting the life I wanted without the distraction of job hunting. For one year, there would be no LinkedIn posting or serial networking. While having the opportunity to reset was a privilege, I earned it by saving for decades, investing wisely, and being financially disciplined.

In that time, I finished writing a children's novel I began nearly twenty years ago but never had the courage or time to complete. I volunteered as a math and science tutor for kids who didn't finish high school and were trying to earn their GEDs. I took vocal lessons, enjoying the experience of being new at something. I started playing piano again, dusting off the music books I used in childhood.

I volunteered my communications strategy skills in my community. I finally got to be class mom. I invested in new friendships and reinforced old relationships. I strengthened my faith by becoming an active part of my church community. I became more present with my kids, family, and friends.

I started writing a book about professional women. In the process, I met dozens of exceptional, accomplished women who generously shared their stories with me. I launched my marketing and branding consulting firm. I earned a fraction of what I earned in the corporate world, but the work felt more rewarding because it was mine. I developed a clear vision of how to grow my business and was loving every exciting, frustrating, and character-building moment.

I am also proud to say I mentored and coached others who were going through similar life and career transformations. Helping others has been one of the most rewarding outcomes of all.

A Life in Focus

One day, history may show that I kneecapped the career I worked so hard to build by following this riskier path. I am confident it will not show that I blew it where my life and sense of purpose were concerned.

Here's what I can say: I feel more fulfilled than I have in a long time. I have invested more in myself and in others. I have given back to my community and to people who needed me. In my consulting business, I feel valued for my talents and expertise, helping me appreciate the skills I took for granted in my corporate job. I have become more fluent in articulating my personal values.

When I started my career, I assumed I would fully retire at sixty. Now, with the options of hybrid work and fractional consulting options, I am challenging that narrative.

I will select the work I do, which will broaden my impact and network. I will commit to continuous learning, welcoming opportunities that challenge me. I will lead a life that is built around volunteerism, philanthropy, creative interests, and entrepreneurialism. As a result of this richer experience, I can envision myself working longer into my life.

I may remain a consultant or embark on a full-time role that aligns with my new goals and sharpened values. As I write this, it's exciting not knowing what my professional future holds.

One thing is certain: I will fit my career around a well-crafted life filled with service, time with family and friends, and room for creative pursuits. I am grateful and excited for what is to come.

JENNIFER'S THOUGHT LEADER LESSONS

Community Service

When I was young, I had time to volunteer. As life changed, my free time became limited. Instead of volunteering, I donated money to causes I cared about, convincing myself it was a good trade-off.

When I began my current act, community service was the first pillar I built upon. I found an amazing local organization that provides tutoring for students trying to earn their GEDs. One student in particular made a big impact on me.

I was assigned to help a young man who had passed all of the other subject tests except for math. He had failed it twice. If he didn't pass the third time, he had to start the program over. We worked together twice a week for three months. The math was challenging for him because he didn't have a solid foundation. We devised alternative strategies for solving every category of problem. His dedication was extraordinary. On our last day, I told him I had never seen anyone work harder to achieve a goal. I was proud of him, no matter the outcome.

When I came back the next week, his teacher had tears in her eyes. He passed! I may have taught him math, but he taught me the more important lesson: people have infinite potential. Our paths to achievement may look different, but those with the courage and dedication to pursue success will always earn it.

Being of service to others can give us a renewed sense of purpose as we progress through our careers and lives. Helping young people achieve goals they may not have considered possible has been life-changing for me.

This experience has inspired me to expand my career. I now have a coaching practice as part of my consulting company. I will always be grateful to my students for this.

Financial Independence
- Invest in your financial future when you are young. Never stop.
- Compounding interest is a powerful accelerator to grow your savings. It is your worst enemy where debt is concerned.
- Whole life insurance is a unique asset class that provides lifelong protection and peace of mind, a cash value with tax-free growth, and low-interest loans to help you achieve your goals. Be sure to have the right disability and traditional insurance as well, or everything you have worked for will be at risk.
- Live below your means for as long as possible. You are funding a long life. Make sure you are prepared so you can live the way you want to live, even if the unexpected occurs.

Health and Wellness
- Protect your health. Start when you are young, before you need to play defense.
- In our youth, we may be more concerned with our looks or bragging about how little sleep we need. We may not realize that what we eat and how we treat our bodies today will demand payment decades into the future.
- The day will come when you no longer take your miraculous body for granted. Good habits will carry you. Bad habits will slowly sink you.
- To age is a privilege. To age with good health is to have immeasurable wealth. Focus on your health span as much as you do your lifespan. Without the former, the latter loses much of its value.

Q&A WITH JENNIFER

Where did you grow up?

When I grew up was even more important than *where* I grew up (which, incidentally, was a special place). I grew up in Montgomery Village, Maryland. In the 1970s and 1980s, young families poured in from everywhere to be part of the Washington, DC, government scene, and to build their careers across thriving industries. Our schools and teachers were exceptional. We had new shopping malls, restaurants, movie theaters, and skating rinks to help us spend our free time. Our parks, bike paths, community centers, and sports teams enriched our childhoods. We had friends our age in nearly every house in our neighborhood. I met my best friend when I was four years old. She is still the person with whom I laugh the hardest.

Every generation celebrates its merits, because every generation has them. I feel lucky to be part of Gen X. MTV, the fall of the Berlin Wall, Atari, John Hughes movies, amazing music, and other parts of our cultural heritage influenced us. So did our grit, imagination, and independence. We loved to play outside. We ate delicious things out of packages we would never touch today. We didn't wear helmets or enough sunscreen. Today, we serve as connectors in our families, communities, and workplaces between the Silent Generation and Baby Boomers on one side and the Millennials and Gen Z on the other.

This year, in 2024, my friends and I will celebrate our 30-year high school reunion. Like the latchkey kids of Gen X, my childhood friendships don't need constant care and feeding. When we see each other, it's as if no time has passed. In a way, we helped to raise each other. I am the person I am today because of their influence.

If you can, try to reconnect with a friend from your youth. The effort may help you rediscover a side of yourself you have forgotten.

As you fasten your helmet and liberally apply your sunscreen, remember that your future will stand on the foundation of the experiences and relationships that have shaped you throughout your life. Keep them close.

What books do you often recommend?

From Strength to Strength by Arthur C. Brooks: I read this to help me prepare for my career transition. It focuses on how we can reinvent ourselves in the second half of life. I used to define my worth in no small part by how successful I was in my career. I now use different metrics to measure my success: my impact on others and my growth from new learning opportunities.

Extra Life by Steven Johnson: This extraordinary book traces innovation in medicine, science, and public health that doubled the human lifespan in the century bookended by the Spanish Flu and COVID-19. It provided me with an impetus to use this extra life for reinvention and purpose.

A Short History of Nearly Everything by Bill Bryson: This book artfully uses clarity and humor to explain how important discoveries about life, the universe, and science shape our lives and world. Read it and you will be the most interesting person at the cocktail party.

What would you tell your 18-year-old self?

- Do the work on yourself. Never stop. Know your non-negotiables. Revisit them often.
- Continuously ask yourself, "How can I be of service to others?"
- Invest in your personal and professional development throughout your life. Your life—and career—won't necessarily be straight lines.
- Everyone can teach you something, even if you can't see the value in their advice or example right away. To learn, we must observe and be open-minded.
- Try new things because you want to try them. Don't always chase expertise: it will hold you back from having important, exciting experiences.
- Act with integrity. Your personal brand is your currency. Make sure it continuously increases in value.

To connect with Jennifer, go to jennifermarchetti.com to schedule a 15-minute introductory call for executive and life coaching, strategy and marketing workshops, and speaking opportunities on topics including branding, strategy, having a growth mindset, finding your purpose, and women in leadership.
Follow Jennifer: linkedin.com/in/jennifermarchettimarketing
Instagram: @marchettijennifer

 Scan to schedule a consultation with Jennifer.

BEN BUZEK

Just Don't Quit
A Soldier's Mindset for Success

Ben Buzek is a family-centric Special Operations veteran and personal finance coach. He's survived bull riding, 28 combat deployments, three vehicle accidents, and a parachuting accident. He thrives on living life to the fullest and helping others to grow through his experience, curiosity, adaptability, and trailblazing new opportunities.

Never Quit Mindset

Mindset is critical in every aspect of our lives. Whether we know it or not, so much of how we navigate life's challenges and opportunities lies in how we interpret situations.

In the US Military Special Operations community, "Never Quit" is the culture that keeps us going when times get tough. Henry Ford is credited with saying, "Whether you think you can or think you can't, you're right!" The power resides in our understanding of a situation and the direction we choose. One of my mentors, Brian Buffini, states "The power of a made-up mind is a force of nature." A made-up mind provides unparalleled clarity and direction.

At the age of 15, I no longer lived with my parents. I bounced around and got myself into some trouble while attending high school until, with the help of a few mentors, I made up my mind to change and found the military at 17. I struggled with the culture of basic training and thought I had made a colossal mistake... until I found Special Operations. In that community, I transformed into a leader and learned the power of sacrifice and perseverance. I had an amazing, challenging, and decorated military career totaling over 24 years.

One of my most memorable and life-changing stories from Special Operations about mindset would have to be my time in SERE school. Survival, Evasion, Resistance, and Escape training prepares service members who are at high risk of enemy capture to survive isolation and captivity. A common mistake people make in a survival situation is pursuing the wrong priority. The priority is not fire, shelter, food, or water. Instead, Positive Mental Attitude (PMA) is the most important need for survival. It doesn't matter how much food you have if your PMA has deteriorated and you decide to quit.

In the book *Man's Search for Meaning*, the author, Viktor E. Frankl, explains the life-or-death importance of mindset. Tragically, for the Jewish people forced into the horrific conditions of World War II concentration camps, the only thing that could not be stripped from them was their mindset. As a psychologist imprisoned in a concentration camp, Frankl found he could identify those who would survive and those who would perish by observing their resilient mindset. Survivors of the Holocaust made up their minds that they would survive, no matter what.

We each have a choice to maintain a level of PMA that keeps moving us forward. If we choose not to, the cost is easily falling prey to quitting.

PMA Made Special Operations Happen

In preparing for Special Operations tryouts, I made up my mind that I was going to make it, and that I'd "Never Quit!" This commitment meant I would do whatever it took to succeed, which came at a significant personal cost.

At the time, I was working a full-time job within the US Army, and my work environment was not conducive to an effective training schedule. I pleaded with my boss to allow me to start work later and stay later so I could train in the morning and still work a full schedule. Unfortunately, the needs of the many outweighed my desires, and my request was denied.

It would have been easy to quit there, but I had made up my mind! With PMA forefront, I woke up at 0300 every morning to complete the necessary physical training and ensure I was at work on time at 0830. I remember rucking (walking fast with a heavily loaded backpack) one morning at about 0430 when a gentleman pulled over on the side of the busy road I frequented to ask if I needed a ride somewhere. I responded with, "No, thank you, sir. I'm actually doing this on purpose."

Despite being exhausted at the end of the workday, I was determined to remain family-centric in the evenings. To complicate things, I had multiple training trips away from home and several injuries, causing significant setbacks during training. It was a very difficult time that challenged my relationships and work/life balance.

That said, when the time came to perform, I felt physically and mentally ready to show up and win. My mindset was the key to accomplishing my ultimate goal of serving in Special Operations. Incredibly difficult scenarios like this make meaningful the success and sacrifice I've had throughout my military service.

Turning PMA Back On

High-achieving people practice PMA and "Never Quit" often. However, it would be foolish of me to say that I'm always in that state of mind. What do I do when my mindset needs to shift?

A previous leader of mine stated that true character comes out in the darkest of times. In my experience, those with steadfast PMA have incredible character, but sometimes we need assistance snapping out of a funk or getting out of our heads. One technique I constantly employ is humor. Almost instantaneously, a quick laugh can change the mood, even during dark times like combat operations overseas. It is my go-to, and I know without a doubt it has saved my team's lives multiple times.

Another way I recalibrate my mindset is by changing my habits. If you have never read *The Greatest Salesman in the World* by Og Mandino and *The Miracle Morning* by Hal Elrod, I highly recommend those as actionable and timeless books that aid in transitioning to healthy habits. A disclaimer though: habits take a long time to develop through small, consistent steps and cannot be changed overnight!

Finding a flow state is another means of bringing myself back into a PMA. Getting into a flow helps my mind either wander or focus intensely on being present. For instance, I practice this by concentrating during my workouts on simply breathing, counting, or the mechanics of a movement. When I am in a physical fitness flow, my mind is sharp and I can clear out all the garbage that inundates me every day.

I believe a large part of PMA resides in the power of the subconscious mind. When one prepares themselves, visualizes, writes down goals, etc., they are actually opening the door for opportunity and success. I have had several premonitions through my practices of goal setting and visualization. It is remarkable, truly serendipitous when your subconscious mind presents a future image of exactly what will occur... and then it happens for you! Challenge yourself to keep a positive mindset and watch your world improve!

BEN'S THOUGHT LEADER LESSONS

Leadership

Jim Rohn says, "Leadership is the challenge to be something more than average." One of my greatest and most challenging life events was when my supervisor selected me over other supervisors and peers for a billet typically reserved for two pay grades above where I was serving. I felt a significant sense of responsibility. As a very junior and inexperienced leader, serving my team for three years in this capacity was one of the most rewarding moments of my 24-year career. Incredible results ensued, as I was able to enhance our team dynamics through one of my leadership tenets, to lead by example. In my experience, when authentic leadership is fortified with leading by example, success is all but guaranteed. I'm grateful for my team and their trust in very dangerous situations in some of the most dangerous places.

Serving

Serving others is my love language based on the book *The Five Love Languages* by Gary Chapman. I, admittedly, am not a great gift-giver. I'd much rather do something for them: help with a project or volunteer my time or expertise however I possibly can. I believe serving is associated with humility. It truly takes a humble person to put the needs and wants of others over their own.

Education

I love the Jim Rohn quote, "Formal education will make you a living. Self-education will make you a fortune." Although I am still awaiting my fortune, I am a big believer in creating value through learning something interesting. The secret is to be curious and take action, something my parents taught me as a child. To date, I've taught myself how to do so many fun and beneficial things like parenting, brewing beer, investing, and growing my understanding of Biblical scripture. Having a business degree from a renowned public Ivy school is amazing, but only through my desire to pursue growth and knowledge will that piece of paper actually hold value in the business world.

Q&A WITH BEN BUZEK

What is your favorite movie?

While deciding on one movie is next to impossible, I love the movie Big Fish because I can closely relate to Edward's desire to leave a legacy through his storytelling despite his son's disbelief. I cry every time I watch this movie.

What is your favorite song or who is your favorite musical artist?

While training for one of the most difficult physical and mental events of my life, the Special Operations hiring process, I found great comfort and motivation in the entire album *Waking the Fallen* by Avenged Sevenfold. I would listen to it while I worked out for hours. When the time came, we were not allowed devices of any sort, and having this album memorized helped me tremendously in maintaining my mindset and pace as I hiked for days through unforgiving terrain.

What are your pet peeves?

Wasting time! It drives me absolutely nuts when others are not respectful of the one resource we can never get more of.

What are a few of your favorite quotes?

I love quotes because I don't believe I've ever had an original idea, and if someone has already articulated a thought well, why try to change it?
1. "You'll never regret the doing. You'll only ever regret the not doing." – Brian Buffini
2. "The reasonable man adapts himself to the world; the unreasonable one persists in trying to adapt the world to himself. Therefore, all progress depends on the unreasonable man." – George Bernard Shaw
3. "When is the last time I let someone change my mind?" – General Martin E. Dempsey
4. "There may be no heroic connotation to the word persistence, but the quality is to the character as carbon is to steel." – Napoleon Hill

Have you had any past challenges that turned out to be blessings?

In my first book *The Transformational Journey*, I discuss the near-fatal accident my wife and I survived. This mishap totally changed the trajectory of our lives. Guilt, anger, losing the control I thought I had in life, anxiety, and depression were some of the many issues I had to work through. It was over a year before I found peace by working hard on my healing, especially my spiritual healing. I was blessed by so many remarkable people who helped me to finally accept and develop a relationship with God. Without the tragic accident and significant work through the traumas, I may have never realized that I truly am not "in control," rather, God has been my entire life!

What is something most people don't know about you?

I was part of a television production team that won an Emmy when we were in high school. It was a teen documentary series with a focus on teen issues and was marketed as "by teens, for teens."

What do you make sure you always do?

I always say, "I love you" to those I love when we depart or end a call. In the early days of the Global War on Terrorism, cell phones were not plentiful, especially for service members deployed to developing countries. We had calling cards and stood in long lines to hopefully spend 10 minutes talking to a loved one. We had to be concise and often only got to leave a voicemail. That might be the last time a loved one would hear your voice so, "I love you" was a must. We never truly know the last time we get to talk with someone, and life is, unfortunately, fragile. Let those loved ones know what they mean to you!

What books do you often recommend?

Think and Grow Rich by Napoleon Hill, *Cashflow Quadrant* by Robert Kiyosaki, and *How to Win Friends and Influence People* by Dale Carnegie.

Ben Buzek thrives on bringing value to others through maintaining a positive mindset and sharing his combat-tested leadership. After a near-fatal vehicle accident for him and his beloved wife, Ben found his Christian faith. Since retirement from the Army, he has developed leaders and coached people to financial freedom. To book or connect with Ben, email info@benbuzek.com.

 Scan to get in touch with Ben!

ALAN STEWART

Engineer to Entrepreneur
Be a Steward and Inspire Others

Alan Stewart is a Catholic Christian, family man, business leader, and 20-year corporate consulting executive turned multifamily real estate syndicator and investor of over 3,400 units. Alan's mission is to help busy professionals and high net worth investors create their own legacies through strategic real estate investment.

Excel Through Hard Work

From an early age, I was driven and always wanted to excel. If I wanted something, I had to work and save the money for it. My first jobs were mowing lawns. At 15, I worked at a farmer's market.

My parents always worked hard, running an automotive parts and repair business alongside my grandpa. When I was in high school, I worked for my parents, delivering parts and as an auto mechanic. I learned to work hard and do something right the first time.

All along, I was involved in church and was studying hard in school with the intent of scoring 100 or higher, if bonus points were available.

Sooner than Planned

I graduated third in my high school and was accepted into the engineering honors program at Texas A&M University. My family and I had big dreams of me becoming a doctor. My girlfriend since high school was attending college three hours away. We were pretty serious and talking about getting married after we graduated.

We weren't talking about starting a family at 19, but we did. When we found out she was pregnant, we chose life, and like any young, first-time parents, we were scared of how to make it work.

We managed to figure it out with advice and support from our family and friends. We got married at the end of my freshman year, and for the next three years, learned the value of being efficient with our time while we finished college and cared for our infant son.

Halfway through college, I thought long and hard about being a physician and decided that wasn't the right path. Engineering, the backup plan, became the primary plan.

My wife and I both did well in school. That's what I understood I needed to do to get a top job and support my family. I graduated magna cum laude with engineering honors and was offered a job at Accenture, thus starting my management consulting career.

Corporate and Life

At Accenture, I learned from so many smart, driven colleagues and clients for almost a decade. I worked hard to deliver client value and, over time, took on additional responsibility and was promoted to a manager of large teams. I continued my consulting career at North Highland where I took on more responsibility for very large projects and became an executive.

When my wife and I graduated, we moved back to the Dallas-Fort Worth metroplex where my wife and I grew up, and where most of our family lived, so our kids could grow up around their grandparents and great-grandparents just like we did.

As a family, we regularly attended church and were involved in several ministries. Our Catholic faith has always been a central part of our family life and has brought us so many blessings of friends, peace, love, and mercy, especially when we needed it most. Despite working all the time and traveling a lot while the kids were younger, I was always involved in their activities. I am grateful we had that time together.

I finished my 20-year corporate career as a managing partner at Gartner Consulting. In a nutshell, I credit my corporate success to working hard every day to solve problems and move the ball forward toward results.

Mindset Game Changer

Three years into my consulting career, I was searching for an alternative way to make money rather than trading my time—a way out of the rat race. I was fascinated by the concept of money making money but didn't have much money to invest. I was pretty tapped out just supporting my family, but I budgeted and started investing some through my company 401K.

In 2001, I attended a conference in Dallas, Texas, where Robert Kiyosaki spoke. Robert talked about his book Rich Dad Poor Dad, and the benefits of investing in rental real estate. He said, instead of working for money to pay bills, you need to buy assets that produce income to pay your bills for you. This was the beginning of my real financial education, a pragmatic financial education not taught in schools. My mindset had changed forever. I started thinking bigger.

I knew I wanted to do rental real estate for cash flow but was afraid. Analysis paralysis started. I lost a good chunk of my 401K during the 2000-2001 recession. I didn't want to fail and didn't know where to start. So between 2001-2005, I attended more investing conferences.

Becoming a Real Estate Investor

In 2006, I attended another conference in Dallas, Texas. One of the speakers, a successful single-family investor, said that rental houses were great, but single-family wholesaling was way more fun. Even better, he offered a training program to get you started. That's what I was looking for, so I signed up.

I started building my wholesaling business nights and weekends. I attended boot camps, bought lead lists, sent mailers, put out bandit signs, and talked with motivated sellers. A few years later, I had basically created a second job for myself that was costing me precious time and wasn't making money. My corporate job paid way better.

In early 2008, I thought I needed to free up some cash to buy some rental houses, and the only way for me to do that would be to liquidate my 401K I still had from when I worked at Accenture, almost all the money I had in the world. I wasn't ready.

The 2008 Crash

In April of 2008, the stock market crashed. I initially thought my 401K would come back up, but it kept going down until, in late 2008, it was down 60%. I had a big pit in my stomach. I'd "let" my professionally managed 401K be decimated by a stock market crash twice now. I couldn't even think about cashing it in, so I focused on my job.

I never stopped learning. I kept listening to real estate investment radio shows and feeding my mind what was possible. Even though I'd been at it for many years with little success, I wanted to be a real estate investor. This really seemed like the way out of the rat race.

Breakthrough

In 2012, a coworker invited me to a meeting about real estate investing. It was great, a local real estate investing company that offered mentoring in exactly what I wanted to do. I signed up that night.

A little bit of serendipity never hurt anyone—my 401K had also just returned to the same value it was four years ago before the 2008 crash.

Through this mentoring, I was introduced to multifamily investing. I always thought some big company or rich person bought apartment complexes. It turns out, many are owned by small groups of individual investors like you and me.

So, I liquidated my 401K and paid the tax. Lots of people thought I was crazy. I've come to embrace being called "crazy." I've found that it tells me I'm on the right track of thinking bigger, growing, and achieving bigger goals in the process. At the time, it was an easy decision for me. That's what I had to do to get started. At that point, I had been in management consulting for 14 years and had risen to executive. I was working long, hard weeks and saw real estate investing as my way out of the rat race.

Make a Decision and Take Action

The best financial decisions I ever made were investing in my financial education and in a multifamily mentor whose experience I could leverage to help me go faster with less risk.

Then the most important thing happened; I started taking action—consistent, small actions every day toward my goals.

It took me six years of early mornings, late nights, and weekends, but my team built a multifamily portfolio of over 3,400 units across 17 properties which I syndicated or invested in, and I finally got out of the rat race.

Thinking Bigger and Reaching the Next Level

Part of thinking bigger often means being a contrarian. What the "masses" think is not always correct. My first eight years in multifamily investing were focused on class B and C value-add apartment deals. Some were really difficult, but we bought and operated them right, and they turned out to be great investment successes.

Over the last several years, I have continued expanding my mindset. I realized what university endowments, institutions, and family offices already knew; that A-class multifamily properties could have better risk-adjusted returns than B and C-class assets.

I finally decided I was going to stop talking about it and start doing it. In 2021, my partners and I bought my first true, A-class, 2016-built, multifamily property in Uptown Dallas, Texas.

It wasn't easy. When I was working on the deal, it was so much bigger, so much newer, so much nicer than anything I had done before. Even so, my partners and I decided to go all-in to make it happen.

We are proud to still own the Uptown Dallas property today and have since bought another large A-class, 2019-built, multifamily property in Fort Worth, Texas' Medical District.

Creating Legacy

My wife and I have now been married for more than 28 years and have two adult children we love very much. Our son is a semiconductor engineer and married, and our daughter recently graduated with a degree in interior design.

My family is very important to me, and my love for them drives me to learn, grow, and expand my mindset so I may be a good leader and an example of the reality that anything is possible with hard work, focus, and consistent action over time.

I want to set an example that is worthy of my kids and others I influence. I intend to continue building my businesses and my real estate investment portfolio to create a legacy for my family, and further, to provide quality investment opportunities that create a path for busy professionals to create their own family legacies.

ALAN'S THOUGHT LEADER LESSONS

Investing

Take ownership of your financial destiny. Your job or the government will not do nearly as good of a job of planning for your financial future as you will for the simple fact that it is your life, and you care more. Some people are called to be employees, and some people are called to be entrepreneurs. One is not necessarily better than the other; be honest with yourself about what you like to do and, more importantly, what you are willing to do. In any case, live at a standard where you are not living paycheck to paycheck and where you have money left over for quality investments.

I prefer investing in hard assets like real estate and other businesses that produce cash flow rather than the stock market. A good rule of thumb I've heard is the concept of tithing. Give the first 10% of your earnings to your church and other worthy causes. Invest the second 10% of your earnings in your financial future. When done this way, starting early and consistently, over time, the power of compound interest will really amplify your investments.

Family and Parenting

Have God at the center of your family and pray together. Be a loving parent and be present (i.e., not on your phone while spending time with family). Your actions make it clear what is more important to you. Play with your kids and be involved in their school and extracurricular activities. Be a leader by example through service at church and in your kids' activities. Let your kids struggle and figure it out; they are going to have to sometime and they won't always be kids at home. Your kids will probably not listen to you and will probably make the same mistakes that you, your parents, and your grandparents made. Remember, we are all humans.

Mindset

Everything starts with your mindset; it's all you can control. Think big, think abundantly and you will live with abundance. Be what others are afraid to be. Stand up for and do what is right, especially during times of adversity. Be your authentic self and let others be attracted to who you are. Remove toxic and scarcity-minded people from your life and don't worry about what they think about you; haters are going to hate, and you can't change them. Always start the day with your top three intentions / goals to focus on for the day and don't let the shiny objects and other distractions take you off your focus.

Resilience

Life can be full of ups, downs, curveballs and what may seem like insurmountable challenges at times. That's when resilience is necessary. Take a breath, take the very first small step, and just focus on moving the ball forward a little each day. It's amazing what you can achieve with small, consistent actions over time, especially over five to 10 years.

Travel

Get out of your bubble and experience different cultures, food, and geographies. Go see the ocean, put your toes in the sand, smell the salt air, and watch the sunset. Go see the mountains, waterfalls, wildflowers, and views that go on forever like you're on top of the world. Go to a US national park. Go see ancient cities; there are relatively "new" things in ancient cities like a 400-year-old clock tower that is older than the USA. Go see priceless art and take in what the artist is trying to convey. Wherever you go, strive to get the local experience—stay in a locally-owned hotel, try the cuisine, visit farmers' markets, talk with local craftsmen, ask locals where their favorite beach or restaurant is, and participate in festivals and traditions.

Q&A WITH ALAN

What are your pet peeves?

People who always want the no-risk, no-work, overnight success easy button. Every overnight success I've met took at least 10 years. Doing something right usually takes effort and time.

What are a few of your favorite quotes?

- "You don't really know someone until money is involved." – Zig Ziglar
- "Opportunity is missed by most people because it is dressed in overalls and looks like work." – Thomas Edison
- "I know one thing: it's either a feature or a user error." – Alan Stewart

What is some of the best advice you've received?

You can't change other people. All you can control are your actions; be your authentic self and do what you know is right regardless of what other people think or do.

Be present and happy with who you are today; you can't change the past, and the future hasn't happened yet. If you can't be happy in the present, you will never be happy in the future.

What do you consider your superpower?

Having a vision and the perseverance to keep working at it until I figure it out or get it done.

What books do you often recommend?

Rich Dad Poor Dad by Robert Kiyosaki. *The 5 Love Languages* by Gary Chapman. The Bible.

What would you tell your 18-year-old self?

Allow yourself to do it wrong. Don't expect to always get it right; that will prevent you from doing anything. Just take the first small step when trying to solve a big challenge; break the inertia and don't succumb to analysis paralysis.

To learn more about real-life multifamily investing, visit AlanStewart.com. To apply to be a part of upcoming passive income investment opportunities and start your journey to financial freedom, contact Alan at info@alanstewart.com or visit AlanStewart.com.

 Connect with Alan

ANNA KELLEY

From Girl in Poverty to Real Estate Millionaire Mom

Anna Kelley, President of ReiMom & Greater Purpose Capital LLC, has active ownership in over $300M of real estate. She is a sought-after real estate consultant, coach, speaker, and author, and a former private banker. Anna invests in apartments to make a meaningful impact for her investors and residents and enjoys changing lives through her real estate ventures.

Escaping Poverty and Abuse

Statistically, you would not expect a girl growing up in Section 8 housing to escape poverty. By the grace of God, I beat the odds.

When I was six, my pregnant mother, my sister, and I left to escape another night of abuse at the hands of my stepfather. We moved in with my grandparents until she found a job as a leasing agent in a Section 8 apartment complex.

A free apartment and food stamps were not enough for us to survive. At nine years old, I began watching my siblings late at night while my mom waitressed. Bad things happened in apartments like ours, and I was scared. The free-spirited little girl, who just wanted to have fun, had to be much more responsible than other kids. I grew up fast!

My mother loved us and did her best to provide, but if I wanted something, I had to make my own money. I sold candy at school, made and sold things door-to-door, and got a job in eighth grade.

My mom remarried and had more children, and the cycle of alcohol, drugs, and abuse continued. We slept in battered women's shelters and on family members' couches multiple times. My only escape was school and music, where I worked hard to be the best at everything I did so I could have a better life "one day." While I tried to fit in, the whispers from kids about how poor I was pierced my heart with shame, destroyed my confidence, and weakened my hope that I could escape the life I was given for one more like theirs.

Determined to Forge a Better Future

At 15, I called my father and stepmother and asked to move in with them. Leaving my mother and siblings was one of the hardest decisions I have ever made. I feared that if I didn't stay to protect them, they would end up dead. The guilt, responsibility, sadness, and fear for what I was leaving behind were at war with the relief, freedom, joy, and hope for the future. I longed for a better life and had a profound sense God would provide it.

Settled in a new school, town, and family dynamic, I discovered that people with higher-paying jobs could afford good food and nicer things, life without drugs and alcohol was more peaceful, and putting Jesus first was the key to an abundant life. My experiences made me determined to do whatever it took to forge a better future.

I became a determined overachiever. I graduated high school and college early while working a demanding full-time job. I then became a private banker at Bank of America and won the award for #1 private banker in Texas. Finally, I landed a high-paying job at AIG. I was convinced my problems were behind me.

New Challenges and Successes

At 25, I got married, and three years later, we had our first child. While I was thriving in my career, I had a deep desire to stay home with my baby. My husband had a $120,000 college debt, and we could not survive on one income. It broke my heart to put my baby in daycare, and as a latchkey child myself, I did not want to be an absent mom. I prayed every day for a way for me to stay home, and HGTV convinced me flipping houses was the way!

With our new baby in tow, we flipped a Victorian house. During the remodel, my husband lost his job and we were scraping by. The flip lost $10,000. I was depressed and wrestled with God through many tears. I couldn't understand His plan.

A year later, we moved to Pennsylvania with our two babies so my husband could start his chiropractic business. We bought a commercial building with three apartments to help cover the mortgage. AIG allowed me to work from home, and we moved in with my in-laws. We later bought a four-unit apartment so we could live in one unit with our mortgage paid by the others. It was cramped and a far cry from our home in Texas.

Just when we were getting ahead, the economy collapsed and AIG was on the verge of bankruptcy. I lost over $200,000 in my 401(k) and borrowed the last $50,000 to buy another four-unit apartment. If I lost my job, at least we would have more rental income. I could clearly see God's protection and provision through this time. Still, I longed to stay home with my babies and felt powerless to make it happen.

Investing in Apartments

After having a few small properties, I was excited to find a conference claiming I could buy large apartments with none of my own money. I just KNEW buying apartments was the answer. I signed up for coaching and was offered an amazing job working from home as a coach. The program's owner would also help me buy a large apartment that would allow me to be financially free. My prayers were answered… I thought. Just before I took the job, I discovered the owner had been dishonest, and I confronted her. She threatened me, destroyed my confidence, and jaded me to the world of real estate. She ended up in prison for fraud. I was protected from unknowingly becoming entangled in her deceit. Still, my dream of being home with my kids was again crushed.

Over the next few years, I had two more children and helped my husband with his practice. The changes in the economy took a toll on his business. I had to keep working and worried that doing so would cause my children to suffer emotionally, intellectually, and spiritually.

Determined to stay home, I decided to buy more real estate. I learned about seller financing and bought, renovated, rented, and refinanced properties using the equity to buy more. I worked my real estate business every waking hour, around my job, and while juggling my children's well-being and activities.

Real Estate Millionaire Investor & Coach

In 2019, I hit my goal of acquiring $5,000,000 in real estate, and our rental income exceeded the six-figure income from my job. I finally retired! While my children were now all in school, I was able to spend much more time with them in the evenings.

Over the next five years, I grew my portfolio to over $300 million of real estate across seven states as a sole owner and general partner. I also created a successful real estate coaching business and became a four-time bestselling author. By God's grace, I beat the odds of persistent poverty and created an income and net worth in the top 1% of Americans today. Most importantly, I created time freedom, allowing me to enjoy significant time with my children, traveling, and making precious memories together.

Greater Purpose Living: Leaving a Legacy

I'm now focused on leaving a legacy for my children and others, including serving on the boards of multiple organizations focused on educating our youth and helping those who are struggling financially.

I'm proud to leave a legacy of a mom willing to do whatever it takes to provide for her children. Through our journey, my kids know they can accomplish anything through hard work, determination, integrity, grit, hope, faith, and a refusal to give up. They know the importance of giving and investing instead of wasting money. Finally, they have learned to make a meaningful impact in the lives of others as they pursue their own God-given purposes.

This is the heart, motivation, and purpose behind Greater Purpose Capital—investing for strong financial returns for my investors and eternal returns in the lives of our residents. It is something I was destined to be part of and a legacy I hope will last generations!

Dave Ramsey said that if you don't like where you are, you can make better financial decisions that can "change your family tree." Thankfully, I have. My motto in life is this: Love God, love people, use money, and NEVER give up!

ANNA'S THOUGHT LEADER LESSONS

Spirituality

I am awestruck by a sunset's majesty, a honeysuckle's sweetness, a rose's perfume, a child's love, and a bird's song. Growing up, I asked a lot of questions about the purpose of life and knew the answers were important. There is something within us that knows we are not here by chance and that life is miraculous. I have observed that all living things are complex, interdependent, and created with a purpose and that humans can find joy, love, and meaning. We can also find and cause great pain and fall into hopeless despair if we think our lives have no purpose.

I found profound answers to my questions in the Bible. It showed me that God is love and the Creator of life, and that man's purpose, joy, and fulfillment come from knowing and loving God and loving others as ourselves. When we discover the deep spiritual truth that we are valuable to God and that He created us for a purpose, we can confidently create a life that brings us joy and fulfillment. Wherever you are in your spiritual journey, I hope you know you are valuable, your life is worth living, and you deserve the best things life has to offer!

Legacy

When people think of legacy, they think of leaving a financial inheritance after they die. The reality is most people have little to no money to leave behind. However, all of us can leave something far greater than money—a legacy of meaningful impact. We all have something special within us, uniquely formed from our experiences, passions, and successes, which give us the wisdom and heart to give exactly what someone else needs to receive. When we design our lives, investments, and businesses to serve a greater purpose than our own self-satisfaction, we discover the joy that comes from helping others and leave a far greater impact on this world.

Embracing our responsibility to leave this kind of legacy before we die results in what I call Greater Purpose Living: investing our lives, time, and finances to make a meaningful impact on others. This impact will become our legacy and has the potential to leave several generations better off than if we had never lived. My hope is that you will discover the joy of greater purpose living and leave the meaningful legacy you were uniquely made for!

Q&A WITH ANNA

What is your favorite quote?

"Character cannot be developed in ease and quiet. Only through experience of trial and suffering can the soul be strengthened, vision cleared, ambition inspired, and success achieved." – Helen Keller

What books do you often recommend?

- *Lifeonaire* by Steve Cook
- *Don't Waste Your Life* by John Piper
- *The Gap and the Gain* by Dan Sullivan
- *The Intentional Legacy* by David McAlvany

Have you had any past challenges that turned out to be blessings?

The Great Financial Crisis and the COVID crisis taught me that the economy and things outside of my control could have a significant impact on financial success. I learned to build multiple sources of income, watch changes in economic cycles, live below my means, hold reserves, and make wise decisions about debt. I learned that with more success comes much greater responsibility. Doing everything with integrity and putting people over profits resulted in greater financial rewards and blessings than I could have imagined.

What would you tell your 18-year-old self?

Trust God to work ALL things together for your good. Don't be afraid to try and fail. Give yourself grace! Challenges lead to growth, wisdom, and blessings. Develop grit and resilience. Enjoy life. Be content with all you have while you work to have all you desire. Enjoy love and relationships; that is where true wealth is found. Prioritize your health. Invest as soon as you start working. Don't invest in what you don't understand. Don't partner with people who don't respect you or whose values and goals are not aligned with yours. There is safety in a multitude of counselors. With God and confidence in all He has made you to be, you have everything you need to create a life beyond what you can imagine!

Anna Kelley is a sought-after real estate speaker, consultant, and coach, and an active multifamily syndicator. Connect with Anna for real estate deal review, financial consulting, coaching, speaking invitations, and passive investing opportunities at www.Annakelleyinvesting.com.
To your success!

PHIL COLLEN

Def Leppard, Persistence, and the World's Fittest Rockstar

Phil Collen is a world-class musician and the lead guitarist for the band Def Leppard which has sold over one hundred million albums. In addition to music, Phil is highly committed to fitness, personal development, and making a positive impact on the planet.

Learning Guitar and My First Band

I was born in Hackney, a borough of London, England, and grew up in a place called Walthamstow. As a child, I loved music but thought it was completely out of reach, until I got a guitar at age 16 and started to play.

I left school and worked in a burglar alarm factory and then as a dispatch rider on a motorcycle while I was in a band called Girl until we got a record deal. We only got about $50 a week, but suddenly, I was a professional musician, and I could concentrate on that. I had something I had to get out. My artistic expression was so rewarding and still is today.

Def Leppard, Joe Elliot, and Mutt Lange

On tour with Girl, we played the British clubs and pubs. When I met Def Leppard, they already had two albums out.

Joe Elliot and I became friends. One day, he called me and said, "Pete is not in the band anymore. Do you want to play some guitar solos on this record?" I agreed and ended up on *Pyromania* playing songs like "Photograph," "Rock! Rock! (Till You Drop)," "Rock of Ages," and "Foolin'" and singing backing vocals. That album exploded. It all changed from that point onward.

Robert John "'Mutt'" Lange had just come off of an AC/DC album, and our management was fortunately able to hook him into Def Leppard's production. He saw something in the band, that we were malleable and something he could improve on. Unlike some musicians who would let their egos get in the way, we listened to Mutt and his suggestions.

Mutt Lange is, without a doubt, the most influential person in my musical career. He is totally inspiring with the highest intellect of anyone I've ever met. This guy is a giant, but he's humble and modest. We learned so much from him.

Singing, Songwriting, and the Muse

Mutt is the reason I learned how to sing and how to play guitar properly. He had a way of introducing you to concepts so you would excel. It was an amazing way to do things that was almost spiritual.

There's no more complete way to express yourself than through singing. It also improves your confidence. A lot of people pick up a guitar because they're a little intimidated by performing, and guitar is a great way to get out of your shell. When you're singing, it's entirely different, especially if you sing in front of people with no effects or band. If you can get up there, sing with confidence, and not really care what others may be thinking of you, it will improve other areas of your life. If you're a musician, it takes you somewhere else.

When you add writing, you're not just a songwriter, producer, or singer, you can be all of the above. I have songs going through my head all the time. I can't ignore them. I could sit down and write all day every day. Music can be so many things, and I find inspiration everywhere. It can be a drumbeat, the sound of a car going by, or any sound that comes to you out of open windows or on the street when you walk around the city. One sound or phrase makes you sing and think of another phrase, word, or memory. I don't even look for inspiration. It practically comes through the air. When the inspiration hits you, it's fantastic, and you're grateful for the muse, whatever it was.

In 2020, I signed with Sony Publishing, and they have been great, hooking me up with a couple of different songwriters. We've been on a storm, working on stuff I wouldn't normally do. It's very inspiring to get into a different type of music. I'm also always writing Def Leppard stuff and am excited about where we are going.

"Pour Some Sugar On Me"

The album *Hysteria* was hard work. Rick had lost his arm in a terrible accident, among many other things. We were moving through different studios in different countries for two and a half years. We went into so much debt that it brought tears to my eyes when I read the breakdown. I thought we would never be able to pay it back to the record company. The album was almost finished, and we had to sell a ridiculous number of albums to break even.

One afternoon, Joe was sitting in the hallway singing something while playing his guitar, Mutt Lange said, "What's that?"

Joe said, "Oh, I don't know."

Mutt said, "Play that again." Over the next 10 days, we wrote and recorded the song "Pour Some Sugar On Me." It was the last thing to go on the record that we had already poured so much into, almost as an afterthought, and it broke the album.

We had three singles out before it and we hadn't broken, even by a long shot, and then that one came out. Dancers in strip clubs would request the song, and then it started getting popular by request on local radio. It became this massive song in Florida, and we had no idea. From there, it just exploded.

Rick Allen's Accident

On New Year's Eve, 1984, our band's drummer Rick Allen had a terrible car accident that resulted in him losing an arm. Our band loves and supports each other like a family, so we asked him what he wanted to do. Mutt Lange went to see him in the hospital and said, "There's all this technology, and you've got amazing kick drum, bass pedal technique. You can use your foot and keep playing." He would have to change one limb for the other and would do double the work with his feet.

Rick was practicing in bed with his one arm and his foot when Steve Clark and I went to visit him in hospital. The three of us lived in a house together in Donnybrook just outside of Dublin. I remember that it was very frustrating for him. He would practice from eight in the morning till about 10 at night, swearing and cursing. Then one day, there was no cursing, and we heard a cool rhythm that was in time. It just got better from there. He got to that next level and was able to keep taking it to another level until it was second nature.

Health and Fitness

I believe if you're going to be constantly traveling and experiencing high levels of physical and mental stress, you need all the help you can get. The best thing anyone can do, especially in this environment, is to nurture and protect their body. This usually has a knock-on effect mentally, too. I try to keep a consistent workout routine going, which really helps, especially when on tour. Diet is as important as a workout routine and serves as a fountain of youth. I feel better than I did when I was 30, and I love the energy my routine gives me in my 60s.

I've been a strict vegetarian for 38 years and have practiced a vegan lifestyle for many years. Becoming a vegetarian was a moral decision because I couldn't eat a dead body. I stopped drinking 34 years ago. I was able to stop, but my best friend Steve Clark wasn't, and it ended up killing him.

Recognizing Addiction and the Benefits of Being Sober

I recognized I had an addiction when I realized I couldn't remember things. There were times I drove blind drunk. I finally understood that I could have hit someone. That really weighed on me, but I couldn't quit cold turkey. I had tried a few times before. I tried things like bringing just one glass of wine with me to the social gathering, but I couldn't do it. I'd bring the bottle instead. And then it was Jack Daniels by the end of the week.

On my ex-girlfriend Liz's birthday in April 1987, we were in Paris having a glass of champagne, and I said, "I'm not drinking after this." We went to India the next day, and I quit cold turkey. That was it, actually. It was easy, and she did it with me.

The benefits were outrageous. I got two extra hours a day that I wasn't spending recovering or just feeling not great. That's when I started working out, because I actually had time to burn. I started running, and it inspired me to do more. I'd run along the shoreline just south of Dublin, even in the cold weather. It wasn't the running itself I enjoyed, it was being in nature and the fact that I just felt different because I wasn't nursing a hangover. I was this clear, cleaner version of me.

Adrenalized Life, Def Leppard, and Beyond

Chris Epting encouraged me to write a book because he thought I had some great stories to share. He received some interest from a few book companies and then Simon & Schuster agreed to publish it. I worked back and forth with their editors, and my wife Helen helped me as well. At one point, we sat down and re-edited the whole thing. When you write it down, you wonder if it's right, if you are getting the point across, if it sounds too highbrow or lowbrow.

I've started writing short stories and plan on writing more. But writing a book, writing a story, or writing a song is a lot more difficult than people think.

PHIL'S THOUGHT LEADER LESSONS

Building Confidence by Overcoming Adversity

When I was a kid, I was told I was asthmatic. My doctor said, "I'm not going to give him an inhaler. I want him to go swimming." When you're swimming, you're thinking about other things, and after a while, I would forget that I couldn't breathe, and my lungs would open up. When I started playing guitar, I gained confidence in myself and started feeling different, and the asthma more or less went away.

I think every little thing you learn creates confidence, an ability to deal with stuff and not feel embarrassed. When I first became a vegetarian, I felt bad because I felt my dietary restrictions would put people out. At some point though, I decided I wasn't going to compromise my beliefs to please others. My vegetarianism became empowering for me. It wasn't ego. It was confidence. You have to accept yourself and your limitations, then make your limitations your strengths. Actually, when you are aware of your limitations, they often become your strengths.

Success and Daily Habits

I think consistency is so important. It's so easy to fall off, and when you do, you have to get back into it, and that's a lot harder. If you maintain whatever you're doing and are regularly inspired by it, you achieve more.

One of the hardest things to do is meditate and think of nothing, especially if you've got songs running through your head and a toddler running around. I struggle with it, but I do it. Meditation is very powerful because it gives you time alone to escape.

I like to have flow in my day and not be rigid. You don't have to fix things. It is what it is. You're on a trajectory. When you're not in that mode, you can overthink things. You can go, *My God, I haven't got any money coming in. I'm not doing this. I'm not doing that. My songwriting has dried up.* You overthink. When you avoid this but keep all the moving parts going in a successful routine, your life runs itself.

Q&A WITH PHIL

What have been some of your musical influences?

Coming from London, the hotbed of the music industry, I grew up on The Rolling Stones, The Beatles, and later the Sex Pistols. All the great bands would come through London. I also love reggae music. Then, I got to America, where they created rock music, which comes from the blues. So I got into the blues, funk, soul, rock and roll, and jazz. I'm a huge fan of Motown!

Do you enjoy touring?

Touring can be challenging for many musicians, but I love the chance to be a tourist. Everywhere we go, I get up early in the morning, find somewhere to have a coffee, and absorb the local vibe. Traveling can get to be a bit much, but if I'm on a tour bus, I'm asleep before we leave the parking lot and usually wake up in the next town.

I have a wonderful wife and five kids, and I'm grateful that my family comes out at different parts of the tour. It may be Europe, Australia, Florida, or Fargo. I remember playing chess in Fargo with my son, Rory, when he was nine. It was winter and cold, and we were playing in a coffee shop, and it's just a beautiful memory. I really enjoy touring and being in new places.

What is something most people don't know about you?

I'm always busy creating and am part of two other bands. One is Delta Deep with Robert DeLeo of Stone Temple Pilots, Debbi Blackwell-Cook, and Forrest Robinson, and the other is Man Raze with Paul Cook of the Sex Pistols and Simon Laffy. I'm always having fun writing and recording. At some point, I might do a solo album.

I did the G3 concert tour with Joe Satriani and John Petrucci from Dream Theater with Delta Deep. Robert DeLeo couldn't make the tour, so Craig Martini stepped in and played bass. Those guys are over-the-top musicians, yet they are so humble.

Phil Collen is the lead guitar player for Def Leppard. For more information on Phil and Def Leppard, go to defleppard.com. To learn more about Phil speaking for your organization, contact info@kylewilson.com.

CLAIR HOOVER

Dream Big, Work Hard, Bless Others

Clair Hoover is a 20-year investor and entrepreneur in self-storage, mobile home parks, car washes, housing, and laundromats. He is the president and CEO of Freedom Storage Management, is a sought-after speaker, serves on the Pennsylvania Self Storage Association board of directors, and is active in men's ministry.

Potential Needs a Push

I was born in the beautiful farming community of Lancaster, Pennsylvania. My early life was spent living and working on our family farm. It was not always an easy life. Finances were never in abundance, but my parents always found ways to find joy in lean times and make the most of what we had.

My dad had a tremendous work ethic. Living on a dairy farm meant working seven days a week, 365 days a year. Kids growing up on farms often experience adult responsibilities early in life. The challenges my dad offered me through tasks on the farm built my character and problem-solving skills at a very young age. I learned what it meant to be a man working by my father's side, and those values have served me well throughout my adult life.

My father encouraged me to choose a different path than he did. Although I showed little motivation and promise through my teenage years, I was frequently told I had great potential. The reality was, I had no real dreams and thus no reason to push myself to achieve.

Cold Toes

Statements starting with "I will never" are much more powerful than "I will" statements. An "I will never" is usually born out of a painful experience and one "I will never" statement forced me to dream big.

After graduating from high school, I decided to take a little time off from pursuing my education. I knew that if I was going to go to college, I had to treat that with a different level of commitment than I did my high school experience.

I spent a few months working for a local construction company. I remember it was so cold that, every hour, they would give us a five-minute break to thaw out our fingers and toes. There were moments when my feet were so cold that I thought it may be wiser to pour the hot coffee down my boots than to drink it.

At some point, during a cold day at a job site, I made an "I will never" commitment: "No matter how hard college might be, if I am warm, I will never quit."

I chose an accounting degree.

They said Intermediate Accounting class separated the men from the boys, and many accounting students chose that hurdle as their exit ramp. I clearly remember staring at that Intermediate Accounting textbook, hating every minute.

Something in the back of my head said, *But you're warm.* That got me through. Having a *why* became very important in my life.

Prior to college, I did not see a clear reason to excel at anything. The effort I could visualize promised very little, if any, benefit. In college, I finally found a reason to apply myself. Good grades meant financial grants and academic accolades with the promise of better-paying career options.

I finally found a reason to work hard, and to my surprise, I was a good student. I was able to graduate with honors in less than three years.

Dream Big

Early in my career, I met some extraordinary people who were doing amazing things with their lives. As I got to experience some other countries and cultures, I began to increasingly value the opportunities I had available to me having been born in the United States.

Growing up, I assumed there were limits on how far I could go because of who I was and where I started. The truth was there were no limits. I could pursue any and every dream I had in this amazing country.

I soon realized that if I continued putting an average effort into planning and living my life, I was going to get average results. However, if I chose to put in extraordinary effort, I could achieve extraordinary results. I developed a passion for seeing how far I could go if I put everything I had into every endeavor, every day. Remember, success is measured not by where you are in life but by the distance you traveled from your starting point.

Work Hard

Two of my favorite quotes about working hard are, "The elevator to success is out of order, but the stairs are always open," and "The man on top of the mountain did not fall there." I was fortunate to develop relationships with some amazing leaders who helped me understand the value of setting goals and the joy of achieving them through hard work. Successful people are often characterized as being lucky. When confronted with that view, I love to explain that I have found that "the harder I work, the luckier I get."

The great philosopher Socrates said, "The unexamined life is not worth living." I love learning from the life choices that other great leaders have made. Every 10 years, I take time to intentionally seek out leaders who are 10 or 20 years older than I am and ask them to speak into my life from their experience. "What can you see about the next 10 years of my life that I cannot? What should be important?" The year of my 50th birthday, I asked: "Now that I have some margin in my life, should I slow down or keep the pedal to the floor?"

I secretly wanted the majority of them to recommend slowing down. But, nine out of 10 said keep the accelerator to the floor because someday your health or other life events will force you to slow down. Another guy said, "Go as fast as you can, for as long as you can, to bless as many people as you can."

Bless Others

One of my mentors told me that I would do well as I built businesses for my personal benefit but when I found the joy of building them to bless others, I would find real success. That spoke to me. My *why* became wanting to create some margin in my life, specifically in my time and finances. Now, when God puts somebody in front of me who needs help, I have the capacity to do something about it. My goal is to be a blessing to family, friends, and organizations dear to my heart.

I have watched people sacrifice the best years of their lives to reach the top of ladders that did not bring them happiness. Every successful person I know understands how to climb a ladder. The best of the best know it's even more important to focus on what is waiting for you at the top of the wall that you have chosen to climb.

If you have been fortunate enough to make it to the top floor in your endeavors, your next greatest responsibility is to send the elevator back down. I am passionate about encouraging others to live the best lives they can live as the best version of themselves because I have been blessed. I realized that "success" is winning, but "significance" is helping others win. As you live this out, you will find that you cannot shine a light on another's path without lighting your own. Blessing others has always led to more joy in my life.

Life is surprisingly short and incredibly precious. Now that I have tasted what it means to dream big, work hard, and bless others, I want that for everyone.

You get one shot to enjoy this thing called life. Why not make the most of it?

CLAIR'S THOUGHT LEADER LESSONS

Financial Independence and Generational Wealth
- Use your wealth and influence to create strong family connections for many generations.
- Money is not good or evil, it is neutral. What you do with it can be good or evil.
- Make as much money as you can for as long as you can to bless as many people as you can.
- When passive income equals or exceeds your living expenses, you are financially independent.
- Relationships are the foundation for the richest parts of life.
- There is no joy in arriving alone at the top of the mountain.
- I have no desire to achieve success at the expense of relationships.
- People will not remember what you say or what you do, but they will remember how you make them feel.

Parenting
- Raise children that you will want to be friends with when they are adults.
- Parent with the goal of knowing that when your children are old enough to choose their friends, they will choose you.
- Encourage your children to be comfortable with failures. You never lose in life. Sometimes you win, and sometimes you learn.

Leadership
- If you want to go fast, go alone. If you want to go far, build a team.
- Delegate and empower to bring the best out of your team.
- Hire great people and then get out of their way.
- Lead efficient team meetings where the only agenda items are things that are new or things that are broken.
- If you are convinced that delegating to another leader will only produce 80% of the results you can achieve, delegate it to two and you will get 160% of you.

Technology
- Technology and automation are the best ways to leverage your time. A one-hour investment can yield thousands of hours of productivity and increase profits.
- A great website never has a bad sales call and can produce 24 hours per day.

Habits or Hacks
- One of the most effective ways to manage your time is to work in sprints with a stopwatch. I do 50-minute work sprints with 10 minutes of downtime.
- Schedule your most important tasks during the highest energy parts of your day.
- Make sure health, wealth, and relationships are balanced into each day's schedule.
- Reflect on your largest challenges then let them go while you enjoy a hobby or time with friends. The answers to the challenges will come to you when you least expect them.

Q&A WITH CLAIR

What is something most people don't know about you?

I have a soft heart. I would throw a competitive win to make sure my opponent is having a good time, and I would give up 50% of my success if it meant not winning at the expense of others.

What are a few of your favorite quotes?

- "Life should not be a journey to the grave with the intention of arriving safely in a pretty and well-preserved body, but rather to skid in broadside, in a cloud of smoke, thoroughly used up, totally worn out, and loudly proclaiming... 'Wow! What a ride!'" – Hunter S. Thompson
- "There comes into the life of every man a task for which he and he alone is uniquely suited. What a shame if that moment finds him either unwilling or unprepared for that which would become his finest hour." – Winston Churchill
- "I am hurt, but I am not slain / I'll lay me down and bleed a while, / And then I'll rise and fight again." – Sir Andrew Barton (High Commander, Scottish Army, 1511)

What is some of the best advice you've received?

- Never fall in love with something that cannot love you back.
- You will regret more things that you didn't try than the things you did try.
- If you are winning at everything, you are not trying hard enough.
- There are no mistakes in life, just tuition to be paid.
- Live a good and honorable life, then when you get older and think back, you'll enjoy it a second time.
- When life kicks you, make sure it kicks you forward.
- Some days you are going to need to be prepared to fight like you are the third monkey on the ramp to Noah's ark and it is starting to rain.

What is your favorite song or who is your favorite musical artist?

- The Eagles – Incredible talent and multiple musical genres in the same band.
- Don Williams – I'm all about the lyrics and melody.
- "Empty Garden" by Elton John – An incredible perspective on life.

What is your favorite movie?

Braveheart – It's the best portrayal I have ever seen of the need for people to live for something bigger than themselves.

Who are your mentors and greatest influences?

Craig Grochelle who is an amazing equipper for leaders and who taught me to live an intentional, focused life.

Robert Kyosaki who taught me to think outside the box.

Have you had any past challenges that turned out to be blessings?

My trucking company was the most challenging company I have built. It felt like a 13-year mistake, but it taught me many of the skills that I believe contributed to my later success.

Being a grandfather to my special needs grandchild—loving a defenseless young child through medical challenges early in life will teach you much.

Who is your favorite sports team?

I'm a life-long fan of the Dallas Cowboys.

What hobbies do you enjoy?

Sailing, scuba, motorcycles, and pickleball.

What books do you frequently recommend?

Rich Dad Poor Dad by Robert Kiyosaki, *The Gap and the Gain* by Dan Sullivan and Dr. Benjamin Hardy, and *The Richest Man in Babylon* by George S. Clason

What would you tell your 18-year-old self?

- Enjoy every minute of the journey.
- Life is short—take the shot.
- Don't wait for the rain to stop—learn to dance in it.
- "Don't judge each day by the harvest you reap but by the seeds that you plant." – Robert Louis Stevenson
- "Anything you do that's new and effective will be met with resistance. Don't worry when you're being criticized... worry when you're not." – Craig Groeshel
- "Always shoot for the moon. Even if you miss, you will land among the stars." – Norman Vincent Peale

What do you consider your greatest achievement to date?

Building family businesses, raising incredible kids, writing my own script, and helping others define and achieve their best lives.

To reach Clair Hoover about investment, entrepreneurship, or ministry, email him at clairhoover@comcast.net. Learn more about Freedom Storage Management at freedomstoragemanagement.com. For details on ministry and the National Coalition of Ministries to Men, visit NCMM.org.

RAJ VENKATRAMANI, MD

From Shadows to Sunshine
My Journey of Resilience and Triumph

Dr. Rajkumar Venkatramani, section chief at Texas Children's Hospital, is a renowned pediatric oncologist and entrepreneur. His journey from humble beginnings to success in medicine and business exemplifies resilience. Passionate about mentoring, research, and real estate investment, his story showcases perseverance and the pursuit of diverse passions beyond medicine.

The Unexpected Privileges of Poverty

Ever walked into a room feeling utterly out of place, thinking *I shouldn't be here; I'm not qualified for this?* I've lived with this feeling for as long as I can remember. But, as I've learned, it's in these rooms of incongruity that we often find our true calling.

My story begins in the modest home of a young couple in India. My mother, a resilient woman, was just 16 when she married my father, and by 20, she was a mother of two. My father, also a man of humble beginnings, was often hustling to change his situation. But his sudden passing in a tragic road accident when I was nine left a void that was more than just the absence of a father. It was the collapse of our fragile world.

Our struggles were not just financial. They seeped into my nights and my very dreams. As a child, I was haunted by nightmares, a morbid tapestry where the dead rose and shadows whispered. But the most heart-wrenching were the dreams where my father returned. In those fleeting moments, my world was whole again, only to shatter when morning came. These dreams remained my secret, locked away from my mother's already burdened heart.

Amidst this backdrop of struggle and loss, I stumbled upon a profound truth—the unexpected privileges of poverty. In scarcity, I found abundance. Every small achievement was a triumph, teaching me to appreciate the simplest joys, to find contentment in mere existence, and to cultivate resilience.

The Road Less Traveled: My Odyssey through Medical School

At the age of 17, I embarked on a journey to medical school, to uplift my family from financial insecurity. My understanding of a doctor's role was rudimentary, shaped by the scant visits we could afford during my childhood. To me, becoming a doctor was a societal elevator—it was about enhancing earning potential and elevating our family's status.

I gained admission to medical school solely on academic merit based on an entrance exam. Without the luxury of cultivating extracurricular skills or volunteer hours, I found this system to be a saving grace. Had the criteria been different, my dream of attending medical school would have remained just that—a dream.

As my medical school journey neared its end, I was confronted with a harsh reality: a failing grade on my final year exam. This was a reflection of corruption that infiltrated the system. Money exchanged hands under the table, determining who passed and who didn't. Unwilling to partake in this corrupt practice, I found myself at a crossroads. This unexpected twist forced me to adapt rather than succumb. The failure propelled me to leave India and venture to the United Kingdom, reshaping my destiny.

At 23, I left India for London with just 800 pounds sterling. The goal was simple: pass the necessary exams and secure a job before the money ran out. The stress of this period was unlike any I had encountered.

The East End of London, with its affordable cost of living, became my home. I shared a modest bed in a dorm for 10 pounds a week, living on a diet of bread and baked beans. The breakthrough came unexpectedly when a doctor, seeking to balance work with new parenthood, offered me a chance to fill in the other half of their schedule. This marked the beginning of my career.

Charting New Horizons: Embracing the Challenges of Pediatric Training

As I navigated the complex landscape of medical training in the UK, an opportunity emerged, one that seemed almost out of reach for an immigrant like me: a position in the highly-esteemed pediatrician training program at King's College Hospital in London.

My mentor advised against setting my hopes on that position. This reflected a hard truth about the landscape for immigrants in the UK. We were often relegated to the periphery, our dreams dimmed by the shadows of origin and circumstance. With nothing to lose, I applied. Though I was initially rejected, I later received an offer due to a last-minute change.

I stepped into King's College Hospital ready to embrace the role that many believed was beyond my reach. The training program assigned a senior doctor as a mentor. Upon meeting, my mentor said, "I'm surprised you've come this far with that name." It carried an undercurrent of bias, an implicit questioning of my place in that institution. I felt humiliated and I completely shut down.

This led me to a pivotal decision—to not let my journey be constrained by the limited opportunities and veiled prejudices in the UK. My aspiration to specialize in pediatric hematology, particularly dealing with blood clots, seemed unattainable within the UK's medical landscape for an immigrant doctor.

This realization steered me toward the United States. My journey led me to Peoria, Illinois, for residency training.

Navigating New Waters: From Aspirations to Achievements in Pediatric Oncology

After residency, I joined the Children's Hospital Los Angeles, specializing in cancer and blood disorders. My goal was clear—to become a specialist in blood clots. This required mentorship from a seasoned expert in the field.

During my first year, I worked with a blood clot specialist who commented that my level of knowledge was less than others. This criticism reflected cultural differences. In India, deference to seniority was the norm. There was a philosophy that emphasized listening over speaking when a more senior person was around. However, the culture in the US encouraged a more vocal and opinionated approach, something I had yet to fully grasp.

When I approached him seeking mentorship, I was met with rejection. This was a pivotal moment— my long-held aspiration seemed to be slipping away.

Life is about adapting to the unexpected. I pivoted my focus to treating cancers of the liver and other soft tissues in children, redefining my professional trajectory.

My mentor during fellowship was instrumental in my growth. I vividly remember the first research paper I wrote. After I spent 13 hours on a Saturday crafting a 2,200-word paper, his feedback was brutally honest—the paper was terrible. This was exactly what I needed. It pushed me to learn, improve, and eventually master the art of medical writing.

In 2014, my wife had to move to Texas to fulfill her visa requirements. Despite my love for Los Angeles and the life I had built there, we moved—she worked in McAllen and I in Houston. This relocation meant starting over professionally, a daunting but necessary step in our journey.

Pediatric cancer is a rarity, with some forms affecting only a handful of children nationwide. I began specializing in these unique cases, understanding that expertise in such a niche area was not immediate but a result of dedication, hard work, and continuous learning. Over time, this led to recognition as a world expert in the field. Requests for my input on treatment strategies come from all corners of the globe.

The Zenith of My Medical Journey: Leadership and Philosophy in Pediatric Oncology

Today, my journey has led me to a position of significant responsibility and influence in pediatric oncology. I was one of the youngest people to be promoted to professor in the Baylor College of Medicine. As the section chief of oncology at Texas Children's Hospital, I oversee a dedicated team of 50 doctors. In 2020, I became the chair of The Soft Tissue Committee at Children's Oncology Group, playing a pivotal role in clinical trials for children with sarcomas across North America. I am the first person of color and first immigrant to hold this position.

A profound piece of wisdom from the Bhagavad Gita resonates deeply with me. "Do your duty, but don't worry about the results." This philosophy underscores the importance of performing one's duty without attachment to outcomes. It teaches that the fruits of our labor are not solely ours to claim—a reminder that success is often a confluence of effort, circumstance, and factors beyond our control.

Adopting this philosophy has allowed me to live a life with significantly reduced anxiety. Whether I'm achieving a long-sought goal or facing an unexpected hurdle, I strive to keep my emotional response measured and constructive. This approach has not only contributed to a happier, more balanced life, but also enabled me to lead and mentor effectively, guiding my team with a calm and steady hand.

Beyond Medicine: Venturing into Entrepreneurship

At the age of 43, I started my first business, REIDOC Capital, a real estate firm that helps doctors invest in real estate. At 44, I started REIDOC Agency, a marketing tool for businesses.

"Why start a business?" my wife asked. We both have fulfilling careers in medicine, earning respectable salaries and living modestly.

The inception of my business venture was fueled by the abundance of opportunities in America and a desire to live without regrets. I didn't want to reach the twilight years of my life wondering, "What if?" I wanted to present my children with a broader horizon, showing they can carve their own paths. Through my journey in entrepreneurship, I hope to instill in them the understanding that hard work can create new opportunities.

In this new chapter of my life as an entrepreneur, I adhere to the same philosophy: focus on the journey, not the destination. The outcome of my business endeavors is secondary. Success or failure won't define my happiness or sense of fulfillment. Life is an unpredictable journey, and today, where I stand was once beyond my wildest dreams.

RAJ'S THOUGHT LEADER LESSONS

The Power of Reliability

Achievement is synonymous with reliability. My wife often points out that while I may not be the most naturally talented, my reliability is my strength. If I commit to doing something, it gets done.

Embracing Imperfection and Delegation

You don't need to be perfect or know everything. My English, for instance, isn't flawless. I still make basic errors, often corrected by my children. This doesn't hinder my ability to lead effectively. Leadership is about finding the right people for the job and empowering them, as emphasized in Benjamin Hardy and Dan Sullivan's book *Who Not How*.

Perspective: The Role of Luck and Satisfaction

An often-overlooked factor in success is luck. Many people possess similar skills and dedication but aren't as successful due to circumstances beyond their control. Recognizing this can keep you humble and appreciative of your achievements.

I also value the transient nature of satisfaction. Significant milestones, like getting admitted to medical school, bring joy that often gives way to longing for the next goal. This keeps me grounded and appreciative of each accomplishment.

The Pale Blue Dot: A Humbling Perspective

The image of The Pale Blue Dot, Earth captured as a mere pixel by Voyager 1, serves as a profound reminder of our insignificance in the universe. I recommend Carl Sagan's book on this topic. This perspective is humbling, reminding us of the triviality of our daily concerns and the importance of a broader outlook on life and our place in it.

Q&A WITH RAJ

What is something most people don't know about you?

Most people think I'm a very serious person. At work I project a very serious image. At home, I'm completely different. My children and wife make fun of me. Great levity is had at my expense!

What is your favorite song or who is your favorite musical artist?

I mainly listen to Bollywood songs. A.R. Rahman is my favorite. A lot of people know him from *Slumdog Millionaire*.

What is your favorite movie?

The movie which influenced me the most when I was little was probably *Gandhi*. The great thing about Gandhi is he was, first, a great politician. He inspired 300 million people who did not speak the same language to unite and fight for freedom through non-violent means.

The other movie I love is: *The Shawshank Redemption*. I think that's a classic.

Who are your mentors and greatest influences?

My greatest influence is my mom, Latha. When my dad died, she took us through life. She went back to high school at the age of 30, graduated, and then did some menial jobs. She's always very calm. She talks very little. But she's my role model. I am grateful to her.

How do you define success?

Success for me is the freedom to do what you want.

To connect with Dr. Rajkumar Venkatramani about real estate investments, digital marketing opportunities, or mentorship, email him at raj@reidoccapital.com or visit his LinkedIn profile https://www.linkedin.com/in/reidoc/

Scan to schedule a call with Raj.

MITZI PERDUE

Architect of My Life

Mitzi Perdue is a businesswoman, prolific bestselling author, and part of a legacy of household name family businesses. She was formerly president of the 40,000-member American Agri-Women and one of the US Delegates to the United Nations Conference on Women in Nairobi. She was a syndicated columnist for 22 years, a TV producer, and an interview show host.

Growing Up in a Business Family

I grew up in the Sheraton Hotel family. My father was the co-founder of the Sheraton Hotels, and we, the family, sold the business after my father's passing in 1967. Even before Sheraton, our family had been in business since the founding of the Henderson Estate Company in 1840.

I am also a businesswoman. I've started multiple businesses, including the family wine grape business, now one of the larger suppliers of wine grapes in California. I also married into a multi-generational family business; Perdue Farms began in the chicken business in 1920.

Challenges Growing Up

Seeing me today, you would think I grew up as confident as they make them. But if you had met me 40 years ago, you wouldn't believe that I'm the same person. Until my mid-30s, I was so shy that I found it difficult to enter a room or use the telephone. If I had to talk to one of my kid's teachers, I would sit on the edge of my bed for half an hour trying to figure out how I could get past hello.

Part of the reason for my shyness was a severe lisp. It was a lisp that you could not just hear but also see. After they knew me well, a few people confided in me that they had initially assumed I was stupid. If each time you met somebody you assumed they thought you were stupid, it does not help develop loads of self-confidence. My lisp was a blight on my life.

Although I had a good education, my shyness coupled with fear of failure meant that by age 38, I wasn't doing a lot with my life. I did have an occupation; I grew rice in California. The great advantage of being a rice grower, if you're shy, is you do a lot of walking in the fields. You have some interaction with a few people, but otherwise, it's solitary. This suited me just fine because I didn't enjoy meetings and was scared of people. My shyness could have gone on forever, but there was a point where it changed.

A Lesson Learned from a Genius

In my rice fields, I had a tenant farmer who had an incredible, unusual gift. He had an IQ of over 200. In gratitude for this gift, he wanted to give back to the world. He wanted to glean, from all the world's wisdom, ideas that would benefit mankind. He even had a title for the great book he would write: *Life, An Owner's Manual.*

He spent a good bit of his life, when he wasn't being a tenant farmer, collecting more and more information for his book. Decade after decade went by, and he didn't start the book. He always felt there was more to learn before actually starting to write.

But, at age 68, something horrible happened to him. He was diagnosed with terminal heart disease. He couldn't walk across my office without crippling heart pain.

It was, for him, a death sentence. His doctors didn't think they could keep him alive long enough to go to the Mayo Clinic for quadruple bypass surgery.

You might think that nothing could be worse than a death sentence, but there is something worse. Peter realized that his whole life had been working towards writing this great book, and now he'd never get to write it.

However, things changed! I influenced him to visit the Pritikin Longevity Center, a spa that had (and still has) an extraordinary record for helping people with heart disease.

Their specialty was diet, exercise, meditation, and every other healthy lifestyle thing that you can think of. My genius friend spent a month there and lost 15 pounds. At the end of the month, miraculously—his heart revascularized. He was in great health when he returned!

I was so happy for him! I told him, "Peter, this is the most wonderful news in the world! Now you can write your book!"

To my surprise, he said, "Yes, I will write it. I just need to do a little bit more research, and I'll be ready." He lived to be 95 and never wrote his book.

I believe what was holding him back was fear of failure. When you spend thousands of hours walking rice paddies with a person, you get to know a lot about them. I knew that Peter was so afraid that he would not succeed at this goal of gifting the world with a spectacular book of wisdom, that he did the one thing that was guaranteed to cause failure: he didn't try.

I Started Thinking, What About Me?

I really wanted to be in communications. My dream had been television. What was holding me back?

I decided that I would turn my life around. If it was fear of failure that held my tenant back, I would redefine failure for myself. Failure would be not giving my all to whatever I wanted to accomplish. Failure would be not giving everything that I was capable of.

Even if I didn't succeed by some people's standards, I would succeed by mine because just in the process of trying, I would be learning things, meeting people, and moving farther along the road to being all I could be.

To start with, I knew I needed to get over my lisp. I went to a speech therapist, and she told me she didn't have the tools to help somebody my age to overcome a lisp. This was the 1970s. Because my new motto was "Try!" I went to another speech therapist and was told the same thing. I went to a third, and again, I was told there was no chance to help somebody with a lisp as an adult.

Redefining Failure

The third speech therapist told me, "I can't help you, but I'd love to take your money!"

That began nine months of practicing half an hour a day and getting absolutely nowhere. It was nine months, a lot of money, and a two-hour round trip to the therapist each week with not even the slightest glimmer of progress. But somewhere around nine months, I began to hear when I was lisping.

When I could hear it, I could work on correcting it. By the end of the year, I was ready to audition for a television show. I fell on my face numerous times, but one day at an audition, the station manager happened to hear me and said, "You're natural for television. Would you like a show?" I went from somebody almost too shy to use the telephone to somebody who had a television show in the space of a year.

I had also always wanted to write, but I had never submitted anything. I began submitting stories about me as a rice farmer to the local newspaper, and soon, 20 newspapers were carrying them. Eventually, the Scripps Howard News Service, which at the time was one of the largest syndicators in the country, was carrying my work.

Before I had decided that I was going to redefine failure, I hadn't tried going for all of these things. It was not being afraid of failure that changed my life.

If fear of failure is holding you back, redefine it. Every time you don't achieve your immediate goal, rejoice, because just the act of trying means that you've become a bigger person, you've increased your talent stack, and you've become more ready to take on the next challenge.

Ethical Will

As I get older, I care more about my legacy. I believe we all do. When we're gone, we would love to have something positive left after us.

I think the people who are most successful at leaving something positive behind are intentional about it. When it comes to family businesses, 70% won't make it to the next generation. That 70% didn't put the effort into creating a culture in which the young ones in their lives learn the important lessons such as:

- You can't always be right
- You're part of something bigger than yourself
- Stewardship is important
- Personal relationships are more important than money

My husband Frank Perdue was extraordinarily intentional about those who came after him. Together, we wrote an ethical will composed of 10 values. He believed if those who came after him would follow these 10 values, they would have a chance of having a happier life.

One value was if you want to be happy, think what you can do for somebody else. On the other hand, if you want to be miserable, think what's owed to you.

I find this is true. Almost every time I'm really feeling down, I'm thinking, "Life is unfair!" or "This should have gone my way!"

But on the other hand, if I'm thinking of a charity, particularly my work to be a part of helping stop human trafficking, or helping to use artificial intelligence as part of a program to help with mental health, I feel good and that my life has more meaning.

Frank Perdue's Ethical Will is sort of like a constitution for the Perdue family. Often, when there's an argument, we refer to it to determine our best course of action. I encourage all patriarchs and matriarchs to create their own version of what has become part of the "family glue" for the Perdues.

Frank Perdue's Ethical Will:

1. Be honest always.
2. Be a person whom others are justified in trusting.
3. If you say you will do something, do it.
4. You don't have to be the best, but you should be the best you can be.
5. Treat all people with courtesy and respect, no exceptions.
6. Remember that the way to be happy is to think of what you can do for others. The way to be miserable is to think about what people should be doing for you.
7. Be part of something bigger than your own self. That something can be family, the pursuit of knowledge, the environment, or whatever you choose.
8. Remember that hard work is satisfying and fulfilling.
9. Nurture the ability to laugh and have fun.
10. Have respect for those who have gone before and learn from their weaknesses and build on their strengths.

MITZI'S THOUGHT LEADER LESSONS

Attitude and Nutrition

The Buddhists say that attitude is everything. Although my birth certificate says I was born in 1941 (I'm 83), I really feel about 40. I may not look 40, but inside, there's a 40-year-old who forgot to grow up.

I'm addicted to reading about health innovations. I've learned nutrition is super important. When you have a choice, pick less processed over processed food. I'm also big on exercise. I believe in cardio. I believe in weight training. I am also a big believer in getting at least seven hours of sleep. The latest neuroscience says you really want that restorative sleep to clear out the metabolites that build up during the day. I also do intermittent fasting. I'm a huge believer in thermal resilience, as in cold showers and going out in the winter without a jacket for a while until you can't stand it. I think putting minor stress on the body, like the cold or the heat or the exercise, helps keep you young.

But I will never allow my diet theories to interfere with my social life because my social life is extremely important to me. When I'm with friends or maybe at a dinner party and somebody's cooked an amazing dessert and put a lot of effort into it, the chances of my turning it down are zero.

Using Wealth for Good

I believe that wealth is power, and I very much want to use the power I have for good. Mother Teresa believed the good that we can do, we must do. I'm not saying I achieve that, but it is something to head towards. I figured out that I have a purpose in life: it's to increase happiness and decrease misery. When there's an opportunity to do something that will increase happiness or decrease misery, that's where I want to be. Emulating President Kennedy back in the sixties is the idea, "Man's reach exceeds his grasp." So, I'm reaching towards this.

Public Speaking and Influence

I was "insufferably shy." The truth is, I was so shy, it literally was hard for me to make a phone call. So, I started taking speaking courses. I bet I've taken maybe 10 speaking courses in my life. Every few years, I take another. Today, there are only a few things I love more than public speaking. I'm living proof that you can change and grow.

I've also taken salesmanship courses because my theory is that a lot of success in life is about having influence. If I'm going to carry out my life's purpose of increasing happiness and decreasing misery, I will need influence, and salesmanship teaches you how to be more persuasive.

Developing Your Talent Stack

Scott Adams, creator of the comic strip "Dilbert," has shared that one of his theories of life is that the more you can develop your talent stack—by that I mean different skills that you have—the more exciting life gets. The more skills you can bring to solving a problem, the more problems become opportunities.

This is one of my personal approaches to life that has really paid off for me. Right after college, I decided that a year would not be complete unless I'd taken a course. It might be in first aid, public speaking, nuclear particle physics, painting, or database programming. It defies statistics how often after I've studied something, I use it or need it. By the time you've taken 60 different courses, you can solve problems with so many more tools.

Q&A WITH MITZI

What is your favorite movie?

Casablanca. I love it partly because it's so iconic. If you watch *Casablanca* today, you'll be astonished by how many phrases came out of it, but that's not the biggest reason. I love that there is great acting, great storytelling, great filmography, and a profoundly moral story. It's people sacrificing what they want most to do the right thing.

What are a few of your favorite quotes?

"If you want to be happy, think what you can do for somebody else. If you really wanna be miserable, think what's owed to you." – Frank Purdue

"There's a divinity that shapes our ends, rough-hew them how we will." – William Shakespeare

What do you consider your greatest achievements to date?

I'm really happy with some of what I've done in human relations. I have occasionally advised family businesses who were, at the time, at each other's throats. I could give some suggestions and help relationships heal. I love, love, love that.

How do you define success?

Success is using your talents, abilities, and skills at their highest level and making progress towards a goal you believe in.

Mitzi Perdue likes nothing better than to share insider tips and actionable advice for successful family businesses. To access Mitzi's books, blog, and podcast, and to engage Mitzi about speaking on family legacies, the end of human trafficking, and her Mental Help Global initiative, visit mitziperdue.com.

SAM ROBINS

Game Changer
How Football, Faith, and Race
Shaped a Green Beret's Journey

Sam Robins is the COO and co-founder of Axios Security Group, focusing on security management. A Gardner Webb University alum, he transitioned from an accounting specialist to a Special Forces Lt. Colonel, serving on seven combat deployments. Now based in Texas, Sam is a family man, married with four children, an entrepreneur, and a man of God.

No Accountability

I grew up near Columbus, Ohio, in a mostly middle-class, homogeneous suburb with my parents and two older brothers. My family has lived in Ohio for their entire lives. My parents even went to the same school together. We played sports and rode bikes. It was a great place to grow up.

Then my parents divorced. I was 11 when my dad left, and everything massively changed. Alcohol and drugs were introduced into my life, and I had no accountability. My oldest brother went to college. My mom remarried and moved with my other brother to South Florida. I didn't want to go, so I moved in with my dad in another town.

He married a woman struggling with intense alcoholism. One night, they both came home intoxicated and fighting. She destroyed every piece of glass downstairs, including the coffee table, and threw knives at my dad. I thought she was going to kill him.

I saw and experienced things no child should. After a year, I had to leave.

I had just turned 13 when I moved to South Florida to live with my mom. The culture shock was intense. I went from "*Leave It to Beaver*," White suburbia to the other end of the spectrum. They filmed the first episode of Cops right down the street from my future high school. My mom couldn't always pick me up, so I took the late bus or had to walk home. People tried to sell me drugs on the way. It was a rough area. God's hand was on me.

I went to Pompano Beach Middle School, one of the worst in Florida. I was new and hadn't had a lot of Black friends before. I didn't care about race, but I was ignorant of different backgrounds.

In gym class, during the first week of school, a few Black kids were throwing candy at another girl. She told them to stop, but they weren't listening. In an attempt to help, I said, "Hey, dude! Stop." After that, I was marked. The rest of that year, kids would randomly attack me. There was a thing called "Cracker Day," a sort of unannounced but known occurrence. A few times in the hallway at the start of school, someone would yell "Cracker Day"—or no one would say anything—either way, a White person was probably getting hurt, and multiple times it was me.

For reasons I don't understand, I never developed hate. I think many would have; I think many did. But not all the Black kids at my school hated me. Some were kind and some were my friends.

High School Football

Ely High School, the one Cops filmed near, was also one of the top 10 high schools in the country for players going into the NFL. When I started there, I decided I would play football.

As I started getting bigger, I got really good. By junior year, I was starting. There were probably three White kids on the team, myself included, so I was an anomaly. But in those four years, I became friends with my teammates. We had a real respect for each other, one I knew to be true because, even through knocking each other down and occasionally knocking each other out, we remained a solid team.

My cultural experience has been unique. There are so many stereotypes about how people grow up. I became the opposite of what I believe most would think. I enjoy spending time and learning from people of all cultures. I have a lot of empathy for those who grow up differently. I realized it's hard for everyone, no matter your background.

Finding God

During the summer before my senior year of high school, my friend Harold started thinking about changing schools. Our mutual friend, Pat, went to Westminster Academy, an expensive, Christian, powerhouse in private school football. Pat's father introduced me to Dr. Daniel Kanell, who offered to sponsor me to attend. His son, Danny Kanell, was an All-American and future NFL quarterback. This was a huge opportunity, but I didn't want to leave my team at Ely. I was in a tough spot.

In the end, I went through with the admissions process. As a Christian school, they asked me about my faith. I remember, "If you died today, do you know for certain you will go to heaven?" and, "If you died today and met Jesus Christ, what would you say about why He should let you into heaven?"

I grew up Catholic but never went to church. My answers were clunky. But the admission counselor was kind and shared the verses Ephesians 2:8-9. You can't earn your way to heaven; it must be by faith.

Two nights later in my bedroom, my world was rocked. This was an amazing opportunity. The Lord was leading me down this path. On my knees, I gave my life to Christ and went on to have an amazing senior year at Westminster.

Nearly Derailed Before College

"Football saved my life, but Jesus saved my soul," is my personal tagline. My faith is so important to me. It's who I am, and I know it's real.

For the most part, football kept me out of trouble. My friends would tell me, "You're the only one who's going to make it out of here. You're going to do something real." Some of them ended up in jail and worse.

I was still young in my faith when I almost got arrested for stealing something valuable. It was a felony and could have derailed everything. The cops were ready to take me away, but the store owner heard what I told the cops. I was headed to college and an arrest would certainly throw that away. He didn't press any charges, and I was let go.

From then on, I made an effort to go a different route. After my freshman year in college, I went home for the summer, and instead of calling up old friends, I looked for a church.

Going to College

My dad went to college for accounting and owned a small accounting firm near Columbus, Ohio. I always knew I would go to college. School came pretty easily to me, especially math.

I ended up at Gardner Webb University (GWU) in North Carolina. I walked onto the team and played sporadically.

I met my wife on summer break at home, and eventually, she attended GWU. While we were dating, we worked on an inner-city mission in South Carolina, about a 30-minute drive from our school. Every Saturday, we knocked on doors and held a Bible class for kids. That was awesome. Before I joined the military, that's what I planned to do with my life.

Military Career

My friend Harold called me about another opportunity during senior year: "Let's join the Army."

I said, "No dude. I'm getting ready to marry Lori. I'm gonna get an accounting job and continue our work with the inner city mission project."

But once I heard the idea, I couldn't get rid of it. I kept seeing the Army everywhere. Even Lori said, "I always thought I'd marry a military guy."

So, I prayed and enlisted, eventually becoming an Officer.

From Accounting Specialist to Special Forces in eight short years, I went on to serve on seven combat deployments. Over 24 years, I was away from home for five or six years at least when you add it all up between deployments, training, schools, and more.

I was fortunate to lead amazing men and women. When you're leading, you're the first one in and the last one to leave. You're constantly thinking about your Soldiers because when you serve them, you serve the country.

I thank God that I didn't internalize hate growing up because being open changed my life. When I became a Christian and started having more love, I looked at every single person as a child of God. We're all human. We have feelings, we care, and we love our children. That helped me culturally in the military. As a Green Beret, I was seeing other cultures and learning different languages.

I'm not colorblind. I see the differences, and I love them. It's a balancing act, but I love talking about it. My experience defines who I am, and I find it's not what people usually expect when they look at me.

Through all my military requirements, I did my best to be around the family. I had a great assignment lined up and was on track to get promoted to Colonel, but I had a new set of small children and wanted to be in their lives more. On top of that, my wife was in a major car accident years prior and needed surgery. I loved our new life in Texas, and the job opportunities were limitless. All of that is why I decided to retire in 2020.

Focus Today

I'm taking a crack at being an entrepreneur. I started a couple businesses with two of my best friends: a security company with Jereme and a kid's ninja gym with Chad.

I'm enjoying being around my family more and building the kind of life I never had growing up. I have two little boys in addition to my two adult daughters and get to take them to school, sports practice, and ninja class. Life is simple, fun, and wonderful.

I want to use the rest of my life to add impact. I went from a punk kid with no future to hanging out with ambassadors and heads of state from multiple countries, and as a Special Forces officer, I had influence with them. I would have never been anything. Even going to college was a big deal for me, and now here I am, an entrepreneur with multiple businesses. It's pretty amazing, and I don't take any credit for it. It all goes to God.

SAM'S THOUGHT LEADER LESSONS

Leadership

When I was a Commander in the US Army Special Forces (Green Beret), I asked one of my Soldiers, a Weapons Sergeant with the job code 18B, to take on a new responsibility, and he offered up that he was "just an 18B," insinuating that he wasn't good enough to complete the task.

I had heard this statement before, but this time, it irritated me. So, I took the moment to mentor him. I encouraged him to instead, be confident. Say something more like, "I am a United States Army Special Forces Green Beret Senior Non-Commissioned Officer capable of leading up to a 100-person armed force to overthrow a rogue nation or resist an occupying power."

He laughed it off and said, "Got it, Sir."

The Special Forces has a motto: "Quiet Professional." Leaders must balance confidence with humility without becoming either conceited or insecure.

We must see ourselves as more so that we can become more, for ourselves and for others. Don't downplay who you are or the skills, training, experience, and attributes you possess.

Health and Wellness

- Vehemently stay out of the inner aisles in grocery stores. All of the dangerous chemicals and "foods" live there.
- Move throughout the day. Walk, run, jump, step, pick up, etc.... Do something! Eat fewer calories than you burn—simple but not easy.
- Everyone needs to lift weights of some kind—bones lose density as we get older.
- Drink lots of water daily.
- Sleep seven hours minimum and get outside when the sun is out daily.
- Limit alcohol or don't drink at all.
- Read 10 pages minimum daily for your mind growth.

Q&A WITH SAM

What are a few of your favorite quotes?

"You must be shapeless, formless, like water. When you pour water in a cup, it becomes the cup. When you pour water in a bottle, it becomes the bottle. When you pour water in a teapot, it becomes the teapot. Water can drip and it can crash. Become like water my friend." – Bruce Lee

"We should not spend much time mourning the men who died. Rather we should thank God that such men lived." – General George S. Patton

"I believe in Christianity as I believe that the sun has risen: not only because I see it, but because by it I see everything else." – C.S. Lewis

What is some of the best advice you've received?

Forgiveness and grace are the keys to fruitful and healthy relationships; without them, you will never have the relationships you desire.

Buy assets; limit liabilities to those that will lead to buying assets.

"I am the Way, the Truth, and the Life. No one comes to the Father except through me...." – Jesus, John 14:6

Count the cost of making commitments. Once made, fulfill them!

What is your favorite song or who is your favorite musical artist?

"Lord, You're Beautiful" by Keith Green: His music is very simple and his love for the Lord is pure.

"Are You with Me" by Lost Frequencies: The music video showcases a strong love for family and the longing for them when far apart.

"Do or Die" by Gospel Gangstaz: Former gang members turned Christian Rap artists. Their music is fire and helped me during my young adult years to transition from hardcore non-beneficial music to music that is inspirational and clean.

Who are your mentors and greatest influences?

Jesus Christ – Savior of the World – He brought salvation, peace, and direction to my life, and I seek to live for and honor Him daily.

Michael Fletcher – Pastor of family, marriage, and parenting – He and his wife taught my wife and me how to be married successfully, raise disciplined and loving children, and in general navigate life together.

George Frost – Faithful and committed father to his family – He was instrumental in helping me be successful in life by taking a chance on me as a young, lost punk kid. Because of him, my life was forever changed and I met Jesus and gave my life to Him.

Maurice Philogene – LinkedIn influencer – He solidified my understanding that we work for things that can entrap us into working forever for things we don't need. He also helped me see that I could take the risk on an entrepreneurial life by taking an honest inventory of my assets and income.

What do you make sure you always do?

Talk to God, pray, and read the Word of God. Whatever you do first thing in the morning and right before bed is what you remember the most.

What philanthropic causes do you support?

- International Missionaries (Philippines, Brazil, Kenya, Nigeria, Cuba) combating child and sex trafficking
- Houston Livestock Show and Rodeo (scholarships)

What books do you often recommend?

- The Bible (Gospels and Romans specifically)
- *How to Win Friends and Influence People* by Andrew Carnegie
- *Relentless* by Tim Grover
- *Psychology of Influence* by Robert Cialdini

How do you define success?

A healthy family in mind, body, and spirit.

Seek first the kingdom of God and everything else will be added unto you! To connect with Sam Robins and learn more about his journey from Special Forces to security leadership, or to explore potential collaborations and insights, email d.sam.robins@gmail.com or call 910-578-3391. Sam is eager to share his experiences and offer guidance to those seeking to make a meaningful impact.

 Sam Robins - ASG Business Card

RICK GRAY

Challenge Yourself Daily

Rick Gray is an Amazon #1 bestselling author, real estate coach, and the sales director for Huzi.ai. He helps Realtors all over the country dramatically increase their sales through systems, processes, and utilizing the power of AI.

How Jim Rohn Led Me Forward

My dad used to get the Nightingale Conant audio series *Insights*, so I grew up listening to Earl Nightingale, Zig Ziglar, and Jim Rohn. There was something about Jim in particular that resonated with me. I loved the stories he told to bring his points to life and I memorized all of his material.

When I was 26, I wrote a letter to Jim inquiring about working for him. About a month later, the founder of Jim Rohn International, Kyle Wilson, invited me to fly to Dallas and meet with the team. I jumped at the chance and, when I came back home, told my wife that I was putting my real estate license and thriving business on hold.

At Jim Rohn International, we traveled to different cities across the US to do 30-minute presentations for sales companies and then promote an event with Jim Rohn. On my second day, one of my coworkers got sick and could not do their presentation for a mortgage company in downtown Dallas, Texas. Everybody thought we'd have to cancel, but instead, I said I'd do it. I didn't even know the talk yet, but I was eager to impress. I spent that whole night doing the talk over and over again in the warehouse where all of the boxes of Jim Rohn books and cassette series were stored. I slept for one hour on the couch in Kyle's office.

The next morning, I was scared and nervous, but I had total confidence in the material. Even if I forgot everything else, I knew when Jim's seminar was going to be and the cost, because that was on the brochure. I also had faith that I knew Jim Rohn. I'd had his material ingrained in me for years. I arrived almost an hour early and sat in my car rehearsing.

There were 10 people at the talk, and I had six sales! This was the start of an amazing four years of traveling the country and doing hundreds of presentations.

Do You Want to Get Business? Or Build a Business?

In 2000, after the seminar business started to wane, my wife and I moved back home to Oregon and got back into real estate together as partners.

Real estate from 2001-2006 was great, but in May 2007, the phone stopped ringing. The real estate market shut down and stayed down. The Great Recession had just begun, and I was blindsided.

Financially, 2007 and 2008 were the most difficult years of my life. But, looking back, they forced me to learn the power of systems, how to actually build a business.

Because my wife and I had been making good money as a team, I thought I was skilled in real estate. After 2007, I realized our success had been the result of a good circle of influence. A lot of people knew who I was. But, I didn't have any systems. Until 2007, I had been good at GETTING business, but I didn't really know how to BUILD a business. If business didn't just come to me, I was stuck. That was a really hard lesson.

Process Outweighs Outcomes

When my son Alex was five years old, we lived in Meridian, Idaho, right across the street from a golf course. One day I took him to the driving range. I wouldn't consider myself a great golfer, but I enjoy playing. Golf is a notoriously difficult skill sport, so I didn't expect much from my son that day, but to my surprise, at five years old, he was hitting the ball well immediately. I thought, *Wow, he's a natural. Maybe I should get him a coach.*

We found a great junior golf program with head instructor Jonathan Gibbs of the PGA. My son's first lesson was one hour, and Johnathan taught him three things: the approach (where the ball should be in relation to your stance), rhythm of the swing, and body position on the follow-through.

During this lesson, I noticed Alex wasn't hitting the ball very well. After watching him be inconsistent for about 45 minutes, I finally asked Johnathan, "At what point do we care where the ball goes?"

Jonathan set me straight: "Rick, we're laying a foundation for his swing right now. I don't care where the ball goes."

That may sound obvious, but I was 42 years old, had played golf most of my adult life, and had never really thought about that. I was always reacting and adjusting to **results**. If I sliced it, I would change my stance and my grip. If I hooked it, I opened the clubface a little and tried to sweep my swing more. Because I always adjust to results, I never developed a consistent golf game.

My son was crushing me at golf by 14 years old. Why? Because he went several years without caring about results. He mastered a process, and then the results were there. Being a process-based thinker rather than an outcome-based thinker is a great wisdom I've learned over the years.

I relate that to business, especially real estate, when I coach agents and brokers. How many agents in the business are constantly chasing the next deal, client, or commission but never stop to build a business? Or to master a system that is duplicatable and scalable? Agents who are always adjusting to results never achieve consistency. Agents who put systems in place that are scalable and repeatable have leverage and thriving businesses.

I've been coaching agents and brokers for over 14 years and have been a licensed real estate broker for over 30 years now. In my coaching business, it's not uncommon for my clients to double or triple their business in one year as a result of a shift in mindset, developing consistent systems, and being focused on the right things.

AI — The NEW Game

After the 2007 recession hit, it took me two painful years to figure out that I had to move in the direction of the market—short sales, foreclosures, and distressed properties. Once I figured it out, I sold a lot of houses again and made my recovery.

When I first saw AI, in the form of ChatGPT in December of 2022, I knew two things right away. One, I had to learn this immediately. I saw a new game coming, and I didn't want to be stuck playing the old game like I was in 2007. Two, I had to teach AI to my coaching clients so their businesses would thrive in the coming months and years. I didn't want it to take two years again to figure this out, so I took action right away. A friend of mine, Eric Post, had just started an AI platform called Huzi, and together, we decided to focus on the real estate industry.

We have created a fantastic platform for real estate agents and are building an entire ecosystem for agents and brokers to become so much better, more creative, and more effective for their clients. In every phase of the business, from lead generation and marketing to transaction coordination and negotiating, we have tools and processes to help the agent be outstanding. We also have tools for the homeowner to have a world-class experience with their home, giving them the ability to interact with every home system through an AI interface. Not only do agents get more work done using Huzi, but the quality of their work is much higher as well. In the end, the clients' experience is better.

We are still in the early adoption stages of AI, and its future is going to be massive. Think about the internet in 1995, major news outlets were downplaying its impact on everyday people and lives. Wow, were they wrong. AI is in that same category, severely underestimated as to how much it will affect our lives. It's coming, so if you want to be successful in real estate, get on board with Huzi.ai now.

RICK'S THOUGHT LEADER LESSONS

Brazilian Jiu Jitsu, Back Pain, Ice Baths, and the Benefits of Doing Difficult Things Consistently

What if I handed you $5 million, but to receive it, you would die the next day? You wouldn't do it. Health is the most precious asset we have. Take care of yourself and make it a priority to live a happy and fulfilling life.

The reason we don't take good care of our minds and bodies is not a lack of knowledge or even time for most people, it's just not a priority. We have a comfort crisis in the world today. Most people are rarely uncomfortable and, as a result, mental and physical health is suffering.

As a distance runner in high school and college, I struggled with low back pain for many years. When I took up Brazilian jiu jitsu in 2021, that back pain became almost unbearable. I was fine at the gym, but each night I could barely walk. I tried so many things to help alleviate the pain! Ibuprofen, turmeric, yoga, stretching, cryotherapy, my doctor prescribed diclofenac (I don't like taking medication for anything), and nothing worked.

In December 2022, I finally tried doing ice baths. I walked down to the river by my house, through the snow in 19-degree air, and into the frigid water. After two minutes, I felt a noticeable improvement. So, I decided to buy a livestock trough, put it in the backyard, and fill it with water.

On December 28, 2022, I started doing ice baths every single day and as of today have not missed a single day. 650 in a row as I write this. My back pain is long gone, which is life-changing in itself, but there are so many other benefits that have come from consistent ice baths. There is real value in doing hard things, and among the most impactful, is more confidence. Confidence affects every area of life.

Doing difficult things on purpose develops resilience to deal with unexpected hardships. Just like the body, the mind adapts and develops resilience. If you never stress your muscles, you won't be very strong or fit. If you never challenge your mind, the same thing applies. Forcing yourself to do difficult things (that are good for you) will have massive positive effects on your life. The key is doing hard things **consistently**. Most people will dabble and challenge themselves occasionally, but consistency wins. Doing things that push you out of your comfort zone **every single day** is the recipe for success.

Commitments should take priority over feelings and motivation. There have been days when doing an ice bath was inconvenient for me as I was traveling. I did it anyway. There have been days where it was -2 degrees out and I didn't feel like an ice bath. I did it anyway. This has really built my self-discipline and increased my confidence in a big way. Forcing yourself to do hard things becomes a habit and you feel powerful. You KNOW you can do hard things, you have confidence and belief (REAL belief) in yourself and there are no setbacks that will stop you.

This mirrors my journey in Brazilian jiu jitsu. It's all about overcoming resistance, getting out of your comfort zone, and pushing yourself to be better in the face of adversity. Being comfortable outside your comfort zone sounds simple but is very difficult in practice. You must evolve and grow, which is not easy. Most people won't do it for long because it's tough! YOU get to decide what you want your life to look like. Just remember, great rewards do not come unless there is great suffering and effort put in.

Start with something simple like reading or keeping a journal. Do a little bit every single day, and eventually, it will become a habit. Then you can expand on what you do and it will start to have a big effect on your life.

Developing a habit like keeping a journal can be life-changing, so get started now. You will be so glad you did. Remember, it's not what you are capable of, it's what you DO that matters.

Q&A WITH RICK

What is your favorite movie?

Groundhog Day. It's about personal development and life lessons. I love the process the main character goes through to finally land on the truth. Happiness and meaning come from being the best you can be and helping others.

What is your favorite song or who is your favorite musical artist?

I love all sorts of music. From heavy metal to country, classical, pop, jazz, and rock. People who write their own music and tell amazing stories are my favorites as I appreciate greatness in all areas. Music is such a mood enhancer!

What are your pet peeves?

People who don't consider others bother me, whether in business, on the road in a car, or just in general. I strive to be a kind and generous person and am disappointed when I see others who are selfish.

Who are your mentors and greatest influences?

Jim Rohn had a big influence on my life! I had listened to and memorized nearly all of his material before joining Kyle Wilson at Jim Rohn International and becoming his top salesperson.

My parents have been married for over 50 years and have been a major positive influence on me as well.

What is some of the best advice you've received?

Learn from other people's mistakes, you won't have time to make them all yourself.

What do you consider your superpower?

Making complex issues simple for others to grasp. Motivating others to take action and feel inspired.

What do you make sure you always do?

Create things to look forward to. Being excited and optimistic about the future is very important to me.

What hobbies do you enjoy?

Jiu jitsu, dirt bike riding, video games, reading to my wife, fly fishing, shooting, slackline, snow and water skiing, and snowboarding.

What books do you often recommend?

Atomic Habits by James Clear, *The Four Agreements* by Don Miguel Ruiz, *The 7 Habits of Highly Effective People* by Stephen R. Covey.

What do you consider your greatest achievements to date?

Marrying Dawn. My life partner is the best thing that has ever happened to me. Raising two beautiful children with hearts of gold. Creating my coaching company. Graduating from university. Becoming the type of person I can be proud of by treating others well and being a lifelong learner.

What has been your greatest lesson?

Your choice of a life partner will have the biggest effect on your life. Choose wisely and work continuously to improve that relationship. Environment and associations are more powerful than knowledge and information.

Find more on Rick Gray, executive coach, speaker, HUZI.ai sales director, founder of Rick Gray International, and cofounder of Gem State Modern real estate at www.rickgray.com Email: Rick@RickGray.com
Instagram: therealrickgray YouTube: @rickgraycoaching
Facebook: https://www.facebook.com/rick.gray.754 and Rick Gray International

 Rick Gray's website.

MARY HAUPTMAN

Resilience and Growth
From Independent Court Reporter to
Entrepreneur & Real Estate Investor

Mary Hauptman is an accomplished entrepreneur and real estate investor from Long Island, New York. She began her career as a court reporter and soon graduated to having her own court reporting school and agency. Today, Mary owns, manages, and develops property in New York and Northwest Florida.

Court Reporter

I grew up on Long Island, New York, in the hamlet of Central Islip. Those unfamiliar with the area may imagine I was among the opulent West Egg and East Egg mansions of *The Great Gatsby* or the 30,000-square-foot "country homes" of the Vanderbilts. I can tell you that the setting of my childhood was a far cry from that frame of reference.

I have fond memories of growing up with my mother, father, and five siblings in our modest, three-bedroom, one-bathroom home. While in high school, I learned more about the opportunities that might come my way if I focused on my studies. I might even be able to have just one job, instead of three, like my dad did.

During homeroom at the start of my junior year, I noticed a flier for a scholarship awarded by W. Clement Stone to aspiring court reporters. Just weeks prior, my father had coincidentally seen a "help wanted" ad for a court reporter in our local newspaper, the *Long Island Press*. Recalling how he marveled at the starting salary, I made a beeline for the guidance office. I picked up the scholarship application and became determined to be its recipient.

My parents had nonchalantly mentioned plans to sell our house and move even further out east to a community called Center Moriches. I always assumed this would happen after I finished school and didn't pay much attention to the gradual disappearance of our furniture. It wasn't until all of the mattresses were gone and we were sleeping on the floor that the reality of my parents' decision to move finally set in.

I was 16. Leaving the district would make my eligibility for the coveted scholarship null and void. There was no way I was going to give that up. But I would have to fend for myself entirely and find a place to live entirely on my own.

I often think back to that day when everything changed—when the sun hung low in the sky over my now-former home, casting a shadow on the ground as my family's station wagon honked and pulled away.

You better believe I earned that scholarship. I was seated on my rickety rollaway cot in the room I was renting for $25 a week when I opened the letter. A jolt of excitement raced through my body like lightning; I knew my life would never be the same.

My court reporting course was 17 months of contiguous classes, equivalent to four years in college. You had to know the vocabulary, the procedures, and how to handle attorneys, some of whom were total hotheads.

At the age of 19, I finished my schooling and finally began my career. My earnings certainly did not reflect what my father had seen in the newspaper, but at least I was starting somewhere.

Starting a School as a Business

There was a legal television show, *LA Law*, with a female court reporter who led an incredibly exciting life. I think she inspired a lot of women to become court reporters. When I was in school, more than two-thirds of the students were men and there were no more than 15 students in each of my classes. After *LA Law* premiered, there was suddenly a shortage of court reporting schools. It was then that the idea of starting my own crossed my mind.

Shortly after I started working, the Long Island court reporting school I attended was closing its doors. The opportunity was clear to me: buy the school. With three other couples, I took up the lease on the space and we opened our own school. I would eventually buy out the partners and become the sole owner of the multimillion-dollar business.

The perk of our school was that we also had a division that was an agency. So, upon graduating, you were virtually guaranteed a job so long as you could get the job done well.

Years into the business, the entire industry started to change. Our reporters were well compensated because they were exceptional. However, once insurance companies nudged their way into the courtroom for medical cases, profitability plummeted. Many of our court reporters specialized in medical malpractice cases because, although it was the most difficult to learn, it often led to the largest paychecks. This was no longer the case.

Additionally, the industry was pointing more toward tape recorders and the use of audio devices. At the same time, I started losing interest. It just wasn't my passion anymore.

Real Estate Journey

By that time, I had begun investing in real estate and discovered it as my new passion. I closed the school and the agency, sold off some accounts, and devoted my time to acquiring larger assets.

Even before I purchased my first house, I was drawn to real estate. I always enjoyed seeing how houses were designed and built, how they were valued, and how location affected those values. I taught myself more about the business by researching listings and listening to audio tapes. In my early 20s, I bought my first rental home, only a couple thousand square feet. Years later, I expanded my holdings to nearly 200,000 square feet—many funded by my earnings from my court-reporting school and agency.

Today, I have focused much of my energy on the Gulf Coast and am in the process of developing my first multifamily projects there.

MARY'S THOUGHT LEADER LESSONS

Discipline

My father, Earl Hauptman, was an austere man who led our household in a strict, no-nonsense fashion. I and my five rambunctious siblings anointed him the "Duke of Earl" as a cheeky acknowledgment of his rigidity. He had high expectations for us including that we take his words seriously at all times. When he established the rule that we must arrive home before curfew if we wished to sleep inside, I didn't dare call his bluff. Indeed, the distinct click of our door latch could be heard at the same time every night.

I admittedly found my father's propensity for discipline rather stifling. It wasn't until I was living on my own and began setting professional goals for myself that I grew to appreciate it. Surely I would not have been capable of living on my own at age 16 had it not been for the strong sense of responsibility that my upbringing instilled in me.

Discipline is the catalyst for confidence. Establishing consistent habits, building resilience, and pushing beyond what is comfortable fosters an unwavering sense of self-worth. Developing a strong discipline muscle is one of the most strategic ways to grow. When it comes to your likelihood of achieving success, I am a firm believer that your level of self-discipline is the guiding factor. While many are quick to abandon their dreams when the going gets tough, those with a strong, guided sense of purpose will likely push ever-restlessly forward until the end. Give yourself the respect you deserve by actively working to improve your level of discipline in all facets of your life.

Investing and Financial Independence

To maintain and expand our healthy real estate portfolio, I have opted to guide our firm's investment strategy rather conservatively. Such caution may have resulted in a few missed opportunities, but I am certain it has also prevented us from engaging in what could have been very sour deals. I liken our conservative investment philosophy to a wall of armor against market volatility, a barrier that minimizes our exposure to the kind of risks I have seen wreak havoc on impulsive investors.

I find it is best to approach potential business partners and investors with an even higher degree of caution. Several years ago, I entered into a partnership with someone who ultimately led our company to lose just under one million dollars. After this tumultuous experience, I have grown increasingly wary of entrusting others to understand and successfully carry out the vision of our company.

Listening to your instincts when making important business decisions is undoubtedly useful, but this should never be the only force guiding your decisions. Always seek to provide yourself with supporting evidence, especially before making a lofty commitment to a new venture. Sometimes, emotions cloud our judgment. Sometimes, we so desperately want to finalize a deal that we overlook important details, fail to ask essential questions, and divert our gaze from the sea of red flags waving right in front of us.

To make the best financial decisions possible, I remind myself: If it seems too good to be true, it probably is. And you can never do a good deal with a bad guy.

Gratitude

When I was 20 years old, I was living in a Long Island town that wasn't necessarily renowned for its safety. At the time, I didn't give it much thought. I was content with being able to afford not just a room, but a full apartment, on my own.

It was October 30, and I was just arriving home after a particularly long day working as a hearing reporter during an arbitration. Finally reaching home, I drove up to the garage of my complex. It had a manual door; the kind you pull open by hand. I hoisted it high enough to fit my Volkswagen and distinctly remember feeling that I was being watched. I turned to take a look, but all that was behind me was the empty street. Momentarily relieved, I hopped back into my car and drove in.

When I exited my car to close the garage door behind me, I froze at the sight of a man holding a pistol hiding behind the outside wall. Before I knew it, the gun was against my head. My screaming—probably the loudest I've ever let out before—was met with demands to keep quiet. His "Stop screaming!" threats grew more aggressive, but I was overcome with terror and just couldn't stop.

Eyes closed, I was sure it was over for me. Just when I thought my life was going to end, a neighbor yelled, "Leave her alone!" from the window above and pointed a firearm straight at the assailant. At the sight of the gun, he ran. He took my purse, but I got my life.

That moment would forever change my perspective; indeed, there is truth to, "you don't know what you have until it's gone." If ever I find myself bothered by miniscule things, I remind myself of that fateful moment and tune into the feeling of intense gratitude I felt to still be alive. Not everyone is so lucky. Had my neighbor not intervened, perhaps I would not have been so lucky either.

If you are not grateful for what you have now, you will never enjoy whatever you think you still need. We have become so accustomed to the need for more and more stuff, and when we do acquire it, our appreciation is fleeting. The desire for something "better" soon takes hold.

Avoid falling into this trap by making a conscious effort to really experience the blessings that surround you every day. No matter how small, there is always something to be grateful for. And if you can't find it, remember this: you're alive.

Leadership

I am certain that the energy a leader brings to the workplace is directly reflected in that of his or her team. It is surprising how quickly employees will decipher a leader's mood after only a few moments of observation. A leader mustn't only focus on his or her actions; tone of voice and body language are equally important.

If I bring any hint of negativity to my organization, I notice the room immediately grows tense. My team becomes, like me, on edge, often resulting in a serious productivity decline.

It is not about forcing a smile while in dire straits; pretending a problem does not exist is not conducive to good leadership. What's important is facing reality from a place of strength rather than weakness. In the midst of a storm, it falls upon the captain to foster a steadied sense of calm and focus. As the captain of your ship, you must steer your crew in the right direction and lead by example. Always keep in mind that you cannot expect something from your team that you do not deliver yourself.

Q&A WITH MARY

How do you recharge?

I recharge by changing my surroundings. A fresh perspective is essential to creativity as it often leads to new ideas and serendipitous inspiration. Even the simple act of taking a walk outside is a strategy I often lean on to recharge and reflect.

What are a few of your favorite quotes?

"Be careful of the environment you choose for it will shape you; be careful the friends you choose for you will become like them." – W. Clement Stone

"Don't wish it were easier, wish you were better." – Jim Rohn

Who are your mentors and greatest influences?

W. Clement Stone, who awarded me my scholarship to court reporting school and completely changed the trajectory of my life.

Have you had any past challenges that turned out to be blessings?

When my court reporting business expanded and I opened a court reporting school, I found—what I thought was—the perfect location. Unfortunately, the deal fell through. The residents did not want a business leasing the property, formerly an elementary school. Just a few months later, a large office building hit the market. Even better than my original idea, it would be one of the greatest financial decisions of my life. That's the moment I really started believing that everything happens for a reason.

What is some of the best advice you've received?

My father would always say, "If you want to have a lot of money, you have to own your own business." Both my mother and my father were very supportive and instilled an entrepreneurial spirit in me at a very young age.

What books do you often recommend?

Ask! by Mark Victor Hansen, *Thou Shall Prosper* by Rabbi Daniel Lapin, *The Power of Positive Thinking* by Norman Vincent Peale, and *Rich Dad Poor Dad* by Robert Kiyosaki.

Explore how Mary Hauptman, accomplished entrepreneur, real estate investor, and developer, can assist you in navigating the dynamic landscape of entrepreneurship and real estate development. With her extensive experience, Mary offers valuable insights and opportunities for collaboration. Email her today at maryhauptman@gmail.com to explore how she can support your journey toward success.

CARLOS DELHERRA

From the Streets of Compton
An Entrepreneur's Path to Prosperity

Carlos Delherra is an entrepreneur, real estate investor, developer, syndicator, and philanthropist in Southern California. His $100 million in total asset value property management and investment firm focuses on student housing. Carlos is married and a proud father of two children.

Don't Hate, Participate!

Growing up in one of the most dangerous cities in Los Angeles County, I faced dreadful public schools, an inept and corrupt local government, and a police force that was feared. When I was 12, a person visibly high on drugs, put a gun to my head. I persuaded him that killing me wasn't worth it and did not lose sleep that night. Deathly violence was numbing.

Most people around me were mad at the world and its injustices. They were angry for being dealt a bad hand. Frustrated that the government had disappointed them. Resentful that they were not afforded the privileges of others who lived in better neighborhoods and had more financial resources. But the worst part was, it seemed to me, they accepted all this as facts of life.

As risky and life-threatening as it was to move to Compton, my hard-working parents boldly uprooted our family for better opportunities. My mother always hustled. She sold clothes at the flea market, sold sweet Mexican corn as a street vendor, and at times collected cans with me begrudgingly in tow. My parents did their best with limited resources. Still, the pain and shame of poverty impacted me tremendously and I was determined to find a way out.

In 1993, I found a pamphlet at my high school about a summer college program at UC Santa Barbara and earned myself a seat and a scholarship. This was just after the 1992 riots in Los Angeles, and I wanted to get away from that hostile environment for just a little while. That summer in Santa Barbara was eye-opening. It was my first exposure to white people outside of the few teachers I had growing up. I met privileged kids for the first time. And guess what? They were some of the nicest people I had ever encountered. They were like me but just happened to win the parent lottery and have skin of a different color. I became close friends with several of them.

They taught me how to properly study. I felt they were rooting for me to succeed. Without their help, I don't think I would have passed my college courses.

They treated me as their own. And they were fascinated to be friends with a kid from Compton. They called me Compton Carlos. I like to think I showed them some things about people with my background. I was friendly and poor but happy and hopeful, and I had the courage to step into that challenging college environment. I believe they were impressed by my fighting spirit as I adapted and put in the long study hours with a positive attitude. After learning about their lives and the contrast with mine, I felt proud of my roots. I didn't have the advantage of good schools and private tutors, but I was willing to put in the work and catch up!

Around this time, I started saying to my friends and family, "Don't hate, participate!" It was my way of telling the world I did not accept things as they were, that hate and frustration were not the best reactions to the environment around us. The opposite of hate is love. Love was not a word you threw around in my tough neighborhood, but I believe a positive, "don't hate, participate" mindset set me apart and made a huge difference in my life.

I left Santa Barbara that summer with more hope and confidence about the world. Not all the things I learned in the ghetto were accurate or as advertised. There were good people in the world willing to help you. You simply had to ask. There were resources available if you were willing to look and had courage. Seek and you shall find.

The problem is that when you are guided by hate, you can't see the love in the world. It was always there, but I didn't have the right lens to see it. If you are willing to participate in the game of life, the opportunities that open up for you are boundless. The limits we perceive in our minds are created by us. The universe is flowing with abundance. You just have to believe it and take action. Hate and anger attract negativity that pulls you down further in life. If you are open and hopeful, the universe will provide everything you desire. This philosophy would later forge a central part of my life, helping me achieve things that I could not have imagined before that fateful summer.

The Advantage of Disadvantaged

When I started my business career, I still wore the label of "disadvantaged" that I took from Compton, but I had learned to embrace my underdog status because it pushed me to be stronger, more confident, and more tenacious. It became a superpower. I loved the idea of being underestimated and going out to the world to prove people wrong. As I climbed the corporate ladder, the shame of poverty I felt growing up turned into a source of pride. When I failed the "first half" of my real estate career during the Great Recession in 2008, this mindset allowed me to quickly rebound from the bottom as it was a familiar place.

Failure is a blessing, the best teacher, and necessary for success. Once we embrace this, we have the freedom to dare to be great. We shed the fear that paralyzes most people and unbottle the courage that is inside every one of us. The only thing holding us back is ourselves. As Ralph Waldo Emerson advises, "Shoot for the moon. Even if you miss, you'll land among the stars."

In 2009, I re-started the second half of my real estate career, and since then, I have amassed a student housing portfolio of 175 units with a total asset value of $100 million. In 2024, I am in the middle of building a seven-story, 57-unit, $55 million ground-up development at the University of Southern California (USC). I am eternally grateful for the success. I have learned to intentionally practice gratitude daily, thanking God for all the little and big things I am blessed to have in my life. It helps me stay grounded and allows me to focus on the truly important things in life, especially my family and health.

Success is achievable for all of us and can be simple, but not easy. We have to be willing to do the things most people will not on a daily basis. Be consistent, determined, and willing to put in the hard work. Success, as Jim Rohn states, "is the result of nothing more than a few simple disciplines, practiced every day."

My next major goal in life is to give back and help other disadvantaged people. I want to help them find their hidden superpowers so they can unleash them much earlier in life than perhaps they would otherwise. I want to remind them that if a poor kid from Compton can do it, so can they. Personal development is where my passion truly lies. And now, after 20 years in the real estate business, I am ready to embark on this new journey.

CARLOS' THOUGHT LEADER LESSONS

Family and Parenting

Being a husband to my wife and father to my son and daughter is my number one job and responsibility. I strive to be not just a good but a great dad. By default, we become our kids' top role models, and they are keen observers, so we need to be very aware of our daily acts.

At Denis Waitley's 2023 retreat co-hosted by Kyle Wilson, Denis said something very impactful that I've heard from a few people I really respect, including Jim Rohn. Denis used to travel a lot, and he said the one regret he had, and he didn't have many, was that he wished he could have spent more time with his kids when they were growing up.

Everyone always tells you it goes fast. I've taken that to heart and try to spend as much time with them as I can. I coach their little league teams and try to be at every sport and school event they have. My kids have a good life, and I am teaching them grace and gratitude and reminding them of the modest roots their parents come from. Our kids are the biggest blessing we get in life, and I strive to be tremendously present and hope to be a mentor for them for the rest of their lives.

Personal Development

Personal development has changed my life completely. I'm a big believer and practice it daily. Every day, I get up and meditate, exercise, and then listen to a personal development podcast or audiobook. I strive daily to get a little better and to maintain and improve a strong mindset. Zig Ziglar says, "Your attitude determines your altitude."

Personal development should end when you take your last breath. The mentors and role models I didn't have growing up in Compton I found in personal development books and audiotapes. Jim Rohn's principles and values have shaped me tremendously. I cannot imagine having the success I have had without his tutelage.

I want to dedicate the second half of my life to serving others using the tools and teachings I have gained through personal development. The fulfillment I get from helping others is authentic and deep. I love to see the fire and hunger in others who remind me of my younger self and get tremendous joy witnessing and cheerleading their journey.

Personal development taught me that attitude and mindset are everything. It all starts and ends in your mind. When I mentor people and I say, "Hey, you should start a business," right away they usually come back with excuses formed in their minds. There are enough obstacles in the world. You don't need to put any more in front of yourself. There's enough negativity in the world, and your mindset is the best way to combat that. Focus on solutions and become a problem solver. That is one of the first steps to becoming an entrepreneur. Once you make that shift, you can conquer the world.

Q&A WITH CARLOS

What is your favorite song?

If I had a pick one, it would probably be U2's "I Still Haven't Found What I'm Looking For" because I feel like I'm on this lifelong journey. I'm always looking for more and never really finishing that process of growth.

How do you recharge?

Each year in January, I do a goals retreat. I do one with my wife for our family goals and one with my business partner for our business goals. There's always an energy of renewal.

Who are your mentors and greatest influences?

Robert Kiyosaki sparked my interest in real estate. He showed me the path in a way that was simple and made me believe I could do it. The Real Estate Guys then took that and helped me really put it into action while wrapping a lot of personal development around it. Then, through The Real Estate Guys, I got exposed to Jim Rohn, which shaped my business and life philosophy completely and profoundly.

What do you consider your superpower?

I'm very calm and level-headed. I don't tend to panic under pressure.

I'm also very good at blocking out all the noise, especially gossip or rumors about what people say and think about you. That includes people telling me I was crazy to start a business. I block that out and just focus on my path and journey. But I do pay attention to people who set the bar high, who I admire and want to emulate.

What is your favorite quote?

"Don't wish it was easier, wish you were better. Don't wish for less problems, wish for more skills. Don't wish for less challenge, wish for more wisdom." – Jim Rohn

Carlos Delherra is the co-founder of Mosaic Student Communities and Mosaic Investment Partners. Contact Carlos about investing, speaking engagements, and philanthropy by email at carlos@livewithmosaic.com and on Facebook as Carlos Delherra Delgado.

LES BROWN

The Deck Is Stacked Against You, So What!

Les Brown is known as one of the world's greatest speakers, motivators, inspirers, and authors. He is the #1 bestselling author of multiple books, including You've Got to Be Hungry *and* Live Your Dreams.

Two Mothers

After giving birth to me and my twin brother, Wes, on the floor of an abandoned building, my biological mother gave us up for adoption when we were six weeks old to Mrs. Mamie Brown. I always say to audiences that I'm on stage because of two women. One gave me life, the other gave me love. God took me out of my biological mother's womb and placed me in the heart of my adopted mother. I feel like Abraham Lincoln who said, "All that I am, or hope to be, I owe to my angel mother."

My adoptive mother was such an incredible force of goodness and love in my life. She is my reason for being, and she has inspired me to do so many things that I had no idea I could do. I wanted to do things for her, and that took me outside of my comfort zone. I believe to do something you've never done, you have to become someone you've never been. She has been the driving force for my success.

Labeled "Educable Mentally Retarded"

When I was in fifth grade, I was forced back a grade by the school's principal after being disruptive in class.

I was labeled "educable mentally retarded." Later, I failed the eighth grade.

My mom taught me that sticks and stones can break your bones and words can never hurt you, but words can hurt you very deeply. Being labeled by others did hurt me.

I had a defining moment when, as a junior in high school, I met Mr. Leroy Washington. I went into his classroom looking for a good friend of mine, and he said, "Young man, come. I want you to work this problem out for us before the class."

He wanted me to read a script, and I said, "I can't do that, sir." He asked why. I said, "I'm not one of your students."

He said, "Do it anyhow." I told him I couldn't, and the other students started laughing. They told him I was "Leslie, the DT... the dumb twin," compared to my brother Wesley. I told Mr. Washington it was true.

He came from behind his desk, looked at me, and said, "Don't you ever say that again. Someone's opinion of you does not have to become your reality." That was a turning point in my life. On one hand, I was humiliated, but on the other hand, I was liberated. He looked at me with the eyes of Goethe, who said, "Look at a man the way that he is, he only becomes worse. But look at him as if he were what he could be, then he becomes what he should be."

I adopted Mr. Washington as my spiritual father. I wanted to be like him. He was a great orator and instructor, and I admired his style. I watched and studied him that year in school. I was never one of his students, but I feel I learned more from him than the thousands of students he taught.

Speaking and Impacting Others

I've been speaking for 51 years now. I believe you were not born to work for a living, but to live your making, and by living your making, you will make your living. I believe I was born to speak. I love it. That's what I do best. I also train speakers.

Most people don't realize speakers get more out of it than the audience does. As Mr. Washington told me, love, hope, and inspiration are perfumes you can't sprinkle on others without getting a few drops on yourself. I always feel when I speak that I leave stronger, better, and more powerful because I was sharing with people a message that I needed to hear. We give a message out of our mess. They say a calling is something that you love so much you would do it for nothing, but you do it so well that people pay you to do it.

How people live their lives is a result of the story they believe about themselves. When we speak, we distract, dispute, and inspire. We distract people from their current story through the presentation of our knowledge, which we gained from what we've experienced. We dismantle their current belief system and inspire them to become, as Mother Teresa would say, "a pencil in the hand of God" and start writing a new chapter in their lives.

Many speakers give information. If information could change people, everybody would be skinny, rich, and happy. So, I come with stories, my story, a story about me, about my mother. A story has a human face, and it touches a person's heart. I use stories to expand a person's mind, to touch their heart, and to ignite their spirit. And that has been my success.

Being Transparent and Authentic

I had a period when life knocked me senseless. When I was going through a divorce, I was diagnosed with prostate cancer, my best friend died waiting on a liver transplant, and my mother died.

My son John Leslie was 10 years old. He came into my room and said, "Are you going to die?"

I said, "We're all going to die one day."

He said, "No, I need to know. Are you dying soon from this cancer?"

I said, "Why would you ask me that question?"

He said, "I don't hear any words coming through the doors, any motivational messages, the room is dark, the shade is down. Where's my daddy? I just want to know where he is. Is he still here, or is he in a slow process of dying?... Will you fight?"

I said, "Yes, I will fight. I'm so glad you asked me that. I'm going to fight."

He let the shade up and said, "Who do you want to listen to?"

I said, "I think I need to listen to my own words right now. Put on Les Brown speaking in the Georgia Dome." He left me with the tape, and I got back into the fight. But sometimes life can knock you so, so silly you can't think. I teach that life is a fight for territory. And once you stop fighting for what you want, what you don't want will automatically take over.

Battling Cancer and Staying Positive

I'm a 20-plus-year prostate cancer conqueror. I'm dealing with stage four cancer under the auspices of the Cancer Centers of America and Dr. Taha. When Dr. Taha told me the cancer metastasized to seven areas of my body, I smiled. Seven is my lucky number. I'm one of seven children. I was born on February 17th. Joshua marched around the Wall of Jericho seven times and dipped himself in the river seven times.

I practice meditation, prayer, upgrading my relationships, and having the mindset that whatever I'm dealing with has not come to stay. I ask, *What's the good in it? What is it that I can discover about myself?*

I think there are four main questions that we have to answer.

1. Who am I?
2. Why am I here?
3. Where am I going?
4. Who's going with me?

Answering those questions allows you to handle the storms of life.

Storms are going to come: Viktor Frankl calls it unavoidable suffering. The concept is echoed in scripture—think it not strange that you face the fiery furnaces of this world, you will. Not you might.... You will have tribulations. They are there to test you. They will bring a strength out of you. They will introduce you to a part of yourself that you don't know. I think that's why Victor Frankl said that adversity introduces a man to himself.

It's part of the human experience. Everybody's going to get their butts kicked. I don't care who you are. As Forrest Gump said, "Life is like a box of chocolates. You never know what you're going to get."

I'll never forget when Dr. Goldson, a top oncologist in Washington, DC, diagnosed me with prostate cancer. He told me my PSA was 2,400, and four is normal. But then, he stopped and said, "But you got this. We determine the diagnosis. God determines the prognosis."

You Have to Be Hungry

The deck is stacked against you. There's no question about it. And to get out of where you are, you gotta be hungry!

Jackie Robinson said, don't level the playing field. Just let me on the field, and I'll level it myself.

People that are hungry level the field. All they want is access to the game. When you are hungry, your gifts will make room for you. Bring what you have, do the best that you can, and God will do what you can't do.

Accomplishments

Les Brown has been inducted into The National Speakers Hall of Fame and is the recipient of its highest honor: The Council of Peers Award of Excellence (CPAE).

Les has received the highest award from Toastmasters International, the Golden Gavel Award.

In 1992, Les was selected as one of the top five speakers in the world alongside General H. Norman Schwarzkopf, Lee Iacocca, Robert Schuller, and Paul Harvey, receiving more votes than all combined.

LES'S THOUGHT LEADER LESSONS

The Key to Influence

The number one key to having more influence is your ability to communicate—to expand a person's vision beyond their mental conditioning, touch their hearts, and ignite their spirits. When you're able to communicate, you can take a person to a place within themselves that they can't go on their own.

As a speaker's coach, I work first on the messenger and then on the message. There are a lot of people who are speaking, but they haven't done anything. They have not lived an achievement-driven life. I think it's very important that you practice what you preach and also preach what you practice. Who you are behind the words is far more important than the words you speak.

Being a Perpetual Student

I heard Brian Tracy say that the average American reads one book a year and that if you discipline yourself to read one book a month, in five years you will have read 60 books, which will make you an expert in a particular field.

Well, I took that seriously. I disciplined myself to read between three to five books a month plus the research I did on corporations like AT&T, Procter & Gamble, McDonald's, General Electric, and IBM that allowed me to break through to speak for these elite companies. That's where 80% of my speaking has come from over the years. Had I not become a perpetual student, it would not have happened. To this day, I still read two books a month.

Authenticity from the Stage

I think, as a speaker, it's important to be transparent. When people get to the last two chapters of my book *You've Got to Be Hungry*, they're often caught by surprise because I talk about the fact that we're three-dimensional. We have a public life, we have a private life, and we have a secret life. And I want to share my secret life. I decided to share about what it takes to become successful. I've also spent a lot of time in my life, kicking myself about the mistakes that I made, and if I had it to do over again, there are some things I would do differently.

On a stage in San Francisco, I spoke about the fact that when I went through a divorce, I couldn't get on stage for a while. I was ashamed. I wondered how I could talk about success when I had failed. Success is more than just earning money or acquiring materialistic things. It's about being a good father, being a good husband, and making a growing family work. And I failed at that. But, I told them, I had failed, but I wasn't a failure.

There was a lady who had been a marriage counselor for 20 years, and she stopped because she went through a divorce. She said she loved providing counseling for couples, but she felt that she couldn't do it anymore because she couldn't make her marriage successful. Because of my transparency, she went back to work. She realized that her career was not over. She failed in that marriage, but she was not a failure, and she still had something of value that she could provide to people.

To contact Les Brown about mentorship and speaking, send an email to LesBrown77@gmail.com. You can get Les' newest book *You've Got to Be Hungry: The GREATNESS Within to Win* through Amazon and all major bookstores.

TEON SINGLETARY

From Poverty to Possibilities
The Journey of Growth and Empowerment

With over 20 years of leadership experience, Coach Teon Singletary embodies a remarkable blend of military skills, executive prowess, and inspiration. Through his TSLE Weekly Live Inspiration podcast, he shares insights on transitioning from a poverty to a growth mindset, empowering listeners to unlock their full potential.

Poverty and Possibilities

Have you ever felt like you were worthless? Have you had life experience that kept you from living your life to its fullest potential? Well, that was me. A little bow-legged, pigeon-toed, flat-footed, squeaky-voiced, asthmatic, stuttering, little, Black boy from the boonies of Trio, South Carolina—a place that creates a mindset of poverty.

I found myself, many times, closing my eyes and daydreaming about the possibilities of my future. What if I had the opportunity to travel, attend college, or even learn from the best in the world? How great would that be? Each time my eyes opened, my mind came back to my hopeless reality. *How could somebody like me become someone special?*

I'm thankful for a few good teachers who encouraged me to dream big. They saw something in me that I couldn't see in myself. I can remember a writing assignment where I decided to write a story of my life through poetry. The sense of pride I felt from the teacher praising me for my creativity is something that stuck with me for years.

For another assignment, I had to create a dream business card for something I'd like to do in the future. I can still remember the name of that business: Teon's Telecommunication Center. It was a business that would create ways for people to connect with others around the world. Before this assignment, I never thought of building a business for myself. This opened my eyes to the possibilities.

My parents are great! They are hard workers who did everything they could to provide a life for me, and my little brother and sister, including sometimes working two jobs each, just to give us everything we needed. As the big brother, I found myself creating a way to bring in extra cash to pay for the little things. I started selling. No, not drugs, even though that was an option. I was selling something to every kid on the bus each morning and afternoon. Candy! Snickers, Kit Kats, and Reese's. I made about $50 a week doing this. Little did I know, this was the beginning of building a business mindset. When I left home, my brother started doing the same thing, and my sister afterward.

Where I'm from, you had four options: 1) be one of the smart kids and be mentored by certain teachers to go to college, 2) become great in a sport and hope you got picked up by a college sports program, 3) join the military, 4) become a drug dealer. Surprisingly, I fell into option one. However, college was not part of my plan. Honestly, I had no plan. I just was going with the flow and surviving. During this time in my life, school had left a very bad taste in my mouth. So, option three became my choice. The choice that changed my life for the best. In the military, I learned more about myself, my capabilities, and my growth potential under proper mentorship. My travels connected me with people who began to share with me other opportunities. One of these opportunities was business building.

Trapped in the Grind

In my 20s, I found myself ensnared in a repetitive cycle of waking up each day to plunge headfirst into the ceaseless hustle, devoid of any vitality. My days were consumed by toil within the confines of a telecommunication center, and I couldn't fathom how I had ended up there. Nevertheless, there I was, trapped in the relentless grind.

With each passing day, the hours seemed to stretch longer, and the task of rising each morning grew increasingly burdensome. I was crumbling into a mere shell of myself. I failed to recognize this mundane existence was a slow descent into oblivion gradually eroding my spirit.

The prospect of assuming the role of lead instructor within the company briefly reignited a flicker of hope within me. I was tasked with crafting a PowerPoint presentation to impart knowledge on a topic of personal interest. A sense of joy permeated my interactions with the managers, and the interviews seemed to proceed swimmingly. Yet, despite my best efforts, I found myself overlooked for the position.

Dejected, I returned to the call center. It was during this moment that a revelation struck me. For the first time, I acknowledged my genuine fondness for creating and disseminating knowledge. Moreover, I recognized the imperative of understanding myself and leveraging my strengths.

During one particular hustle and bustle workday, I queried myself incredulously, *Why are you here? They compensate you far less than your true worth, and you possess the capability to forge your own path.* In 2011, with a surge of determination coursing through my veins, I made the impulsive decision to depart.

The Odyssey of an Entrepreneur and Coach

Thus commenced a new chapter in my life—an era fraught with uncertainty yet brimming with untapped potential. Was I apprehensive? Undoubtedly. I found solace in the wisdom imparted by my mentor, John C. Maxwell, who espoused that personal growth is the most invaluable investment one can make. Indeed, one cannot hope to effectively lead others without first mastering the art of self-leadership. My journey of self-discovery commenced in 2012, and from that moment on, I never glanced back.

In 2015, I established my first business specializing in graphic design and book publication. In 2020, amidst the turmoil wrought by the pandemic, I boldly ventured forth to create a second enterprise. This business specialized in professional leadership coaching and speaking.

Among the myriad decisions I encountered along this odyssey, none proved as pivotal as my unwavering commitment to investing in my personal development. To date, I have devoted countless resources—both financial and temporal—towards this pursuit, spanning several avenues, including books, courses, programs, schooling, and coaching. As a result of my unyielding dedication to investing in fostering my own growth, I find myself in a state of fulfillment and empowerment. Armed with newfound wisdom and insight, I stand poised to inspire and embolden individuals to embark upon a similar voyage of self-discovery and empowerment. I became a life coach: to help others do what I have done.

One of my favorite sayings is, "Every day is a great day to be alive. Why? Because you are greatness made from greatness."

Every day has challenges and potential for greatness. Success depends on whether our attitudes are positive or negative. Life's journey is full of obstacles and fears that hinder our goals. Overcoming these fears is key to reaching our full potential and achieving our dreams.

Your fear could be:

- fear of the unknown
- fear of stepping outside of your comfort zone
- fear of speaking up for what you really want out of life
- fear of not knowing your purpose in life and what you want to do for your career
- fear that you don't have the resources needed to achieve your goals or
- fear of failure and falling short of what you want to accomplish in life.

Your fears may differ, but I am confident you have the inner strength to conquer them and achieve your own success.

COACH TEON'S THOUGHT LEADER LESSONS

Self-Development

Self-development means a lot to me, and I want to share three important steps here (out of five I often share) that can help you discover yourself and grow personally.

Step One: Awareness. We all have things we struggle with. For me, growing up, it was a speech problem and being teased by other kids. At first, I let these things define me. But when I realized these challenges were not my identity, I could start figuring out how to deal with them.

Step Two: Preparation. This is where you make a plan to grow. It starts with your mindset—believing in yourself and your ability to succeed. Positive statements like "I am capable" can help build that mindset.

Step Three: Action. It's not enough to just be aware and plan. You have to actually do something. In my experience, taking action—even when you're scared—is crucial. One motto I follow is "Do it afraid." It means taking risks and trusting that things will work out.

C.H.A.M.P.I.O.N. Mindset

To become a champion and excel, you must embody these essential attributes.

C. Confidence is the cornerstone of the champion mindset, empowering individuals to navigate challenges with unwavering belief in their abilities and resilience in the face of adversity.

H. Honor is the bedrock upon which success is built, fostering authenticity and accountability, thus empowering individuals to achieve their goals with grace, dignity, and ethical fortitude.

A. Attitude. A positive mental attitude drives success by shaping perceptions, actions, and resilience, enabling individuals to overcome obstacles and achieve greatness.

M. Morale fortifies individuals' belief in their potential, enabling them to navigate challenges with courage and optimism, ultimately propelling them toward their goals with resolve and tenacity.

P. Possibility. Embracing possibility thinking empowers individuals to transcend limitations, innovate, and focus on opportunities, driving relentless excellence and success.

I. Integrity guides individuals to foster unbreakable honesty, trust, respect, and self-respect, ultimately building a foundation of moral excellence and good character.

O. Opportunities. Seizing opportunities empowers individuals to grow, build resilience, and reach their highest potential, unlocking success and fulfillment with courage and determination.

N. Never Quit. It instills resilience and perseverance, empowering individuals to overcome adversity, pursue their dreams, and emerge victorious, embodying the essence of champions.

Q&A WITH COACH TEON

What hobbies do you enjoy?

I enjoy video gaming and a good round of golf.

Who are your mentors and greatest influences?

Undoubtedly, my father, Leon Singletary, stands as the most profound influence in my life. He has shaped the positive aspects of my character. From him, I learned the essence of being a strong African American man, grounded in morals and values. The most enduring lesson he imparted to me is the importance of taking ownership of my decisions and accepting their consequences with maturity.

I owe a debt of gratitude to several teachers from my school days. During my early education, I struggled to grasp many of the lessons presented to me. Their dedication and patience instilled in me the necessary skills to thrive. They fostered the development of my character, guiding me along the path to becoming the person of integrity I am today.

What are a few of your favorite quotes?

"Be before you do. Do before you have." – Zig Ziglar

"Let go of yesterday so you can reach for tomorrow." – John C. Maxwell

"For things to change for you, you have to change." – Jim Rohn

"If you can look up, you can get up. You've got comeback power!" – Les Brown

How do you recharge?

When I need to recharge, I do something to get away into my own world. That could be going to the beach or putting in earbuds and listening to some good tunes.

What would you tell your 18-year-old self?

I would tell myself to never be afraid of failure, to seize every opportunity that comes along, and to invest in self-development now.

Investing in yourself is crucial, so feel free to connect with Coach Teon Singletary for support. He's excited to provide you with further resources to enhance your life. Download complimentary gifts like his Reflection Time & Goal Setting ebook and a lesson taught by Dr. John C. Maxwell. Access Coach Teon's exclusive Building Stick-to-itiveness Email Training at teonsingletary.com.

 Growth comes with dedication and commitment. Commit to your personal growth today.

CRAIG MOODY

Find Your Why!
From Self-Doubt to Business Leader

Craig Moody is a serial entrepreneur, bestselling author, speaker, and business coach. Craig built a contracting business and sold it in 2021. He is managing partner in a skincare business with his daughter Taylor. Craig also owns The Business Climb where he coaches small business owners to amazing heights. Craig and his wife Angela have three kids and two grandkids.

Entrepreneur Mindset

In 2003, I bought into a contracting franchise: just myself, a briefcase, and a dream. Ten years later, I exited the franchise system and started my own brand. Overcoming imposter syndrome was a big step towards achieving success.

That entire time, deep, deep down, there was a tiny voice screaming out that this was all a lie—that truly, I was a phony. For several years, I believed myself a failure, phony, and fraud.

Work hard, save everything you can, and probably even then, it won't be enough. Don't get your hopes up, and don't go for your dreams, because you will be disappointed.

Self-doubt and risk avoidance owned me. I needed help but was too scared to admit it.

The Beginning

Before I ever started a franchise, I had a long period of dead-end jobs and bad decisions. Then I worked as a sales representative for a printing company in Arizona.

One day, in 2003, my brother called me and said he had found a new franchise opportunity out of Florida. They were trying to grow and were willing to fly out and meet with us.

I was scared. This would be leaving the comfort of my job, although it was no longer serving my needs, to invest in my own business. I had no confidence.

My brother kept calling. "I'm gonna do it," he said. "Let's go to the training together." My loving wife believed in me and urged me to do it. We had equity in our home and could take out a second mortgage. Still, I had serious doubts. Deep down, I was still a failure.

What if this doesn't work? What if I fail? What would happen to the house? Our marriage? My reputation?

More importantly, at that time, our oldest child was sick and required surgery. After the procedure, the doctor said that in addition to kidney reflux, he had a blood disorder. We were so scared. However, after more education, we started to realize we were lucky. We would eventually take our child home, and he would live a long life.

My parents visited the hospital as much as possible. I was talking to my mom when she asked me what I thought about starting a business. I told her it was just not the right time. Then she said the words I will never forget: "You're just not a risk-taker, are you, honey."

The last afternoon before my son's discharge home, as I stretched my legs on the top level of the Phoenix Children's Hospital parking garage, I decided life was too short to not go for it. I called my brother and told him I was in!

Walk the Walk

The first few years were slow growth. My favorite part of being a franchisee was the conventions. I loved meeting people in the industry and listening to motivational speakers. I started buying their books, and for the first time in a decade, I read a book.

Another franchisee introduced me to a leadership teacher named John Maxwell. I dove into his teachings. He was a former church pastor who saw a need for growing leaders. On the plane ride home after a convention, my brother and I made our first business plans on notepads. I would have my entire team watch Maxwell's videos.

I loved it. I learned that to grow financially, we must first grow personally and professionally. It took a while, but my business started to grow.

The first few full-time technicians I hired did their jobs well enough, but I knew I needed people operating on a higher level. Maxwell taught me that if you are a four on a scale of one to 10, you will only attract a three or lower. I had to grow myself to attract people on a higher level. I did just that. My first stellar employee freed me up to work on my strength: marketing.

It did not happen overnight. With debt, franchise fees, and a failing business, I was on a financial rollercoaster.

"You are always so stressed," my wife would tell me. I was only stressed when it was really busy or really slow. The problem with emergency restoration is, it is either really busy or really slow. There is rarely in between.

The Road to Passion

Ten years after my original agreement with the franchise, there was a massive exodus of franchisees due to the owners splitting up. I was able to buy my way out of the contract and start my own brand with additional services.

I learned over time that good business is a series of risks and decisions made daily. I kept thinking, *Once I do a million dollars in revenue in one year, I will have arrived.*

Well, that year finally came. It felt good. I had a little breathing room, but not a lot. Budgets helped that going forward.

My mastermind group was amazing. One day, after explaining part of my story, my buddy Andrew said, "Craig, I have heard you tell this story several times, and I believe you suffer from PTSD."

What he said was so freeing: You had trauma in your life, and it is okay to admit it and seek help. This was a huge milestone.

Andrew also told our group about Darren Hardy. I watched him on YouTube. He was amazing. I read his books and joined his program. Through Insane Productivity, I learned how to stay focused, stay on schedule, and work hard. He was just what I needed, a no-nonsense, tough coach.

In 2018, I rejoined personal training and went on a diet fueled by Darren Hardy saying, "You absolutely need to do this to focus, get your mind right, and go to the next level." To get in shape, I repeatedly told myself Brian Buffini's axiom, "the power of a made-up mind." Eventually, I lost 50 pounds.

In the next few years, I dove into insane production, even through the COVID-19 pandemic and having my youngest still at home. I built a solid management team, implemented better job descriptions, and grew the fleet. In a little over three years, I increased my annual sales by $2.4 million. I became debt-free, began traveling, and started coaching others. I developed a routine, and I hammered it: 4:00 a.m. wake and devotion, 5:00 a.m. workout, 6:00 a.m. inspirational writing, meditation, Darren Daily videos, podcasts, etc.

Everything culminated when I sold my contracting business in 2021 for more money than I could have ever imagined.

I never dreamed of being a contractor. Since selling that business, I have focused on my dream of coaching, speaking, and writing.

I have also been fortunate enough to help my daughter with her new business.

And I am now a grandparent.

I started coaching other small business owners with the goal of not letting them make the same mistakes I did. It is so rewarding. Seeing my clients' success is just as rewarding as seeing my own. I named my coaching company The Business Climb. Growing a business is just like climbing a mountain, and what is the quickest way to the top of the mountain? Easy, ask those coming back.

With all my experience I felt motivated to share with others. I recently started keynote speaking. Experience has taught me that I am going to make mistakes. I need more experience. With each keynote, I improve a little. I also make sure to receive feedback from the event providers.

Please, forgive yourself for your past. Leave it there. I had to. Only look forward. Fix what needs to be fixed, surround yourself with good people, distance yourself from the negative, never stop learning, study the greatest leaders and motivational teachers in the world, and find your why!

CRAIG'S THOUGHT LEADER LESSONS

Leadership

Everything rises and falls on leadership. Families, schools, cities, teams, businesses, non-profits, states, and countries are only as good as the leader and the vision to have leaders developing other leaders.

Business and Entrepreneurship

The thought of ultimately being your own boss, working for yourself, that's the goal. How we get there and the plans we make are ultimately what make or break us. Of all businesses, 66% will ultimately fail. This is way too much. There has to be a better way: a roadmap, a cheat sheet, a course on how to be successful. It starts with the entrepreneur admitting they are going to need help from day one, then seeking advice and the vision of others.

Mentorship

I would not be where I am today if it were not for the mentorship I received from others. Whether I paid for the advice and accountability or not.

Seeing my clients grow their businesses and implement my ideas is the most gratifying work I have ever done. A lot must go right. You must have a lot of trust, follow-up, effort, and implementation.

Q&A WITH CRAIG

What is something most people don't know about you?

I was fortunate enough to be a "guest swamper," meaning I was a laborer with a commercial outfitter, and I rafted the Colorado River through the Grand Canyon on three separate occasions in the early 1990s. The trip was free, but the work was hard, and it was all well worth it.

What are a few of your favorite quotes?

"Smooth seas do not make for skillful sailors." – African Proverb

"If you want to go fast, go alone. If you want to go far, go together." – African Proverb

"You are most qualified to help the person you used to be." – Ed Mylett

What is some of the best advice you've received?

You're going to fail, and that's okay. It's the only way to learn.

When starting a business, surround yourself with really good people, especially a good lawyer and a good accountant, and then meet with other like-minded business owners on a regular basis. They are the only ones who understand the struggles you will face. They also are the only ones who will pat you on the back and say "Good job."

What is your favorite movie?

Lonesome Dove. It glorifies true friendship and highlights how hard life was back in the 1800s. It was a struggle to stay alive every day, much less thrive.

Who are your mentors and greatest influences?

John Maxwell – He was the first to teach me about personal growth and development.

King David – He became King against all odds. He made huge mistakes, then admitted and corrected them. He ruled and kept Christianity legal.

Darren Hardy – He's a NO-nonsense, tough-shit type of business leader who taught me how to stay focused, driven, and productive!

What hobbies do you enjoy?

College football tailgating, fishing, camping, and hunting.

What books do you often recommend?

The Miracle Morning by Hal Elrod – This book taught me the rituals of the successful.

The Compound Effect by Darren Hardy – Small, consistent, day-to-day progress will add up to great success in the long run.

Extreme Ownership by Jocko Willink and Leif Babin – This book rids you of excuses!

What would you tell your 18-year-old self?

Take care of your health. Do not stop exercising. Do not get overweight. Also, do whatever it takes to solve your anger management issue.

What do you consider your greatest achievement to date?

Overcoming a self-sabotaging, negative-Nelly attitude to build and sell the largest restoration company in Northern Arizona.

What has been your greatest lesson?

People don't care how much you know until they know how much you care.

How do you define success?

When others often seek your advice.

Craig Moody – Your Strategic Business Advisor – craigmoody.co.
"Make me your next hire and elevate your business to new heights."
Mention any of Craig's books to receive a free "Discovery Call" with him on how he can help you overcome your business's greatest challenges.
craig@thebizclimb.com
Instagram/LinkedIn @thebusinessclimb
https://hihello.me/p/8b251fb0-233e-4a12-8b96-bcaa331a3b27

 Connect with Craig

SANDHYA SESHADRI

Creating Wealth While Building Communities

Apartment syndicator, underwriter, and hands-on asset manager Sandhya Seshadri is a Dallas resident with an immigrant mindset of extreme gratitude to this country, especially the Lone Star State. Sandhya is passionate about serving her residents and building wealth for her investors by creating neighborly communities and impacting lives.

The Amazing Land of the Free

In the mid-1980s, I arrived in New York City. Thanks to a kind uncle, I was able to have this summer vacation as a teen. I would help him with his kids and get a glimpse of life in the United States.

Standing atop the World Trade Center, I remember looking down in awe and deciding that I would do everything in my power to experience more of this amazing country. *But how can I turn this dream into reality?*

We were living a comfortable middle-class life in India. My parents are highly educated. However, due to the exchange rate, their monthly salary was about $60 US. At the time, colleges in the US cost at least $10,000 per year. Even if they were to give me their life savings, my parents would not be able to afford to send me to school in the United States. So, I needed a scholarship.

When I returned to India, I worked hard in high school, made the best grades I could, and excelled in competitive tests to get admission to a school in the United States with a scholarship. I landed in Dallas, Texas, with two suitcases and never looked back.

I had the honor of studying electrical engineering at Southern Methodist University (SMU). I fell in love with the beautiful campus and experienced my first taste of Southern hospitality. The Lone Star State welcomed me and made me feel at home.

From Corporate America to Trading Stocks

Soon after my graduation, I was offered a job at a local Fortune 500 company. They were kind enough to pay for me to go back to school part-time and earn an MBA. That's where I got all my financial acumen. The insights served me well for many years both in the corporate and entrepreneurial worlds.

I belonged to multiple investor groups where we discussed stocks, and I traded on a regular basis. What I eventually realized was that as much as corporate America served me well and helped me with a salary plus benefits, it was my investments that made me wealthy.

Stock Market to Large Apartments

Between corporate America and trading stocks, I was not doing anything to reduce my tax burden.

I knew 90% of all millionaires become so through real estate. I analyzed single-family rentals and didn't find it lucrative enough to justify a recourse loan and the headaches of being a landlord. There was no economy of scale in single-family rentals to justify paying a third-party property management company.

A weekend seminar led me to apartment investing.

Today, after five years in apartment investing, I have invested in over 4,200 doors which I syndicated as a general partner or invested in as a passive investor. Between the tax savings and profit earnings, I was able to exceed my salary in corporate America while having the flexibility to choose my schedule.

I was shocked that so few people knew about this avenue for investing in real estate passively. Why is only the stock market promoted as a vehicle to invest? The market is so volatile and subject to fluctuations from factors well beyond control. Apartment investing is such a great way to diversify one's portfolio from Wall Street to Main Street.

This led to my multifamily journey with Engineered Capital. Today, we engineer the capital of our investors to make money work for them while they sleep or pursue exciting adventures.

I am keen to give back to this wonderful country and the state of Texas. I am focused on improving communities in the Dallas area—one apartment complex at a time.

The best part is providing safe, affordable places to live. More than that, we strive to foster communities where people feel connected with their neighbors and proud of where they live. When I came here as a student from India, I lived in a place like the apartment buildings I own now. I want the people living there to feel they can have, or already have, a good life.

When I focus on taking care of my residents as well as my investors, my two main customers, great things happen. We are fulfilling a vital human need by providing shelter, a need the government cannot fulfill alone. By taking these apartments to the next level, making them nicer, better, and safer, and by building communities—we are impacting the world.

Why I Started a Mastermind

The biggest challenge in 2023 and 2024 was rising interest rates. It was a rough time. I couldn't pay back my investors the amount of cash flow I had hoped. But, I was not facing foreclosure—when you don't have enough money for a deal to pay the mortgage and are in negative cash flow.

When all hope is gone, that's when your creative juices have to flow. Never lose hope. Never surrender until the very last second. This time has shown me that what I'm doing is good and useful and that I need to continue doing it.

People told me, "You're doing things very hands-on. It's too slow. You can't scale that way." But I'm paying attention to the details like the owner of a little, boutique store.

A lot of people were struggling. Those who neglected operations found their deals in trouble and foreclosure. Some lost 100% of their investor capital.

The minute you start seeing negative cash flow or low occupancy, you have to figure out why. *Why are people not wanting to stay at my apartment complex? Why are we not serving them the right way?* Take care of your property and serve your residents well. They'll never leave if you maintain a good community, and ultimately, that's the way you make money in real estate. Create a place that everyone wants to live in, that always has a waitlist, and you will stay profitable. If you have happy residents you will have happy investors. It's happiness and win-win all around.

Many people came to me for help. I wanted to share everything I've learned by writing a book. Kyle Wilson, my business coach said, "You're going to give away all your knowledge in a $12 book? Launch a mastermind." Kyle has definitely influenced me for the better.

At first, I was very uncomfortable with the idea of a mastermind. I was full of imposter syndrome. I haven't lived and breathed real estate for decades. But, I started helping people, and in just one call, I can improve their operations by $10,000 a month. If they implement all my suggestions, a one million dollar property value increase is something I've now done for every mastermind member.

I realized you don't need a PhD to teach fifth-grade math. There's never going to be a time when everything is going to line up and be perfectly ready. You have to try anyway, because if you keep fearing failure and never start something, then you never know what works and what doesn't.

I made the price a no-brainer and had 44 people apply. I accepted 17 of them who I felt I could truly help. It's been phenomenal. After eight months, nobody has left, and I'm thinking of growing it.

SANDHYA'S THOUGHT LEADER LESSONS

Financial Independence

As an immigrant, I felt the need for financial stability. I came here with nothing. Once I got my degree, I started with a $36,000 annual salary, and my Fortune 500 company was kind enough to pay for me to get an MBA. I started investing $100 here and there, and within a few years, I realized that my investments were making more than that starting salary. That's when I learned the power of investing and achieved true financial independence.

Making work optional was never something I imagined. I didn't see that growing up in India. In the US, people work until they're 70 or can't work anymore. No matter how you earn money, it is important to have a second stream of income. Now, I'm doing it with real estate and stocks and helping others do the same.

Education and Knowledge

Always be a continuous learner. There's something you can learn from every person you meet, book you read, and thing you do. Use feedback to continuously improve because sometimes to achieve that big, hairy, audacious goal, you have to evolve. The person you become is the best part of the journey, so never stop learning.

Parenting

My kids were born and raised in the US. They don't know what it's like to be raised in a place where hot water and 24/7 power are not a given. I want to teach them to keep a gratitude journal and to appreciate all the little things in life.

My parenting philosophy is that children must learn to be financially independent because money does solve a lot of problems. I don't want my adult children to be dependents in this society. I tell them to ask themselves, *What is my contribution to this world? What am I giving back?*

Be independent, give back constantly, and be grateful no matter what you face in life.

Attitude and Mindset

If you can have a positive, problem-solving attitude, 90% of problems can be solved. There's always a solution. Somebody has solved it. We just have to find that person or that solution.

Step outside, even if it's a rainy or snowy day. The plants need the rain. After winter comes spring. The sun will come back. You have to wait…hang in there.

If necessary, phone a friend or a mentor. The question is what will it take for them to give you their time? Be nice, beg, bake cookies, whatever it takes, and get yourself help.

Resilience

Know when to seek help. But don't give up on the first try. Look at many famous people. How many times did they have to try before they so-called succeeded? How many shots did Michael Jordan miss versus how many he made? He definitely missed way more. That's the reality of life. So, don't give up.

Keep persisting. You will find creative ways. With a positive attitude and persistence, you will find a way. Just shine your light and never give up.

Q&A WITH SANDHYA

What is your favorite movie?

Top Gun. I like Tom Cruise's character. He's nowhere close to perfect, but no matter what, he doesn't give up. You see all his struggles and the demons in his head, but he still comes through by doing what he has to do, even if it means losing his life, to save the mission.

What is your favorite song?

I like "Danger Zone" from *Top Gun*.

I also like "Titanium" which reminds me that I'm unbreakable, I'm stronger than I believe I am, and I can keep going.

What are your pet peeves?

When people don't realize just how blessed they are to live in this country. We have 24/7 running water and electricity. We have highways, bridges, and parks, all free. Yes, you pay taxes, but so much of this country is so beautiful and so free.

How do you recharge?

Nature. I love to go for walks by the ocean, lakes, ponds, and creeks. Movement and being outside help me a lot.

What are a few of your favorite quotes?

"Success leaves clues." – Jim Rohn

"You can have everything in life you want if you will just help enough other people get what they want." – Zig Ziglar

"Don't be penny wise and pound foolish," meaning, get the big picture and do the big things first.

Who are your mentors and greatest influences?

I'm a big Jim Rohn fan. I love his philosophy.

I've been following Ryan Holiday. The way he writes about stoicism in many of his books has really helped me.

Rich Dad advisor, Tom Wheelwright, from a very tactical tax perspective.

And, of course, Kyle Wilson.

What is something most people don't know about you?

I used to ride motorcycles as a teenager. I love riding on the beach. I don't do it anymore because I have two kids that I'm responsible for. Maybe one day, I'll go back to it.

What philanthropic causes do you support?

I strongly believe in anything related to literacy for children, including financial literacy. And then women: abused women, women's shelters, and combating human trafficking.

What are some favorite places you've traveled to?

I love Fiji, New Zealand, Iceland, Hawaii, Kangaroo Island, off the coast of Adelaide in Australia, Alaska, and various parts of Europe. Traveling is my favorite hobby.

I always look for bargains, like I flew round-trip to Fiji for free. I fly economy, but we usually find ways to get upgrades. I save points, and I know when points are at a discount. I'll maximize all my loyalty and credit card points for one thing I want for that year. It's cheapest if you travel off-peak times (mid-January to mid-March and September to November). And, if possible, befriend an airline employee!

What books do you often recommend?

I still like Tony Robbins' *Unleash the Power Within* and *Awaken the Giant Within* to get rid of your limiting beliefs. I love James Clear's *Atomic Habits*. I like *The Win-Win Wealth Strategy* by Tom Wheelwright. I think the strategy in it is even better than in Tax-Free Wealth. And then, if you're a diabetic like me, *The Diabetes Code* by Dr. Jason Fung is unbelievable.

What would you tell your 18-year-old self?

Be confident. Don't blindly believe older people—just because somebody is older than you doesn't mean they are wiser than you. Only take advice from people who have actually done what you want to be doing.

What is your image of an ideal world?

An ideal world is where women feel empowered, strong, and confident. Where they don't have any limits keeping them from their highest level of achievement.

My little way of impacting that is by tutoring kids for free for over a decade now, especially in math. Grocery shopping, buying airline tickets, or anything else, how do you do that well without basic math? Without math skills, you do not have basic financial skills. If you win a lottery ticket, you're going to go bankrupt if you're not educated.

To join Sandhya Seshadri in growing your passive income through real estate investments with a feel-good component of impacting communities, and to receive a free checklist for vetting a deal, email invest@engineered-capital.com

CHRIS GRONKOWSKI

From the NFL to *Shark Tank* as the Founder of Ice Shaker

Chris Gronkowski played four years in the NFL along with his three brothers, Rob, Dan, and Glenn. Chris graduated from the University of Arizona. After leaving the NFL, Chris appeared on Shark Tank with his company Ice Shaker in 2017 and made a deal with Alex Rodriguez and Mark Cuban. Chris lives in Southlake, Texas, with his wife, Brittany, and three kids.

Growing Up in Buffalo with Four Competitive Brothers

My parents raised five boys. In Buffalo, New York, we lived in this awesome neighborhood. Every couple of houses there was another kid our age. We had that house where everyone came over, and we would make up games in the backyard and play against each other. Every sport you can imagine, we competed in. I believe that bred competition among us brothers and the neighborhood kids.

As we got older, we started playing competitive sports in leagues, mostly hockey, baseball, and football.

My dad started a fitness equipment company from scratch and worked long hours. My mom was in charge of getting all five of us to school and sports events. Five boys. We all played multiple sports for multiple teams and were on travel teams. I still don't know how she got all of us to all our practices. She physically could not bring us all to every practice and game. Plus, we were going to church and other functions too. She had to bring in coaches, friends, and family from other neighborhoods. Thinking back on it, she did all that without a cell phone.

Ivy League or Football Scholarship

My dad played college football, and at one point, he had a Bills contract hanging on the wall at home. He was a good player but then got injured.

All five of us brothers grew up wanting to go to college and play pro sports, and all of us did.

I wanted to play college football but wanted to make sure I also got a good education so I could become a CPA and make good money if pro sports didn't work out.

I committed first to the University of Pennsylvania. My dad was excited. I would be the first Ivy League son in the family. We wouldn't just be the family of dumb jocks. And I was the one to prove it.

At the last minute, I ended up getting a full scholarship offer to play for the University of Maryland. I wanted to play at the highest level, but at the same time, I also didn't want to pay for college. At the University of Pennsylvania, I would probably graduate with $200,000 in debt. So, two weeks before the summer ended, I accepted a full D1 scholarship to Maryland.

That scholarship really came about because a bunch of their players were about to go on academic probation and some of the incoming players didn't make it because of grades. So, they gave it to the guy who had good grades that could bump up the GPA for the football team a little bit. I tell people all the time, I got my first athletic college scholarship by having good academics.

I ended up transferring to the University of Arizona where my younger but much bigger brother, Rob, had also decided to go play. He was a coveted 4-star recruit. I was just hoping to make the team. Since I was a transfer, I had to sit out a year. So, that first year, I played baseball, and after two years, I went full-time in football.

I never thought I'd make it to the pro level, but I got my chance.

NFL for Four Years

I was undrafted. I was fortunate to have an agent believe in me and sponsor me to train for several months in Miami for the NFL Combine. That led to an opportunity to try out for the Dallas Cowboys.

My wife is from Buffalo, but her dad got transferred to Dallas-Fort Worth six years before I went to the Cowboys, and everyone fell in love with the area.

I made the team. I hoped I would be playing for the Cowboys forever. It lasted a season before I started bouncing around to other teams.

I made it four seasons in the NFL, which locked in some nice benefits. After I retired, we came back to the Dallas area. We love it here. It's a great business environment and having family around is really important.

Life After the NFL That Led to *Shark Tank*

I wasn't rich by any stretch, but I had a pension and a nice 401K built up (the NFL offers a nice double match). Plus, you get severance pay and healthcare benefits. So, I had a good chunk of money without debt. I had gone to school and only had to pay for one semester. At age 26, I was leaving the NFL far ahead of everyone else my age.

I had this money that I could invest into whatever I wanted. I first went into business with my wife. She had started a business and Etsy shop while I was playing with Denver so she could work from home. She did really well. I helped her, and we ended up making more money than when I was playing in the NFL.

It was a good transition for me, but having grown up in fitness and having played football my whole life, making wedding gifts wasn't really me. After five years, I thought of the idea for Ice Shaker.

I love a shaker bottle, but the shaker bottle wasn't perfect. I took what I loved, like being able to blend powders and an easy-open pop top, and added insulated, kitchen-grade premium stainless steel to keep drinks cold or hot and a handle to make it easy to carry. Through my wife's business, I could customize Ice Shakers and fulfill bulk orders fast.

I could go to the gym, and I could call it work by making product videos around my workout. It was awesome. I thought, *Let's start this as a side hustle. Let's see if it gets to a place where we can make this a full-time thing. Let's go all in and see where it goes.*

Lessons from the Tank

I remembered getting an email in 2012, when I was with the Broncos, that said ABC's *Shark Tank* was looking for current or former NFL players to pitch them. Four and a half years later, I emailed back. That spark got me the opportunity to pitch to the Sharks.

That was about three months into the company's life. We only had $20,000 in sales, but at least I had proof of concept. They asked me to submit a video. I did, and they liked it. They said I had three months before we would film and that I should get ready. My focus became to get all the revenue I could so I could get the best valuation possible.

When I went on the show, we had around $80,000 in sales, and I was asking for $100,000 for 10% of the company.

After I did the initial pitch, I had all my brothers come on. They brought a lot of energy, and we had fun with the Sharks. One of the big lessons is to just show up with confidence, have fun, and know what you're talking about!

I watched every episode. I wrote down every question they ever asked. I felt like I was best friends with each Shark. So, when I walked out there, instead of being nervous, I could say, "Hey, I feel like I know you guys."

I ended up getting a deal with Mark Cuban and Alex Rodriguez. Later, my brother, Rob, bought Alex's position.

With their help, I got Ice Shaker into The Vitamin Shoppe, Lifetime Fitness, GNC, and Walmart as well as to appear on QVC, *Good Morning America*, and many other outlets.

We then secured a licensing partnership through Wincraft, which was purchased by Fanatics, bringing Ice Shaker into the NFL, NBA, NHL, and MLB! With that new audience, we realized the power of licensing. We now have a license with the US Army license and many more.

Learning from My Dad

I have a family, a wife, and kids, so working a hundred hours a week doesn't work for me anymore. That forced me to put people and processes in place, which takes time!

My dad has more than 30 years in the fitness industry, and in that time, he built 17 retail stores. When he wanted to be a mentor to me in sports and business, at first, I didn't listen. It took time for me to realize the value of his wisdom.

When the pandemic hit, things slowed down. There were no processes in place. There was no budget. I could only come in the store when half of my employees were there because of the COVID restrictions and my kids at home. I realized I had better figure things out pretty quick.

It was time to figure out how to do this the right way and to build the team. I went to my dad and said, "How'd you build your business to 200 employees? That's insane." At the time, I was trying to manage eight employees.

My dad said, "From day one, I asked you, what's your game plan? What's your budget? What's your forecast? How are you incentivizing people? Tell me that first, and I'll tell you how to fix it."

That's exactly where I was going wrong. First, there was no team. It was me making every decision and me with all the responsibilities. I thought that was how it was supposed to be because it was my business. When it couldn't be like that anymore, I was forced to delegate, which was one of my dad's keys from day one.

When I started to share the responsibility, I realized that people responded well. They felt like they were part of a team. They could make their own decisions. They loved it and wanted more.

Next was figuring out how everyone could win. I had to figure that out with the whole team. We had a fulfillment team that wasn't feeling the win when we made sales. They didn't have a piece of that pie or input on the goals we set. We had to realign all the goals, and rather than incentivizing certain individuals, we had to incentivize everyone as a team.

Once we did that, I would walk in with a big sale, and everyone in the entire company was pumped. That's when I knew we had figured this thing out.

CHRIS'S THOUGHT LEADER LESSONS

Fitness, Working Out, and Nutrition

When you own a company that's all about health, fitness, and protein shakes, being fit is part of the brand image, so you better live that image. But also health and fitness were ingrained in me growing up and playing sports. It feels like an accomplishment to get a workout in every day, and without it, I feel like the day hasn't really been completed. A workout is a mental release for me as well, to help get the stress out.

I think fitness is also an opportunity for me to be a role model. I coach kids in football and baseball, and the first thing they say when I walk out there is, "Man, let me see your muscles!" It earns immediate respect, and I think being in shape sends a good message for these kids.

My real journey with nutrition started after I was done playing football. I had to figure out how to eat healthy and what healthy eating really was. Because you can say eating a banana is healthy, but eating two or three bananas before bed is not always the best choice.

After the NFL, I dug deep into what to eat and when to eat it—breaking down the macros of protein, carbs, or fat—helped me fuel my body. On average, I'm burning 3,500 calories a day. Since I'm not trying to gain or lose weight, I eat right around that mark most every day.

Family

Family makes a massive impact on everything I do. Having four brothers definitely set the tone for everything I did. With us, it was always a competition, whether it was who could lift more, who could eat more, or who had better grades. You couldn't lose to your little brother and you had to try to beat your older brother. That all-day, every day competition took us all to another level. As we got into high school, we became more friends than enemies, and working together to beat the other team helped us excel on the field.

Now that I have a family, I see my boys already competing. It's a lot of fun to watch, and I'm here all day, everyday coaching them on how to be the best they can be and how to be great teammates like my dad did for my brothers and me all those years.

Preparation

When you prepare, you will be ready versus nervous. You can't play fast unless you know what you're doing.

Philanthropy

We started the Gronk Nation Youth Foundation about 10 years ago. Through that organization, we do fundraisers every year and give to youth sports programs and children's hospitals. My brother is building a new playground in Boston, MA, which is a more than a million-dollar project. Some of the youth sports programs we helped might have shut down if someone hadn't stepped in to buy the football and weightlifting equipment they needed.

If you purchase Ice Shaker through our website, you have the opportunity to choose between three different foundations to give money to. It's 1% of the sale, and it comes out of our end. We've donated thousands of Ice Shaker bottles to active military members, made a Guinness World Record to raise money for a local youth football program, and donated to local schools because we love representing and helping kids live an active and healthy lifestyle.

Q&A WITH CHRIS

How do you recharge?

Definitely with a gym session. Also playing pickleball. Having a big workout on a weekend morning is definitely my go-to for a recharge.

What is something most people don't know about you?

I got accepted into the University of Pennsylvania's Wharton School of Business. I also took an official visit to Harvard and missed only one question on the math part of the SAT.

How do you define success?

It's about the whole team winning. If everyone on my team has the opportunity to win and we're winning as a team, to me, that's success. It's like winning a Super Bowl.

You can follow Chris Gronkowski on Instagram @chrisgronkowski and go to Iceshaker.com to order your own Ice Shaker. You can also order in bulk and have your order customized with your logo. You can order from Chris's wife's company at EverythingDecorated.com.

 Snag the best, ditch the rest. Ice Shaker's 26oz Shaker bottle is third-party tested to hold ice for over 30 hours, and the patented twist-in agitator will help mix your favorite drinks and powders.

BRETT BINKLEY

Leaving a Legacy
Transformational Leadership in the Family Business

Brett Binkley has served as CEO and vice chairman of Binkley & Barfield|DCCM, a civil engineering firm, since 2002. Having spent 30+ years as an advisor, mentor, and principal-in-charge for clients in the public and private sectors, Brett engages others in building strong and committed teams through role modeling and transformational leadership.

Working Smarter

I started my first job when I was 11 years old. I did newspaper delivery in Houston and then became a solicitor selling newspapers door to door, sometimes in not-so-nice neighborhoods.

My mom would take us to Alfie's Fish and Chips now and then. I started nagging the owner Mr. Jackson for a job, and when I was 14, he finally acquiesced. After school, I would ride my skateboard to work. Mr. Jackson had five kids, like the Jackson 5, which I thought was great. He was always trying to make me work harder, and I was always showing him that I was just going to work smarter. One day, he had this massive, floor-to-ceiling stack of peanut oil in five-gallon plastic drums packed in cardboard boxes. He wanted me to rotate the new shipment to the back and the older oil to the front. I said, "Yes, sir." He was chuckling, thinking about this scrawny kid dragging five-gallon boxes. When I started stacking them on my skateboard and rolling them to the back, he just rolled his eyes, like, *I can't believe this kid.*

Growing Up in the Family Business

In junior high, I took drafting as an elective which piqued my interest. In my junior year of high school, I gave up all my high school electives to start a work-study program in vocational drafting. In my senior year, I got a car and started a drafting job at the family company Binkley & Barfield, a civil engineering firm. I would go to school in the morning and work in the afternoon.

When I graduated, I got an apartment to experience independence. I worked full-time and paid my own bills for a year, then went on to college. In my senior year of undergrad, I chose to attend the Business in Britain program at Queen Mary College, University of London. Back stateside, I met my future wife, Robin, and I stayed at school to be with her and to earn a master's degree. Over summers and holidays, I would come home and work for the family company.

In 1990, with my new degrees, I started working at the company full-time. My first job was as a business manager. When our IT guy quit, I took on a secondary role as the IT director. Computers were in their infancy; I implemented our first website and email, moved us from DOS (the command prompt) into Graphical User Interface (GUI), which we all enjoy today, and took us through the world's Y2K scare. My role kept changing and growing to add under my management marketing, support services, and our leasing company. Before long, I was a vice president and managing four jobs.

I craved mentorship, and I wasn't finding the depth of mentorship I needed within my organization. Knowing the same skills I started with wouldn't take me to the next level, I sought out structured opportunities. Through several Chamber of Commerce Leadership programs, The Greater Houston Partnership, and Leadership Houston and American Leadership Forum, I launched into my personal development journey.

BRETT'S THOUGHT LEADER LESSONS

Leadership

In 2002, I became the CEO working under my father who was the founder, the president and chairman of the board, and the executive vice president, the latter of whom is still my business partner today.

In January 2006, our founder, my father, passed away. He lived a good life, but his death was a surprise. He was still coming into the office just days before. This was a major, life-changing moment. I had lost my father, and now, I was in the patriarchal role of my family as well as the business.

It didn't come easily for me. Even though I was already in the role of the CEO, up until that point, I was under his shadow and unable to develop or express my own leadership. I remember, at my dad's eulogy, standing up and describing my father as a great oak. Well, it's hard to reach the sunshine under the canopy of the great oak. I quickly learned that God equips the called more than he calls the equipped. My success would be based on setting a vision that others believed in and creating a "people first" mission within the organization.

Following my father's death, there was a legal dispute over the execution of his will. Going to court to defend his will was embarrassing and humbling for me, but as I look back, this time was one of the greatest growth sectors of my life because of the intimate nature of this disagreement. I believe we're always trying to find the easy place in life, but the reality is we were not made for the easy place. I think we were made to work through the struggles. Working past that was the foundation of my leadership skills that took me forward. I would find strength in scripture and support in a network of followers who, over many years, would help accomplish my vision and goals.

To be the leader I wanted to be, I worked on developing leadership from deep within, committed to my values and beliefs. To this very day, I continue to seek wisdom, guidance, and counsel through professional coaching, CEO groups, and ACEC's Senior Executive Institute.

I never considered leaving the family business. It was always about growing into the person that could make things work no matter what. I have always felt I had a three-word job description: "Whatever it takes." It was often very hard, but the only way was to keep pressing forward and to never quit. My dad would always tell me, "Just keep doing what you're doing… stay the course." I can look back today and see this as sound wisdom.

Legacy

When my father passed away, there wasn't a long-term plan in place for how to take care of the company going forward. We had to figure it out on our own. That worked out, but I swore I would do the work required to continue the family business honoring both tradition and progress after I was gone. I had always thought about transferring ownership internally to the employees, so we implemented an ESOP where everybody gets ownership in the company. Over time, we realized that ownership transition through acquisition was best for the organization and sold the company in August 2021.

After the sale, there were realities that I never really thought about. I signed an employment contract, and when two years passed, it dawned on me that I had completed the ownership transition, but I still had to complete the leadership transition. I had been working on it, but I had not taken my mind to the place where it was final. I realized in my gut that I was working myself out of a job.

The final phase of leadership succession is the giving stage: sharing knowledge, empowering the new generation, and witnessing creativity curated over years flourish. It is rewarding to see others flourish as I move into a new season of mentorship. I am opening doors for others, imparting wisdom, displaying values-based decision-making, and demonstrating how to avoid the trap of short-term, reactionary thinking.

The greatest trees take decades to grow, and the strongest trees grow in some of the most adverse conditions. Sometimes our greatest character development comes because of that slow, continuous growth through experience and hardship.

Q&A WITH BRETT

What makes a family business different?

Growing up in a family business, I gained industry knowledge and business sense at a young age. I realized that there are different levels of commitment when it comes to business and family but that both are parts of a greater whole. Working in the family business can create an innate sense of purpose and meaning in your life. Typically, when people disagree with how things are run in a company, they get another job. When this happens in a business you run with your family members, there is a feeling of disconnect from something you were born to be. When your professional and personal lives are intertwined, your own identity can be overtaken by the daily demands of family and work. There tends to be a higher level of emotion in decision making, and some of the personal dynamics and shortcomings of a family tend to make their way into the workplace.

At a very early age, I realized the financial burdens that transcended the workplace and made their way into the home. Financials, developing business, and entertaining clients were standard parts of my responsibility, so happy hours and extended dinners became a regular occurrence.

Having witnessed my parents' broken marriage, I should have seen the warning signs. Never let business success come at the cost of family. But, at the time, I didn't realize, one is replaceable, the other priceless.

I had seen the damage alcohol had done to our family growing up, and although I knew better, I carried these same actions into my adult work and family life. I was skilled at remaining high-functioning and even found that I could enhance my already outgoing personality with a couple of drinks. I was known in college for being "the life of the party" and for "spontaneity."

This outgoing personality combined with a never-quit attitude translated into building relationships and following through in business and in my personal life. As my family grew and the demands of business got harder, the stress relief alcohol provided became a welcome release. Over time, this played real havoc on my marriage. But the allure was so strong that I just couldn't abstain for long periods. I tried many times to convince myself that I could drink socially, but that never seemed to last for long.

Finally, the stress brought my marriage to the point of destruction. Thankfully, through time, commitment, humility, and a lot of prayer, I was able to turn my life around and do my part to restore my marriage. The work that I had been doing on leadership and personal development had encouraged an inward journey of self-discovery. This, coupled with a book called *Life's Healing Choices*, allowed me to uncover my life's hurts, hangups, and habits that were holding me back and keeping me from being my best.

We all tend to have something from our family's past, even if we don't work in our family business. I am resolute in breaking the generational curse and carrying my family forward into a transformed life. It's not what happens to us but how we respond that shapes our future as we move forward. I, like so many others who have struggled, can face the decision, accept the humility, and make the change that deep down inside we know we need to make.

Today, I am blessed with the forgiveness of my family, a thriving marriage of 31 years, the legacy of productive and beautiful children and grandchildren, and restoration we are continuing together. As I like to say, "He's not finished with me yet."

As a recovering CEO, Change Equals Opportunity, I feel my life's work is to share leadership principles with others. I want to help those who may be struggling on the inside while the world sees their success as "having it all together." I am stewarding today's leaders through difficult decisions with business acumen based on Biblical principles. The generous heart will multiply grace exponentially.

For further insights and guidance, contact Brett Binkley at Brett@realequityip.com or find him on LinkedIn or Facebook. He is dedicated to helping others navigate their leadership journeys, incorporate values-based decision-making, foster growth, and create transformational lasting, positive change.

NEAL BAWA

The Data Scientist of Multifamily
Profit with a Purpose

Neal Bawa is CEO/Founder at Mission10K and Grocapitus, two commercial real estate investment companies. Neal's companies use analytics to acquire or build large commercial properties across the US for over 1,000 investors. Current portfolio around 4K units valued at $700M. Neal speaks at real estate conferences across the country and virtually.

Big Tech Background

I ran a technology company from 1993 to 2014. It was growing fast, and I had a big, fat tech salary. I lived in California, so I was paying a huge chunk of my income to the tax man.

In 2003, we started building campuses for our company, and by 2011, we had built or improved half a dozen campuses. In that process, I had a chance to understand the extraordinary depreciation benefits of real estate and its tremendous positive impact on my take-home salary. That made me a huge fan of real estate investing.

By 2008, I had saved a bunch of money because now I wasn't paying a huge amount of tax, and I wanted to invest in real estate. I am a data scientist, so naturally, I focused on the data. I started asking simple questions like: What is the best city in America to invest in? How do you tell which city is the best? Which city is the worst and why?

When I would ask people, even real estate experts, these kinds of straightforward questions, I would never get answers that made sense. It seemed no one I met had actually gone through data for every US city, found effective ways to compare them, and finally backtested to see how the results compared to real estate profits. When I realized there wasn't anyone looking to do this, I decided I wanted to be the first.

So, I started mining various websites and then backtesting the data to connect it to real estate profits. Slowly, I started to discover the metrics that matter the most. Home prices were obviously connected to real estate profits. Metrics like population, income, jobs, and crime were very interconnected and powerful ways to rank cities by growth. I built a decision matrix and started to make public predictions. Many of my predictions have successfully identified small cities that have gone on to become blockbuster cities. That process got me notoriety in the industry.

The Mad Scientist of Multifamily

While I was publishing real estate data science from 2009 to 2013, I was not a professional investor. I was buying for my own portfolio and publishing data science for geeky investors through a Meetup group and a Udemy course with 13,000 students. People who were like-minded, who were nerdy and geeky like me, started to coalesce around me. That group eventually helped me invest $300+ million in equity to buy and build real estate.

In 2013, I sold my tech company and had this huge tax liability. How do I reduce it? I started looking at multifamily. *Hmm, maybe instead of buying one single family home, let's buy large multifamily properties.* I put properties under contract and shared what I was doing with the geeky folks in my database, people I had been influencing for years. They loved it, and everyone wanted to invest with me because they understood my math-driven approach.

Someone then gave me a nickname, The Mad Scientist of Multifamily, and soon, I was being called to present at conferences. Somebody put one of my hour-long presentations on YouTube, and that video ended up having hundreds of thousands of views.

That's how the ball got rolling. The investor list kept growing. Each year, I would publish a list of cities I thought people should invest in, and people were making investments and sending me thank you emails a year or two later. I used the list in my company which had two divisions: one that built apartments and one that bought and rehabbed older apartments. I've been lucky enough to be involved with a large number of projects of each kind, almost 5,000 units altogether.

Profit with Purpose

I am an immigrant, and I love my adopted country. I feel like I shouldn't just be making money for investors, I should be doing good in general. Over time, I became driven to have a mission, a profit with a purpose. Initially, the mission was taking older properties and improving them or building beautiful buildings. For years, I thought both were improving lives. After about five or six years, I came to a realization: both of the approaches had issues.

By the time I finished rehabbing an older building, rents were raised so much that I was pricing out a lot of tenants. The same thing happened with the buildings I built. To make a profit for my investors, I was adding gyms, infinity pools, and clubhouses. As a result, rents were pricing out middle-class Americans. I needed to change something to get back on mission. By 2019, I felt I had to try something different.

I started to do a lot of research about what Middle America really wanted. The short answer was most Middle Americans didn't really want to live in apartments. They wanted single-family homes. But post-COVID, interest rates dropped to zero and single family home prices rose dramatically. The difference between what Middle America could pay for a starter home and the actual mortgage payment ballooned, which marooned millions of families from ever having their own homes. They became "forever renters."

I realized the right mission for me was to find the most efficient way of building rental townhouses for these forever renters. Townhomes are as close to a single-family home as you can get. You've got a backyard, a garage, and no one living above you. And townhomes are significantly cheaper to build. I felt the townhome was the missing solution for America.

Mission 10K Cities

I started doing research on where I could build townhomes at a reasonable price. I tried building in Texas, but the cost of construction and the property taxes were too high.

So, I ranked every city in the US by "buildability." This made-up word, "buildability," allowed me to match up my townhome construction price to the income of the people living there. In the majority of cities, it was completely out of whack. There was no way the cost of building a rental townhome would match what someone in Middle America could pay.

But, I started finding cities where it could work, where I could build profitably for a certain rent number that would not burden Middle America—a rent number that they would be happy to pay and stay for a long time. I called these Mission 10K Cities because it was now my goal to build 10,000 of these homes.

This isn't subsidized housing. This means it has to be attractive enough for people to want to pay to live in it. In Idaho Falls, for example, we built a Mission 10K community with nine-foot ceilings, granite countertops, custom cabinetry, and a Starbucks in the building next door. And rents were only $1,700 a month!

In 2022, I took my mission to my investors, and they loved it. By 2024, I had invested $60 million from 300+ investors into building Mission 10K communities.

10,000 Townhomes

The incredible investor support I built really made Mission 10K doable. Now that we have completed several communities, I have an extremely high level of confidence that I will build 10,000 rental townhomes.

Every day I wake up and ask, *Is there anything stopping me from building 10,000 townhomes?* At this point, I don't believe there's anything in the way. Affordable townhomes are true profit with a purpose. Bottom line: I don't believe the government is going to solve America's housing crisis. The private sector must step up, which means making profit for investors. Data is the core of everything we do, and Mission 10K was designed to use data to make profit without burdening the tenants. We are absolutely going to help 10,000 families.

NEAL'S THOUGHT LEADER LESSONS

Health and Wellness

My beliefs around health and wellness are slightly nutty. I believe in continuously measuring everything going on with my body. For example, most people do a blood test once every couple years. I do a battery of blood tests three times a year. I want to live my peak life, and to do that, I have to measure continuously. For example, in March 2024, I had a stressful argument with a business partner. After my next blood test, I saw that my thyroid function was depressed. I visited my doctor who, in light of my results and a family history of thyroid issues, recommended a thyroid medication. But, I correlated my thyroid hormone level with the stressful argument. My research showed that stress has a tremendous short-term effect on thyroid. So, I removed stress by pulling away from that difficult situation. A month and a half later, my thyroid was normal. It still is. Bottom line—focus on the cause, not the symptom.

Another example. I am over 50 years old, and there are parts of my body that ache. My doctor says: Take this pill and exercise. But, I do pilates and yoga 3-4 times a week. After years of that routine, I didn't think I should be hurting or popping pills for the ache.

So, I started looking into it, and I realized that 50+ year old people should do ten times more physical therapy (PT) than they do. But a single session of PT costs $150+. So, I started researching and came across an Indian website called YourPhysio.in. To have an Indian doctor of physical therapy for a 45-minute session, the cost was incredibly low, $12 a session in packs of 30. With four PT sessions a week, I have fixed my shoulder, tennis elbow, wrist, and extreme tightness in my hamstrings. Outsourced healthcare!

Philanthropy and Giving

Because I am in the housing business, I was donating money to organizations building homes in the US. But, I wasn't happy with the inability to measure my impact.

I'm well off financially, and I fly business class around the world. This creates a huge amount of carbon emissions, which have a negative environmental impact. I became very concerned about my carbon footprint. Research showed that my carbon usage is five times higher than an average American's. So, I became obsessed with getting to net carbon neutral.

Research, research, and more research. I came across articles about planting trees to lower your carbon footprint. I started doing math: *How many trees does a person need to plant to become net carbon neutral for life?* The answer is very tangible: 918. If you plant 918 Douglas Fir trees, they will grow and act as carbon sinks, over time pulling harmful carbon out of the air equivalent to the amount you are responsible for emitting over your lifespan. I needed to plant 4,300 trees because of my bigger carbon footprint.

Ok, so how much will it cost to plant these trees and where can I plant them?

I looked at Brazil and India, and unfortunately, it was clear that Americans were donating trees, and later they were being cut down for lumber. I wanted a tree that would be there 100 years after I died. Then, I came across One Tree Planted. They plant in California, Oregon, and Washington on protected land. I donated enough to make myself carbon neutral for life, then enough to make my family carbon neutral for life. Then, we started offering our employees a 50/50 match, and a number of our employees took us up on it. It was a very interesting way of doing philanthropy. Very satisfying.

I also spend philanthropic dollars each year on an Indian charity called Sankara Eye Foundation. Each year I donate, they send me the list of the people who are no longer blind. They have 20 hospitals in India where they do operations for free. For $30, someone who was blind and dependent becomes a productive member of society. That's an incredible bang for my buck.

Education and the Pursuit of Knowledge

When I was nine years old, I was diagnosed as autistic. My mom was panicked. She thought there was something wrong with me because I would randomly start uttering numbers. My father was a fighter pilot, so they took me to the Air Force hospital in India. I was very lucky, because a doctor there conducted tests and told my mom, "Your son has a gift. The worst thing you could do is suppress this gift with medicine."

He told my mom that I was continuously measuring the world. The numbers were not nonsense, they were my measurements. Even today, there's a portion of my brain doing math, measuring everything in my environment around me. Often this math has no real meaning, but my brain is doing it all the time. Over time, my doctor was able to teach me how to continue measuring while also acting normally. I learned I can have two channels. One channel is doing this math, and the other channel is like any normal person taking in their environment. I'm proud of the fact that my brain is continuously doing two things.

The diagnosis and the decision not to put me on medication was a turning point. I was allowed to freely pursue math-driven knowledge. I think it was the greatest gift in my life.

Q&A WITH NEAL

What are a few of your favorite quotes?

"You can only manage what you can measure."

I'm continuously creating dashboards for everything. A data dashboard should be like a car dashboard. You look down for 1/10th of a second, understand, and then return your eyes to the road. A quick glance leads to new insights. So, I do not allow my team to send me large spreadsheets. I only want to look at data that I can get insights from within a second or two. If I fail to get insights in 1-2 seconds, it's the wrong dashboard. I have the simplest, almost childish dashboards. My obsession is continuously making them simpler. You can only manage what you can measure.

"The Bible got it wrong by one letter. It is not the meek that shall inherit the earth. It's the geek."

Richest man in the world, geek. Second richest, geek. Third richest, geek. See the pattern? There was a time when being an oilman was the way to be the richest man in the world. That time has passed. Now, it's the geeks that are ruling the world.

What are some favorite places you've traveled to?

I've been lucky to travel all over the world. The place that was the biggest surprise and became a favorite was Bali, a large island in Indonesia. Indonesia has a mostly Muslim culture, so I was expecting Muslim mosques in Bali. But I found that, of the 4.3 million population, 87% were Hindu. There were 10,000 Hindu temples on an island. Bali felt extraordinarily spiritual. I felt they have kept the original tenets of Hinduism alive. It's one of the most beautiful places on Earth. I am returning for my 25th wedding anniversary. I'd like to learn from these people. They have so much to teach.

Neal Bawa, known as the Data Scientist of Multifamily, invites qualified investors to explore innovative opportunities in real estate with Mission10K and Grocapitus. To learn how data-driven strategies can maximize your investment potential while making a positive impact, visit www.grocapitus.com or email Neal at neal@grocapitus.com.

 Scan for smart investing made easy with Multifamily University.

CAROLE SOUZA

Worthy of Life by Your Rules

Carole Souza is a mom, wife, real estate broker, certified life and business coach, mentor, and advisory board member for the largest coaching company in the world. She has raised three children and with resilience, strength, and unwavering determination successfully navigated the rough waters of living two lifetimes in one.

Rules of Life, My First Life

As a little kid, I just wanted peace in life. I can remember thinking that if everybody would just get along and be connected in some way, there'd be so much less turmoil. The idea of connecting has carried on through my life and each of my careers.

My childhood was also a lot of people telling me what I couldn't do. I never really believed them.

I grew up in the '50s in a very close-knit, Italian-Portuguese family and graduated from high school in the '60s. In our Italian neighborhood, there was this unspoken set of rules. Kids went to school. Boys were encouraged to go to college. Girls were not.

I went to Catholic school for 12 years and got married when I was 19 to the boy who lived across the street. He had gone off to the Air Force and come home in uniform, and I thought that was really cool.

We had two kids, and by the time I was 26, I was divorced with an 18-month-old and a five-year-old. I was also unemployed and owner of my first home.

I had a picture of what life was supposed to look like. I was supposed to get married, buy maple furniture, have babies, and live happily ever after. I was still young. I didn't have a strong sense of who I was. But, I knew I wasn't like what everybody said I was supposed to be. I wasn't the perfect mom or the married person anymore.

When my ex-husband left, one of the things he said to me was, "You'll never amount to anything." So, that became my marching order. I knew I could be good.

Day to day, I started making decisions about what my life should look like. And, before long, I found that somewhere inside me from the beginning was this belief system of "I can do anything."

Corporation President by 30 in the 1970s

I started taking big risks. When I was 27 years old, I opened my first business with a friend and business partner—an interior plant rental company named Mother Nature's Hang-Ups in the California Bay Area town of Walnut Creek. That turned out to be a very big business. By the time I was 30, we formed a corporation, which I became the president of, and had operations all over California. Nobody had told me I couldn't. Ten years later, I sold the company before moving ahead to the next opportunity.

I started working in the mortgage credit industry, and over 10 years, ended up moving all the way up to senior vice president of what became Fidelity Corporation. Eventually, I retired and that is when I found a new passion for real estate.

On Regrets

In the late 1980s, my father retired after 50 years of working at the same job. He was now free to do all the things he wanted to do and was so happy. Then he was diagnosed with cancer, and unfortunately, he passed in 1990.

In 1992, my mom got sick, and in '93 she was diagnosed with ALS, Lou Gehrig's disease. I spent six months taking care of her, and it was a life-changing time for me. I had been so busy running around being important to other people that I hadn't spent a whole lot of time with her.

We talked a lot, and I asked her about what she regretted. She listed a few things—the most important was paying too much attention to what other people thought. The other one was not having a career.

She had watched my career and said she would've liked to have had that opportunity. She said her life was about being a mother, wife, daughter, and sister, and she would have loved to have had a part of her life that was just about her.

That was earth-shattering to me. I felt really sad for her. It made a huge change in me and in what I was doing with my life. The doctor said my mom was only supposed to live for six weeks, but she lived for almost six months. I think it was because she had my brother's and my attention, which she had not had in this way for years. He too had a big job and family and moved all over the world.

A Huge Risk Conversation and a New Life

When I was caring for my mom, I was in a relationship with my current wife, Laura, but I was not out as a gay woman.

The day my mom died, I called my daughter, Sherri, and asked if she would have dinner with me. I sat down with her, and after we talked for a while, I took the biggest risk I've ever taken. I came out.

Sherri looked at me and said, "Well, Mom, first of all, we know. Scott knows, and so did Grammy." (Scott is my son.) I was surprised, to say the least!

Then she asked, "Why did you have so much trouble telling us?"

"Well," I said, "I was afraid you wouldn't love me."

Sherri said, "You taught us... that no matter what we do, you may not like it, but you're going to always love us. Why would you think we would feel anything different?"

That's when I called my son and talked with him. He told me he loved me too. That same day, I quit my corporate job of 10 years.

The shame of thinking that you're "other than" is dark. But when you tell the truth... you're truly in the light. From that moment on, my mantra became, "Where I live, you can't touch me." I had already taken the biggest risk I could take. *What could anyone possibly do to me now?* I was free.

That brought me into my second life. I was in my late 40s, and starting over.

Laura and I met in 1994. We celebrated our 30th anniversary of meeting recently and have now been legally married for 15 years.

After I came out, we began to live our new life integrated with my life with my older kids. A few years later, we had our son Max, who is now 24. Being able to parent again has been a privilege. Parenting in your 20s and parenting in your 50s is very different. I didn't ever think that was going to happen, but it has been amazing. Max and my older kids have always been close, and now that they're all older, I love that they're all friends.

Coaching the Core Self

I've done a lot of things. It hasn't always been great, but I have lived a lot of life, an amazing life. In fact, I've lived two amazing lives in one lifetime. I've been in positions of power, of controlling my destiny, and of being in places where I can make a difference.

Today, Laura and I are actively working as real estate agents in Omaha, Nebraska, and southwest Iowa. We love serving people through life transitions, specifically when buying or selling homes. Over the years, I developed a team and worked in the corporate side of brokerages, training, mentoring, and coaching. Coaching and sales with my wife became my primary focus.

I am a certified coach and leader, helping people grow in business and in life. It has been amazing. I help people by asking questions and letting them guide themselves to their greatest selves. I am a professional "Question Asker."

I love watching people discover how freaking awesome they are. I believe who you are is good enough to be great. So simple and what I really believe. That's the impetus for my coaching. For me, coaching is helping people own who they are and what they're driven to do. It's helping people get where they want.

CAROLE'S THOUGHT LEADER LESSONS

Personal Development

I worked for 10 years in personal growth workshops, The Life Trainings, with Dr. Louis Stolis, as a facilitator. When I started these trainings, I was a senior vice president for a big corporation, and the president thought it was so valuable that he gave me 10 days a month to facilitate the workshops and make personal growth available to leadership throughout the company. Ten years as a facilitator in personal development had a huge impact on my life and my ability to become a thought leader.

I experienced people of all ages, genders, and backgrounds, and all had one thing in common. Between the time they were born and the time I interacted with them, their experiences in life had given them a message, which they believed: they were not loved, not worthy, or not capable. Whatever it was, they showed up with it at the personal growth training. These false beliefs were keeping them from being who they really are. We are loved. We are worthy. We are free. Coming out through those beliefs myself was life-changing. I think I had to do that first to have the courage and strength for the next seasons of my life.

Business and Entrepreneurship

I've had many businesses. My wife, who is a trained executive chef, and I have owned two restaurants. One was a coffee house in the Shakespearean theater area of Ashland, Oregon. The conversations with the Shakespearean actors we served were incredible. I had a consulting business, was a trainer for a non-profit, and then became a Realtor for the past 22 years. We've been very successful.

We've also been unsuccessful but always kept going. From 2007 through 2012 were very difficult years. We just kept going. We worked harder and made things happen. That's what an entrepreneur does. You go up, you go down, but you are always going forward, and eventually, you get to that success, and you lean into others because you go further together.

Q&A WITH CAROLE SOUZA

What is your favorite movie?

Elf is a hilarious movie with a lot of powerful messages. We watch it every Christmas when my kids are all together. My two sons know the movie by heart. It's a happy time.

What is your favorite song or who is your favorite musical artist?

Since childhood, Barbara Streisand has been my favorite. At my high school graduation in 1964, we sang "Somewhere," my favorite song ever. The lyric "somewhere there's a time and a place for us," tells the story of how I've felt my entire life.

What are a few of your favorite quotes?

My absolute favorite quote is from Maya Angelo: "When someone shows you who they are, believe them." And then, I personally add, "the first time."

My dad used to always say this to me, and I hated it at the time, but now I understand: "Show me your friends, and I'll tell you who you are."

Who is your favorite sports team?

Indian Fever and the whole WNBA. I love the awareness Caitlin Clark has brought to women's sports in general but also her ability to bring a team together.

What are your pet peeves?

My biggest pet peeve is probably conversations of small talk when I feel people are not really engaged and connected.

How do you recharge?

I connect. Deep connection with people is my recharge. One intentional place I do this is an amazing group, The Peak Pros, I meet with on Monday mornings. There are 25 of us, and we're able to be vulnerable with each other. We always get into a deeper conversation than our topic. It's the thing I look forward to more than anything all week.

Who are your mentors and greatest influences?

Brian Buffini is probably my greatest mentor and influencer. There's also the people representing the Brian Buffini organization and my coaches, who I've had for 22 years. They have all been influencers in different ways and at different times. The coach that has probably had the most impact on me is Dave Mcgee, vice president of coaching, so, the coach of coaches. He was my personal coach for two years through COVID. I am a professional coach, but he didn't let me coach him. He would force me to face myself, even when I tried to avoid it. I cried many times on our calls.

Jolie Johnson, who has since passed, was the first agent I worked with in real estate and an amazing woman. She was always giving first, before she asked for anything. She taught me three things: 1) nobody gets in your car who's not pre-approved, 2) you have to take one day off every week, and 3) you need to get a coach. Those keys are probably the best advice I could have ever gotten.

Have you had any past challenges that turned out to be blessings?

My generation didn't know it, but we kicked in a lot of doors and shot holes in a lot of ceilings for the next generation. I'm proud to have been a part of that. It took a lot.

What is something most people don't know about you?

I've never really gotten rid of fear, but I walk into it. It's harder to walk into the older I get. But you practice and you learn to do it, because on the other side, there's so much more. I'm afraid to stand up and talk in front of people. I'm afraid to make a video or to approach somebody to ask for what I need. But I do it anyway.

What philanthropic causes do you support?

I support human rights, specifically LGBTQIA+ causes. I also support anything that has to do with getting rid of opioids, drugs, and alcohol abuse. Finally, I support causes that advocate for the well-being of animals.

What are some favorite places you've traveled to?

Bermuda and Portugal are beautiful and surrounded by water, which is my love. My daughter lives in Portugal, so it has a special place in my heart.

Sedona is a wonderful place to recharge. When I was working in personal growth workshops, the trainer and I took 40 people to all of the vortexes. Then, at a church carved into a mountain, we held a ceremony where they married themselves. It was out-of-body amazing.

What books do you often recommend?

The *7 Habits of Highly Effective People* by Stephen R. Covey is my favorite book ever. If you could never read any other book, this one would give you enough lessons to get through life.

The Greatest Salesman in the World by Og Mandino

Anything by Mel Robbins, especially *The High 5 Habit* and *The 5 Second Rule*.

What would you tell your 18-year-old self?

You don't have to live the life your parents, family, or friends lived, or the one others thought would be right for you. Seek to **Be You**.

What do you consider your greatest achievements to date?

I think it's living the life I've lived, the life that my family and I have lived together, without asking anybody for permission and doing it well, with respect from others. That's a huge achievement—not apologizing at all for who we are. I came out at 48 years old, successfully raised my children, which I did by myself for years, and then alongside my wife, raised our son in a world that didn't really understand our marriage. We do it anyway.

Carole Souza has a huge heart to lead and inspire. As a former SVP of a major corporation and lifetime entrepreneur, she has served on numerous non-profit boards. Carole also partners with her wife of 30 years to serve people transitioning in life, buying, and selling homes. Call Carole at (402) 871-9817 or find her on LinkedIn, Instagram, or Facebook.

ERIK MIKKELSON

Reeling in Wisdom
For Your Financial Future®

Erik Mikkelson is co-founder of Monona Docks and Waterfront LLCs, founder of RMR Wealth Advisors and Financial Future, LLCs, board member, and real estate investor. As a Certified Financial Planner™ professional, Erik is passionate about helping others grow, utilize, preserve, and protect their family's wealth, so they can then enjoy life and create their legacy.

Gifts from My Grandparents

Some of my best childhood memories are of going to stay with my grandparents every summer and being at their cabin on Bass Lake in Southern Minnesota. I learned to operate the boat, and, most importantly, to fish! "Give a man a fish, and you feed him for a day, but teach a man to fish, and you feed him for a lifetime." That applies to so much in life, including being around entrepreneurs and absorbing how they treated their customers in a small, rural town.

My grandparents grew up in the Great Depression. My grandfather eventually became a butcher, which paved the way to my grandparents becoming owners of a SuperValu grocery store in Blue Earth, Minnesota.

I remember my grandparents with the newspaper in their sunroom most mornings, reading the previous day's stock market report. Based on what SuperValu and other stock holdings of theirs had done, they would say, "Well, we can keep the lights on!" or "We might need to keep the lights off today." I received my first stocks and bonds from them. That is when I started learning about investing in publicly traded companies based on profitable and viable businesses.

This is also when I learned the importance of knowing the competition. My grandfather would take me "undercover" (Everyone in town knew him!) into the nearby "dirty bird," Red Owl grocery store, to check on pricing, produce, product displays, etc. I would get to buy a candy bar to see how I was treated by the checkout person. That was my pay for helping!

I also began to learn about real estate ownership, although I don't think I realized it at the time. I remember when my grandparents bought the actual SuperValu store building and parking lot. It was a huge deal for them. I remember them putting in a restaurant, them owning a residential rental home and a cabin, as well as them looking at properties they eventually decided to pass on. Looking back, all were based on utilization value, investment potential, and some form of lifestyle value. I have been a big believer in owning real estate ever since, especially waterfront properties.

The importance of providing great service and value was exemplified by how my grandparents conducted business and lived their lives. I believe those same values are at the heart of what makes so many entrepreneurs' businesses successful. I am blessed to have had such great role models to learn from.

Economics and Finance in Practice

It was time I learned to fish. I studied economics with a minor in accounting at St. Olaf College in Minnesota while I gave up my knees to Division III college football. During those years, I enjoyed a unique work experience as a bouncer and eventually became the wharf manager at Lord Fletcher's on Lake Minnetonka. I was allowed to work on a feasibility study my senior year for converting the downstairs bar into a restaurant-bar combination. That idea looked to be a good return on investment, and the downstairs bar was renamed Granddaddy's, which remained a key part of Lord Fletcher's for decades.

After college, I went into logistics management and manufacturing with Kimberly Clark and moved to Paris, Texas, then California, and then back to Texas. The hours were long, but the experience of working in the consumer products industry was insightful. I gained additional experience through roles with Newell Rubbermaid in Ohio, at Anchor Hocking Glass, and finally in Wisconsin working for Fiskars, a small publicly traded company best known for the orange-handled scissors on many desks across the country.

As a member of and eventually a leader of the Fiskars corporate operations team, my team and I would fly all around the US and Europe working with a conglomerate of many small consumer product manufacturing and assembly businesses on efficiency, quality, and of course, profitability. I was also able to gain some merger and acquisition experience in my role as the operations lead for multiple projects.

From there, while flying to different locations, I found myself reading about estate planning, investing, and personal finance. I was finding my true passion.

Persistence, Patience, and Setting the Hook

On one trip, I went to a leadership center in Colorado with a group of colleagues, and during the exit interview, the leadership advisor asked me if I had ever considered being a financial professional. The line was cast!

My first daughter was born, and it seemed traveling so much was not right for me anymore. Armed with the notion of a career change, I called a great friend, which led me into conversations with his network of coworkers in the mutual fund industry.

I once again jumped on airplanes to meet and interview some industry leaders. As I learned more about many aspects of the financial industry, I found myself a bit disgusted with commissions and greed, yet drawn more and more to helping business owners and families with anything financial. Around that time, a good friend and real estate partner of mine said, "When are you going to stop doing what you're doing and become a financial guy so you can manage our stuff?" With that, the hook was set!

Becoming a Full-Time Fiduciary

I got into the finance industry and began assisting one of the earliest established registered investment advisors (RIA) and certified financial planners (CFP®) in the state of Wisconsin just as the tech bubble was deflating, fast! He came to my desk and said, "Guess what? I need you to pay rent and become a full-blown financial advisor."

So, I became a tenant, began investing money into the business, and became a family wealth advisor. I studied to earn my CFP® designation and started finding people to help, or more like, they started finding me—thankfully!

My goal became to work with a relatively small group of people as a fiduciary to help them enhance, utilize, preserve, and protect their family assets. I wanted to help people meet their family's financial and lifestyle desires, achieve their retirement and wealth accumulation dreams, and envision their legacy wishes.

I eventually departed from my position to form my own firm and serve families. Prior to this, I was a big student of *The Millionaire Next Door* and the demographics it was based on. I had a vision of serving people with that mindset and lifestyle, much like my grandparents. I formed a business registered as an RIA, charging our clients fees for advice and service, not commissions.

This path led me to develop what had been a self-created job into a small business, much like as described in the book *The Cashflow Quadrant*. I give that book, *The Millionaire Next Door*, and *Freakonomics*, a lot of credit for the foundation, values, insight, and guiding principles we operated the business by.

Serving the Millionaire Next Door

Just as I had envisioned, a lot of families we have been fortunate to serve are self-made millionaires next door. You would never know their paper wealth by running into them in public. For the most part, they are fiscally responsible, meaning they have established habits and behaviors to keep themselves spending less than their resources, saving the difference, and in most cases, investing in some fashion.

Oftentimes, this involves investment in markets, real estate, and businesses, and often becoming entrepreneurs themselves.

My grandfather used to tell me to make sure I always took care of my own old man, meaning save for myself, for my future, first. Armed with that mindset and the power of compounding returns, I believe most can achieve a financially rewarding future.

Unfortunately, a problem most of us face is that, as humans, we behave emotionally, especially when it comes to our money and investments. For whatever reason, when we find that something we really need to buy or want to buy is on sale, we often enthusiastically buy it. However, when it comes to investments that go down in price and are "on sale," we get scared and often sell instead of buy. To have a successful investing strategy, we need to have a system of saving and investing we believe in and adhere to through both good and bad, sometimes downright terrible, times. Having a process that guides us to have the conviction to invest even more when times look the bleakest, often leads to above-average performance in the long term. Indeed, rebalancing or adding to investments coming off of lows is where you can get exponential growth. This can often be the foundation of great wealth creation.

As people approach retirement, I strongly believe the most important thing they can do is have a well-thought-out lifetime cash flow strategy. Investments are important, but without a good cash flow strategy that holds up through both up and down markets, there is a large risk of jeopardizing a person's retirement. I believe this is very misunderstood by many as they head into retirement and sadly even ignored or neglected by many professionals in the industry.

Plan for the Worst, the Rest Is Upside

To help explain and manage investment portfolios and retirement cash flows, we have copyrighted *Capturing Profits and Preserving Wealth*© and service marked *3 Barrels and a Bucket*sm. The most stable barrel is structured to preserve wealth and be the resource to draw both peace of mind and cash flows from when needed throughout one's retirement. The comfort, peace of mind, and conviction for retirees who are surviving, and even thriving, during rough economic times as a result of following this process is priceless.

Taking advantage of different markets through this consistent, strategic, and thoughtful approach can be a cornerstone of a lifetime of wealth creation and utilization.

When faced with major decisions, imagine the worst-case scenario and plan for it. As soon as we can deal with the worst, the rest is upside! I believe this frees one to focus on achieving the upside and true financial freedom.

Get Up and Get Doing It!

I was truly fortunate to get some one-on-one time with my grandfather when he was in his late 80s. We went fishing, of course! But we also just talked, remembering past times together. Then, at the top of our stairs leading down to the dock on the lake, he had a tear coming down his cheek. He said, "Dammit, Erik. We spent our whole life saving and investing, and all she wanted was a new dock and some things remodeled. What was I waiting for?!"

"She" was my grandmother. I just gave him a hug, and we went fishing.

A few years later, in his 90s, I got to visit with him again, but this time we didn't go fishing. We were having coffee in the morning, while he was, of course, looking at the business section of the paper. I asked him if he had any words of wisdom for me. He thought, and he said that there were still many things he would have liked to do. He paused; "I think my best advice is, if there is anything in this world you would like to do, you had better get up and get doing it!"

Years ago, while reflecting on the words of my grandfather while sitting quietly alone in the woods, as I so often enjoy finding time to do, it occurred to me to pursue registering *For Your Financial Future*®, and I got it done. *For Your Financial Future*® guides my purpose, direction, and actions whenever I have the honor to serve others, hopefully helping them to get up and get doing whatever it is they find most meaningful!

ERIK'S THOUGHT LEADER LESSONS

Wealth
is having enough to be able to utilize your time, the 24 hours per day that we each have, in the manner you find most meaningful, purposeful, and satisfying to you.

Investing
Begin early and often. Be persistent and have a well-thought-out, straightforward approach. Think about and be able to answer what, why, and by when. Understand what is enough—enough to be able to live without worry of having enough. Be systematic, diversified, and relentless until you achieve "enough." Part of understanding and achieving enough is embracing "just because you can, doesn't mean you should."

Business & Entrepreneurship
Be focused. If you chase two rabbits, they will both get away. Develop healthy paranoia of what could go wrong and create contingency plans. Be ready. When opportunity presents itself, recognize it and act. Proper prior planning prevents poor performance.

Daily Habits
Strive to learn and do three important things to plan for tomorrow: be responsible, be reliable, and be ready to act.

Hobbies & Passions
I have love and respect for the outdoors, nature, and the real-life chess matches that can be found in both fishing and hunting, especially archery.

Q&A WITH ERIK

What is your favorite song or who is your favorite musical artist?
"In the Air Tonight" by Phil Collins

Who is your favorite sports team?
Vikings – Just win a Super Bowl (or five) before I die!

What are your pet peeves?
Hearing someone say they are bored.

How do you recharge?
Time in the woods, on a mountain, or on the water.

What are a few of your favorite quotes?
"Just because you can, doesn't mean you should." – Proverb

Have you had any past challenges that turned out to be blessings?
Needing to split from business partners.

What is some of the best advice you've received?

Be genuine, be honest, be reliable, be resilient, and do meaningful things with enthusiasm.

What do you consider your superpower?

Persistence.

What are some favorite places you've traveled to?

The South Island of New Zealand, the Australian Great Barrier Reef, and Belize.

What would you tell your 18-year-old self?

Save and invest even more.

What has been your greatest lesson?

If you have plans for the worst-case scenarios, you are able to enjoy focusing on the upsides!

How do you define success?

Accomplishing what you set out to do, one meaningful accomplishment at a time, while being true to yourself.

To get in touch with Erik Mikkelson, you can email him at mikkerik@gmail.com or call him at 608-436-0206.
For Your Financial Future®

NEWY SCRUGGS

Beyond the Broadcast
The Emmy-Winning Journey

Fifteen-time Emmy-winner Newy Scruggs has been the sports director at KXAS-TV (NBC) in Dallas-Fort Worth, Texas, since 2000. Stops along the way have included gigs in Myrtle Beach, South Carolina; Austin, Texas; Cleveland, Ohio; and Los Angeles, California. Newy combines his media expertise with a commitment to personal growth and lifelong learning.

My Big Dream

If I wanted to make it a Hollywood script, I'd say, "It was winter. It was the cold, brutal winter of December 1970 in war-torn West Germany when this newborn of African-American descendants from Alabama came into the world. The baby boy was sick, but he recovered. He healed up and made the trip to America as a youth, learned the English language, graduated from a Native American university, and became a decorated television sportscaster in the United States." Cue the music.....

The facts are all correct—embellished a bit but, hey, everyone likes a feel-good story.

My father was serving in the United States Army when I was born, on a base in Wiesbaden, West Germany. We moved back to the States when I was very young. I was an avid sports fan. We were stationed in Savannah, Georgia when I was called to participate in a mock newscast in my fifth grade class. It was Mr. McDuffie's class, to be exact.

I played the sportscaster role, and I loved it. I had found my calling. Well, almost. I wanted to play for the Dodgers. If that baseball thing didn't work out, I would go do this television sports thing. I was 11 years old and had it all figured out. I was going to be the guy giving you the sports on the six o'clock news or on this new thing called ESPN.

It was my dream.

Tenacity

I pursued TV sportscasting the way Kobe Bryant would chase his basketball dreams. I did work in Los Angeles and covered Kobe's time as a rookie with the Lakers up until he won his first of five NBA titles.

Today, I tell people that had I known then how small the odds were of making it to a top two TV news market and how hard it would be, I would have never done it. Fortunately, I just had the drive and the guts to pursue this dream.

How did I make it? I read a lot of books. I found the teachings of Henry David Thoreau, Ralph Waldo Emerson, and the NBA Hall of Fame coach Pat Riley when I was a junior at Westover Senior High School in Fayetteville, North Carolina. Yes, *the Ville*, which would later produce the rapper J. Cole.

I also met the legend of WRAL-TV in Raleigh, North Carolina, Tom Suiter. He was the best sportscaster on my local channels. We met at a student council meeting and became pen pals. I will always remember the advice he gave me about college.

Tom said to attend a school where I could get hands-on training. I was focused on going to the University of North Carolina (UNC). I loved North Carolina, and that was billed as the top school in the state to get a journalism degree.

Many a Carolina intern roamed the WRAL studios under Tommy's watch. His criticism was that they didn't really get experience until late in their college career. He was in favor of going to a place where a student could get hands-on training as soon as possible.

I found that place at Pembroke State University (PSU). It is a Native American institution in Southeastern North Carolina the next county over from where I was going to high school.

I got a chance to be on the air my freshman year, and I just attacked my work. Like Michael Jordan, I was relentless. I worked my craft, did two internships before my senior year, and eventually was handed a key to the TV studio.

One month into my senior year at PSU, I was making money shooting Friday night high school football highlights for WBTW-TV in Florence, South Carolina. Then, when the weekend sports guy was fired, I said I would do the job.

On Air Success

So, there I was, at 21 years old, just ten years removed from the beginning of my dream, working full-time as a local TV sports anchor and reporter. I was instantly the richest man living on campus because I was making $300 a week.

After nine months in South Carolina, it was on to Austin, Texas. The other sports jobs I had were in Cleveland, Los Angeles, and my last stop, Dallas-Fort Worth, Texas.

Today, with 15 Emmy awards and memories of numerous trips to the biggest sporting events in North America, I can say I lived the dream. I found success. God blessed me in many ways by allowing me to use this gift and the passion that burned inside of me and to welcome me into the homes of thousands.

NEWY'S THOUGHT LEADER LESSONS

The Pursuit of Knowledge

Jim Rohn, Les Brown, Brian Tracy, Ryan Holiday, Robert Greene, John Register, Dr. Delatorro McNeal II—I could go on about the great self-help authors whose books I have in my personal library.

Reading is one thing. Taking massive action is another. Most of us can get inspired quickly. But can you follow through with that inspiration to reach a goal or desire? Can you really make that change you have wanted for a long time?

For years, I wanted to get an MBA degree. I would talk myself out of it because I was terrible at math. I thought it would be selfish to invest six figures in a graduate degree when I have three children who will need to get their own college educations. In other words, I was full of excuses.

The late, great business philosopher Jim Rohn said that people change for two reasons: inspiration or desperation.

Despite having an award-winning career as a sportscaster, I had a boss who wanted to fire me about 17 years into my run at my station. I watched this cowardly man fire many hardworking journalists in our newsroom. He had my name on the chopping block, and I was not handling it well mentally.

I was working in fear. I became angry and took it out on the people I love. I was really mad at myself for not having gotten the skills I needed to be prepared for life after television.

As it turns out, that terrible boss was fired. Many of my coworkers and I were relieved. But it did stay in my mind that I didn't have the skills to pivot past the job I had held since I was 21 years old. I was comfortable and didn't push myself in the ever-changing field of education.

At 50 years old, I enrolled at the Texas Christian University (TCU) Neeley School of Business. I earned my executive MBA. It took 18 months of being uncomfortable in courses like finance, accounting, analytics, and strategy. In-person classes were held from 8:00 a.m. to 5:00 p.m. on Fridays and Saturdays.

I can't express how much confidence I gained from completing that program. Growth truly does come from being uncomfortable. My school-aged kids were able to see me struggle in my studies. They saw my grades, which were good. I shared with them my adventures from Portugal and Spain as I completed the international business course. Walking across that stage at TCU to receive that MBA degree was one of the top ten moments in my life.

Knowledge is power. Learning gives you confidence. Never stop trying to gain wisdom.

Personal Development

"You must be an active participant in your own rescue." – Pat Riley

I keep a copy of Pat Riley's book *The Winner Within: A Life Plan for Team Players* in my personal library. It's one of the most influential books I have ever read.

That quote about being an active participant in your own rescue was his plea to his 1986-87 Lakers to look within themselves to fix their club and get better. Riley was the head coach, and the Lakers were coming off a season in which they got put out of the playoffs unexpectedly.

The premise is simple. Stop looking for and waiting on a calvary to come over the hill and save you from your situation. You must be an active part of the saving, the turnaround, and the climb to redemption.

Notice the adjective word "active."

In many cases, we can feel sorry for ourselves if we have a setback or receive bad news. We can find ways to complain or express frustration.

Riley is telling us that we must look within ourselves first. Things have a better chance of going the way we want if we are working and trying to make them better. Faith without work is dead. Get active and work to make things the way you want them to be.

Q&A WITH NEWY

What is your favorite movie?

Days of Thunder with Tom Cruise. I first started covering NASCAR around the time it came out, and everybody who covered NASCAR loved or hated it. "Oh, it's Hollywood! It's not real." But it was my introduction to the sport. I love Tom Cruise, the dynamic between him and Robert Duval, and the way Tom Cruise as Cole Trickle fought to become a race car driver.

What is your favorite song or who is your favorite musical artist?

If I have to pick, Stevie Wonder is fantastic. Being discovered in the '60s, breaking out and becoming the artist he was in the '70s with *Songs in the Key of Life*, and to be able to keep making music for so long, and to be so good for so long, is unmatched. There's really not an occasion where you can't pull out a Stevie Wonder song, whether it's a wedding, a funeral, or a party.

Who is your favorite sports team?

I grew up a Cowboys fan. I was the kid who had the Cowboys lunchbox, pencils, raincoat, pajamas, curtains, and leather jacket. I was the person who wore the royal blue Cowboy jersey when they couldn't win in them and it was considered a curse. I had the blue Tony Dorsett, number 33. I also loved Roger Staubach, Drew Pearson, Harvey Martin, and "Too Tall" Ed Jones.

That was one of the reasons I wanted to get into the business, and luckily enough, I got to end up covering my favorite team. I am going on 30 years of covering the Cowboys and am grateful to say that these guys know me.

I also grew up a fan of Jackie Robinson, and to get to cover the Dodgers was special as was being around Tommy Lasorda when he managed the team.

Plus, covering the Lakers, watching them on TV, then going to the Forum and actually watching Magic Johnson play in his final season and being there when Kobe and Shaq were there—those are incredible memories.

What are a few of your favorite quotes?

Ralph Waldo Emerson wrote, "What I must do, is all that concerns me, not what the people think." In 1988, I learned in Mr. Stanton's English class at Westover High School, and that carried me, really challenged me, and helped me understand who I was.

Pat Riley's book *Showtime: Inside the Lakers' Breakthrough Season*, Chapter 13: Motivation, says, "Be so good at what you do that they can't think about replacing you."

Pat Riley also says, "What do you get when you squeeze an orange? Orange juice. Put anything under pressure and you'll bring out what's inside."

Bill Parcells: "I don't have to be fair, I have to be right."

What do you consider your superpower?

My ability to and wanting to learn and read books. There lies the power to do whatever you want to.

What would you tell your 18-year-old self?

Read The Book of Proverbs and then reread it, highlight it, and journal about it.

Follow fifteen-time Emmy-winning sportscaster and sports director at KXAS-TV (NBC) in Dallas-Fort Worth, Texas
Newy Scruggs on X: @newyscruggs | Facebook: NewyScruggsSports

GREG ZLEVOR

Pause and Prosper
How Slowing Down Can Propel You Forward

Greg Zlevor, president of Westwood International and HopeMakers founder, has worked with Johnson & Johnson, The Singapore Police Force, Volvo, General Electric, and many other high-profile companies, co-authored eight #1 bestselling books, and shared the stage with greats including Jim Rohn, George Land, and M. Scott Peck.

In Pursuit of the Mind and Spirit

I was born in Milwaukee, Wisconsin, and grew up in Racine, just a short distance south, near Lake Michigan. I'm a cheesehead, a Packer fan, through and through. My whole family is still in Wisconsin and religiously cheers the Pack.

For college, I enrolled at Lawrence University in Appleton, Wisconsin. I was a biology major and hoped to go to medical school. But halfway through, I realized my life was going to unfold differently than I'd always thought. In my free time, I was reading books by authors like Mohandas Gandhi, M. Scott Peck, and Dietrich Bonhoeffer. Many books were science-related, but more were about psychology, spirituality, and development. I came to understand that I was more interested in personal growth than physical growth and I'd rather work with the mind and spirit than the body. I stuck with my biology degree but decided not to go to medical school.

Even though I knew I was following my passion, I wasn't sure how to translate that into a career. Luckily, a local school needed some help. For four years after college, I was a science teacher and football coach at Xavier High School in Wisconsin. In the back of my mind, the desire to go to graduate school wouldn't go away. I just didn't know what to study.

Someone said to me, "Why don't you go for what's important to you?" I came to realize nothing was more important to me than my spiritual journey. It had been a gradual awakening, but there were some peak experiences, like the summer I'd spent living at Madonna House, a Catholic community in Ontario. I made up my mind and decided to get my master's degree in spirituality.

One Step at a Time

I started applying to graduate schools. I was most excited about the University of San Francisco. The program would kick off with a 40-day silent retreat.

As I pursued the program, the priest who had taken on the role of spiritual director in my life asked me, "Greg, have you been on a 10-day silent retreat?" I had never been on any silent retreat. He asked, "Don't you think you should go on a three or five-day retreat before you go on a 40-day?"

I took a left turn, skipped San Francisco, and decided to go to Boston College. The program included classwork, reflection, and a master's thesis but did not have an intense silent retreat component. That mentor changed my life with a 10-minute conversation and a simple question. It's a reminder that in spite of the fast-paced world we live in, sometimes it's best to take things at a slower pace. Starting graduate school with a 40-day silent retreat could have gotten me on the right foot faster, but it could have burned me out just as quickly.

For nine years, I stayed at Boston College, first as a graduate student, then as a chaplain designing and running leadership programs, mission trips, and retreats. Within a few years, I was hosting community-building workshops and studying group dynamics. Based on my work, companies began asking me to work with them. When a few of them offered me retainers, I realized each would pay more than I made in a whole year as a chaplain. I decided that I had better give training others a try. I left the university and embarked upon what has become my career.

I didn't plan any of it in advance, nor did I think that one step was going to lead to the other. But the combination—my degree in biology, my training in spirituality, and my work in mindfulness, meditation, and emotional intelligence, merged with my understanding of the importance of serving and building communities—led me to where I am today.

It was crucial that I slowed down when the instinct was to act fast. The world changes. We change. Often, building the lives we want to live isn't about meticulous, years-in-advance planning, but in slowing down, reflecting, and adapting.

Taking the Journey

Spiritually, we're individuals from different traditions and paths, yet most of us struggle with the same questions. We want to serve, be happy and content, and use the most of our gifts. Getting there is a journey of questioning, practicing, and discovery.

I've worked with quite a few mentors and spiritual directors in my life. Their role is to open up your conscience, not tell you what to do. The spiritual journey is one you walk yourself, and increasingly, that journey is relevant to other areas of your life. I find it fascinating how businesses, even masterminds and personal development circles, are being called upon, not necessarily consciously, to do work that used to be handled by churches and spiritual centers. How do we, as business leaders, fill that role in a way that has integrity and depth? It's not an easy question.

In the corporate world, I rarely mention the word spirituality. Yet, I teach values and skills imperative to a healthy spirituality. It is important that I listen, serve, and stay calm in a crisis, and it's important for the people I work with to know there's something bigger than themselves. When they do, and when they share their personal agenda in a calm way, they can bring others together. That's the ultimate form of teamwork and connection. Listening, leading, and partnering. It's also human spirituality. We have learned this through the centuries, and today, we can adopt these truths within the framework of technology to fit our 21st-century world.

Living Wisely by Breaking the Emotional Chain

As a consultant and speaker, I travel a lot for work. After one particularly long week on the road, I hustled to the airport, excited to get home for my son Daniel's birthday party.

As I was sitting at the gate for my connecting flight, I heard the announcement, "I'm sorry ladies and gentlemen, we are slightly delayed. The crew isn't ready yet."

Ready yet? You've had all week to get a crew ready.

Nervous, I looked at my watch and started calculating. I had a tight connection for my next flight. *I better make my next flight.* Time ticked by.

"Sorry about the delay. We are ready to board."

I calculated again. *Uh oh, I might not make my connecting flight home.*

I was sweating the whole flight. We landed. I only had nine minutes.

Frantic, hoping my connecting flight was delayed too, I rushed out of the jetway and asked the attendant, "Where is the gate for the flight to Boston?

"Right there," he said, pointing to the next gate. The door was open and the plane was still at the gate! *I just made it!*

I ran over. "This is my flight. I can't believe I made it!" I panted to the gate agent.

"Sir, I'm sorry. The flight is closed."

"No, I see the plane right there. The door is still open. The flight's not closed."

"Sir, you don't need to raise your voice. Calm down."

Now, just a little note: in the history of calm down. No one's ever calmed down by someone saying calm down.

"That door's open. The plane is here. The flight isn't closed!" I gestured angrily toward the jetway. I leaned toward the door.

"Sir, if you go to get on that flight, I will call security."

"Your company is the one who made the mistake and didn't have the crew ready. I'm getting on this flight!" She reached for the phone.

Arrghhhh!!!! I turned and stomped two big steps away.

Suddenly, I realized, *I teach this stuff.*

In my journey, I had come to understand that all my "ouch" times I made worse when I held onto the emotion and the story that fueled it. What if there is something else that matters more than the emotion? What if emotions are simply messengers? What if the main role of emotions is to bring a message? What if, when a difficult emotion shows up, I ask, *What is important to me? What really matters?*

Hello, Anger, what's the message?...

It's been a long week and I really want to be home and celebrate Daniel's birthday. I don't want to argue or fight; I just want to get home.

I turned back to the agent. "Ma'am, I'm really sorry that I raised my voice. I know you're just trying to do your job. My apologies. It's been a long week. If I can get on that flight, I can make my son's birthday. Can you help me get on that flight?"

She paused, "Let me check with the pilot."

When she returned a moment later, she said, "The pilot said you can board."

I learned again—don't get caught up in the emotion. Don't hold onto the messenger. Get the message, pause, and intelligently pursue what matters.

The wisdom is in the message.

Emotion. Pause. *Hello, Emotion. What message do you carry? What's important to me now?* Get the message and let the emotion go. That's the wise move.

How to Create Miracles

One of my favorite phrases from entrepreneur and motivational speaker Jim Rohn is, "You do not have to do extraordinary things to get extraordinary results. You only have to do ordinary things extraordinarily well to get extraordinary results." Miracles aren't random or reserved for rare geniuses; they happen when people diligently practice the ordinary. Teams are looking for these miracles, to accomplish the extra-ordinary, and helping them is priceless for me.

We live in a world that simultaneously worships the idea of "move fast and break stuff," a phrase made popular in Facebook's early days, and the expectation that you have your five- and 20-year plan sharply in your headlights. Neither is realistic. Committed, slow discipline gives you the expertise to create miracles in your work. It's wildly underappreciated. But it works.

I've gained immense advantages in business from obtaining a graduate degree in spirituality and serving as a chaplain. I recommend getting good at contemplation. Everyone's looking for a better bottom line, more productivity, better efficiency, and ways to find and retain talent. The tricky part is that when problems show up, many executives are quick to find and implement solutions to relieve the pain. They don't stop to breathe and contemplate. When I work with companies, I'm there to show them that their real challenges, and their solutions, are likely on the inside.

People who have spent years meditating can tell you that there is beauty, wisdom, and strength in slowness. As it turns out, turning inward may also be key to solving some of the most pressing issues that face your business. Slow down and give your challenges the reflection they need. A simple pause can save you a relationship, deal, key employee, or strategic mistake. Our success is determined more by how we handle the difficult not how fast we move. Proper pausing leads to prosperity.

GREG'S THOUGHT LEADER LESSONS

Daily Habits

My rituals include:

Meditation. I begin every morning early with meditation. It helps me stay focused and calm even when things get difficult. I started with 15 minutes and now I am consistent with 45 minutes every morning.

My tribe. I seek trusted, respected, and beloved supporters who keep me on track. They are asked not to collude but to challenge any foolish thinking. You just need one to three people in this critical role: your first call group. I also maintain a broader, candid, creative, and action-oriented community that listens, appreciates what works, and prioritizes serving over taking. They foster an atmosphere of engagement, meaning, and achievement. Both of these circles have been indispensable to my journey!

Journaling. Keeping a productivity journal where I map out my intent for each day and my schedule helps me get clear and stay focused. Since I have implemented this practice, I have seen huge improvements in my mindset and what I can get done. It allows me to set and accomplish realistic tasks every day.

Reframe. When a difficult situation arises, or a troubling emotion shows up, I ask these questions: *What story am I telling myself? Who would I be in this moment without that story? What's a better true story? When have I experienced this or something similar in the past? What can I do more of, better, or differently this time? What do I want? What will move me toward what I desire?* Pausing to observe and ask resourceful questions is a super skill.

Q&A WITH GREG

What are some favorite places you've traveled to?

I spent a semester studying overseas in London. I worked for three years in Singapore with the Police Force. I traveled across the world, working on five continents, for multiple global enterprises. That said, my favorite place in the world is Taize, France. It's a village and global community dedicated to bringing reconciliation to all corners of the globe. It's a well for the soul.

What books do you often recommend?

The Road Less Traveled, The Tao of Leadership, Transforming Problems into Happiness, The Alchemist, A Heart That Trusts

Contact Greg Zlevor about his books, coaching, leadership development programs, and speaking at gzlevor@westwoodintl.com, or look for Greg Zlevor on LinkedIn. To learn more about HopeMakers, go to www.hopemakerscollective.com.

 Learn more about Greg Zlevor, Westwood International, and HopeMakers.

LINDA GRIZELY

Thinking Bigger
Anything Is Possible

Linda Grizely is a financial planner, motivational speaker, and money mindset mentor who has emboldened hundreds of people through transformational journeys. She thrives on empowering and inspiring people and is known for her ability to connect, gracefully hold space for others, and foster an atmosphere where people feel seen and heard.

My Younger Self

When people ask me what I would tell my younger self, my answer is always, "Think bigger." I didn't know what I didn't know, and my world was very small. Now that I am older, wiser, and have more life experience, my world is bigger, yet it is still small. I continually strive to keep thinking bigger.

Growing up in a lower-middle-class household, we lived paycheck to paycheck. My parents never really talked about money, but I knew most of my friends did more and had more than I did.

As a teenager, I had no direction and was an underachiever. I'm smart, but I did as little in school as possible. When I was 16, I became pregnant, so I dropped out to have my daughter. It was an easy decision for me and a good one for many reasons. The first is that I became an overachiever. I had a purpose now.

I was blessed to have an opportunity to go to community college through a local grant for single moms. While I was a single mom and working, I completed a two-year degree. When I applied to graduate, they informed me that I couldn't receive the degree because I didn't have my GED! I rushed to take the GED exam, and afterward, I got a letter that said I scored so high that I was up for an award! If I'd known there was an award, I would have studied! I received my associate's degree, had a successful first career, and got married before eventually taking a break to be a stay-at-home mom.

A Pivotal Moment

After 23 years of marriage, I got divorced. At the time, I owned a business that I had built from scratch. It was like a baby to me, but it was a new business, and it wasn't turning enough profit, so I had to sell it. Fortunately, I was lucky enough to land what I thought would be my dream job.

I loved the job itself, but soon, I was driving to work with a pit in my stomach every day. The culture was toxic and a bully was working against me, dividing the community. I also wasn't making enough money to survive. I was looking for another job under the radar, but I couldn't get through. All the jobs seemed to require a bachelor's degree. The more I searched, the more dead ends I came to. I realized I needed to do something drastic.

I never thought going to a four-year college was an option for me, but at this critical point in my life, I took a leap of faith. I got a home equity loan, cashed in a small retirement fund, quit my job, and enrolled in college. As a financial planner, I don't recommend doing that, but I wasn't a financial planner then!

Major Growth

In that first semester, I took 11 classes at four different schools. I was on a mission to graduate by the end of the year. I earned my bachelor's degree—a dual major—on schedule, when I was 49.

I set out to find my next career. I was getting interviews and making great connections. I went through multiple months-long interviews, and I always seemed to come out as the second choice or to get an offer lower than I was willing to accept. It was frustrating!

During that process, I was stacking my resume through education. A friend offered me a chance to attend a mastermind on one of John Maxwell's leadership books that completely opened my eyes. I experienced a major mindset shift and realized that I needed to do a lot more introspection. I was already on an external growth journey, and now I was kick-starting my internal growth journey and thinking bigger.

Books were my mentors. I started with John Maxwell's books, which were amazing. I also loved *The 7 Habits of Highly Effective People* by Stephen R. Covey, *Think and Grow Rich* by Napoleon Hill, and *The Tipping Point* by Malcolm Gladwell.

I realized that even an overachiever can only achieve to the level of their mindset. I kept asking myself, *How do I think bigger?*

I had been looking for a job at a nonprofit because I really wanted to help people. I figured in that space I would have the biggest impact. I enrolled in the Chartered Advisor in Philanthropy program through the American College of Financial Services. It taught legacy planning and charitable giving strategies, which served nonprofit fund development professionals, financial advisors, and tax planners.

When I put that pending credential on my LinkedIn, financial services recruiters started contacting me. After a few conversations, I realized this path made a lot of sense for me. I could help people through financial planning.

Key Mindset Shifts

Back when I started my bachelor's degree journey, a local financial services team reached out to me about a job doing marketing for them. They knew me and recognized my capabilities, but I declined so I could focus on school.

A year and a half later, when I decided to go into financial planning, we worked out an agreement where I would do marketing for them and become a financial advisor at the same time.

I earned my master's degree in financial services at age 52.

It was only a few years before I knew it was time to think bigger again. A well-known, large brokerage firm was opening a branch near me. I reached out on LinkedIn to the person who would be managing the branch and set up a one-on-one networking meeting. Ultimately, I landed a job and started making more money than I ever thought I would.

During that time, I was helping my elderly parents a lot. My mom was having medical issues that caused her to be in and out of the hospital for a few months. My dad, who had already suffered a brain injury, started to develop dementia and needed someone present to be an advocate for him. My husband was taking them to appointments while I was at work. My husband's wonderful, but he's not my parents' daughter, and he doesn't have the legal power to make decisions. I needed to be there. I was making fantastic money, but I was not serving my family.

So again, I took a leap of faith, left that role, and embarked on a new journey. This time, I set out to build a life where my devotion to family, friends, career, and clients could harmoniously coexist. I embraced the power to shape my future.

In that period, a tremendous amount of internal growth was happening. I was working incredibly hard and thinking very big. Even though I wasn't looking, it wasn't long before bigger, better, opportunities started to come my way.

Financial Planning, Speaking, and Money Mindset Mentoring

In my financial planning career, my commitment is to engage in a collaborative process with integrity and prioritize my clients' well-being. I provide guidance and education driven by a dedication to offering the high-quality service I would expect as a client myself.

Being a motivational speaker is all about empowering and inspiring others to reach their full potential. Sharing messages of resilience, personal growth, and tenacity brings me a deep sense of fulfillment.

As a money mindset mentor, I host an online course where I empower people to transform their mindsets about money. It's about helping them to recognize and clear internal obstacles to success. Through introspection and self-realization, I unwittingly shifted my money mindset. This program is for people who want to change theirs in a guided, deliberate, structured way.

Lessons

Being a teenage mother was a challenge. Getting divorced after half a lifetime was difficult. Quitting my job and going to college was a risky move. Leaving the most lucrative job I'd ever had was a bold move. However, each time I made big decisions, they allowed me to expand, think bigger, and make progress.

I didn't let limiting beliefs of being too young or too old get in my way.

Many things I have done, I once thought I would never be able to do. I seized the moment, created opportunities, and facilitated change.

There are no failures, only stepping stones. You can take a downturn, dwell on it, and let it bring you down, or you can learn from it and move forward with intention.

Strategic pivoting, being willing to modify your course, and staying open-minded and flexible can help you weather the storms and emerge stronger on the other side.

The story is never over. Bigger thinking is still happening, and greater growth is ahead!

LINDA'S THOUGHT LEADER LESSONS

Giving

My father taught me the joy of giving. When I was about 12 years old, I spent my Friday nights at the roller rink. My mom had bought me a cheap pair of skates that were two sizes too big. I set out to earn money so that I could buy some new skates. I did all kinds of jobs around the house and, eventually, I earned enough. I couldn't wait to show off my new skates.

When Friday came, a friend of mine came over so my dad could drive us to the rink. My friend didn't have skates of her own, so I let her use my old pair. They fit her better, and I told her she could keep them.

On Saturday, to my bewilderment, my dad told me he was going to buy my friend a pair of roller skates. I told him I had given her my old ones, but he insisted that she have a new pair like mine. I was confused and a little upset. After all, I had just worked so hard to earn the money to buy mine, and he was just going to give her some.

One simple question opened my eyes to a whole different view of life. My dad asked me: "Do you think that she has a way to earn the money to buy her own skates?"

My answer was, "No." At that moment, I understood the joy of giving to others.

Resilience

Even if you've got a great life, you are going to have ups and downs. You must decide what to do with these challenges. Do you run from them, ignore them, blame them on external circumstances, or think of them as obstacles you can't overcome? Or do you acknowledge them, approach them positively, and take them head-on?

Resilience is about finding ways to internally boost your spirit and improve your life. It's taking ownership of the problem and focusing on things you can control.

Personal Development

I believe in ongoing introspection as the foundation of personal development. It is important to define your purpose and values. When you feel a sense of unrest in a situation, chances are you need to assess how that situation is related to your purpose and whether it aligns with your values. If you haven't defined these, you may not be able to determine what has you feeling stuck or unhappy.

Q&A WITH LINDA

What is your favorite song?

Triumph's "Magic Power." It encompasses all that music is and does for the soul.

Where did you grow up?

Colorado, on the front range of the Rocky Mountains. My favorite memories include amazing sunsets, walking in fields, wading in creeks, and mountain adventures.

What is something most people don't know about you?

I once owned a pole fitness studio. It was the most amazing experience seeing the transformation of women and the confidence and self-love they gained. Many people think of pole fitness as objectifying women, but it is the opposite. It gives them their power back. It was the most rewarding thing I've done. My students still talk about how much it changed their lives!

How do you define success?

To me, success isn't just an achievement; it's a feeling. It's when you feel a resonance, deep within your core, that you've arrived.

Linda Grizely has spent a lifetime thinking bigger, overcoming challenges, and empowering others. If you aspire to get clarity on your finances, would like Linda to speak at your event, or are ready to embark on your own money mindset transformational journey visit LindaGriz.com/connect and take the first step towards thinking differently, unlocking your true potential, and achieving greater success.

 Follow Linda on LinkedIn

KUNAL DEWAN

Building Dreams
A Tale of Immigration, Education, and Entrepreneurial Resilience

Kunal Dewan is a real estate investor and entrepreneur in Southern California. Originally from India, he completed a master's degree in structural engineering in the US then grew a tax franchise firm while working full-time. His goal today is to help other investors gain the freedom of time, which he enjoys spending with his wife and two children.

From Dreams to Steel Skies

I was born in the heart of India with dreams that stretched across oceans. Armed with unwavering determination, I embarked on a quest for knowledge, seeking post-graduate opportunities in the land of possibilities—the United States. Scholarships were my lifeline; without them, my dreams would remain grounded. I meticulously researched universities, applied to seven programs, and held my breath.

Two acceptances arrived—one with a golden ticket: a full scholarship. With $400 from my father, I boarded a plane, leaving behind generations of soil-tethered roots. The unfamiliarity of a foreign land greeted me, but my heart brimmed with ambition. Structural and civil engineering became my canvas, and I painted my master's degree in five intense quarters. Alongside, I juggled internships, building both savings and bridges.

Post-graduation, I crisscrossed the East Coast on a Greyhound bus, tasting accomplishment. Then, reality nudged me—I needed employment to stay. So, I donned my best attire, marched into engineering offices, and introduced myself boldly. "I am looking for an engineering position at your firm," I declared, handing out resumes. The dot-com crash lingered, but my audacity bore fruit—I secured three jobs.

Then, a call from a friend beckoned me to California. I repeated my audacious approach, applying to five places. Two job offers materialized—one promising visa sponsorship. I crashed on a friend's couch near the University of Southern California (USC), my dreams now anchored in the City of Angels. For seven years, I sculpted skylines, my immigrant spirit soaring alongside the structures I helped create. One project that still brings me a lot of joy—the pavilion at The Natural History Museum of Los Angeles.

My journey—from a cramped plane seat to the pinnacle of engineering—defines the audacity of dreams. I am the embodiment of resilience, a testament to the magic that happens when passion meets opportunity.

Bridge to Entrepreneurship

My work was good, and I was fortunate, but contentment eluded me. Perhaps it was the ambition. A restless fire burned within, urging me toward something different, something other than "average." That inner flame ignited my entrepreneurial journey.

Being in the construction industry, I knew the real estate market was down. Fear surrounded buying a house or investing in real estate between 2008 and 2010. However, somehow we knew internally that: "This is the time."

My wife and I took a leap and invested everything in our first real estate property in Ventura County, California. We lived in a small apartment in Pasadena, but Ventura County was where we could afford.

Our bank account was empty, but our aggressive mindset kept us going. We worked tirelessly to make it work.

In 2012, I decided to diversify. I started a tax business while still working full-time. The plan was to earn extra income and invest in more real estate. The first year in business was a success.

Then came the second year. I expanded to a second tax office, thinking I had it all figured out. But reality hit hard. Running a business with 10 people was different from running a team of two. Financially, it was my toughest year.

To succeed, I had to go all in. I left my W-2 job after obtaining my green card. It was a tough decision, but necessary. I needed time to learn, consult experts, and build myself before I could build the business.

The key lesson? Leadership. I shifted from working in the business to working on it. Over the next three years, we grew from one office to five, with 42 employees.

The Mindset of a Parent

In 2016, after eight years of marriage, and nine years of togetherness, my wife and I finally grew our family with our first child. That changed the game. The way you think as an entrepreneur without kids is totally different from the way you see things when you're an entrepreneur and a parent. Your risk profile changes. I believe that new way of thinking is for the better.

That was the first year I went all remote. I wanted to spend all my time with my wife, who started working from home too, and our baby. It was a life choice, and by making that choice, I learned an amazing business lesson. Without my hands-on, daily involvement, my tax business accelerated on a J-curve in 2017!

Yes, I was the roadblock! When I got out of my people's way, they flourished. The business went from 12 people to 32 people to 42 people. They built the team by themselves. I only brought in the first five people. That was a huge awakening—a lesson in leadership.

Growing My Circle of Influence

After the first few years of building my businesses, I have been fortunate. When the business went on autopilot because it was able to fly itself, my real estate started growing as well.

Over time, my neighbors, coworkers, and family became interested in what we were doing. They trusted us and wanted us to invest their money like we had been doing for ourselves. That's when I decided to start a syndication business.

Soon, I was looking into how I could grow and invite more people outside my circle of influence. For the longest time, I was not comfortable talking about myself. I felt like I couldn't tell people that when I came to this country I picked up the mattress next to a trashcan to sleep on during my first three months. I was very embarrassed to even talk about it. I was embarrassed that 21 years ago I had accepted invitations into people's homes and allowed them to feed me. God bless their hearts! How could I talk about that? But before I built a business, that was my reality.

But, as I talked to people about real estate syndication, they asked me, "Who are you? What have you done?" So, slowly, I started opening up myself, and my story resonated with people. In turn, they opened up to me and told me their story. That's how I grew my circle of trust.

Goals for Growth

There's a power to financial independence, especially if you have family and young kids.

Ambition is the relentless pursuit of excellence. Courage is the fuel that propels dreams into reality. Visualization is the art of creating mental images of your desired outcomes. When you vividly imagine achieving your goals, your brain begins to pave the way.

It is in the intersection of visualization, courage, and ambition where lies the path to greatness. The path to financial freedom.

I want to help, guide, and share my lessons of financial freedom with others.

KUNAL'S THOUGHT LEADER LESSONS

Embracing Fear: How You Feel About Money Matters

Imagine a person haunted by fear—fear of money, fear of taking action, fear of losing what they have. The weight of ambition presses upon them, urging them to do something meaningful in life, yet fear holds them back.

This fear, I've discovered, never truly dissipates. Even today, as a business owner, I grapple with the uncertainty of each year. Accepting this fear was the toughest part of my journey.

My story began with a meager paycheck after graduation—$4.80 an hour. In 2004, minimum wage was $6.50. I worked tirelessly—an engineering internship from 6:00 a.m. to 4:00 p.m. at $10 an hour, followed by another job from 4:00 p.m. to midnight at $4.80. Survival was my sole goal.

A decade later, our real estate and tax businesses flourished, yet the fear persisted. Oddly, it had little to do with my bank balance. It was a mental construct—an illusion that "enough" remained elusive.

My upbringing shaped my relationship with money. As an Indian, frugality was ingrained. We saved diligently, living below our means. But how we feel about money influences our actions. Some find satisfaction in spending, while others harbor guilt.

The "not enough" mindset propels growth, but at what cost? Missing family moments? Sacrificing time with loved ones? Not for me anymore. A decade ago, perhaps, but not today.

For those from humble beginnings, money is either seen as evil or perpetually insufficient. My fear stems from the dread of returning to a harsh life if everything disappears. I crave security—a comfortable bed, privacy—yet I seek it not through reckless spending, but by wise investments.

Fear persists, but it needn't paralyze us. Our mindset shapes our reality. Embrace the fear, acknowledge it, and channel it into purposeful action. After all, security lies not in hoarding, but in wisely navigating life's uncertainties.

Investing and Financial Independence

One of the easiest ways to make an emotionally-regulated investment is to have a long time horizon. And one of the safest ways to sustain a long time horizon is to have a portfolio that yields cash flow.

Researchers concluded that a human's emotions and their capability to make a rational decision are deeply intertwined. In other words, a person cannot make a logical decision without emotions. Emotion and reason are so interwoven that one cannot behave normally if one aspect is missing.

How do you make your investment decisions? Be aware that every investment decision you have ever made, and every investment decision you will ever make, is deeply governed by your emotional state and emotional intelligence during that stage of your life.

The secret is not to lose the emotion but to rather regulate it.

The Power of Compounding

It is unfortunate that the human mind cannot intuitively visualize the power of compounding. For example, we can easily calculate $5 + 5 + 5 + 5 + 5 + 5 + 5 + 5$ is 40. But when asked $5 \times 5 \times 5 \times 5 \times 5 \times 5 \times 5 \times 5$, it is not easy to visualize. The answer is 390,625. A human mind cannot even fathom that number.

Warren Buffet is a great example of this. He is not the best investor of all time. Buffet has been successfully creating returns at an annualized rate of about 22%. On the other hand, a gentleman named Jim Simmons has been compounding at an annualized rate of 66%. Jim is truly one of the best investors in the world, yet Jim is not one of the wealthiest people in the world. As a matter of fact, Jim has about one-third of Buffett's wealth. This is because Jim did not find his investment stride until he was in his mid-40s. On the other hand, Buffett has been investing since he was 10 years old. That is the power of compounding.

People who understand the power of compounding in their relationships, careers, skills, business, and investments, are the people who live a very prosperous life.

A happy marriage of 10 years does not hold 10 times the love it did when the couple got married, but rather numerous investments of commitment, humor, sacrifice, forgiveness, persistence, and patience.

A successful career is the result of time invested and compounded over decades.

A successful investment of 1% growth every day leads to an annualized growth of 3,800%.

Grow slow. Grow consistently.

Multifamily real estate is boring but predictable. Start investing in multifamily real estate now and let it compound.

Q&A WITH KUNAL

How do you recharge?

I love stories. I enjoy watching movies and listening to books.

What are a few of your favorite quotes?

1. "Consistency enlarges ability." – James Clear
2. "I trained for four years to run nine seconds." – Usain Bolt
3. "When you focus on problems, you'll have more problems. When you focus on possibilities, you'll have more opportunities." – Zig Ziglar

Who are your mentors and greatest influences?

Darren Hardy (*The Compound Effect*) – This book changed my life because it helped me to "start" what I wanted to do.

Napoleon Hill (*Think and Grow Rich*) – This book shattered my limiting beliefs and ignited my ambition.

What is some of the best advice you've received?

Think long-term.

What do you consider your superpower?

My ability to talk to strangers.

What do you make sure you always do?

Check up on my parents every day and find alone time with my spouse and kids.

What philanthropic causes do you support?

I run a non-profit that provides financial education and other basic needs to families. I also support a spiritual non-profit in India that focuses on providing free education, healthcare, and other basic needs to families.

What are some favorite places you've traveled to?

Botswana, Kauai, and some super-remote villages in India with no power or running water.

What hobbies do you enjoy?

Reading. Actually, listening to audiobooks. Also, I greatly enjoy working on my business.

What books do you often recommend?

The Psychology of Money by Morgan Housel
The Almanack of Naval Ravikant: A Guide to Wealth and Happiness by Eric Jorgenson
Start with Why by Simon Sinek
How Will You Measure Your Life? by Clayton Christensen

What would you tell your 18-year-old self?

Take risks.
It is okay to fail.
Every rejection gets you closer to your goal.

How do you define success?

Let me first define what is not success:

- If you have a lot of money but not great relationships with family and friends, you are not successful.
- If you have great relationships but not sufficient time to nurture those relationships, you are not successful.
- If you have plenty of time but not good health to enjoy your time, you are not successful.
- If you have great health but not enough financial resources to leave a legacy for the people whom you love or for the causes you believe in, you are not successful.

Success means prosperity in every aspect of life, not just one.

Kunal Dewan is the founder of Liberty Capitus and an experienced commercial real estate investor helping busy professionals spend more time with family and leave their legacy with hands-off real estate investing. To take action on your financial goals—Reach out to Kunal at KUNAL@LibertyCRE.com or on LinkedIn at /kunaldewan.

 Virtual Coffee with Kunal

TC CUMMINGS

Mind of a Navy SEAL

TC Cummings, US Navy SEAL, has passionately translated soft skills used by SEALs since the 1990s to business executives, individual performers, and corporate teams. TC founded Noble Warrior Training to simplify leadership, communications, accountability, and more.

Childhood and Early Emancipation

I was born in the Midwest, but my father's job with Eastman Kodak moved us to Rochester, New York. Known for its high concentration of PhDs, it was a white-collar city. Along with the philharmonic and the best hospitals, there was a strong emphasis on education.

I had a challenging childhood. After a long, drawn-out divorce, Mom moved us to Buffalo, New York, during the collapse of Bethlehem Steel. This blue-collar city was under a great deal of pressure, and survival was a daily struggle. As a laborer, I was taught work ethic from the traditional plaster-of-Paris workmen and escaped in other moments by reading novels. Mom was doing all she could just to take care of herself, so I did my best to care for my kid brother.

Success leaves clues. At the age of 12, I had written in my personal journal, "On the opposite side of adversity is benefit. Like any mathematical equation, the greater the adversity, the greater the benefit."

When I was 14, Dad invited me to come live with him and his new wife. Remarkably, I said yes on the condition that he send me to the toughest school! The all-male, Jesuit Catholic college prep school that kids were dragged into kicking and screaming.

I still remember Dad shaking his head in disbelief. But you and I know "on the opposite side of adversity is benefit."

Two years later, my stepmother and I reached an impasse, and my home became an unsafe place from which I was legally emancipated. I chose to continue going to school and worked to pay for food, heat, rent, and all. Coming home from work six or seven nights a week between 1:00 a.m. and 3:00 a.m. with Homeroom at 7:40 a.m. allowed about four hours of sleep each night. Summer breaks were harder as I took on three jobs a day to make ends meet. I had the stress of moving 12 times in 22 months—including one month I spent homeless living in my tiny, rust bucket of a car (a gift from my dad). I would sneak into school before anybody showed up so I could use the showers, then sneak out of the locker room before anybody saw me. I like to think the faculty knew but just turned a caring blind eye.

This grind was exhausting and lonely. There were moments when despair nearly consumed me. One Saturday afternoon between work shifts, I determined I would swim out into Lake Ontario with the intent of disappearing. I just felt so tired. A phone call from my best friend, Probir, turned me back from the door. With understanding reverence, he simply said, "Hey, TC. We haven't heard from you in a long time. I just wanted to see how you are doing."

When I got off the phone, I fell to the floor and bawled my eyes out. It was love. Somebody expressed love to me at the right moment.

Navy SEAL Training

"On the opposite side of adversity is benefit." In 1986, I sought the greatest adversity I could find: the previously secret US Navy SEAL Teams.

Getting into the "basic" training (known as BUD/S – Basic Underwater Demolition / SEAL) is not easy. First, you have to commit to service in the US Navy, then you must meet stringent physical, psychological, and intellectual qualifications and secure orders to BUD/S, knowing that there is an 85% chance you will fail and be employed somewhere else in the fleet. To fill his quota, my recruiter tried to push me into the nuclear program because my ASVAB (Armed Services Vocational Aptitude Battery) test score was in the 99th percentile. As demanding as that branch of the Navy is, I remained resolute to my purpose and eventually received my orders.

About a third of the people who try out for BUD/S qualify. Maybe only half actually get and accept orders. It is a serious commitment.

Day in and day out, BUD/S is a grind: six-and-a-half months of the world's toughest training where every day is harder than the last will chisel every aspect of your being. Each day began well before dawn on the beach or on the grinder. Half-way through a 90-minute calisthenic workout, we heard, "Feet off the deck until… the sun comes up." This easily meant 45 minutes of abdominal exercises. When (not if) you fell out, you earned extra attention, which may look like an instructor with a water hose on your face.

BUD/S was unrelenting, but I learned to push beyond exhaustion. If (*when*) you fell behind during the six-mile beach runs, instructors circled back, giving you a chance to catch up (requiring you to dig deeper and pay the price). Leadership lesson for life: always give people a path back into honor.

Then, we'd jog one mile to the chow hall for breakfast. We'd have eight miles under our belts by 8:00 a.m. At about 8:15 a.m., in the warm classroom, the temptation to drift off is strong. Somebody would fall asleep, and immediately, an instructor would help you learn not to let yourself fall asleep. Incentives were provided like the inflatable boat full of ice water outside of the classroom for you and a swim buddy, who didn't do anything, to immerse yourselves in, fully dressed, and return to class.

This is all to prepare for worst-case scenarios. Even with as much as we train, real life is going to be different. After that, we'd run another two miles for lunch.

In just this half-day of the 27-week BUD/S, we see opportunities to quit. The truth is, BUD/S instructors are SEAL Operators often working this job spend more time with their families. At the end of three years, they return to a SEAL Team where they will deploy. The last thing they want is somebody unqualified on their team. SEALs embrace the axiom that *the team is only as strong as its weakest link*. There is always going to be a "weakest link." The question: Is that link strong enough to achieve the mission and get everyone home?

My BUD/S class started with 153 men; only 18 of us became SEALs. This meant completing another six to nine-month Advanced Tactics Training in which candidates demonstrate proficiency in working together as a team—both safely and effectively. Not every stud is capable of being a teammate. If an individual will quit during the stress of combat, it is preferred that they quit during basic training, not when lives are on the line.

This is when the operator receives their Special Warfare insignia badge—the Trident, marking them a SEAL. And since *the only easy day was yesterday….*

Authenticity and Ownership

We had a situation where my platoon had suboptimal leadership. We did the best we could with what we had, but we didn't have a say in anything.

Once the Persian Gulf War was concluded, we were tasked to stand by in the area. After about a week and a half of boredom, our senior leadership canceled morning musters. It was sort of like a perpetual snow day! Initially, it felt wonderful, but intellectually, I knew that *the devil finds work for idle hands*.

Not being in charge, I made an announcement: "Tomorrow morning before breakfast, I'm going to lead a workout on the deck of the ship at 0600 hours, if anybody wants to join me." Eighty percent of my platoon came to sweat, and they all thanked me. It was camaraderie and working together, and they unanimously agreed to meet daily.

I announced a late morning offering of advanced first aid training. The same 80%, including my future leaders, showed up. Being a certified armorer with the Department of Justice, I alternated daily morning classes of medical or weapons care. Afternoons, we did weight training and began a book club.

This inspired others. One of my greatest personal joys was when Kyle, a teammate, asked if he could lead the workouts. That's the dream! Someone else to carry the torch while you then focus on building the next thing. Another guy came and offered to do a class on dive calculations. Another on radio communications.

Stepping up when it mattered, taking initiative, and contributing authentically—this act silently opened the door for others to do the same! Months later, when I first walked back into the command, I was congratulated for saving the morale of the platoon. It's nice to be recognized—and I was just being myself.

Where morale had been sinking quickly, I, a mid-level leader, demonstrated ownership of my team by contributing my authentic self, with no attachment, to be of service. That inspired the other mid-level leaders to also contribute. When there's ownership, when somebody is sick, someone else with ownership is going to jump in and take over. It was an unbelievable compliment from my peers.

Noble Warrior Training

I approach all people as **multidimensional, holistic, and dynamic beings often embroiled in messy relationships (sometimes with ourselves)**. I developed the two-part coaching paradigm of Noble Warrior Training a decade after separating from the Navy. Based upon my own life experiences and standing on the shoulders of giants who came before me, I looked back to discern what we were doing right in the SEAL teams, why it can be so elusive, and how to use leverage for greater autonomy!

Why would you ever allow your life experiences to be determined by someone else? Your Worst Enemy tantalizes and seduces you with the rush of energy. Even the vigilant are vulnerable because this enemy never sleeps, knows you better than you know yourself and most often fools you into believing you are in control.

Claiming the command of yourself is an active engagement, requiring effort. Making this effort, you contribute your special, different, uniqueness to all your relationships. You gain access to the exponential power of synergy while simultaneously reducing the detrimental stress from your life. SEALs thrive on synergy! *"The difficult done immediately, the impossible done by appointment only."*

My purpose is to participate in leading a shift in mindset from *effect* to cause, leading to "outrageous authenticity." Synergy in all relationships provides exponential fruit while reducing negative stress. I accomplish this by increasing awareness and providing "the right tool for the job" for your noble battles.

TC'S THOUGHT LEADER LESSONS

Communication Is Your Responsibility

Navy SEALs are a brotherhood with tremendous love for one another. A pro tip: we don't always like each other! Being liked is not a prerequisite. Trust is paramount on a team.

To engender trust, you have to be an effective communicator. Part of my Noble Warrior approach, which leads to Outrageous Authenticity, includes taking one hundred percent ownership of your communications. I believe if I say something to somebody I want them to hear, and they only understand a portion, then I have failed.

We have various battle-tested tools at our disposal—such as *Confirm and Verify* to ensure effective communications. If I instruct Joey, "Three packages are to be picked up from the helicopter pad at 2100 tonight and transported to the submarine with urgency," and Joey responds, "Got it," do I truly know what Joey heard? Is it responsible of me to entrust this operation and my career to someone who gave me a head nod? Using the *Confirm and Verify* tool, I ask Joey, "How well am I communicating: what did you hear from me?"

People are lazy or distracted. Effort is required to go through this process. It is so much easier to spout off words and walk away, thinking you did the job. Only after you've developed trust in communications can you simply head nod back and forth. When you achieve this level, you become more efficient—less time and effort, allowing you both to focus on additional things. Synergy.

Ego in Relationships

Accountability and coaching require humility. The student needs to be ready. Both the coach and student take 100% ownership of the process and outcome.

Love is a superpower. Love doesn't have to be the gushy, romance stuff that we read about or see in stories. In India, there are 81 different words for distinct types of love. Tough love is hard on the person delivering it more so than on the person receiving it. Otherwise, it's egotistical. That's why they call it tough love. Love yourself and the relationship enough to say "no" where boundaries need to be set.

In healthy relationships the power of the whole is greater than the sum of the parts. I believe there are two sides of ego: a constructive and a destructive side. One side contributes while the other separates. Ultimately, we are facing the same enemy.

Using rough numbers, there were never more than 80 SEALs in Vietnam during the war, yet they accomplished the most successful number of operations of any unit. Synergy allows you to "do epic shit" with little resources. "The difficult done immediately, the impossible done by appointment only!"

Accountability and humility set you up to harness your ego and gain power. *Carpe diem*!

Q&A WITH TC

Who is your favorite sports team?

I love my New York Rangers. The greatest sport, ice hockey, combines individual talent with the dynamics of a team. I can think of no position more demanding or less appreciated in global athletics than the goalie!

How do you recharge?

I enjoy my travel, yoga, exercise, mediation, breathwork, gardening (and composting), books, shows, introspection and quality time with family and friends.

What are a few of your favorite quotes?

"I'm not telling you it's going to be easy. I'm telling you it's going to be worth it!" – Art Williams
"Your greater potential is a threat to your current comfort." – TC Cummings

What is something most people don't know about you?

I'm a big fan of the definition of courage: feeling fear and doing it anyway. I've had a lot of fears in my life, and I've demonstrated courage time and time again. Many people have this illusion that Navy SEALs are emotionless. It's more accurate to say we compartmentalize very well and are willing to go through the pain. I've really developed the habit of opening the kimono and developing lasting relationships instead of hiding (all) my fears.

To learn more from TC Cummings, to ask any questions about the mindset of Navy SEALs, Noble Warrior Training, or to inquire about engagements that might be a good fit for your group, contact him via email info@TCCummings.com. Follow TC on LinkedIn and visit TCCummings.com.

 TC Cummings: Leadership and Teamwork soft skills translated from US Navy SEAL Teams

DR. LEE NEWTON

A Road Less Traveled
My Connection Between Health Care and Real Estate Development

Dr. Lee Newton is an optometrist, saxophonist, and real estate developer. His experiences have taught him how to build, develop, and invest profitably in real estate. He loves to help others solve their real estate challenges.

A Road Less Traveled

I have always loved to learn because a product of learning is growth.

An insatiable desire for acquiring and applying new information and skills has prevented me from accepting that we were meant to do one and only one thing in life. I have intentionally ignored the tired mantra "go to school, get an education, get a job, make a comfortable living, save money, retire, and live frugally." I never thought that advice applied to me.

Though I enjoyed playing the saxophone, I chose eye care as a profession due to my interest in science and healthcare and because most career opportunities for saxophonists involved teaching—and I only wanted to perform. Some of my fondest memories include meeting Grammy award-winning musicians Bruce Hornsby and Branford Marsalis and performing at the Hard Rock Cafe in Las Vegas and Times Square.

A few years into my career, I became interested in real estate. This was a logical consequence of owning my office building, my home, and other commercial and investment real estate. By owning real estate, I developed a working knowledge of construction and building science—the physiology of how buildings work.

Building science was fitting given my background. I remember the event that stimulated my interest: after having a new roof installed, I noticed an intermittent drip of water. Not wanting to draw inaccurate conclusions (the roofer was well-respected in the community and a friend), I asked him to help me determine the source of the drip. "Do you see that metal flashing up above?" he asked as we looked above the ceiling. "The warm, moist air from the office is condensing on it and dripping." Building science told us that an imperfect air barrier was the culprit, not an imperfect roof.

Sometimes, people seem confused when they learn that my hobbies aren't typical for someone in my profession. Once, a friend said: "Your Facebook profile shows optometry at the bottom of your list.... Those who don't know you well will think you are unfocused on your real profession."

I couldn't help but think: *My patients generally aren't Facebook friends with me and I don't believe I have any choice in determining the order of attributes on Facebook. Finally, who is to say that I can't do more than one thing well?*

"Jack of all trades, master of none" refers to a person superficially competent in many areas rather than proficient in one. Many grew up in an era where learning, polishing, and practicing one skill was the norm. But times are changing.

Les Brown stated, "You have to develop at least three core competencies." In other words, we don't have complete control over our segment of the economy. Some industries evolve and others fade away. Having multiple skills and abilities allows one to pivot when necessary.

When I moved my eye care practice into a new facility and later expanded that facility to accommodate new tenants, I was the project's general contractor. Later, as general contractor, I put up an 8,600-square-foot office building with two other investors. These experiences taught me powerful lessons in value engineering, which I define as refining the scope of the project to save costs without compromising intended functionality.

Experience Leads to a New Opportunity

I was asked to help the owners of a therapy practice who were looking to expand and construct their own facility. It was an exciting time for them as they envisioned their hard work and practice growth leading to a brand new facility of their own design.

At this time, I was chairman of our local DDA (Downtown Development Authority, a quasi-governmental entity that uses tax revenue to entice economic development). Our DDA stimulated economic growth by purchasing vacant commercial land and then giving it away in exchange for developing it. In that scenario, everyone won: the building owner received the land for free, and the local municipalities saw their property tax revenue increase forever. It was a beautiful mechanism for progress and development in the community. As chairman, I had a fiduciary responsibility to act in the DDA's best interest, which was to stimulate interest in developing the DDA's only remaining vacant lot.

So, I introduced the therapy practice owners looking to build to the DDA's vacant lot, and their exciting new construction was planned. When the design-build firm failed to meet their budgetary needs (the two parties were over one million dollars apart), they asked me to step in and construct their facility for them, knowing that my recent experience would help them save money.

The savings were immediate. Instead of starting over with construction drawings, my engineer was able to modify the structural prints of my previous build to suit their needs for the new construction. This was value engineering at work!

I have found that almost every area of the construction process can be value engineered: the layout of the build on the property, the footprint of the building, the foundation, the framing, the superstructure, the rooflines, windows, doors, the wall and roof assemblies, the interior layout, all the mechanicals (plumbing, electrical, heating/cooling) as well as where they are placed, the modularity of interior wall construction, the ceiling height and layout, and the finishes.

The initial construction documents proposed a building design with a footprint shaped like a cross, with eight outside corners and four inside corners. By changing the design to a rectangle and altering the rooflines to add visual interest, we experienced savings in materials and labor during every step of the construction process. As an added bonus, the final design had a much smaller heating and cooling load, meaning lower utility bills for the life of the structure. The practice owners were pleased, having accomplished what they originally set out to do and spending one million dollars less than the other bid.

Reputation Leads to Another Opportunity

An optometrist colleague of mine knew I had been successful in helping others with their facilities, and he requested assistance with his practice relocation. He had rented for his entire career and desired a newer, larger facility as well as ownership of the real estate.

We initially looked at new construction; I had recently done a land assembly and had access to a great build site. However, cost analysis revealed that new commercial construction wasn't favorable to his budget.

There was a tired, old, but well-positioned civic facility across the street for sale. It was a perfect location for his practice but would need a lot of work. Taking a leap of faith, he purchased the building and asked for my help with the renovations.

With rehabilitation, there are no "potential" unforeseen circumstances. Unforeseen circumstances are an absolute guarantee.

This job involved having to deal with surprises including:
- Demolition to an extent that exceeded anyone's estimate;
- Structural problems due to poor water management;
- Other structural problems due to previous poor workmanship;

- Mold due to poor air management and faulty cooler construction;
- Cutting up a 1,800-square-foot dance floor with a chainsaw;
- Removing more than 50,000 pounds of concrete for the underground services;
- A municipality that seemed to thrive on making the entire process more difficult than it should have been.

On the way to the finish line, after numerous delays, the bank told us that we were reaching the very end of the construction loan term and that they could not extend the timeline any longer. Fortunately, we were already wrapping up.

In the end, I was proud to report that we had acquired and remodeled an 8,300-square-foot facility, transforming it from a kitchen/dining hall/dance floor/bar into two medical suites for less than $120 per square foot all-in, which is unheard of in today's inflationary environment. Further, we were $20,000 under budget. Finally, my friend acquired a solid commercial tenant, another healthcare firm, to subsidize his costs of financing and operating.

Reflections

Why are societal expectations considered "norms?" Why isn't it considered normal to follow where our passions lead? Why do we place limits on ourselves? Should I worry about what others think if they know that their eye doctor put up that new office building?

I have learned not to dwell on the cognitive dissonance of this type of thinking. I still enjoy optometry after more than 23 years of practice growth. But dollars are only marks on the scorecard of one's passion, drive, and skill; they shouldn't be a source of motivation. If I were not successful in my primary occupation, I would not have developed the connections that provided these opportunities.

By leveraging lessons from building science, value engineering, and many real estate development projects, I am able to help other healthcare providers save money on designing and building their new facilities. I am often sought to consult on construction and development challenges. And I relentlessly pursue the concept of affordable workforce housing—this will happen in my lifetime.

Never underestimate your ability to redefine the limits of your comfort zone and accomplish something remarkable. By looking for opportunities to help others, you can solve problems, experience incredible personal growth, and change lives.

LEE'S THOUGHT LEADER LESSONS

Vision

I cut my teeth investing in real estate with used single-family homes vis-à-vis the "tenants and toilets" method. That quickly got old because it is difficult to attract the best tenants to an older, less efficient structure.

I cut my teeth developing real estate with commercial builds and remodels. While on one hand it could never really get old because I love it, realistically, there is a limit, and that is defined as the prevailing demand for commercial space. This may go up and it may go down.

The product of all my education and experience thus far is my passion for affordable housing design, and I apply the lessons I've learned in the building science and value engineering realms toward this goal. My vision is to redefine affordable housing means, techniques, and costs in my lifetime.

Investing

We are taught that we should invest to amass wealth in the form of a nest egg and capital appreciation. However, our bills arrive with monthly regularity, and a mountain of cash either stagnates, grows, or is decimated when it is liquidated to pay one's recurring expenses of living. If one invests to produce passive income, one can pay recurring bills with the cash flow produced by the investment.

Business and Entrepreneurship

I observe so many who operate their careers as if they are on some sort of countdown to the day they can retire, and it makes me think that they must hate their jobs. Given that a career may consume 20, 30, or more years of a life, it is a shame if one does not actually love what one does for a living. There are so many opportunities available—I feel sad if someone does not absolutely love what they do.

Business Philosophy

Recognizing that complacency is always our enemy, I try to constantly remember to ask myself: *What can go wrong and how can I mitigate that? What did go wrong and what caused it to go wrong? How can we do better?*

The Environment & Sustainability

We only have one Earth, and our activities on Earth—particularly construction—make a big difference in the longevity of the planet and the prevailing environmental conditions. There really is no green building—every construction project leaves the environment a little less green than it was before ground was broken, so how we treat our built environment with respect to carbon footprint and energy consumption really matters now and in the future.

Q&A WITH LEE

What is your favorite song or who is your favorite musical artist?

I love music and have so many favorite songs. My favorite artist is Bruce Hornsby for many reasons, not the least of which is that I have had the opportunity to meet and hang out with him. He initially called me when he read a paper I wrote about his music when I was in college.

One of my favorite songs is "Tropical Cashmere Sweater" by Bruce Hornsby and the late Grateful Dead lyricist Robert Hunter. In particular, the lyric "The door to forever is open wide…when you dare to step outside," has huge meaning for me in my life and I think about it every day. To me it means that one may never experience all that life has to offer until one has the courage to pursue a new opportunity or challenge.

How do you recharge?

My day job requires me to be at my best with respect to my state of mind and appearance. I usually start my day early at the gym because if I don't work out early, I won't find the time later. What a great start to the day, mentally, and physically!

I also love to have an occasional "mental health day," which I define as a day that I don't have to "look good, smell good, smile, and be nice to people" and during which I can work on some of my own projects, get my hands dirty, or simply take a break from the realities and challenges of life and work; and use my mind in other, less stressful, more relaxing ways. This may involve physical labor, researching a better way to solve a real estate or construction challenge, or performing due diligence on a property I intend to purchase.

What are a few of your favorite quotes?

"Keep your heart on fire and your mind on ice." It is expected that you will be passionate about what you are doing. However, don't be so passionate that you lose focus on the logistics and the intricacies of your performance—at work, in music and the performing arts, etc.

"Good judgment comes from experience. Experience comes from bad judgment." Learn from your mistakes.

"If you are not practicing, your opponent is. And when you play them, they will win." This originally came from a college athletic coach. I cannot remember whom. It was paraphrased by Bruce Hornsby years ago in an interview about really learning your craft, trade, or perhaps instrument, in his case.

What is some of the best advice you've received?

Don't waste time and energy worrying about things beyond your control.

Don't sign up for more than you can handle. If you have to think about it, you're probably over-committed.

What hobbies do you enjoy?

Being outdoors, riding my bike, working with my hands, finding a better/more cost-effective way to build something, improving my home and office, listening to music, and playing music.

What would you tell your 18-year-old self?

Keep an open mind and experience a lot of things in life. Don't get too set in your ways; your brain isn't fully developed yet.

What is your image of an ideal world?

Inflation has ravaged our economy and the ability of many working-class people to afford a comfortable home. My past experiences and education have allowed me the opportunity to redefine affordability as the term pertains to single-family residential housing, and I am beginning to apply the lessons I've learned with respect to building science and value engineering toward promoting and constructing efficient and cost-effective home designs for both the for-profit and the not-for-profit sectors.

How do you define success?

To me, the attainment of success is realized by helping others succeed and achieve their goals.

Dr. Lee Newton maintains a successful optometry practice while building, developing, and syndicating real estate. He is the author of *A New Housing Paradigm*. Dr. Lee is an expert in building science, value engineering, indoor air quality, and affordable, energy-efficient construction. Learn about opportunities for connecting and consulting by emailing Lee@DrLeeNewton.com.

COURTNEY MOELLER

The Power of Mindset

Courtney Moeller is a US Navy veteran, a speaker, an entrepreneur, an oil and gas expert, and the CEO of ATS Assets, an investment platform revolutionizing the way people invest. Crafted by investors for investors, everything needed to confidently turbocharge wealth creation, from specialized tax assistance to powerful calculators, is on ATS Assets.

From the Depths of Loss

Mindset is more than just a state of mind; it's the heartbeat of our aspirations and the breath of our achievements.

My journey to understanding this began amidst a storm of challenges that threatened to, and nearly did, upend everything I had worked for. During this difficult time, the action of positive thought and a steadfast belief in possibility became my guiding light.

About a year ago, I was involved in a deal with people I loved and trusted. It was an opportunity I was excited about investing in and raising money for because it was moving the needle financially for so many!

Unfortunately, I ended up losing a significant amount of money in this deal, in the seven-figure range. This put me in the two-comma club in a way I never wanted or expected.

Losing your own money is horrible, but there are no words to describe being responsible for losing someone else's. I can't even begin to portray the level of pain and betrayal I felt because of what happened with that deal.

These were very dark times for me. I gained weight, I couldn't sleep. There was a week I didn't get out of bed. I almost quit doing what I love so much—helping others build a legacy for their families. I was humiliated and embarrassed and felt like a massive failure.

Failing Forward

People often talk about how successful they are and how great things are, but I rarely hear successful entrepreneurs talk about the challenges they face: how they're navigating and overcoming trials, difficulties, and failures. Really, nobody wants to talk to other successful people about losing millions of dollars, including myself.

Every day, I dwelled on what had happened. I replayed everything in my head over and over again. And I stayed in this state of anger, frustration, and hopelessness.

But the problem with focusing on the loss and the negativity is that doing that *keeps* you in a state of frustration and resentment. You CANNOT go on to do great things and be successful and fruitful when you are stuck in that state.

This realization didn't happen overnight. It took time to truly understand and implement. But once I did, it was powerful, and I want to help as many others as possible do the same.

I'm going to share my biggest takeaways and what I learned, because no matter how great or how bad the experience is, there is always the potential for powerful lessons and positive outcomes. We learn great strategies from mentors and read books with great advice, but it is in the face of hardship that we learn the true value of the information. And, most of the time, it is easier said than done!

Your network matters. I mean, it REALLY matters. Jim Rohn said, "You are the average of the five people you spend the most time with," and this is pure gold. I have spent the last several years being very intentional about who I spend my time with. I want to be surrounded by people who are more successful than I am—people with an abundance mindset who want to see others achieve. I find great value in people who are willing to brainstorm ideas, share processes that work for them, and discuss strategies.

Fortunately, I had surrounded myself with incredible people who played a key role in me getting through this time. They built me up and refused to let me quit. They boosted my confidence when it was all but gone. They showed me why my actions mattered. They truly gave me a hand out of a deep, dark hole that I had put myself in, and I will be forever grateful to my circle.

During this period, I spent a lot of time working to build up others who had gone through the same ordeal. I was sending uplifting quotes and urging them to see beyond the circumstances to realize what great people they were. It tore me up to see bad actors taking out great people.

But as I was trying to lift others up, I was falling deeper and deeper into my own abyss. Eventually, thanks to my circle, I had an epiphany and realized that I needed to apply the advice I was giving to others to myself.

The more I opened up to the people I trusted, the less alone I felt. Knowing that other people, including people who I looked up to, were going through the same thing didn't change my feelings about them or my respect for them. I didn't see them as failures—I really appreciated how they were navigating the events. This caused me to take a step back and focus on *the solution* instead of *the problem*.

This is a big deal! Once I switched from focusing on what went wrong, got rid of my victim mentality, and started honing in on how I was going to move forward, I was invigorated with new life and motivation. I found purpose and drive. I was on a mission, and I was excited to get going. I have gone on to build relationships and start things that never would have come about had the "unfortunate event" not occurred.

These trials and failures don't define who we are. They don't determine our futures. They present opportunities to learn, grow, and be better all around.

I never thought I would be thankful for this event that crippled me, but I have grown so much because of it, making me a better entrepreneur, mother, wife, and friend. And for that, I am truly grateful.

Sharing: A Catalyst for Change

Sharing my story has been powerful, and I have recently started sharing it with larger groups. I am truly humbled and honored to have people come up to me and tell me that they are going through a similar situation and that they appreciate me sharing my story because now they don't feel alone.

I have always wanted to come up with my own version of the word "failure," as it has such a negative connotation. I haven't come up with the perfect new meaning yet, but I saw someone post a picture breaking down the meaning by letter, and I felt it was very fitting. **FAILURE** – **F**eedback **A**nd **I**nvaluable **L**essons **U**ncovered by **R**eal **E**xperience. Wow! Failures are the lessons we need to propel us forward and make us better. The only way you can actually be a failure is if you quit.

The Sky's the Limit

A year ago, I was devastated and humiliated and felt like a massive failure. Today, as I continue to focus on the future and being solution-oriented, I am thrilled to share that I have so many wonderful things happening in my life. Because of this experience, I am a better syndicator, partner, and investor. I demand honesty, integrity, and transparency in my partnerships. They are non-negotiable.

Today, I am proud to share that I have partnered with an amazing oil and gas company to bring unique, excellent opportunities in the oil and gas space that are making a massive difference in people's lives. And, if that weren't exciting enough, we are building an incredible investment platform that will allow investors access to CPAs, background checks, and financial calculators. It truly will change the way people invest, and I can't wait to unveil it!

Sometimes it is so hard to find the good in certain experiences. Sometimes it just takes time. You aren't failing unless you give up, so I urge you to keep going! Find your tribe, and remember, the only thing holding you back is YOU!

COURTNEY'S THOUGHT LEADER LESSONS

From Failure to Feedback

I love and highly recommend the book *The Gap and the Gain* by Dan Sullivan and I have gathered many great lessons from it. We either focus on the gap, where we think we are falling short and failing, or we focus on the gain, the positive things that come from any circumstance. Where we focus affects our mindset, which affects our physiology. There are some great examples of this in *The Gap and the Gain*. It is so easy to focus on the negative things that are happening and what we feel like we aren't accomplishing instead of our accomplishments.

So, how do we fix this?

1. Read books like *The Gap and the Gain* which will help you shift your mindset and see the good in every situation.
2. Be solution-oriented. When you focus on the problem, it keeps you there. To move forward, you have to focus on the solution.
3. Get rid of the self-limiting beliefs you have put on yourself. One of my favorite activities is listening to paraliminals which help us change our mindset and break through limiting beliefs.
4. Stop comparing yourself to others. Sit down and determine what your internal markers for success and happiness are. Stop taking into consideration what the world thinks and set your own standards.
5. Set goals! I set goals for my professional life, my personal life, and my family, and then I put them on a vision board. Every night before I go to sleep, I visualize what it will look and feel like when these goals are accomplished.
6. At the end of the year, write down all of your accomplishments, no matter how small or insignificant you think they are, and reflect on them. You will be blown away by all you have gotten done. And remember to celebrate your wins! As successful entrepreneurs, we are our own worst critics and have a difficult time realizing and celebrating our success, but it is necessary.
7. Approach everything from a state of gratitude. I refuse to let a circumstance or another person dictate my happiness or derail me from my goals. I control these things within myself. When things got ugly, I made a decision within myself to not stay there. I knew negative thoughts weren't serving me, so I let them go. I am here to tell you that you can accomplish as much or as little as you think you can. The only limitation you have in this world is your mind.

Q&A WITH COURTNEY

What do you make sure you always do?

The first thing I do when I wake up in the morning is thank God for giving me another day. Several years ago, I had somebody ask me, "If all you had right now is what you thanked God for this morning, what would you have?" And wow, that hit me like a ton of bricks! I am grateful for everything. I think it's very easy to get complacent and forget how fortunate we are for small things that have such a big impact on our lives, so I make sure to be grateful every day.

Before I go to bed, I think of three events from the day that I'm thankful for. Sometimes it's as simple as the opportunity to pick my kids up from school because one day they're going to be grown and gone and I'm going to wish I had more time. Then, I think about the three things I need to accomplish the next day. That sets my intentions for the next morning and I am much more productive.

Who is your favorite musical artist?

George Strait is timeless. I grew up in West Texas wearing jeans, boots, and a cowboy hat, and his music represents home. When my dad came home on a Friday night, we would play George Strait and two-step together in the living room. My dad was 10 feet tall with his big old black cowboy hat, and I can still hear his voice and see his excitement when certain songs would come on. It's a wonderful memory. My dad was one of my best friends, and I thought he was the smartest man on Earth. I have a ton of admiration for him and wish he were here to talk oil and gas with me today. I know he's proud of what I'm doing!

Contact Courtney Moeller to get information on her investment opportunities and projects at www.CourtneyMoeller.com. Get early access to her new investment platform at ATSassets.com. Download her oil and gas report at oilandgasreport.net. Connect with Courtney on LinkedIn (Courtney Moeller).

 Scan to connect with Courtney and get access to tax-incentivized investments.

AARON CHAPMAN

Riding Through the Storm
From Broke to Broker, Defying Expectations and Embracing Identity

Aaron Chapman is a highly productive real estate investment financier, author, real estate investor, and contrarian. He lives with his wife of 28 years and children in Arizona.

The 2008 Crashes

I opened my eyes. Blinking in an effort to focus in the bright, fluorescent light, I could make out someone sitting in a chair next to me. A hoarse, labored "Where am I?" escaped my lips.

"The hospital. You've been in an accident," came the voice of my wife Rizzo.

"What day is it?" I asked.

"August 8, 2008," she said. She explained that both my legs were shattered. I had road rash, burns, broken ribs, and a shattered clavicle, and I would need to get right with being in a wheelchair for a while.

She'd been through this explanation with me a few times, but this time it began to stick.

That morning, I left my home as an athletic person with a net worth on paper of over three million dollars. I was taking three days to get my head clear on a Harley. At 12:24 p.m., an inattentive driver at over 80 miles an hour sent me skidding on a sunbaked Arizona freeway.

Now, I laid in a hospital bed, drugged up, with external fixators to position the bone fragments. I was facing multiple surgeries and extensive rehab, while the global market was teetering on a precipice.

Free Diapers and Loose Change

I come from an extremely blue-collar background. My dad worked in all types of different things, mainly the mines and some cattle ranching in the '90s. After high school, I worked in the oil fields of Wyoming then in heavy equipment operation, as a semi-truck driver in Arizona, and in the mines in northern New Mexico with my dad. Underground, hard rock mining was something I wanted to do since I was a kid. I loved the job.

I got laid off when I was 23 years old. I hunted for a new job but was not finding one. I heard of an opening as a $10-an-hour truck driver hauling landscape rock in Phoenix, Arizona. I didn't want it, but I needed something. My wife and I were penniless, and we'd just had our first kid. But, they told me I was overqualified.

I remember walking out of that office to my truck wiping tears from my eyes. I had to go get diapers. I had a coupon to get them free from a grocery store.

As I drove, my gas light came on. I pulled up to the pump on the corner by the store and ran my debit card. It was declined. I was overdrawn.

I started looking through my truck for change. I found a few coins and then spent the next two hours wandering the parking lot to find more.

Eventually, I found enough to buy two gallons of gas. Then, I went into the store, found the diapers, and redeemed my coupon.

As I walked out, I ran face-to-face into a guy I used to work with, Keith. He ran the office, and I was one of the heavy equipment operators in charge of an excavation crew. He asked me how things were, and I explained my situation.

Keith suggested we go to dinner. I told him I couldn't afford dinner out, but he had a gift certificate to Red Lobster from a client.

When he took my wife and me out the following night, he explained the mortgage industry and slid me the card of a mortgage broker branch manager.

In an effort to look professional when meeting this potential employer, I cut off a foot of my hair, shaved my beard, and dressed in new clothes purchased by my mother. They started me as a telemarketer that December.

It was absolutely miserable going from working in the mines to telemarketing, but within 10 days, I was able to create some good leads. Then, I convinced them to allow me to work as a trainee loan originator.

Rebuilding and Making Changes

Everybody took a beating in the 2008 crash. There were plenty of people who lost businesses or their houses. Some had losses so extensive they took their own lives.

I left the hospital a skeleton of my former self. The market shift and my crippled business pushed my net worth from three million dollars in the black to one and a half million in the red. Then the medical bills started to come. The first week alone was invoiced at almost two million dollars.

Because of the circumstances, I could negotiate with my creditors. I was blessed to be able to negotiate and settle all of my debt from my wheelchair. In my opinion, I got out of it cleaner than most people who were in similar circumstances but without a story of physical devastation to illicit compassion.

For a second time, I was penniless. In this case, less than penniless. I had an extreme negative net worth. I couldn't stand on my own financially or physically. But that accident provided me with the divine gift of an accelerated education.

With some highly concentrated effort, we worked our way out from under that debt. With more focused effort, I learned how to walk, and I started building myself up. By carrying a notepad to write down conversations, phone calls, and tasks to complete, I tediously re-trained my short-term memory.

I've learned an abundance of lessons, financially, physically, and mentally. Now, I say that getting the hell kicked out of me by the pavement at 80 miles an hour was one of the greatest things that's ever happened in my life.

Defining Moments of Clarity

That nasty accident forced me to re-evaluate my direction in life. When you've got the noise of the world turned down and you're left to your own thoughts, you have the opportunity to decide if you like the person you are and the direction you're going in.

Coming back to the lending industry, I narrowed who I sought out as clients. I was done putting on the show that most in my industry did—trying to dress, act, and speak in the way they believed the world expected them to. My clients would get the real, raw me. If they didn't like that, okay. Being myself allowed me to sort through masses quickly to those I could develop a relationship with.

I found I was now well aligned with investors coming into Arizona and buying property at the bottom of the market because of the crash. It wasn't long before those investors migrated from Arizona to Indiana, Texas, Tennessee, Missouri, and many other states. My business started spreading across the country. Now, having done hundreds of millions in closed transactions across 30 states and, in an industry of over 300,000 licensed individuals, I am ranked in the top ½ percent of people for number of transactions closed.

AARON'S THOUGHT LEADER LESSONS

Daily Ritual and Habits

This is your bedrock of success. If you can first build the habits and character traits you need to be successful, your efforts compound and everything becomes easier.

"Time management" is just another way to say manage yourself, your mind, and your focus.

We are extremely creative beings. A lot of people discount themselves and what powerful creators they are. We can decide what we want, write that down, and create it. Just keep trudging towards it, and you will eventually get there.

Business Philosophy

In 2014, I was in line at Chipotle. When you ordered, five people would construct your burrito. I thought that was very interesting. It took 11 people total to complete your transaction at a fast casual restaurant, yet there were only two people, me and my processor, working on intricate financial instruments like real estate investment loans.

Creating a system that was unheard of, I re-engineered the loan construction process on one assembly line, and it changed everything for the better. The industry had been doing the same thing forever: separate departments, separate systems—nobody interacted.

Still, I had to prove the value of my idea. In 2015, I read *The Goal* by Eliyahu M. Goldratt. It's about the theory of constraints. Like a flowing creek, your business will only flow to the level of its tightest bottleneck. My goal became getting everybody to understand that and get behind it. It took years. Eventually, in 2016, the new way started to take off.

To do that, you have to believe in yourself and be able to show that you can control yourself when things don't go your way. When you stay at it, slowly, one at a time, people start to respect that and get behind you.

Relationships

There's an authenticity that comes when you decide who you are, what you're about, and what you're willing to do every day. And you earn respect when you maintain that. The guy who is a certain person at work, another after work, and another at church is hiding. Now, if you can walk into a bar and run into the person you were at church with yesterday and introduce him to the guy you hang out with on the weekends and have a nice time, you probably have a pretty consistent idea of who you are. You will still evolve. We're not going to always be the same person we were in our 20s, but figuring out who that person is and then being that person allows you the ultimate relationship with yourself.

The world is a very treacherous place with a narrow pathway to walk. We wander off of it all the time, but as long as we keep sight of the path and return to it, I think we're going to be okay. You're a human being. You'll do something stupid on occasion, and you have to be okay with saying you were wrong and not feel less of yourself. We're all just figuring it out. Some of the most successful people in the world have just figured it out faster by being wrong more. Make moves and make mistakes.

Q&A WITH AARON

What is something most people don't know about you?

I was an extremely shy child, definitely one to sink into the background. I used to stutter heavily, and I cheated my ass off to get out of high school.

What are a few of your favorite quotes?

My absolute favorite quote is, "Good judgment comes from experience and experience comes from bad judgment."

I love to use that to explain to people that in life, you're going to take a beating in some form or another, and that's the way you're going to get educated. We learn from the beatings we take.

In the movie *Rounders*, one of the characters shares another of my favorite quotes, said by the poker player Jack King: "Few players recall big pots they have won, strange as it seems, but every player can remember with remarkable accuracy the outstanding tough beats of his career." Wisdom is garnered by getting your ass kicked. We'll retain those scars forever.

What is some of the best advice you've received?

At a time when I was looking at all these different opportunities to make money, I had a mentor who said, "Stick with what got you here." He was saying that there would be many opportunities and many shiny objects, but that I shouldn't throw away what gave me the wherewithal to have those greater opportunities or shiny objects.

That's what I've done. I've stuck with what got me started in 1997. I've compounded from being an average guy in my industry to being ranked number seven in the United States when over 1.1 million people do this job. That's because I've stayed very, very focused.

Who is your favorite musical artist?

Tool. I'm amazed by everything they do with instruments. It's very unique individually, but it blends with everybody else. They're the only band I've seen live that duplicates precisely what's on the album.

Who are your mentors or greatest influences?

Abraham Lincoln is a great influence because he took a beating all through his career and still became successful at an older age. He was extremely persistent and became president of the United States after a lot of tries. He was also a storyteller. That's what I do. When my client asks me a question, I'll tell them stories about what other clients have done and the outcomes so they're more informed in their decisions.

Darren Hardy is another mentor. I've been listening to Darren for years and getting a lot of great data from him which I share with others daily.

What hobbies do you enjoy?

I've been hunting around the world. In the middle of Alaska with no cell phone coverage, you have to be present. Every sense has to be on high alert because your life could be snuffed out in a second. We are an apex predator, but we're also prey. I love the danger.

What would you tell your 18-year-old self?

It's all possible.

I was cattle ranching starting at 14 or 15 years old, and I questioned what I was capable of. I was always crushing myself, worrying how I was going to make things happen.

You'll know how to do it when it's done because there's no formula. You just have to start. As you start, you'll adapt. You're going to fail and you're going to make mistakes, and then you're going to find out that's not a failure or a mistake, that's just what not to do. If it takes you 20, 30, 40 years, who cares? It does not matter because you're gaining experience. Gain the experience, retain the experience, and share it with everybody you possibly can.

How do you define success?

It's being able to wake up every single day knowing that I can go about making that day what I want it to be. When I have a bunch of calls lined up or my calendar is booked solid, it's because I choose to have a booked solid calendar. If I choose to take time away from that calendar, I will take time away. I don't, because I drive myself crazy if I'm not not doing something, but it's my choice. When I go to the grave, I'm coming in hot.

To contact Aaron Chapman, visit https://www.aaronbchapman.com/. Check out his YouTube series https://www.youtube.com/QuitJerkinOff and QJO Initiative Book Series with all booksellers.

KENT RODAHAVER

Humans Over Houses
A Real Estate Broker's Route to Success

Kent Rodahaver is a nationally recognized real estate professional, entrepreneur, and endurance sports enthusiast. As the founder of a thriving real estate brokerage with multiple offices across the state, he is known for his relationship building, customer-centric approach, and exceptional service. He lives in Florida with his lovely wife, Laura.

The Way I Started

I grew up in rural southwestern Pennsylvania. It was not unusual to see an Amish horse and carriage on our common roadways. We never locked our car doors or our houses. Church pews were full, our elders were respected, work ethic was instilled from an incredibly early age, stores were closed on Sundays, and family reunions consisted of hundreds of aunts, uncles, cousins, grandparents, and great-grandparents and lasted an entire weekend! The nearby town of Addison had a population of 270 people. I had 45 in my graduating class. We were a blue-collar family; my stepfather was a truck driver, and my mother stayed at home. Our family did the best with what we had. As a middle child, I wore many hand-me-downs, which never included the latest fashion trends. I was frequently teased about my outfits. You can imagine how motivated that made me.

At a young age, I became quite competitive and would frequently immerse myself in music and my curiosity to learn. In elementary school, I learned that I could solve problems and that I could sell. I used to take old bicycles, disassemble, customize, repair, and paint them, then sell them for a nice profit. I also had a neighbor who would bring me broken yard sale finds with the confidence that I would be able to fix them. I embraced the challenge and loved the confidence that she had in me even more.

I attended college in Florida. While in school, I took a part-time job at UPS loading trucks every morning at 4:00 a.m. There was a time when I had three jobs and was taking classes in the evenings. When you are 18, it is okay to function on a few hours of sleep a night. I actually did that for several years.

Then came the opportunity to go full-time as a delivery driver at UPS. The salary and the benefits made it an exceptional job, so I took it.

At 21, I was the youngest driver in our building, and I was earning well above the median income. Before I was 30 years old, I built a new house. I had nice cars and flashy things and did everything we do in society to impress.

The Magic of Real Estate

I got married, had two children, and eventually, unfortunately, found myself in a long and contentious divorce. I needed to make other living arrangements. I left a beautiful, custom home with a three-car garage and swimming pool to rent a rundown studio apartment. I soon realized I could not even afford that. I ended up sleeping on my friend's couch for nearly a year.

Working at UPS, I saved some money and bought a small bungalow that needed work so my friend could have his couch back. Unwittingly, I purchased in what was about to become one of the most popular up-and-coming neighborhoods in St. Petersburg. I did some renovations while living there, sold, and nearly quadrupled my investment.

I met my beautiful wife, Laura, during that time. She was managing a paper store, and I brought her daily deliveries on my UPS route. I still vividly recall the little bell that rang when I entered her store's front door. Today, we have been married for 22 years.

We sold the small bungalow and found a house in a prestigious neighborhood. It was in rough shape, but we knew we could create something amazing there. While we were working on it, a writer for *The St. Petersburg Times*, one of the largest newspapers in the nation, did a story about real estate investing. My wife and I were on the front page of the Sunday edition and inside, they had a full-page picture of us working. I was about 14 years into my career at UPS, real estate was making us exceptional returns, and we figured if the newspaper was doing a story on us, they must see something special in us. We embraced this whole real estate investment idea and invested in several other properties.

Can I Retire?

As I was approaching 20 years with UPS, I started thinking about retiring. I just had to wait until the time was right.

In 2005, my financial advisor and business coach said to me, "The market is great. You have saved up adequate money. Jump!"

I remember the day I announced my retirement as the scariest but happiest of my life. I can remember clearly how my pulse was thudding. My entire adult career, I had someone provide the opportunity for me. I punched the time clock, did the work, and in return, they gave me a paycheck, 401K, health insurance, and paid vacation. In an instant, my income and success were up to me.

I immediately got my general contractor's license and started a commercial and residential development firm. Over the years, we completed several profitable projects, so we had the experience to make this successful, and the investment returns were exceptional.

Hard Lessons

2008 hit us like a sucker punch. Two of the properties we owned were condominiums leveraged with adjustable-rate mortgages, which we thought were awesome—until they adjusted up. The mortgage payments went up, the condo fees went up, and our tenants were not paying rent, so we were losing money every month. We did not walk away or short sell, but we did have to sell them at a loss. That is when I realized I hated being a slave to a lender and that I despised debt. Over the next few years, we worked very hard to become debt-free.

Soon thereafter, I acquired my real estate license. This would save $20,000 or $30,000 on each of our company and personal investments—an average of 6%. By leveraging my contractor's license, I was saving an additional 20%. A combined benefit of 26% before doing any actual work was a huge win!

As a Realtor, I enjoyed the marketing aspect of buying and selling. Soon, people sought me out to list and sell their properties, and I found myself gravitating more toward sales and less toward investing. With the real estate investment returns in decline, transitioning into the real estate sales associate role felt like a natural step.

The more I focused on real estate sales, the more people gravitated toward me. In my first year, I did seven times more volume than the average Realtor in our market.

A Customer-Centric Brokerage

Once I received my sales associate license, I crafted a plan to open my own brokerage.

Opportunity presented itself in 2019. I acquired my broker's license but was not sure when it would be time to venture out on my own. Then, an agent I met in a broker class months earlier called me. I will remember this phone call for the rest of my life.

She said, "I am not sure why I am calling you. I just feel like you are a person I need to talk to." She was exceptionally talented, previously nominated as Realtor of the Year by her local board, and a wonderful person, but that day she was down in the dumps. She said "I had a horrible year last year. I am thinking about taking a job that is not even real estate related."

We talked for an hour and a half, and I felt God put us together to have that conversation at that moment.

A month later, she called me again and asked if I was still planning on opening a brokerage because she would love to come work with me. That was what I needed. She, myself, and one other agent started my first real estate brokerage in 2019.

We expanded from there. I opened another office, added agents, and then another office. Today, I have four offices across Florida and about 60 agents. For the past four years, we have been voted the best real estate company in the Tampa Bay area.

The culture within our team makes our company special. There are large national brokerages that brag about being "agent-centric." I pride myself in running a company that I consider "customer-centric." We focus on our customers and relationships. My organization uses a hashtag that we created several years ago: #humansoverhouses. We live by that mindset.

Relationships are critical. I do not want to have a 400-agent brokerage. I want to always be available and accessible. The more I pour into my people, the more they reciprocate and the more fulfilled and successful we all become.

KENT'S THOUGHT LEADER LESSONS

Investing for Financial Independence

I have realized financial independence through investing—mostly in real property, investment homes, and commercial buildings, but also in businesses. I have built and sold start-ups, and my wife and I own and operate several companies—all generating profit and 100% debt-free.

None of this would be possible without educated, intentional action. We invest in what we know and do not subscribe to "get-rich-quick" schemes or the countless "pie-in-the-sky" investment offerings. I have taken my share of risks. I have lost on an investment or two. I am ever-evolving, always learning, and have an instinctive nature I lean on to find and recognize new opportunities.

Fitness, Health, and Wellness

I am an endurance sports fanatic. Not only am I a huge advocate of an active lifestyle, but I am also a multi-Ironman finisher and have completed several ultra-marathons. With over 400 sanctioned races under my belt, I have never competed in an event I did not finish.

I feel an individual cannot be at their mental best if they are not intentionally focused on being at their physical best. Sometimes work or family responsibilities do not allow for suitable exercise or nutrition. We have all felt sluggishness or misalignment. Sometimes we need to reset. Simple focus on good nutrition, healthy physical activity, and a night of sound sleep is all it takes to get back on track.

Relationships

Real personal relationships and authentic business relationships are imperative. One of the larger businesses I own is my real estate company. In our profession, I often see real estate agents relying on expensive online leads to supply their customer base. My philosophy is to have a network of people with whom I have an actual relationship, for instance, past customers and fellow real estate professionals in a different market. I do business with experts in complementing fields, such as attorneys, title agents, mortgage lenders, contractors, home inspectors, etc. Solid referrals result in reciprocation. If you give and refer freely, others will gladly return the favor.

Once you get the opportunity to provide exceptional service to this new customer, and you impress upon them your unparalleled work ethic, character, and amazing results, they also become a human relationship, a raving fan, and the newest member of your personal marketing agency.

Mentorship

At a real estate conference, I presented a keynote on the importance of mentorship, coaching, and having an accountability partner. Even as a professional coach, I seek the direction of a professional coach. I have had a business coach for the past 10 years. No matter how much we know, no matter how much coaching we receive, we will never be perfect, nor will we ever be 100% proficient. I also have several accountability partners I meet with on a regular basis. We make each other better.

Q&A WITH KENT

How do you recharge?

Physical activity: Swimming, cycling, or running. My mind instantly shifts from work stress to an endorphin-filled, detached paradise.

Who are your mentors and greatest influences?

The greatest influence on my life has been my junior high wrestling coach, Coach Barton. There has been no one on Earth who has challenged me to the extent he did. He always encouraged me to push harder when it hurt, be patient with the process, show up and work my tail off every single day, pay extremely close attention to what others are doing (both successes and failures), and allow myself to be coached. We were consistently among the absolute best in the state every year. To this day, I channel many of those philosophies in my personal and professional life.

What is some of the best advice you have received?

My mentor and dear friend Jim Fischetti advises that "work works." Simple, profound, and accurate, yet still not easy for many to incorporate into their daily lives.

What is something most people do not know about you?

I used to be a professional musician. Even though I play multiple instruments and sing, the majority of my musical career was spent as a percussionist. I have played with several well-known bands, did a large amount of studio work, performed live on the radio, studied under some of the largest names in the industry, and recorded a full-length album.

What philanthropic causes do you support?

Canine Companions, Friends of Boyd Hill, NextHome Disaster Relief Foundation, and Preserve the Burg. I am also in the preliminary stages of creating my own foundation that will provide scholarships to those who wish to pursue a career in the construction trade. We have a serious shortage of qualified tradesmen/tradeswomen, and a large majority of these career opportunities can be very lucrative.

Several of my mentors frequently state, "To whom much is given, much is expected." I am a true believer that the more you give and the more you pay it forward, the more you will be blessed and rewarded, both personally and in business. I love to give of my time, talent, and treasure!

What are three books you often recommend?

The Greatest Salesman in the World by Og Mandino
The Go-Giver by Bob Burg and John David Mann
Rhinoceros Success by Scott Alexander

What do you consider your greatest achievements to date?

Enjoying a happy and healthy marriage with my very best friend in the entire world. I have been married to my wife, Laura, since 2002. Much of the success of our marriage is due to the qualities that Coach Barton instilled in me: You get out what you put in. You must work extremely hard in the present for the celebrations and successes in the future. Things are not always easy. Acknowledge and lean into the strengths of your teammate. Celebrate both large milestones as well as small accomplishments.

Follow entrepreneur, speaker, coach, and business leader Kent Rodahaver on LinkedIn, Instagram, and Facebook. If you have any questions, need advice, or want to share your story, Kent would love to hear from you. Feel free to reach out via email at Kent@NHSouthPointe.com or visit his website at KentRodahaver.com. Be intentional, stay focused, and keep striving for success!

 Scan to connect with Kent.

BOB BURG

The Go-Giver Way of Business

Bob Burg is the author of numerous books on sales, referrals, and influence. His bestselling business parable, The Go-Giver, *coauthored with John David Mann, has sold well over a million copies and been translated into 30 languages. He speaks for companies internationally, including those in financial services, real estate, and direct sales.*

Finding a System

I began my working life as a sportscaster for my hometown radio station, eventually moving to the Midwest to work as a news reporter and then late-night news anchor for a very small ABC television affiliate.

Soon realizing that this was not going to be my life-long profession, I took a job in (or as I like to say, "graduated into") sales. Having no prior formal sales training and with none being provided by the company, I was really on my own. Indeed, I worked hard at it—knocked on a lot of doors, made a lot of calls, and told a lot of people about my products and services—and failed miserably. As Jim Rohn would have said, "I had the motivation, but not the information." Both are necessary.

After floundering for the first few months, one day while in a bookstore, I came across two books. One was by Zig Ziglar and the other by Tom Hopkins, two of the icons in the field of sales.

It was encouraging just seeing the titles. This was 40 years ago and I had no idea that sales teaching even existed. I got those books and devoured them. Every day after getting home from work, and well into the night, I'd read, study, highlight, take notes, practice, drill, and rehearse.

Within a few weeks, my sales improved dramatically. I now *had* the information. I had a methodology. I had a system.

I define a system as "the process of predictably achieving a goal based on a logical and specific set of 'how to' principles." The key is predictability. If it's been proven that by doing A you'll get the desired results of B, then you know all you need to do is A and continue to do A, and eventually, you'll get the desired results of B. That was truly inspiring to realize, and from there, sales became a fascination for me. I'd found my profession.

It also became obvious to me that a big part of sales involved personal development: building yourself on the inside so that success could manifest on the outside. This prompted me to read all the recommended classics like *How to Win Friends and Influence People*, *Think and Grow Rich*, *Psycho-Cybernetics*, *As a Man Thinketh*, *The Greatest Salesman in the World*, and so on. I loved it! Several years later, I became sales manager of another company and eventually began a speaking business with a focus on sales and business development.

Success in sales is about being focused on bringing immense value to others. We need to be inwardly motivated, but outwardly focused. It's about them, not us. As I suggest to my audiences, "Nobody's going to buy from you because *you* have a quota to meet. Or because you need the money. Or just because you're a nice person. No. They're going to buy from you because they believe that *they* will be better off by doing so than by not doing so." Those salespeople and entrepreneurs who understand this are positioned to succeed.

The Go-Giver

My first major book, *Endless Referrals*, was written for the salesperson or entrepreneur who knew they had a great product or service, one that brought fantastic value to others, but either they didn't feel comfortable and confident going out into their community and building relationships, or they simply didn't know how. *Endless Referrals* was the "system." Its premise was that "All things being equal, people will do business with, and refer business to, those people they know, like, and trust." The book was a step-by-step guide on how to build these relationships so that people wanted to do business with them directly and refer them to others.

My book, *The Go-Giver*, is a business parable. Stories have a way of connecting with the reader on a deep, heart-to-heart level, making it easier for people to receive and embrace the message. So it seemed like a good idea to take the basic premise of *Endless Referrals* and write a book in that format.

That's when I asked the amazing John David Mann, at that time known mainly within a specific niche (now co-author or ghostwriter of numerous bestselling books with many different co-authors) who is an absolutely brilliant writer and storyteller, to co-author *The Go-Giver* with me. We wrote the book in just a few months. One year and 24 rejections later, we came across our perfect publishing partner, Portfolio, a division of Penguin Random House.

Interestingly, the initial adopters of the book were the very people who didn't need it. These were people who had built immensely successful businesses and organizations long before the book was ever published. John and I would often receive emails saying, "This is exactly how I built my business," "This is how I built my fortune," and "This is how I built my company, but none of my people believe me." So they would then simply either recommend that their team members get the book (the power of "third-party credibility,") or they'd buy it for them. We had companies and leaders buying hundreds, sometimes even thousands, of copies. It's something we felt greatly honored by.

At heart, I believe *The Go-Giver* was a hit because it validated how people instinctively wanted to do business and receive abundance as a result. Most people truly want to bring value to the world. As human beings, we're built that way; we want to feel our lives have meaning and purpose. We want to know we have contributed and that we have made a difference. Salespeople and entrepreneurs tend to do that through their products and services.

The way you're going to earn a lot of money through your business is by first being genuinely focused on the *other* person and the immense value you're providing them. It comes down to understanding that "Money is an echo of value. It's the thunder to value's lightning." Thus, the money you receive is the natural result of the value you've given others.

Selling The Go-Giver Way

While *Endless Referrals* can put people in front of you, you've then got to be able to communicate the value of your product or service during your sales conversation in such a way that the other person understands and chooses to buy.

Selling is simply "Discovering what the other person needs, wants, or desires... and helping them to get it." The most important part of the process is the discovery, which involves asking questions and listening; deep listening past the surface, and continuing to ask the right questions to understand the issues at their core.

Then, before ever moving on to the part where you connect the benefits of your product or service to their end goals, you must be sure to confirm that what you heard and understood is exactly what they meant. Failure to do so will practically always come back to haunt you later, mainly in the form of "unnecessary objections."

Speaking of objections, it's so important to know that despite how often the following term is used, you cannot "*overcome* objections." Because to overcome is to *conquer*, and no prospect wants to be conquered. What you can do is work correctly within the stated objection to—in partnership with your prospect—understand their actual concern, the true root cause of their objection, and from there, effectively advance the sale forward.

The best thing about selling The Go-Giver Way is that when you get to the part where you ask for the sale, there is absolutely no pressure on either of you. You are simply asking them to take action on something they've already told you they want to do.

A Final Thought

I'd like to share something taught to me early in my sales career by a wise, elderly man I hardly knew. He said, "Burg, if you want to make a lot of money in sales, don't have making money as your target. Your target is serving others. When you hit the target, you'll get a reward. That reward will come in the form of money, and you can do with that money whatever you want. But never forget, the money is simply the reward for hitting the target. It's not the target itself. Your target is serving others."

What I realized was that great salesmanship is never about the salesperson. It's never *about* the product. It's *about* the other person and how their life becomes better just as a result of you being part of it.

I believe that when we approach sales from that perspective, we're nine steps ahead of the game… in a 10-step game.

BOB'S THOUGHT LEADER LESSONS

The Five Laws

There are five laws, or guiding principles, in *The Go-Giver*. They are the Laws of Value, Compensation, Influence, Authenticity, and Receptivity.

The Law of Value says, "Your true worth is determined by how much more you give in value than you take in payment." This is really the foundational principle. It sounds counterintuitive at first. "Give more in value than I take in payment? Isn't that a recipe for bankruptcy?" Here, it's important to understand the difference between price and value. Price is a dollar figure, a dollar amount. It's finite. Value, on the other hand, is the "relative worth or desirability of a thing to the beholder or end user." In other words, what is it about this product, service, concept, idea, etc., that brings so much worth, or value, to another human being that they will willingly exchange their money for this value, and be very glad they did, while you make a very healthy profit?

The Law of Compensation says, "Your income is determined by how many people you serve, and how well you serve them. So, while Law #1 is all about the exceptional value you provide, Law #2 is about *how many lives you impact* with that exceptional value. This is one major reason why building a referral-based business is so beneficial.

The Law of Influence says, "Your influence is determined by how abundantly you place other people's interests first." No, absolutely *not* in a way that is martyrish or stelf-sacrificial, but in a way that simply demonstrates your desire to make it all about them. Moving from an "I-focus" (or "me-focus") to an "other" focus is the fastest, most powerful, and most effective way to elicit the know, like, and trust feelings toward you that are so necessary for cultivating that powerful and desired relationship.

The Law of Authenticity says, "The most valuable gift you have to offer is yourself." All the skills in the world—sales skills, technical skills, people skills—as important as they are (and they are all very important) are also practically worthless if your words and actions aren't congruent with your true, authentic core. But when they are, it's a force multiplier for every other law.

The Law of Receptivity says, "The key to effective giving is to stay open to receiving." You breathe out, but you also must breathe in. It's the same with giving and receiving. A big part of that is the *willingness* to receive. By following the first four laws, you've created the "benevolent context for your success" and earned the right to receive. Now, you must be willing to do so comfortably and gratefully. From there, your world expands. You are in a position to give even more and receive even more, and give even more and on and on.

My Passions

I'm an advocate for the free enterprise system. I truly believe that the amount of money one makes is directly proportional to how many people one serves. Free market capitalism is the greatest economic system that humankind has ever had. Please understand that when I say "*free market* capitalism," I'm not talking about cronyism, where big businesses and other special interest groups, through their lobbyists, buy the influence of politicians in exchange for special favors that diminish competition and create an unfair advantage. That is not free-market capitalism. Again, that's cronyism. Unfortunately, many people don't understand the difference. This is something I wish would be taught in school. After all, how will people be able to distinguish between the two if they're never taught the difference? Free market capitalism, where people do business with one another voluntarily, has brought more people out of poverty than any other economic system by far. It's not even close! And to the degree it's permitted to operate, it's a beautiful thing.

I also have a passion for animals and am an unapologetic animal fanatic. I just love them, and I believe it's a shame the way we as humans have treated them over the past 12,000 years and continue to do so, and in so many ways. I work hard to do my part to educate the public about being kind and good to animals, who are always so good to us.

Q&A WITH BOB

How do you recharge?
I'm really an introvert, so I recharge by being by myself. I also recharge by reading. I love to read.

What is your favorite quote?
It's Zig Ziglar's perhaps most famous and often misquoted: "You can have everything in life you want if you will just help enough other people get what they want."

Who are your mentors and greatest influences?
My dad definitely was my number one mentor and influencer. Just a wonderful human being. I was blessed with two great parents. Being their son was a privilege and an honor.

What do you consider your superpower?
I think my superpower is my ability to encourage others and make them feel genuinely good about themselves.

What do you consider your greatest achievement to date?
Professionally, it's probably the universal success of *The Go-Giver* book and series.

How do you define success?
Let me define happiness first because success ties into that. The dictionary definition of *happiness* is a mental feeling of well-being. Pretty much everyone, consciously or unconsciously, wants a mental feeling of well-being. I take it a step further and define happiness as a genuine and ongoing feeling of joy and peace of mind; the result of living congruently with one's values.

I believe success, then, is a genuine feeling of happiness; the result of having done one's best to live up to their potential.

To read a sample chapter of *The Go-Giver* and other books by Bob Burg, access lots of resources including his blog, podcast, Daily Impact email, and online video courses, or to schedule Bob to speak at your next event, visit burg.com.

JEFF MCKEE

It's Not too Late to Use These Powerful Alternative Asset Investing Strategies

Jeff McKee is a syndication investor in 2500+ apartment units, an ATM passive income fund manager, and an oil and land syndicator. Jeff was a 30+ year sales and business development executive in the software industry. He is passionate about introducing alternative asset investing to family, friends, and those wanting higher returns to achieve financial and time freedom.

Never Too Late to Start Investing in Real Estate

After college and starting my career in tech, my high school sweetheart and now wife of 36 years and I started a family. We were focused on raising three kids and working. We assumed our 401Ks and social security would be enough for a good retirement.

At the age of 52, I found myself 30 years into a successful career in tech with a single source of income from my W-2 job. I heard about others investing in real estate and creating multiple streams of income while continuing to work, but I was a typical investor with a company 401K and holdings in stocks, bonds, and mutual funds. That year, I read Robert Kiyosaki's *Rich Dad Poor Dad*, and it shifted my mindset about real estate investing and spurred me to action.

At the time, our net worth was less than $1M, with two streams of W-2 income between my wife and me.

After hearing about others becoming financially free through real estate investing, I dedicated myself to becoming educated in this area. Over the next three years, I read more books than I had in the prior 30 years.

With my newfound wisdom, in 2018, my son, Brice, and I attended a local REIA (Real Estate Investment Association) meetup in Austin, Texas. Later, my son and I, plus my wife, attended the workshop where we became excited about single-family investment opportunities and ultimately joined this group.

Scaling with Multifamily Investing

After one year of executing our single-family homestead build strategy, fix and flip, wholesaling, and buy and hold plan, I learned we could scale faster with multifamily apartment syndications, so we quickly pivoted.

What I like about multifamily apartment investing is the cash flow generated when taking over an existing apartment community and improving operations to increase the NOI (net operating income). With apartment investing, unlike single-family homes, we can "force" appreciation through increasing rent once the exterior and interior have been renovated. Single-family homes are valued on "comps" (comparable sales per square foot), whereas commercial properties such as apartments are valued on NOI, which can be increased through improved revenues and decreased expenses. Like single-family homes, in multifamily the tenants are paying down the principal on the loan, thus we are using other people's money to increase equity in the asset.

One of the most important benefits of multifamily investing is the ability to scale. We decided to partner with others to syndicate apartment investments and became part owners of 100+ unit apartment communities instead of trying to buy and hold 50 single-family homes as investment properties.

Joining Multifamily Ecosystems

My wife, son, and I attended a weekend multifamily real estate seminar in Dallas then joined that apartment investing syndication group. The primary takeaway was learning the impact of dramatically increasing the value of an apartment community by increasing the NOI with small reductions in expenses and small increases in revenues. The general partners (sponsors) of these multifamily syndications, partnering with the property management team, have a direct influence on executing the business plan for the property and improving the NOI. This contrasts with how single-family homes are valued on comparable properties and the lack of influence investors have on stocks, bonds, and mutual funds.

Over the next six months, we invested as passive investors with this group in five deals across Dallas and San Antonio, thus becoming limited partner owners of 1,000+ apartment doors across five apartment communities.

We started evaluating other programs that were focused on helping families, including children, join in on the education and investing benefits. Due to the COVID-19 pandemic of 2020, my wife and I were able to attend an event in August 2020 and joined our second multifamily apartment investing group. After returning to Austin, my wife started listening to the recordings of their latest group calls.

Our First Deal as General Partners

On a recorded group call, one of the general partners was sharing his new deal and asking for volunteers to join the on-site due diligence of a deal under contract in Fort Smith, Arkansas. My wife and son drove out that week and supported the due diligence along with analyzing the competition in the area. We ultimately became co-general partners on that deal and helped raise capital, including investing as limited partners ourselves. That deal closed in December 2020 and led to partnering with others in the group on many deals from Arizona to Florida.

We have been fortunate to have capital to invest in these deals and are glad to share the opportunity by bringing new investors to these opportunities. We also bring value to the investment team by putting in time to support the on-site due diligence and providing multifamily real estate experience.

As mentioned, part of our capital has been generated from single-family strategies such as our homestead forced appreciation strategy. This plan did involve some risk, but the rewards for us have been tremendous. We would rather have 10% of a 200-unit deal than 100% of a 20-unit deal.

Larger deals with experienced partners can grow your wealth faster than doing smaller deals on your own. Within three short years, through massive education and action, we have more than doubled our net worth through real estate investing, and we have built more than eight streams of passive income from real estate while lowering our federal tax burden.

Life Is Short

My dad died suddenly from a heart attack in 1998 when he was only 55. That was a difficult time for our family. He was such a family man. Fortunately, he was able to spend a lot of time with all seven of his grandkids before he died.

In 2020, when I turned 55, I realized on a new level how short life really is.

I am a cancer survivor. I was diagnosed as part of a routine physical in 2009. I had the cancer removed, followed by treatment, and have had no recurrence.

Based on my family history and my health scares, I do not take tomorrow for granted. Now, I balance enjoying family time, sports, traveling in our RV, vacationing, and building our real estate legacy to last well beyond when I am gone.

One of the legacies my dad instilled in us is camping, so my wife and I have camped a lot over the years with our kids and are passing this legacy down. My dad loved camping so much that we donated a playscape at Inks Lake State Park in Texas with a plaque dedicating it in his name.

Over time, I've realized experiences with friends and family are more important than material items.

What I Learned

1. It's never too late in life to learn new skills such as real estate investing. For our family, having both my wife and I on board has been a key success factor. Involving our children helps us ensure we build a legacy of investing that will continue for generations.

2. Having a good W-2 income(s) can help you qualify for single family loans to generate capital for other real estate investments such as scaling with multifamily. For us, the homestead strategy has been a catapult to our investing.

3. You can't use debt with your 401K/IRA, but you can leverage debt in a solo 401K to invest in multifamily apartment syndications, which use 60% - 75% low-cost debt, thus driving up your returns.

4. Being around like-minded people and the power of partnerships have accelerated our real estate investing path.

5. If one strategy isn't working for you, learn from that and quickly move on, applying those lessons learned to your next strategy.

JEFF'S THOUGHT LEADER LESSONS

Investing and Financial Independence

After five years of passive and active investing outside of Wall Street assets, my wife and I were able to retire from our W-2 jobs to focus on our passions, such as traveling and our multiple family-owned small businesses. We were able to achieve this by learning from others, including by joining mastermind groups, paying for advice from other professionals (in tax planning, asset protection, passive investing, active investing, etc.), reading relevant books, and listening to relevant podcasts. Through multiple investments, including multifamily apartments, an ATM fund, and oil syndications, we were able to build more passive income than our expenses to reach financial freedom, then spend time on our family-owned companies to leave a legacy for our family. Having this "side hustle" outside of our W-2 careers was critical to our achieving financial and time freedom early while we could enjoy being active and traveling.

The Pursuit of Knowledge

Reading some of the top books (*Rich Dad Poor Dad*, *Rich Dad's Cashflow Quadrant*, *Tax-Free Wealth*, and *Who Not How*) enlightened us about the possibility of retiring early to spend time with our family and the activities we most enjoy and **ways** to retire early outside of the traditional method of saving in a 401K plan. Podcasts about different asset classes and business models have been another source of great learning. The idea that "your network is your net worth," (Porter Gale) enabled us to meet and engage with people further along in the financial freedom journey. We have been able to learn from these people to accelerate our progress and exit the W-2 workforce.

Business and Entrepreneurship

"Risk more than others think is safe. Dream more than others think is practical." – Howard Schultz, CEO of Starbucks

"Financial freedom is available to all those who learn about it and work for it." – Robert Kiyosaki

We originally focused on single-family investing in 2017. Then, in 2018, we took a calculated risk and paid $500K to buy a teardown house on our street in South Austin. We hired a team (general contractor, architect, and interior designer) to help us build two houses on this property. The construction loan was $700K, and we persevered through COVID-19 in 2020 to finish the two houses in mid-2020. We had some other challenges along the way, but we believed this was a solid investment and an opportunity to become developers. Ultimately, the after-repair value was $2.5 million. This launched our short-term rental business with the back house and then the front house.

We lived in the main house and managed to net $50,000 per year in revenue on the short-term rental, which my wife managed. She quit her W-2 paralegal job in July of 2020 after we moved into the new property to focus 100% of her time on real estate. After I retired, we traveled for large portions of the year, renting out the main house as well. We did not sit on the sidelines but rather took a risk which paid off for us.

Q&A WITH JEFF

What is something most people don't know about you?

I nearly died when I was eight years old running through a sliding glass door. I'm a cancer survivor.

What are a few of your favorite quotes?

"The best way to predict the future is to create it." – Peter Drucker

"Believe you can, and you're halfway there." – Theodore Roosevelt

"The true entrepreneur is a doer, not a dreamer." – Nolan Bushnell

"You may delay, but time will not." – Benjamin Franklin

"Every problem is a gift—without problems, we would not grow." – Tony Robbins

What are some favorite places you've traveled to?

I've traveled to many places across the world. Some of my favorite places include Hawaii, Australia, Canada, Cabo San Lucas in Mexico, Singapore, Japan, Iceland, Scotland, Ireland, England, France, Portugal, Spain, Italy, and Greece.

What hobbies do you enjoy?

I enjoy golf, tennis, pickleball, racquetball, swimming, and games with family and friends.

What books do you often recommend?

Rich Dad Poor Dad by Robert Kiyosaki

Rich Dad's Cashflow Quadrant by Robert Kiyosaki

Who Not How by Dan Sullivan and Dr. Benjamin Hardy

What would you tell your 18-year-old self?

Take more risks when you are young. Start a side hustle that you are passionate about. Explore entrepreneurial activities early before deciding on a career. Work as an intern during summers in fields where you are interested in spending your career. Travel abroad to learn more about other cultures and create memorable experiences.

What do you consider your greatest achievement to date?

Being married for 36 years and raising three great children.

How do you define success?

Doing what you want to do, when you want, and with whom you want.

To download Jeff McKee's free eBook about multifamily investing, generating multiple streams of cash flow, and achieving financial freedom, please visit www.mckeecapitalgroup.com. To connect with Jeff directly, please email: jeff@mckeecapitalgroup.com

 Jeff McKee's Contact Information

MAI DUONG

The Will to Change

In memory of my father, Can Quang Duong

Mai Duong, CPA, is a real estate investor and global trade coordinator with 25 years of corporate finance and Big 4 audit experience in the US. An emerging fund manager and developer helping real estate investors achieve financial freedom, Mai is also passionate about freedom, liberty, and children. Mai and her husband live in Tampa Bay area, Florida.

A Mango for My Dad | The Will to Survive

I was born in Saigon, the capital of the Republic of Vietnam (RVN) or otherwise known as South Vietnam. As a little child, I had a sheltered life with Catholic private school, live-in nannies, and a family car. I hardly knew anything about my native country's political or economic climate until the fall of Saigon on April 30, 1975, the end of the Vietnam War. My world immediately turned upside down when, as the late Senator John S. McCain said, "the wrong guys won." McCain said *in Saigon* on April 29, 2000 (quote) "I think the wrong guys won. I think that they lost millions of their best people who left by boat, thousands by execution, and hundreds of thousands to reeducation camps."

My father, magistrate of the Supreme Court of the Republic of Vietnam (RVN) and director of the center of law research at the Supreme Court, was taken away to communist prison, deceivingly called a "re-education camp", for eight years, seven months, and 16 days. Publicly, this was a "30-day education" program in Saigon to prepare the RVN administration's personnel to "better serve" the "unified Vietnam." In reality, it was a big lie! My two cousins, my cousin-in-law, my mom's cousins, my husband's brother and brothers-in-law, my uncle, and my father… if I put together the years all the men in my extended family were imprisoned by the Vietnamese communist party, the number would be staggering.

Extreme starvation, mental and physical torture for those who dared to attempt escape, and harsh living conditions, including exposure to disease and no medical care… destroyed many souls. Many of the brightest men and women of the RVN never came back.

However, my dad did (come back).

The day he left Saigon for the communist 30-day "re-education" trap, I planted the seed of a mango in front of our home. Maybe it was a sign, since I had never done any gardening. I was nine. Dad did not come back to us until years later when I was about to begin college. The mango seed grew into a little tree, one foot, two feet, then three feet tall, and always skinny like the five of us siblings who did not have enough to eat for a long time. The mango tree witnessed numerous seasons of missing our dad on Christmas, New Year, and Tet (Lunar New Year), and the hardship endured in a society cut off from civilization. For example, Saigon only had electricity three times a week for many years.

When the mango tree was six and a half years old, it gave its sweet first-season fruit. My youngest brother, Hung, took the best one of those mangoes to my dad in prison when he was moved back to a southern province closer to home. My dad shared that first-season mango with his cellmates and "tears flowed down inside" when the sweet mango juice freshened his hungry throat. My dad told me later that it was "as if a knife were ripping apart my heart when I heard from your mom that the mango came from the seed you planted the day I was away. I was so fearful that I shall be rotting in that inferno for the rest of my life."

Eventually, in 1983, with only four teeth left, my dad was released from that small prison back home to the huge prison of the country of Vietnam, then called the Socialist RVN. He finally went home to my mom and "only four kids left," since while he was away my sister lost her young life to asthma in a "free healthcare" system which had no medication nor doctors.

Journey to Freedom | The Will to Be Free

In March 1994, when beautiful cherry blossoms were in full bloom, our family arrived in Seattle, Washington, USA, as "refugees by plane." We were not the stateless Vietnamese refugees, nicknamed Boat People, risking their lives for freedom in the late '70s nor the Vietnamese immigrants sponsored by families beginning in the mid-'80s in the Orderly Departure Program (ODP). We landed in America as political refugees in a program that sent over thousands of Vietnamese families of long-term re-education camp survivors in the '90s. The official name was Humanitarian Operation (HO) – Former Re-Education Center Detainees.

Just shy of 20 years earlier, according to the Department of State (DOS), there were only 671 Vietnamese people who chose to live in the US and became citizens. The DOS provided this number to my father when he visited the US Supreme Court for a three-month exchange program with the RVN's Supreme Court in 1971. Back then, he was a middle-aged Supreme Court magistrate with many dreams for his native country. In 1994, he was now an old refugee who came here for the future of his adult children.

I shall never forget the 11-year-long process that brought our family to America. In 1990, I incredulously saw our files on the AS 400 computer screen in the ODP Bangkok office when I visited from Saigon, a chance no one in our situation could ever have, simply because leaving Vietnam still largely meant an escape at the cost of one's life. A few years later, we were interviewed by US immigration officials who flew to Saigon in the morning and out to Bangkok that same night due to the lack of diplomatic relations. My mom, a lifelong French language high-school teacher, was asked to resign due to "applying to go to America." My entire family languished for more than a decade waiting for the actual departure.

Yet, when we wanted to find some communist official to bribe in exchange for passports, as many people did, my dad told us that *if his fate were to die in his homeland, then so be it*. He could not commit bribery. He would not know how. He could not compromise his values, even if it was for getting out of hellish Vietnam.

Eventually, my dad got his turn in line. It was four years later than we had hoped, but we did get our turn. We came to America a few months before President Clinton shook hands with the Vietnamese communist government promising an unconditional diplomatic relationship. The four-step roadmap President Reagan demanded of Vietnam (freed political prisoners, a free market, land ownership, and a multi-party election) was abandoned for good.

Thirty years later, Vietnam today remains a one-party communist country and a police state where my high school classmate, prisoner of conscience Tran Huynh Duy Thuc, was imprisoned for over 15 years simply for promoting a society under the rule of law and free of widespread corruption.

From Bus Ride to First-Class Air France | The Will to Thrive

Compared to where we came from, everything in America seemed superb.

Just like all first-generation immigrants, we had a humble start in our new homeland. My parents, my grandma, three siblings, and I all stayed together in a tiny rental home, cooked at home to save money, and watched little or no TV for years. My siblings and I excelled in college, and with time, we all graduated from the same alma mater, the University of Washington.

Within my first few weeks in America, I managed to get a job offer as a flight attendant on US-Japan routes. It was a great opportunity, as I love to travel. But to my surprise, my dad advised me to go back to school, choosing "the type of work less demanding on health and less time away from home." Before I knew it, I started with PricewaterhouseCoopers, LLP as an auditor and landed a multi-year audit project in Paris, France, as I speak French. I literally switched from riding a bus to flying first class on the Concorde supersonic! Instead of serving food, I had fun ordering food from the a-la-carte menu on Air France.

Devoted to my corporate job, I traveled around the world for work. I then graduated from Cornell with an MBA and Harvard Business School's Executive Education Program, Mergers and Acquisitions. As director, senior director, then controller, I worked for major companies, including two Fortune 500s, doing consulting work on major projects, with the aspiration to ring the New York Stock Exchange bell one day as the finance chief of a company going IPO!

But while my corporate life appeared to be successful, I felt very lonely inside. The rat race was wearing me out!

Since my husband and I were childless, we spent most of our free time in his music hobby and my non-profit causes involving everything child-related, including children rescued from sex trafficking with One Body Village and, more recently, Child Liberation by Paul Hutchinson, helping poor children in Asia with Messengers of Love, educating children with Sunflower Mission and Community Family Centers, Youth Leadership Len Duong camp, and Sunday school.

Beyond Paycheck | The Will to Transform

I was yearning for a change, and the authoritative shutdown of the US economy in 2020 accelerated the change for me. Pivoting from corporate finance to commercial real estate and partnering with people from all walks of life, I found my new passion and a sense of freedom never experienced before in the confines of corporate America: I transformed from a stressed-out corporate CPA to an everyday American investor who tries hard to follow God's teachings in her daily activities.

Against the so-called conventional wisdom, I reached out to new investors, the less connected, less wealthy, or less experienced… because they needed and appreciated my help the most. Nothing is more satisfying than serving those who truly need help. I created a small volunteer group to help others underwrite deals and other tasks related to commercial real estate. My company Manna Capital Group, named for *manna* from the Bible, offered a pro-bono class on underwriting, and we had people call in from as far as Holland and Israel!

In my efforts to help others, I grew from a novice to an experienced investor. I went from zero to partnering in nearly 2,900 units of multi-family apartments within three years, got accepted to a few development projects, joined a global trade group, and was invited to speak at a few real estate events.

I can't help but make a comparison.

Thirty years ago, when we left the Socialist RVN for good, we were not allowed to sell our own house in Saigon. The Socialist RVN ordered us to either "offer" it to the communist government or "leave" it to our relatives.

In America, my right to private ownership is protected by the Constitution. So, I am buying real estate!

When I became an entrepreneur, I became creative again: composing poetry, singing on stage, participating in fashion shows, creating an online business, and putting together music shows with my husband. Working out hard to drop nearly 20 pounds and be in Mrs. Vietnamese Community Florida 2024, where I placed in the Top 5, I fit back into my wedding dress, the traditional Vietnamese formfitting Ao Dai. When I was walking on stage in my nearly two-decade-old Ao Dai wedding dress, I had no idea some other pageant contestants in designer Ao Dais were one full generation younger than me. Talk about a challenge!

I broke away from all the inner inhibitions and saw myself change for the better.

Above Yourselves | The Will to Serve

Over the years, I found myself supporting the ideals of self-governance and small government. "A government big enough to give you everything can also take everything away from you."

I want to clean up corruption and help good people go into public service.

Devoted public servants remind me of my late father. He taught me since the tender age of six, back in Vietnam, that President Kennedy told youth, "Ask not what your country can do for you. Ask what you can do for your country."

Patriotic sentiments always inspire!

In Vietnam, my native country, I helped educate youth to the extent possible. For nearly two decades now, I have been involved with the 501(c)3 *Institute for Civic Education in Vietnam*, translating classics and other articles into Vietnamese to educate youth in Vietnam via online books and courses. My only goal *there* is to help make concepts like separation of powers, constitutional rights, and freedom of speech a bit less foreign to people who have lived under communism for nearly 50 years.

In the USA, my adoptive country that I have called home for 30 years now, I have volunteered as a strategist with campaigns, from city council to state legislature, congressional and gubernatorial races, wherever I live. My only goal *here* is to help good candidates win to serve for the right reason and protect our country against *all* enemies, foreign and domestic.

Why does it matter? Because "Freedom is never more than one generation away from extinction." And I know just what President Reagan meant!

MAI'S THOUGHT LEADER LESSONS

Spirituality

Love your neighbors.

Excerpt from a poem I wrote in memory of a priest, the late Catholic Cardinal Thuan Van Nguyen, that led me to Christianity:

> *...In all my matters I didn't use my heart but just my mind.*
> *I believed in the survival of the fittest*
> *The hardest worker deserves the best.*
> *Believing in competition,*
> *I tried so hard to be the winner.*
>
> *Yet you said "God is a bad manager"*
>
> *"Regardless of the working hours*
> *He rewards everyone with the same coin of silver"*
> *To me, it seemed an absurdity,*
> *It didn't seem to be fair any bit!*
> *I was half amused and half confused!*
>
> *But then you explained:*
> *"To love, there's no such thing called fairness*
> *There's no strength, there's no weakness,*
> *Love is to give and to accept,*
> *Love is something one cannot measure*
> *What seems unjust to man is just to the Creator."*
>
> *I was surprised, then turned interested,*
> *Knowing little about Bible.*
> *But through your voice I heard God's words.*
> *A simple thing now means so much,*
> *I now see 'just' in different ways!*
> *A new journey began that day...*

Leadership

A leader needs to lead at times and follow at times.

Mindset

The right mindset takes you to the right place.
Make extra efforts, because it's the extra step that will take you very far. Don't give up.

Team Building

Reprimand in private and praise in public. Apply the Golden Rule.

Q&A WITH MAI

What is your favorite movie?

I saw the movie *Gone with the Wind* in Saigon, Vietnam, in the mid-'80s, a time when nothing but communist propaganda was allowed in the country and VHS was a novelty. It was unforgettable due to the background of the Civil War and the captivating heroine played by Vivian Leigh. I already read the book in my native tongue and was overwhelmed with the chance to see such an American classic *clandestinely*, at the high school where my mom was a teacher.

What has been your greatest lesson?

In business, have an open mind. Go for what excites you, and do everything you can to achieve it, and you will achieve it.

What is some of the best advice you've received?

Guard your heart (The Bible).

What are a few of your favorite quotes?

"Be the change you want to see in the world." – Mahatma Gandhi
The Golden Rule – The Bible

What would you tell your 18-year-old self?

Be brave and explore the world. Don't live within too many boundaries.

Mai Duong's journey from Saigon to the world of commercial real estate is a testament to resilience, determination, and success. She's eager to share her knowledge and empower the next generation of investors.
Email: Mai@mannacapgroup.com | Website: www.mannacapgroup.com
Phone: (425) 535-5223 | FB: https://www.facebook.com/maiduongcpa

 Scan to schedule a call with Mai

JIM JOHNSON

Keys to Leadership from a 30-Year Head Basketball Coach

Coach and speaker Jim Johnson developed winning high school basketball teams for 30 years, taking over three losing varsity programs and quickly turning them into winners. Of his 428 career victories, one game in 2006 captured the national spotlight and has been seen by millions. Jim was named Coach of the Year in 2006 by several Rochester-area organizations and received a National Sportsmanship Award.

My Hometown and Becoming a Coach

I grew up in Greece, the largest suburb of Rochester, New York. My family was very athletic, with my dad being a physical education teacher and basketball coach in my high school. I went to college at Slippery Rock in Pennsylvania before transferring to Cortland State University. I met my future wife my junior year in college, we got married after graduation and had our son Tyler.

My dad was my hero. I wanted to follow in his footsteps: teaching, coaching, and administration. I earned my certification in administration, but I just fell in love with coaching; that was my passion. I spent 35 years as a basketball coach and was a head coach for a total of 30 at four different high schools—the last 20 of those years were at Greece Athena High School in my hometown.

The J-Mac Game

In 2003, Jason McElwain, a student on the autism spectrum known as J-Mac, didn't make the high school basketball team but became the team manager. After trying out again in his senior year in 2005, once again, he did not make the team. However, I surprised him by giving him a uniform for senior night. Despite his small stature, J-Mac made an impressive impact in the game, scoring six three-pointers and captivating the crowd. His performance was so remarkable that it brought tears to my eyes and earned him a standing ovation from the crowd.

The night culminated in J-Mac scoring a memorable three-pointer from well beyond the arc, solidifying his status as the lead scorer of the game with 20 points. The heartwarming scene of the team lifting him onto their shoulders and celebrating his success showcased the power of teamwork and sportsmanship in the face of adversity. J-Mac's incredible display of skill and determination left a lasting impression on everyone present, including his mother, who expressed heartfelt gratitude for the unforgettable experience.

The game's outcome, a resounding victory for the Greece Athena Trojans, was a testament to the unity and support within the team. The camaraderie and sportsmanship displayed by the players, as well as the overwhelming response from the crowd, highlighted the transformative power of sports in bringing people together and inspiring moments of triumph. J-Mac's remarkable performance not only made an impact on the game but also served as a reminder of the resilience and spirit of individuals who defy expectations and achieve greatness against all odds.

Huge Media Attention

The day after the game, I felt numb at school. During my physical education classes, we watched the VHS recording of the game all day. The local newspaper's article focused on the Trojans tying for the division title, barely mentioning Jason's incredible performance. Jason's speech pathologist, who had never attended a game before, was moved and contacted a local TV station. They aired the game footage that night, leading to widespread attention. National TV stations picked up the story, including *CBS Evening News*, *Good Morning America*, ESPN, and others. The coverage went viral, especially on YouTube.

The team's success continued with a win in the quarter-finals and a historic victory in the semi-finals and finals. The media frenzy and celebratory calls continued until the end of the season and included an invitation to appear on Oprah's show for an interview.

Big Heart

After the pivotal moment, Jason returned to his role as team manager with enthusiasm, showcasing his big heart and selflessness. His humility and dedication to the team were evident. His impact was profound, with players willingly passing him the ball without my coaching them to do so.

The season culminated in a historic Section 5 Championship win, a moment cherished by all. For Jason, this achievement stood out as the highlight of his senior year. His incredible performance and the team's success made the season a unique and unforgettable experience for me. It was a reflection of the resilience and unity within the team.

A New Calling: Sharing the Lessons

I coached for 10 more years after that. Jason returned and helped me with my last eight. We ended up winning four more Section 5 Championships together. He became my good luck charm. I retired from coaching in 2016 to pursue a full-time speaking career.

Speaking was something I'd never really thought of, but people started to reach out. After several events during which I simply told J-Mac's story, I developed a motivational keynote called "Dreams Really Do Come True." The keynote includes Jason's story alongside my keys to being a team player, perseverance, and goal setting.

When I met my speaking manager, she helped me make my dreams come true in much the same way I helped Jason. Having spent over 30 years in a leadership position, I created another keynote, "Leadership Lessons from Half Court." Leadership is crucial for team success and can either build or break a team. In my career as a basketball coach, I initially focused on strategy—the X's and O's. However, when I realized the significance of enhancing my leadership skills, I was led to develop seven key leadership principles, which I now share in my leadership presentations:

1. Clarifying vision
2. Building trust
3. Creating the edge
4. Communicating effectively
5. Leading by example
6. Leaving every situation better than you found it
7. Being a servant leader

I also emphasize that while everyone agrees on the significance of trust when building a team, many struggle with implementing a plan to build trust effectively. My three-point plan for building trust includes aligning words and actions, fostering a culture of honesty, and recognizing and praising positive behaviors. It is essential to understand that building trust is a gradual process that requires consistency and effort and that trust can be easily shattered with a single wrong decision.

My mission is to be an outstanding role model, who makes a positive difference in the world by helping others make their dreams come true. When I get up every day, I ask myself, *How can I live my mission?* There are days I don't hit my mission, not even close, but it's always a foundation to come back to.

JIM'S THOUGHT LEADER LESSONS

Team Building

If I hadn't been a skilled team builder, I wouldn't have been a varsity coach for 30 years. As a coach, knowing the sport of basketball was important, but understanding how to cultivate team culture was crucial, requiring daily attention.

Team building involves inspiring a group to believe in a vision and establish shared goals while respecting individual objectives. A leader must grasp everyone's goals and how they contribute to the team's objectives.

Living near the school allowed me to host team lunches after finalizing the roster. At the first lunch of every season, we discussed our mission and core values and set team goals. I provided typed copies for everyone and showed a Jim Rohn film on goal setting.

I held weekly captain's meetings, which evolved from a focused agenda to prioritizing their input, with me asking questions like, "How's team chemistry?" and "How can I improve as a coach?" I emphasized the importance of their feedback, becoming the primary questioner to enhance their development.

I came to understand that if you're in the business of leadership, then you're in the business of creating and maintaining good relationships with the people you work with.

Habits and Personal Growth

Studying habits is crucial, as they form the foundation of your life. Leaders must set an example by cultivating habits that promote personal growth. For instance, we instructed our players in mental imagery before games.

To excel in your field, look for opportunities to learn. Surround yourself with like-minded individuals for mutual improvement. Establish daily non-negotiable habits like exercise, prayer, meditation, reading, and journaling. Start with two minutes for consistency and block out time in your schedule to focus on these habits.

Implement a "two for one" strategy by listening to audio programs while doing daily tasks. This maximizes productivity and learning opportunities in everyday activities.

Attitude and Mindset

Focusing on controlling what you can control is key. Your attitude and work ethic are within your power, even when facing life's challenges. Accepting what you can't control and learning from mistakes are vital. Analyze errors, identify improvements, and strive to be your best in areas you can influence. It's normal to feel upset during this process, but acknowledging your limitations while maximizing your strengths is essential for personal growth.

Q&A WITH JIM JOHNSON

What is your favorite movie?

Remember the Titans

What are your pet peeves?

I'm a real stickler about being on time.

What are a few of your favorite quotes?

"There are no traffic jams on the extra mile." – Zig Ziglar

"Attitudes are contagious. Is yours worth catching?" – Bruce Van Horn

Who are your mentors and greatest influences?

In personal growth, it's Jim Rohn.

In basketball, it's UCLA basketball coach John Wooden. Growing up, I studied both his leadership style and coaching methods and so I listened to, and read, everything I could from him.

What is something most people don't know about you?

I'm an avid tennis player. Today, I actually watch more tennis than basketball.

How do you define success?

Success is continuing to grow myself while serving and growing others. If I can become a little bit better and help others become a little bit better each day, to me, that's success.

When I share a message, I want to convey that hope is alive. It's not a strategy. It is something you've got to believe. Things can get better. I'm trying to be the antithesis of the news, which draws eyeballs because they highlight the negative. I'm trying to consistently share good information to help people improve their lives.

Coach Jim Johnson is a heartfelt speaker who relates the story of a basketball game that went viral. His messages about leadership principles, teamwork, and sportsmanship are in demand by schools and universities, non-profit organizations, and corporations.
coachjimjohnson.com | (585) 210-9194 | speaking@coachjimjohnson.com

Scan to visit Coach Johnson's website to learn more about his presentations, to read his blog, or to sign up to receive his monthly newsletter.

KEVIN EASTMAN

Leading in the NBA, Business, and Life

Kevin Eastman, a professional speaker and author, spent 13 years in the NBA as assistant coach with the World Champion Boston Celtics and as assistant coach and vice president of operations for the Los Angeles Clippers. Kevin was inducted into the hall of fame of his high school, university, and home state of New Jersey. His bestselling book Why the Best Are the Best *is used by sports and corporate teams across the country.*

Losing My Mom, Finding Basketball

My mother died tragically when I was six years old, so my dad worked long hours to provide for my brothers and me. He did his best to balance running his company and providing for three kids... not easy for anyone. Consequently, I had to figure out many things about life and growing up on my own. Sadly, I have no memories of my mom and wish I could have had more time with her. I wish I remembered the lessons she taught me, but I'm sure they are part of who I have become. Fortunately for all of us, my dad was a tremendous role model.

I don't know why I fell in love with basketball, but I am so glad I did, as it has been a huge part of my life. I was a shy kid, and basketball provided something I could do on my own. You don't need anybody else in order to get better—just a boy, a ball, and a dream. I was that boy, and I had the ball; the dream was to play basketball for as long as I could.

I went from having fun in the driveway shooting hoops to becoming passionate, then all-in-committed to basketball. That commitment earned me a college scholarship and a short professional career following college.

When my playing days were over, I had to figure out what was next. Coaching became my new passion, and that passion, along with the same commitment I had to playing the game, has allowed me to experience coaching at the highest level.

What Creates Greatness

I had the good fortune to coach in the NBA for 13 years and to win a World Championship with the Boston Celtics in 2008. I was alongside the best of the best, all the while keeping notes on what I learned from the players, coaches, and others in the organization. I wanted to figure out what made "the best" the best, and I set out to do so through observation, listening, reading, discussing, and learning from others.

I have been around several great leaders during the course of my life, and each one has left a significant impression on me. Among other shared traits, I believe that they are all thoughtful and caring people.

One of the most important things we can do as coaches and leaders is to provide positivity and hope. We must understand, people want to be appreciated, recognized, and valued, so we must do our part to make sure that is part of our leadership philosophy as well.

I was fortunate in that my dad was a great leader. Like other great leaders and parents, he led by example, helping my brothers and me make our way by showing us that he lived his values every single day.

Leadership Velcro

How do you get your followers to stick to you? I call that leadership Velcro. After studying some of the best coaches, CEOs, and VPs, many of whom are close friends of mine, I have found a few common qualities among these successful leaders that create loyalty from their followers and separate them from the pack.

Humility. Great leaders find a way to be "in charge" and lead effectively while still being humble.

Vulnerability. The leader doesn't have to have all the answers, but someone in the organization should have those answers. Great leaders are open to ideas and suggestions brought by others.

When I first took over as vice president with the Clippers, there was a culture of "no." New ideas brought by anyone were met with negativity and were routinely rejected. After years of this treatment, some had understandably stopped giving their best to the organization. So, I wondered how I could let the staff know that our new culture would be different.

In our first meeting, I said, "I know it's been a tough time these last few years. Some of you have told me exactly this. But I need to tell you one of the staples of our culture. We are going to live this every single day, and it's going to be great. We now have a culture of 'know.'"

I could see all the air go out of the room as they heard the last word. I said, "Under Doc Rivers' leadership, we spell that word differently. The old regime spelled it N-O. We will spell it K-N-O-W. We want to know what's in your head. When you have an idea, you have to let us know. I'm here to tell you, as the vice president, I do not have all the answers. But I've seen you guys work. I know what you're capable of. The answers are in this room. Don't be afraid to let me know about a good idea."

Likability. Many say, "They've got to trust and respect me. Who cares if they like me." In my mind, there must be some level of like. Fortunately, likeability is easy. Be friendly. Know names and use them; people love to hear their own names, especially from a leader.

Empathy. As leaders, we walk in two pairs of shoes every day. The first pair are the ones from our closet. Man, do they feel comfortable. They fit. But there's another pair of shoes. Those are the shoes in your employees' closets. You may wear an 11. They wear an eight. Those size eights are uncomfortable, but you must learn to walk in those shoes, too. We need that empathy more than ever today.

Values. People follow people who have strong values and who live those values every day. Values aren't just those things you have on the wall or on your website. A true core value is something you're willing to be fired over.

What are your core values? When people know them and see you live them each day, that's when leadership Velcro happens. That's when those you lead want to meet the challenges you put before them. They want to stick with you, to follow you wherever you lead them.

How to Work with People

We always hear that we need to know what makes people "tick." I believe we must care about what makes them talk, because if we can get them to talk, we have an opportunity to find out what makes them tick. We also must care about what makes them listen, because if we can get them to listen, we have a chance to influence the way they tick.

It all comes back to relationships. Who cares if we have a Hall of Fame player on our team if he won't listen to us and won't do what we've asked him to do to win the game that night? You have to develop relationships to become successful in any arena.

I use an acronym, REAL leadership:

R   **Relationships.** You can't lead people properly unless you have a strong enough relationship with someone such that you're comfortable talking about what matters to them.

E   **Example.** Simply put, be who you want them to be.

A   **Attitude.** We need a positive attitude so we can provide hope for the people we lead. Sometimes it's not what you know but what you bring that day.

L   **Listening.** This is critical to leadership. Do you listen to respond or do you listen to understand?

To become real leaders, we want to cover the four attributes in REAL. Sure, we have to have a vision and processes, but to me, the REAL acronym defines true leadership.

Leaving a Legacy

I have a list of what leaving a legacy means to me—my "elite eight." A legacy is others-driven, not me-driven. I don't want to leave a legacy so my name stays around. I want to leave a legacy because I want my lessons to help someone 20 years after I'm gone. A legacy is built one conversation, one touch, one word, one person at a time.

To me, a legacy is about listening. A legacy is about sharing. A legacy is about depth... staying a little longer in conversations with people. Legacy starts with the person in front of you. No one else. I have spoken to crowds of thousands and to leadership teams of 12. The people in front of you are the most important people in your legacy at that moment.

KEVIN'S THOUGHT LEADER LESSONS

Daily Routines

My daily routines are most important to me in two areas of my life. The first is what I do with the start of my day. The second is what I do before a game I coach or a speech I give. For every speaking engagement, or every game when I was coaching, my routine allowed me to always be in a relaxed and prepared state of mind.

If you ask any great athlete if they have a game day routine, you would get a resounding "yes" from all of them. As we used to say to our players, "Your routine travels no matter who we play or where we play." Once you get into your game day routine, it brings a consistency to your day and a calm to your mind. You know you are ready.

My morning routine is locked in. I first ask myself two questions:
- Did I waste yesterday?
- How will I feel if I waste today?

If I had an unproductive day the previous day, then question number one gets me to reset my mindset and make sure I am productive today. Question number two is always answered the same way: I would not feel good if I knew I was about to waste today, so it instantly puts me into a mindset of making sure I get something out of my hours.

I make sure I include two very important "must do's." In the first hour or two of each day, I go to a coffee shop and get in my reading and uninterrupted thinking. The environment I choose has to be one where I know my mental juices will flow and my curiosity gene will be activated. The coffee shop setting does it for me.

Pursuit of Knowledge

The pursuit of knowledge is a characteristic of every successful person I have ever met. They know they have more to know. They are not embarrassed by recognizing this. They have that curiosity gene that energizes them to continue learning.

I pride myself on going through life with big eyes, big ears, and a small mouth. This allows me to stay alert and aware of what I hear and what I see, which leads to the possibility of what I might learn.

One thing I know for sure is that everyone we meet knows something we don't. So, why wouldn't we pay attention?

Finally, I always keep in mind to not just acquire knowledge but also to apply that knowledge. If we are only in "knowledge acquisition" mode and never get to "knowledge application" mode, our knowledge is never fully utilized. As a matter of fact, I would also add that knowledge not shared with others is also knowledge that is never used to its fullest extent.

Every audience I speak to, I encourage to become all-stars at acquiring, applying, and most importantly, sharing knowledge.

Development

We have a choice to keep things comfortable or to challenge ourselves to grow, develop, and improve. I don't believe anybody wakes up in the morning saying: "I want to be the very worst in the world at what I do." I believe we all have thoughts of: "I can do better. I can be better."

The challenge is that it's hard to admit this to yourself and to others. But, I believe there's more inside each of us, and that begs the questions: *Am I willing to pull that out? How do I pull that out?*

My "personal development system" is the following:

- Admit I need to develop in a given area.
- Research people who are successful in this area.
- Read or talk to people as much as I can so I can begin to see how they did it.
- Make a plan to develop from what I've learned.
- Commit to that plan.
- Take action. The best way to start is to actually start.
- Give myself a chance by putting in the work.

Mentors

None of us knows all we need to know. We are not finished products, and all of us can use some help. All the highly successful athletes I have coached or worked with have had mentors and coaches to help them get to where they are.

In my formative years, I was a little hesitant to ask for help. I saw that as a success flaw or as "he's not ready yet." So, I decided to seek mentors who were successful coaches and read everything written by or about them from books, magazines, and newspaper articles. (Remember that I grew up pre-internet.)

I knew I would never meet these mentors, but that didn't mean they couldn't mentor me, teach me, and show me how to do things.

There is no "I don't have any mentors" excuse. With the internet today, the mentors are limitless. So, start your mentor search now. I don't know how many YouTube videos, podcasts, and Facebook posts I have taken in from people in my industry like Nick Saban, Steve Kerr, Pat Riley, Tony Dungy, Andy Reid, Danny Hurley, Shaka Smart, and many more. They have all been mentoring me these last few decades, sometimes without them even knowing it.

Go. Start. Grow. Develop. Improve. Now!

Q&A WITH KEVIN

What are a few of your favorite quotes?

"He who angers you owns you." – Grady Rivers, Dad of Doc Rivers

"It's not just about what you want. It's what you do every day that counts." – Brad Stevens

What do you make sure you always do?

- Read two hours every day
- Workout every day
- Sit and think every day

What books do you often recommend?

The Four Agreements – Don Miguel Ruiz
Call Sign Chaos – Jim Mattis
The Leadership Secrets of Nick Saban – John Talty
It Takes What It Takes – Trevor Moawad
Think Like a Winner – Yehuda Shinar
Gold Standard – Mike Krzyzewski

How do you define success?

Doing your best—no matter the circumstances—to make sure you are getting the most out of your God-given talents.

What would you tell your 18-year-old self?

- If you put in the right type of work, why can't it be you?
- Make sure you win way more at home than you do at work, but know you do need to win there too.
- Never let doubt or fear be the reason you don't try.
- Relationships are extremely important. Work at building them in a first-class way.

Kevin Eastman is a professional speaker, author, and NBA World Champion coach. His bestselling book *Why the Best Are the Best: 25 Powerful Words That Impact, Inspire, and Define Champions* can be found at www.kevineastman.net. To inquire about speaking engagements, email wendy@kevineastman.net. Follow Kevin on Twitter @kevineastman.

BILL MALCHISKY

Persevering and Thriving with Chronic Illness

Bill Malchisky is the president of Effective Software Solutions, LLC and an author, international presenter, and entrepreneur. He co-authored two top IBM® Redbooks® on Linux®. By bringing global consulting experience to his roles as senior product manager and senior solution architect, Bill helps his larger clients realize seven and eight-digit returns.

It Was All Going So Well

Upon graduating college, I landed an entry-level position with a prestigious company on Wall Street. I took this position not because it was the most lucrative—it was not—but because it provided the greatest opportunity to learn. I appreciate the metaphor of being a distance runner rather than a sprinter. For me, long-term potential outweighed short-term gains.

Many nights at work, especially in the winter, I would sit on the large window seat, look out at the New York Stock Exchange, and just soak in where I was and what I was accomplishing. I found it deeply moving and motivating.

I was on my way up. The job was a good fit, and I did well. My internal clients nominated me for several significant accolades. This level of achievement in one's first year was quite rare. It made me exceptional but also an outlier.

It became apparent that at least one person above me was concerned with how quickly I might rise, so I was forced out.

The company's outplacement office helped me land my dream job, which due to company reorganization, vaporized. Needing cash, I picked up a few short-term tech gigs.

Doing well and being let go would repeat itself in the next few years. That's how I found consulting.

After initial challenges in building a consulting business, I decided to start my own company. Now, I was in control of my destiny and moving steadily forward again. This decision started me on a life-long journey of growth, contacts, successful projects, and accolades that would lead to experiences, memories, and relationships for which I am thankful.

Life Tests Your Resolve

Five years post-graduation, I was debt-free, had a significant sum saved in the bank, was in a great romantic relationship, and was riding the consulting wave through Y2K and into the new millennium.

Five years later, the consulting market was dry in the wake of the 9/11/2001 terrorist acts, I was in debt, and I was quite ill. My symptoms had cost me that great relationship and made me physically unable to do the same type of consulting work. My life had quickly turned 180 degrees, and circumstances weren't letting up.

My illness had started with difficulty getting out of bed. I felt incredibly tired each morning—which was out of character for me. It was hard to catch my commuter train. I would finish tying my necktie once I was onboard and then sleep. This progressively worsened over the next few months. I went to multiple doctors who all came back with the same diagnosis: stress.

In my soul, I knew that was inaccurate. I went through so much stress early in life, and I knew how I responded. In six months, I had gone from solving complex puzzles to struggling to write a check in the doctor's office. My life had followed a sinusoidal curve, from graduating from a top technical institute, succeeding in my first job, and starting a business to my current cognitive decline. So, I kept searching for answers.

By this time, I was in a fog almost 23 hours per day. What seemed like a few minutes to me was, in fact, hours. I had about one hour of clarity, and I made the most I could of it. I stopped taking on large, complex projects with well-known financial firms. Right at a time when people knew my reputation and wanted me, I disappeared.

I started doing computer system installations, which worked with the fog because this was typically done at night when businesses were closed. If a two or three-hour evening job (as agreed and invoiced) actually took me eight hours, no one would know it, and the work got done. I didn't make much money during this time, but I maintained my credit score and paid my bills.

In the middle of this time, the IRS came calling. Essentially, they wanted to know: *How is it that you went from growing your business three successive years to declining your business the next three years with pretty similar expenses?* They asked questions. Physically, I could not provide what they needed, so I hired an attorney.

The legal team didn't understand my condition and eventually lost interest in the case. What they didn't tell me was that the IRS called them multiple times... and they didn't call the IRS back. So, when I called the IRS to check in, I got an unpleasant surprise. Because they had been ignored, they filed a lien against me. I had no idea. Preparing to protect myself and do right with the IRS only put me in a hotter pool of water.

I found a CPA who did handle things well and was ethical with the process. It took almost five more years to get everything settled correctly. I'm in good standing now.

Listening to Your Body Is Sage

My then-girlfriend suggested I see a naturopathic doctor (ND). I'm not arguing for or against a naturopathic doctor over a medical doctor (MD), but I realized I needed a new perspective. This doctor was in demand, and it took nearly three weeks to see her. During that time, the fog got worse and worse.

When I finally got to meet the doctor, she knew exactly what I had. She ordered tests that would confirm the diagnosis, and I left with medicine I could start taking as soon as the results were returned. Unusual, but given the severity of the infection consuming me from the inside, prudent.

I was told it would be a three-month recovery and made a three-month adjustment for projects and cash flow in my business. After three months, I was nowhere close to being well. It took almost 10 months of visiting several doctors to resolve the infection. Additionally, several new health complications appeared, each needing a specific treatment and doctor. The last doctor was a gem and became a close friend of 20 years I still see today. The truth is, though, the extra recovery time I needed crushed me financially. With knowledge from my college finance class, I kept myself afloat.

Due to the infection, my diet had devolved. Many foods fed the infection and had to be eliminated. But it was also diet that allowed me to heal and regain my strength. Advanced nutritional knowledge became compulsory for me. Several years later, my dietary discipline permitted increased choice, and I regained the 40 pounds I had lost during my health decline. My distance runner's point of view provided a long-term perspective and holistic approach which aided in my recovery.

"Strive Not to Be a Success, but Rather to Be of Value."

I really appreciate that Albert Einstein quote. An eternal optimist, I knew the illness and succeeding events would help me help others. My purpose in life was revealed: Stop focusing on how much money I could make and focus on how much value I could add. If done properly, one can have both. This mental transformation changed me in ways I could never have imagined.

Post-recovery, adding value became my model. It took many years to get the fundamental systems executed, but I evolved into a solution architect. Now, I help my clients solve business challenges around technology. My resume includes some amazing opportunities I've had to work with incredible people. Each project helped me grow.

Every few years, my approach to what I offer clients evolved further. The work I do now is very different from when I started my business. Some changes are correlated to changing market conditions and others are a result of situations forcing my hand, as with my illness. In the end, seeing the opportunity in every challenge lends itself to greatness—or at least a better outcome than if you focused on the negative in the moment.

Despite being incredibly challenging, testing my integrity, patience, drive, and creativity over many years, the illness became one of the best things to happen to me. Perhaps divine intervention is at play, but this extended chapter in life shifted my focus to being healthy first and then adding value to others. If you live a life with an abundance mindset, it is easier to find the opportunity in any challenge.

BILL'S THOUGHT LEADER LESSONS

Health & Wellness

So many health-related ailments people experience can be avoided with a clean diet.

While at a health retreat, I witnessed a 40-ish woman using a walker 100% of the time. In a week, she decreased usage by about 20% with a nutrient-dense, clean, organic diet, gained leg strength, and with help getting into the hot tub and plunge pool, she enjoyed an evening outing with the group. After three weeks, she didn't need the walker.

As we age and our bodies change, what we eat and how much we need to eat to maintain the health metrics we enjoyed when younger also changes.

Proper hydration resolves several health conditions and improves one's overall quality of day-to-day life. That is a pithy statement that many people do not understand fully. From my research combined with personal results including friends and family, I am comfortable providing this data point.

Entrepreneurship

Successful entrepreneurs have a value-based mindset, whereas employees tend to have a cost-based mindset. Although seemingly counterintuitive, the annals of business history are sprinkled with companies that either did not evolve to value-based thinking from cost-based thinking and companies that achieved it, but when a new senior leader or executive arrived, they reverted the business to cost-based thinking. In the cases I've studied, it did not end well for these companies: many either declared bankruptcy or lost their independence as a result of becoming an acquisition target.

Though costs are important in business decisions, successful firms, in my experience, have it as around number four or five on their decision-criteria list—with value, cultural fit, reliability, and risk ranking higher.

Peter Drucker's famous quote, "Culture eats strategy for breakfast," is apropos here.

Cybersecurity

Many people who started businesses outside of technology are now realizing that technology is deeply intertwined with both their business and daily lives. Knowledge of cybersecurity provides the peace of knowing that you are part of the solution rather than compounding a problem. Many outages occur due to poor training in cybersecurity, lack of knowledge, or inconsistent adherence to what was taught. I have witnessed clients' team members who are more diligent in their professional lives than at home, which can cause challenges later.

With the steady annual increase of cybersecurity breaches, one vulnerability people commonly underestimate is email. Though a great, convenient communication medium, email is insecure. Cybercriminals can (and do) set up sniffers (tools to capture emails) entering and leaving companies. Always presume that businesses in the investment, medical, document management, accounting, banking/finance, insurance, real estate/title management, government, legal, and pharmaceutical arenas have sniffers directed at their external email server(s); these verticals are easy pickings for bad actors. Be safe with your data and request your vendors do the same. Just because it's easy, does not mean it's safe.

At the end of the day, if you do not protect your identity and well-being when online, who will? If a vendor is cavalier with your data and someone takes advantage, ultimately, you—not the vendor—are responsible for the clean up.

Four basic steps to help increase security when online:

- Use a 12-character minimum, complex password
- Use dual-factor authentication (sometimes written as Multi-FA) with a secure authentication tool—SMS and phone calls are suboptimal
- Use a VPN on your computer—especially when on a public WiFi network (e.g. when in an airport or coffee shop)
- Avoid sending PII (personally identifiable information) over email—including SSN, birthdate, and financials; upload to your vendor's portal or use a secure transfer medium.

Q&A WITH BILL

How do you recharge?

"No Alarm Clock Saturday" is my favorite day of the quarter. When that day comes, I appreciate the opportunity to disconnect and disappear until my body says, "Okay. Let's go."

Being in IT, causes one to utilize multiple computers and be online more than most. Recently, I found the simple pleasure of being offline more. Being offline affords me the cathartic opportunity to be present and to focus on what's in the room.

Saturday night fitness and making time to visit friends and family during business trips or engaging in intellectual dialogue for hours with a friend means the world to me.

Have you had any past challenges that turned out to be blessings?

- My illness.
- My car accident, which I was lucky to survive when I was a teenager.
- I learned and grew from each personal relationship after college, including how to be a better man. I am indebted to the wonderful, intelligent women I've met on this journey.

What is some of the best advice you've received?

You don't get what you deserve, you get what you negotiate.

What do you consider your superpower?

Saving troubled IT projects and vendor relationships.

Not all of my projects are corporate rescue or corporate firefighting. Many are smooth, well-planned efforts. But when things go awry and I am called in, that's where I shine. With vendors, poor communication or mismatched deliverables can cause strained relationships. I like to help get things moving again. If the product is good, it is much cheaper to save the relationship with the vendor than to migrate and start over.

Over the past 25 years, this theme emerged numerous times with several high-profile projects. This created significant risks for my clients. In the end, when I have management backing, being placed in a sea of corporate chaos then creating calm is comforting for me.

If a team is behind schedule, a developer is ready to quit, and the project is over budget, I'm happy to smooth everything out. What to do and how to proceed is very objective for me. In the end, I find the problem, target the root cause, remove emotion, and solve it. I clear the carnage, cultivate the land, plant, seed, water, and provide care, and when I'm finished, not only does the client have a quality deliverable, but the problems that existed are long forgotten.

What hobbies do you enjoy?

Many people speak of relaxing on a tropical island. Skiing is my island. For me, the panoramic views, remote locations, quiet, and good-natured people in small quantities is picturesque.

What books do you often recommend?

Authored by Kate Wendleton, founder of The Five O'Clock Club: *Targeting the Job You Want*, *Mastering the Job Interview*, and *Packaging Yourself: The Targeted Résumé* is an incredible job management series—especially the latter book. The content is timeless. Several friends and colleagues have moved on to incredible careers as a result of these books.

How do you define success?

If you are doing what you want to do in life and have achieved the sought-after level of advancement or accolades therein, then you are successful. The example I often use is, "If you want to be a forest ranger, and you are the best forest ranger that you can be while feeling gratified with your work, then you are successful." It has less to do with money and more with impact. There are wealthy people who have little impact on the world and lower-income people who create an everlasting impact on the lives they touch.

To learn more about how Bill Malchisky can help your business thrive through effective technology solutions, to invite him to present, or to ask a question, please contact him at 203.374.2973 or book@effectivesoftware.com. Bill enjoys sending the elevator back down, helping small business owners solve problems so they too can achieve success. LinkedIn: billmal; X: @billmalchisky

 Tech Teasers

RITA GAMIL KECHEJIAN

From Stay-at-Home Mom to Real Estate Business Owner

Rita Gamil Kechejian is a real estate broker with over 18 years of guiding people to build wealth and financial freedom that will create a generational legacy through home ownership. She is a firm believer in education and giving back to her community. Rita and her husband George have three children and live in Orange County, CA.

Legacy and the American Dream

Coming from Armenia was a family dream. Armenia was part of the USSR at the time, and everything was controlled. It was my family, my uncle's family, and my grandparents. We didn't have much money but, as kids, we didn't know any better. The way they were talking about America, it was like the ground in America was paved with gold.

My grandma's sister in Hollywood sponsored us. We were supposed to come to California in 1980, but the legal doors to the US closed, so we waited until '88. All 11 of us sold our belongings and gave everything up for our dream.

It was a nearly three-week journey through Russia and Italy and my first time on a plane. I remember lots of paperwork. I never heard my family complain. This was what we were doing to have a better future.

On my first day at my huge, American, public junior high school, I was nervous. The only English I knew was, *I love you, thank you,* and *goodbye.* My little cousins (I call them sisters because we all lived together) were going to the elementary school, and my brother was going to the high school, so I felt alone. Thankfully, there were a lot of Armenians in Hollywood. I remember sitting in a multipurpose room, understanding nothing being said. When I saw this little Armenian girl who looked just like me standing on the side, I knew she would be my best friend. You just need one good person to be your friend. We went through a lot together and still keep in touch.

At 11 years old, I didn't realize how my family's American dream of owning a home would impact me and what I now do for a living. We didn't have much, so we couldn't afford much. Our first home was in Palmdale, California, in the Mojave Desert. Now, I'm on the other side of the table. As a real estate broker, I get to help others with their dream of owning or selling a home. It's unreal. I love what I do. With housing prices, interest rates, and uncertainties, many are afraid it can't be done, but people still want the American dream. It warms my heart to be involved in their journeys.

My husband and I started in a little townhome. It doesn't have to be big, but you get your foot in the door and start to build your equity, which can eventually become your legacy. It's amazing when you think of the big picture—when you're gone and still helping the people you love, even just a little bit. That's the undercurrent of what I do. People are not only getting a house, I'm helping their families for generations to come.

Stay-at-Home Mom

My niece asked me, "When you were a kid, what did you want to be when you grew up?" I told her I've always wanted to be a mom.

I met my husband on a blind date. He says he knew he was going to marry me from day one. Today, I've been married to my husband four times, with zero divorces. The first time was at a chapel in Las Vegas, and the second was the big Armenian wedding. We were both very young and grew up together. Our third wedding was renewing our vows for our 10th anniversary on a Disney Cruise with our kids, and the fourth was our 30th anniversary. I want my kids to see the value of family, the unity.

As young as I was when my husband and I met, I was always very clear on what I wanted my life to look like—I was going to be a stay-at-home mom, like my mom was for me.

We were very clear on our roles. My husband was responsible for providing for our family. There were challenges with being a one-income household, but it was our choice. I supported my husband in working long hours and weekends and was where I wanted to be as a stay-at-home mom, enjoying and raising my kids. To this day, my kids are my biggest accomplishments. We are still very clear on the idea that as a family, we're a unit.

Starting a Business

I want my kids to know, you can be everything. You can have it all, just not all at once. I was a stay-at-home mom for 13 years, and I loved every second. Then, the kids grew up. When my third and youngest son started kindergarten, the house was too quiet. I didn't want to be home alone during the day. I wanted to work. Actually, I wanted to build a business.

As I got started, impostor syndrome came on strong. *Who do you think you are? You have no talent and no degree. You were home for 13 years. Who's going to hire you or want to work with you?*

Fortunately, my mom gave me the gift of reading and loving books. When I was a child, I always saw her reading. I remember her holding my hand in Armenia as we walked to bookstores or the library. I still remember the "old book" smell. And now, when I feel uncomfortable or don't know something, I turn to books.

I read this little book that said—If you think that, as a stay-at-home mom, you have nothing to provide, think again. You're a multitasker and all the jobs you do are valuable.

This little reminder really helped my confidence. And that's when I found real estate and became a real estate agent.

Getting started was still intimidating. I was lucky that I knew many of the parents in my community. When you're sitting at a little kids' baseball game that lasts hours, you talk to parents and get to know them. They get to know you, then they like you, then they trust you. It takes time to build that trust. Then they come to you when they have a question or could use some help with real estate.

As I continued, I read more books, got coaching, and kept learning and getting better. I never had the opportunity to pursue a college degree, so I took every class I could, mostly paying for them myself. I have my real estate broker license and designations like the Graduate, REALTOR Institute (GRI), which only 2.7% of agents have. For months, I took Dale Carnegie in-person live classes. I also completed the Master Certified Negotiation Expert certification (MCNE). I think it's fascinating to learn how everyone negotiates, from different generations, like baby boomers and millennials, and from different cultures. When you understand what people need, you realize it's not about you, it's always about the clients and their needs. I sent lots of handwritten notes, made lots of calls, and hosted client parties. I'm so thankful to my clients. In this business, there's no ceiling, but there's also no floor. I work a lot and long hours, and I'm okay with that because my clients put their trust in me and I don't take that lightly. I love my job and my clients.

After almost two decades, I'm very comfortable in my experience, expertise, and knowledge. I don't think of myself as a salesperson. I'm in the service business. With my clients, I'm their trusted advisor. I'm here to educate them on the market and their options. We're a team, and when they are ready, my clients get to decide what's best for them and their families. Then I can help them make their real estate dream a reality.

Goal Setting in Real Estate Investing

I love setting goals. In 2022, I accomplished one of my biggest 15-year goals when my husband and I bought a triplex in Los Angeles!

Another big goal is for our kids to each have a home for themselves. When our oldest moved out of state, we went with her to look at places. She was looking at renting, but we ended up calling a friend of mine. (It's nice to have friends everywhere. That's one of the beauties of the coaching company I belong to. We have real estate agents nationwide.) We looked at a few homes, wrote three offers, and bought a house for her to live in. That was very rewarding. We know she's safe, and if she wants to change the paint color, she can!

We bought those properties when people, and even the news, were saying it was the wrong time to buy. But I believe in real estate. I absolutely plan to continue investing in buying properties. Now, my goals include paying off the properties we own to produce passive income.

I believe real estate is safety, financial freedom, and building a legacy. For me, freedom is the most important. If my kids live out of state and I'm financially free, I can fly to go see them and I don't have to worry about it. The long-term goal for me is that we get to travel the world and still help my clients buy and sell homes.

RITA'S THOUGHT LEADER LESSONS

Generational Wealth
We did not come from money. Eleven of us lived in a four-bed and two-bath home of 1,300 square feet. There was always noise and a line for the bathroom.

It takes a while, and it's hard to stay on the path, but every day, little by little, results will come. Then, you look back and see what you accomplished. The key is having that
big goal that scares the crap out of you and then working toward it every day one bit at a time. People overestimate what they can do in the year and underestimate what they can do in five.

Identity and Self-Belief
Sometimes there is a little, quiet voice inside us. Don't numb that out. If you listen to it, it's constantly saying you have more potential. You have more gifts and talents to use.

A lot of times I feel like we're waiting for permission from someone. I've always been the big personality in the family. I laugh big. I talk big. My hair is big. Everything about me is big, including my big, passionate personality. The culture I grew up in is traditional. Kids are supposed to be seen, not heard. They tried to make me fit in this box. Well, my big hair alone can't fit in that box. I had to learn to be okay with that.

I know I'm not everybody's cup of tea. They're not mine, either. As women, we are taught to think we have to please everyone. I had to learn that we don't. At the end of the day, when the door closes, and it's just you and yourself, what other people think of you is not important. I think some of that wisdom comes with age. We have to get comfortable in our skin.

You need truth-tellers. I have found that the secret to being successful in life is surrounding yourself with people who are not worried about hurting your feelings. Having the right tribe and somebody to believe in us helps!

Q&A WITH RITA

What are a few of your favorite quotes?
"I stand here as one, but I come as 10,000." – Maya Angelou

That quote resonates with my heart because I am where I am not because of my successes, but because of my parents, grandparents, and ancestors! They've come from genocide and a struggle to survive. I have them to thank. If I don't take the opportunities in front of me that were not available to them, shame on me!

Who are your mentors and greatest influences?

My parents. I saw them struggle and still be so God-loving and always recognizing their blessings. In traffic, they would say, "Thank God we have a car and can be in the air conditioning." I do what I do because of the lessons I've learned from my parents. They were always there for me no matter what!

Have you had any past challenges that turned out to be blessings?

Losing my mom was heartbreaking. She was 43. I was 19. My whole world shifted upside down. The unconditional love she gave me was suddenly gone. I had to learn to get by without her and to rely more on myself. The big hole is still in my heart but you learn to live with the pain.

I learned so many lessons. She used to save everything for later! Enjoy everything now. Use the good dishes. It's ingrained in me to experience and enjoy every second of life.

What is some of the best advice you've received?

"Put your head down and work." Whether it's at home or work, you said you're going to do this. Honor your word.

When you're in the midst of a challenge, or if you're having the best time of your life, "This too shall pass." We have seasons in life. I try not to get stuck in the ugliness or the blessings.

What philanthropic causes do you support?

With RE/MAX, I'm a huge proponent of donating to the Children's Hospital of Orange County on behalf of my clients when we close escrow. And I donate to our elementary school for 6th grade camp.

What hobbies do you enjoy?

Cooking. I love feeding people. That's my love language. When I've had a long day, cooking is how I decompress. I never measure and it's my way of connecting with my mom. And I've got to have my music.

I'm getting into pickleball and back into photography. I have a couple of photos from places I've traveled printed on canvas. I'm not an expert. I just love capturing the moment.

Buying and selling real estate can be daunting and Rita Gamil Kechejian is ready to help. Email Rita4Homes@outlook.com or visit RitaGamil.com with your questions. Ask for free real estate courses "What's Ahead… Housing Market" and "Free Market Evaluation of Your Home." Find Rita on social media: Facebook /RitaGamil Instagram @Rita4Homes

 Scan for more info.

BOB BEAUDINE

Challenges You to Think... Differently!

Bob Beaudine, CEO of Eastman & Beaudine, is a nationally recognized search executive, author, and entrepreneur. Sports Illustrated *named him "The Most Influential Man in Sports You've Never Heard Of!" Bob is the bestselling author of* The Power of WHO! *and* 2 Chairs, *which provides a definitive roadmap to personal transformation.*

Early Lessons

I thought growing up with a mom and dad who loved, hugged, and encouraged you every day, was the norm. Unfortunately, for far too many, that's not the case. Looking back, I think God gave me great parents so I could write books and speak to remind people that each of us has an assignment, purpose, and dream all our own that we need to discover or rediscover.

I'll never forget my dad taking me backstage to see Frank Sinatra. I was about 13, and it made an *indelible imprint* on my approach to business and life.

Frank Sinatra was the greatest singer of the day, so going backstage and meeting him was not only improbable but also something most normal people would find intimidating. But not my dad! He wanted to show me something: **"The greatest limitations in life are not external, but internal."**

When we got to the backstage door, there was a large man guarding the entrance. My dad announced, "The Beaudines are here to see Frank Sinatra."

The guard snickered and said, "Mr. Sinatra is not available."

My dad then said, "Tell him Frank Beaudine and his son Bobby are here."

He said, "Mr. Sinatra is not seeing anyone!"

It was then that my dad forcefully and confidently leaned in and said, "Tell him Frank Beaudine from Chicago is here!"

The guard's face changed when he heard that! You could see him think to himself: "I wonder. If I don't tell Mr. Sinatra, will I lose my job?"

Now, we didn't know Frank Sinatra. We never said we did. But the guard didn't know that.

What happened next was AMAZING! The doors (BAM) opened, and Frank Sinatra walked toward us and said, "Frank, Bobby! How are you? How's Chicago?" And we marched in!

"Where's the wife?" Frank asked.

My dad said, "Martha arrives tomorrow!"

Mr. Sinatra then told someone named Joey to make sure there were three tickets/VIP—out-front tomorrow, on me!"

I was stunned! We sat for 20 minutes talking with Frank Sinatra!

What's my takeaway? "Every dream you and I have has an obstacle at the door saying, "No Entry!" But we're going in!

How? You have to know WHO you are, just like my dad. You have to look at them and say, "Frank Beaudine from Chicago!" **Life is made up of moments and choices—don't miss yours!**

Pursuing Your Highest Value

My dad was one of the pioneers of the executive search industry, having started back in 1967 out of McKinsey & Company. He and I worked together for 20 years. My dad had a simple mission statement for our firm, and we still live to this statement some 50-plus years later: **"Make friends. Help your friends in every way possible. Don't be surprised that you do a lot of business with your friends!"** I'm proud to say, "My dad was my best friend, my dad, and my business partner!"

Are you doing what you love? With people you love? In a place you love? Where your family loves it? And are you doing it for all the right reasons?

I was in my late 20s when I first joined my dad's executive search firm, Eastman & Beaudine. I never really thought about this being "the job." I was just seeking a field where I felt I could excel and where I loved the people I worked with and they loved me. After several years of doing the same thing, I noticed in myself a growing uneasiness and a longing for "something more." I liked executive search, but I loved sports. I often wondered if there was a way to involve my passion for sports with my career as an executive recruiter.

One day, I approached my dad with the frustrations I was feeling. He asked me two very simple, yet direct, questions. "What do you want to do? What do you love?" Those questions awakened my dream, and in a flash, I began to speak with clarity about how I would love to develop a division in our firm that would accommodate the worlds of sports and entertainment.

His response: "Go get it!" The rest is history. All it takes is one thought, one idea, or one friend, and you can change the entire trajectory of your life—if "love" is the operative word.

A Dream Not a Job

When I was young, my dad was out of work for eight long months. Each day, he'd get dressed in a suit and head to the office. At least that was what we thought he did. When we finally went off to school, he'd circle back home to look for a job. He just couldn't bear for us to be worried; it was a different generation. Years later, when I worked for my dad in executive recruiting, if people came to our office looking for a job without an appointment, we'd always treat them as though they had one. We'd welcome them to the office, get them a cup of coffee, sit and talk. Dad taught us how vulnerable it felt to be out of work. My dad always told me, "There's something great in everyone, Bob, it's your job to find it!"

From time to time, I have friends ask me to meet with one of their family members or friends because they were fired or downsized or their company was acquired. They're hoping I would encourage them and possibly point them in the right direction for their next job. When they come to my office and tell me about their trouble, they're usually shocked when I tell them, "Congratulations! This is the greatest day of your life!"

They say, "What are you talking about?"

I remind them, "You never liked that company; it was just a job! Isn't it about time to do something you love? Wouldn't it be great to come home with joy on your face and happiness in your heart when you finish work? What if you could do something that is not just a job, but a dream?

Of course, they all say, "YES!"

But then, ask: "What does that look like? Is there something great people look for in a dream job?" There are five things leaders look for in a dream Job, and you should too!

1. People – Go where you're **celebrated**, not where you're **tolerated**.
2. Tools – They want to be able to do the job they're hired to do. This involves factors like staff, budget, and being empowered to make a difference.
3. Family – Success is geographical. No leader can maximize their potential if their family isn't excited and on board with the opportunity.
4. Legacy – Feeling a sense of significance as it relates to job and life satisfaction is important. Find the opportunity to do something that hasn't been done before and leave it better than when you found it.
5. Money – Being paid commensurate with the role and then being rewarded financially for great results.

BOB'S THOUGHT LEADER LESSONS

True Success Is Love

Bestselling author Max Lucado wrote an endorsement for my book *The Power of WHO!* He said, "People matter most. God teaches us. Our heart teaches us, but we forget."

Do you know that you have friends right now who are out of work or in trouble who will never call you or tell you they need help? Why? Unexpected change can be overwhelming! When a crisis comes, people do the craziest things. They go bonkers and begin to bunker. There's something inside us that just hates to "ask for help!" That's so interesting, because, if you and I were best friends and I asked you for help, would you help me? The answer's always yes! So, why would you deny me the same joy of helping you? It never works in reverse! That's why we have to stay in better touch with our friends! If you're pursuing your highest value, you must remember—that the core of "true success" is love!

The Power of Who! It's Not About Selling, But Alignment

In *The Power of WHO!*, I challenged many widely held, preconceived notions. One of which is the popular concept of Networking, which is Not-Working! Why? Because the concept is filled with cold calls, mass emails, and 15-second elevator pitches instead of with people WHO know and love you! Add to that, it's faceless. It's handing out business cards to strangers like they are mints! I get thousands of resumes sent to me: Dear Sir, To Whom It May Concern, and Dear Recruiter. "Dear Recruiter" is an oxymoron. In 40-plus years of executive recruiting, I've never placed anyone from a resume.

But what if I told you that you didn't have to go any further than the people you already know!? Hear me on this: it's all about your inner circle of friends! Did you know that over 80% of jobs come from "one" phone call from a friend? References, endorsements, and testimonials are your greatest allies. My purpose in writing *The Power of WHO!* was to introduce you to a revolutionary concept that would get you moving toward your goals and dreams in ways you never imagined possible. This strategy has been time-tested and has worked successfully for over 50 years. This idea of the WHO is really important! These are the people that know you, know what you really want, and in fact, they may know WHO you are and what you want even better than you might remember!

My greatest honor is to be there for my friends on their worst days. They have been there for me, and I am always looking for ways I can be there for them. Friends are treasures! When you start to understand the Power of WHO and the magnitude of 2 Chairs, everything changes! Step out of the box and into your WHO. And then take a seat across from God WHO always has something helpful to say if you listen!

Q&A WITH BOB

What is your favorite movie?

It's a Wonderful Life. Bailey is in trouble. And of course, who's he going to turn to in his worst of troubles? Is he going to go to his friends? No, he goes to Mr. Potter. When Mr. Potter says he won't help him, what does Bailey do? He's going to jump off a bridge. In the end, it's his brother, his friends, and his wife who come to his aid and say he's the richest man in town. What is he rich with? Friends!

How do you recharge?

I leap out of bed to get to my 2 Chairs!

When I was about to graduate from Southern Methodist University, I had a lot of questions surrounding life goals, dreams, finding a mate, and what to do in times of unexpected trouble!

I had this feeling... I needed to talk to my mom. She said, "Oh, Bob, those are good questions. Of course, I don't have the answers. But I know WHO does! I'm going to teach you a 'secret' that was passed on to me—a 'secret' that I'm not sure you even know is a possibility."

She then said, "If you set this up and do it every day, it'll change your life! Let me ask you three questions. I believe they will lead you in the right direction. Now, these questions are simple. Simple in the fact that you can't believe you haven't asked them. But they're also disruptive."

These three questions became the premise of my book *2 Chairs: The Secret That Changes Everything*. I am excited to say that this book has gone big! I have people all over the world sending me pictures of their 2 Chairs. When you apply this "secret," I believe you'll find God's plan for your life.

1. **Does God know your situation? Yes!**
2. **Is this too hard for Him to handle? No!**
3. **Does God have a good plan for you? Yes!**

Take a deep breath and think about the magnitude of the opportunity. God is *calling you* to an intimate conversation at 2 Chairs! He's not mad at you, He made you, and He makes no mistakes! In fact, what He desires is a deep and intimate relationship; He calls you "friend!" Once you meet with Him, you'll discover something amazing! He has a fantastic plan for you! But to know these plans, you have to stop and listen. Five minutes in the presence of God changes all our best-laid plans.

How do you get started? Simple! All you need is 2 Chairs. One for you, one for God. You sit and have a conversation first thing in the morning. I always start out by saying, "Good morning! Thank you for coming! I'm a mess!" I tell Him all that hurts, all that's bugging you! He knows! Then, I make the exchange! I give Him the problems, and He then gives: peace, joy, insight, wisdom, power, and favor for the day! It's a good trade! My countenance changes because I have sat in the presence of God. That's how I recharge. Mom was right!

What would you tell your 18-year-old self?

You're only remembered in life for two things: the problems you solve and the problems you create. When I heard that, I first thought to myself, *I don't want to create any problems. I am in the problem-solving business of helping others.*

I just want to help. I'm going to stop, pause, pray, and believe that God will give me the right words at the right time. Each of us has had people who have crossed our paths who have helped us in our worst moments—who have helped us with a loan, who gave us a job when we didn't deserve one, who when we stuck our foot in our mouth still loved us and put their arm around us. That gives us an opportunity to be that moment-maker for others today.

Find *The Power of Who!* and *2 Chairs* at all major book retailers. Learn more about Bob Beaudine as a speaker, author, and search executive online and through social media: bobbeaudine.com, eastman-beaudine.com IG: thebobbeaudine
YouTube: @BobBeaudineYOUGOTWHO | Facebook: BobBeaudine.WHO
LinkedIn: Bobwho

 Scan to visit bobbeaudine.com

ANDREW ROSENBERG

Pushing Past Good Enough
Finance, Startups and Investing

Andrew "Andy" Rosenberg is a Hawaii-native, podcast host, and serial entrepreneur who has founded three successful ventures. His businesses span asset classes from oil and gas to real estate, hedge funds, commodities, and more. Today, Andy serves as a mentor and a discerning real estate investor.

My Childhood Fascination with Investing

Most little boys enjoy bedtime tales of slaying dragons. I enjoyed tales about the Hunt brothers trying to corner the silver market, the risks of a margin call, and betting the house on Chrysler stock when it was in bankruptcy.

I loved sitting on my grandfather's lap and reading him the stock quotes from the newspaper. He patiently explained daily volume, dividends, and 52-week highs and lows. While friends collected trading cards, I collected the annual reports of public companies. My father explained his investment in mutual funds and his limited partnership position in a fund lending money to fast food franchisees.

My mother wanted to buy an apartment each year. It was a wise choice, as Hawaii was experiencing a building boom. My parents financially sacrificed, owning one car, and eating in more than most young couples. My parents got up to owning two apartments before they sold them when they were just too busy to be landlords. My father's business was flourishing and I was a handful for my mother. Unfortunately, no one told them about third-party property managers.

I loved reading the periodicals my father subscribed to: *The Wall Street Journal, Fortune,* and *Forbes.* I loved reading about current events from the lens of investors, the successes and failures of publicly traded companies, and macroeconomics. My bedroom was full of every book I could find on stock market investing. Peter Lynch and Warren Buffet were my idols. It was a happy childhood for an only child and bookworm.

For my Bar Mitzvah, six family friends pooled their money together to give me a joint gift, with the caveat that I MUST use it to buy stock. These wise ladies valued the analysis, research, and mindset this gift would impart upon me. J.M. Smucker's stock went from $60 per share to $80 per share, and I was hooked. This was well before the internet, and I was a minor, so my father would call in my buys and sells over the phone for me.

Imagine my excitement upon seeing Gross Anatomy of Finance as an elective high school course. We learned about personal finance and numerous asset classes. However, the most important lesson imparted by my instructor Mr. Gross was, "All this [finance and investments] is great, but just remember, it's like a great sauce added to a steak. Without the steak (family and health), what's the point of the sauce? Does anybody just eat sauce?"

My Surprising Accounting Education

I was so thrilled to be studying finance at a hyper-focused business college renowned for entrepreneurial studies. My grandparents and parents, themselves entrepreneurs, were proud. My maternal great-grandfather owned a liquor distribution company. My maternal grandfather owned an army surplus store and promoted musical big bands. My father owns his court reporting agency.

But, fate would intervene. Most of the professors within the finance department abruptly departed. So, I pivoted to majoring in accounting—close enough, right? It would be one of many fateful pivots that turned out to be a blessing. I benefited from outstanding accounting professors.

Upon graduation, I landed a job in Lucent Technologies, Inc.'s financial leadership development program. I completed three one-year rotations within the company, which was one of the hottest tech stocks at that time. I thought I was on the express ladder to being a corporate executive.

I learned cost accounting at a fiber optics factory in Georgia, treasury operations in the Netherlands, and the madness of supporting sales teams in New Jersey.

From Corporate Career to Real Estate Investing

When the 2000 tech bubble burst, the crash brought me down to Earth. It was the best "bad thing" that's ever happened to me. I didn't enjoy living in the mainland United States or the stifling phoniness of corporate. You can take the island boy off the island, but you can't take the island out of the boy. I returned to Hawaii where fate smiled on me again.

Right before I experienced the next stock market crash in 2008, I sold all my equity holdings to buy an apartment with my fiancé as we were expecting our first child. That's when I realized I needed to learn another asset class for diversification.

We bought two properties in northern Idaho. The first property was a complete disaster, but we sold it for a profit. The second property almost made me give up on real estate investing. Our property manager embezzled a few months of rent. Fortunately, family members talked me into persevering. With the help of a new property manager, our investment flourished. More rental properties and apartment syndication investments followed... but something was missing.

The Constrained Threshold of Success

I read in a collection of interviews with famous traders, *The Market Wizards* by Jack Schwager, "... all losers want to lose and all winners who fall short of their goals are fulfilling some inner need for a constrained threshold of success...." That line by Ed Seykota kicked me in my stomach. I lost a night of sleep after reading this—thanks, Tony Conflitti, for the book recommendation.

Admittedly, I had accepted a constrained threshold of success, or "good enough." It was easy to rationalize. I was financially comfortable working in the family business. I had my wife and one child on track to go to college, a suburban house with a white picket fence, and two dogs. I had largely accomplished the American Dream.

I lost my mother early, first when dementia took her mind and again when she passed away. She was my biggest cheerleader, instilling an absolute belief that I could do great things if I dared to and worked hard enough. I wondered if I would have accepted a constrained threshold of success if I hadn't lost her.

Two years flew by fast, and I found myself hosting my own podcast, appearing as a guest on numerous podcasts, co-hosting a Zoom CRE Meetup with Christina Stevens, CRNA, and posting daily on LinkedIn.

One of my mentors, Ethan Gao, suggested that being a passive investor didn't truly suit me and that I should consider an active role. It seemed crazy at the time. Most active investors aimed to become passive investors, not the other way around. However, if someone I respect so much thought it was a good idea and that I was worthy, I figured I'd better give it a shot. I ended up tripling down by joining three startup ventures.

Douglas Dowell called me and said, "I'm starting my own real estate syndication. Will you come and join me?" I initially told him he was "absolutely bonkers," but now, I'm a co-general partner with Eagles Flight Equity Group.

Third, I'm a co-general partner with Chris Perkins and Dylan Clark at Abundance Asset Management, an investment fund utilizing the QQQ, a large cash position, and zero debt selling options contracts (we don't buy options).

My favorite poem is "Our Greatest Fear" by Marianne Williamson. My favorite lines are, "And as we let our own light shine, we unconsciously give other people permission to do the same. As we are liberated from our own fear, our presence automatically liberates others."

I hope that this story of dream chasing, however deferred, encourages others to chase their own dreams now.

ANDY'S THOUGHT LEADER LESSONS

Investing and Financial Independence

There's a lot of bad advice out there in print, online, in social circles, and even in families. I've been passionate about investing for 33 years. I'm not a registered investment advisor and can't offer financial advice. What I can do is encourage people to question their assumptions, empower them to take control of their wealth, and refer my friends to trustworthy members of the investment community. Most investors base their perception of risk more on narrative than facts. I enjoy walking investors through facts with real-world examples to help them challenge what are often dangerous assumptions. My greatest satisfaction is seeing investors make better choices and not feel dependent upon their advisors.

The biggest obstacle I overcame in my journey of transitioning from passive investor to active investment business ownership was my fear that I'd lose my ability to be objective and unbiased. In each business, there's one rule: I only work with ethical partners driven to do right by our investors, who take our stewardship of people's hard-earned money earnestly, and who zealously ensure that our fiduciary duties remain our utmost priority. Our investors deserve to know that we'll explain the full spectrum of pros and cons.

Mentorship

In Hawaii, we say, "Live aloha." I'd translate that to "Pay it forward." I've asked numerous mentors, "Why me? Why help someone when it's unclear how it could benefit you?"

Most often, when they're done chuckling, they tell the same story. "I benefited from wonderful mentors. I would be disrespecting their legacy by not helping others." There are two things about mentorship. One, the mentee must be worthy and willing to be mentored. Two, the mentor must believe that they are worthy and capable of mentoring.

It sounds obvious, but how many people have you met that could be described as askholes? They ask for advice, but pride or limiting beliefs render them unable to implement sound advice. How often has pride slowed us down from asking for help or even admitting we need help?

As a dad, I've watched the *Harry Potter* movie series countless times, and my favorite Dumbledore quote is, "Help will always be given at Hogwarts to those who deserve it." The mentee must be worthy. How do I define worthy? It's a sense that the person is driven and hardworking and gives freely and frequently. Ethan Gao, a serially successful friend of mine explained, "I can't divorce being able to enjoy working with someone and being able to enjoy being with them socially. The two are the same. It's the same for me when it comes to mentorship and my inner circle."

The first few times I was referred to as someone's mentor, while I was deeply touched, I couldn't accept the idea. I said, "Me a mentor? I'm just a regular guy and your friend." Fortunately, I was called out on this limiting belief and excessive modesty bordering on insecurity. More than one of my inner circle and mentors explained that "Mentors come at different stages of a person's journey." Who will tell you hard truths like this if you don't intentionally nurture an inner circle and open yourself up to being mentored and mentoring others?

Q&A WITH ANDY

What is some of the best advice you've received?

My maternal grandfather told me, "You could stand on your head and spit pennies into a jar and still not everyone would like you."

What is your image of an ideal world?

An ideal world is one in which people take accountability for informed decisions with an understanding of history. There are no solutions, only trade-offs. I dream of a world less driven by hate and fear, no longer manipulated by those who "never let a good crisis go to waste." I'm a traditionalist and anti-establishment at the same time, a champion for having the wisdom to embrace paradox and ambiguity, a numbers guy who loves poetry.

How do you define success?

Waking up in the morning excited about the tasks at hand.

Find investor and entrepreneur Andrew "Andy" Rosenberg on LinkedIn www.linkedin.com/in/andrew-rosenberg-791a0a202. Discover his insights on business, mentorship, and real estate in his podcast, *CRE Spotlight*, available on YouTube.

JAMES BLAKEMORE

Digging Deep
The Persistent Pursuit of Entrepreneurial Gold

James Blakemore is a serial entrepreneur active in oil and gas, real estate investments, mergers and acquisitions, and other diversified businesses. He is the founder, president, and CEO of Road Canyon, LLC, Iron Mountain Capital Group, and Blakemore and Associates of Midland, Texas.

Mining Unexpected Value

In *Three Feet From Gold*, my good friend, author Greg Reid tells of Mr. Darby, who found gold but lacked mining knowledge. After losing the vein, he quit and sold his equipment to a junkman, who used his expertise to find a rich deposit just three feet away. This story, similar to Russell Conwell's *Acres of Diamonds*, mirrors my real-life experience.

In the late 1800s, near Salt Lake City, Utah, a US Army officer discovered the Emma Mine, a fabulously rich silver mine and the greatest of the time. Millions of dollars of silver were harvested from the Emma Mine, until one day, the ore just stopped.

As in the story, the operators of the mine didn't understand the geology of the area. There were major faults that cut the silver deposit into pieces, and the operators had no idea that their silver had been displaced only about one hundred feet. The treasure lay undiscovered for over 50 years until a geologist who studied the area found the continuation of the ore and mined it, until again, it was apparently exhausted.

Years later, I had the opportunity to run the family company by virtue of my uncle, a mining engineer and geologist familiar with the mine, and his brother who took a stock position in it to help finance it. I turned what was then a virtually worthless company into a $1.75 million profit.

How did I do this?

The company had been stagnant and considered worthless for many years with no production due to no proven reserves and the low price of silver. My uncle, the geologist and mining engineer, studied the geology of the area and deduced that there was more ore left to be mined.

We set about proving this. We did the exploration, drilling, sampling, etc., and began to demonstrate the possibility of a new silver discovery.

This mine is in one of the most environmentally sensitive areas of Utah, a canyon used primarily as a watershed for Salt Lake City and a recreational area. These two qualities were pretty incompatible with a major mining operation. We were under the great scrutiny of many people, most of them not too interested in us reopening a major silver mine, bringing with it trucks, dust, dirt, pollution, and noise.

Sometimes your most valuable product may not be the most obvious. I realized that reopening that mine was nearly impossible. The forces that would align against us were so vast and well-funded that even if we could raise the necessary capital, win the countless court battles, and finally get the necessary permits, that would come long after I had passed. It seemed to me that the actual value of this company would be to sell it to a buyer who intended to make sure that there was never any mining in that canyon again. That is exactly what I set out to do and what I ultimately succeeded in doing.

This process took time, money, and energy. LOTS OF TIME! I could easily have quit at any time, and no one would have blamed me. After all, the company had been dormant for nearly 40 years. But, I hung in there. I knew I had something and just needed to study, learn, take my time, and most of all, NEVER GIVE UP! Ultimately, my persistence paid off when I took an all-but-abandoned company and sold it for a $1.75 million profit.

Entrepreneurial Roots

I can trace my entrepreneurism to one occurrence. While I was in college, I had a job that I truly loved. One day, I was called into the manager's office and terminated. It broke my heart. On that day, I determined that I would never be put in a position where someone else had such power over my life and future. To this day, I have never worked for any company that I didn't form or have ownership in.

I am a serial entrepreneur. I love taking an idea and making it into a successful enterprise. I am also an unabashed capitalist. I fervently believe that entrepreneurship and the capitalistic system are the fundamental basis for creating wealth in this country and the world. Every major enterprise—from the oil and gas industry to the auto, tech, and entertainment industries—has its roots in entrepreneurship and capitalism.

My great-grandfather came to Texas from Mississippi as a child in 1880. From his humble beginnings, he built a business empire that included ranching, banking, lumber, oil, real estate, newspaper publishing, and broadcasting. Only through entrepreneurship and capitalism can the son of a subsistence farmer with little education create such an empire worth millions of dollars. I am honored to be his great-grandson and endeavor to follow his example.

I've been involved in numerous ventures including professional photography, radio broadcasting, oil and gas exploration and production, ranching, mining, and real estate rental properties (single and multifamily), manufacturing, and more. All this time, I maintained my involvement in the family business in oil and gas and ranching, descended from my great-grandfather's original business empire.

Current Endeavor

This past year, my life took a turn. Due to differences of opinion with my brother about running the business, I exited the family business which I had grown up in and still loved. As a result, I no longer have access to the family ranch where I grew up.

The silver lining was that this exit provided me with significant capital and time with which to pursue other ventures. This brings me to the next phase of my life. Despite my life-long family history in the oil and gas business, I've always been fascinated by real estate. The famous saying, "They aren't making any more land," kept haunting me, drawing me to the immense potential and wealth that real estate investments can generate.

Over the years, I've accumulated significant experience in this field, from building a real estate development company to owning single-family and multifamily rental properties and operating a workforce housing community. Along the way, I've formed close, beneficial friendships with highly successful operators in various asset classes.

While the oil and gas industry can be extremely lucrative, it is also fraught with significant risks. In real estate, I found a more stable and secure avenue for investment that serves me and my clients. Thus, Iron Mountain Capital Group was born. This project is strategically designed to develop a portfolio of real estate investments tailored to meet the needs of today's busy non-real estate professionals who are looking for lower-risk investments with reasonable returns. Our aim is to deliver exceptional service, mitigate risks effectively, and provide long-term returns for those seeking investment security, generational wealth, and a diversified real estate portfolio that requires minimal time and effort to manage.

My expertise lies in identifying and partnering with the highest-quality, highly experienced operators who have lucrative opportunities across various markets, leveraging in-depth market analysis and employing rigorous due diligence processes to assess the potential of each operator and their investments. I collaborate with this network of experienced, ethical, and highly successful operators in the multifamily, mobile home and RV park, and self-storage asset classes to provide significant returns on risk-mitigated investments. In addition to offering high-quality investment options, I am committed to providing the utmost service to our clients. Consistent, timely, and highly personalized updates on every project are a cornerstone of our approach. This diligence not only safeguards the interests of my investors but also fosters long-term, successful partnerships.

Many times I'm asked why I'm working so hard at this new venture when I just concluded a successful exit from the family business and can take it easy. Many people retire from the business they spent a lifetime in and immediately start to wither away. I can't do that. I value high productivity and being of service. Another successful entrepreneur and speaker friend of mine, when asked when he would retire, replied that the definition of retire was, "To remove from useful service." I certainly don't intend to go down that road.

I have a legacy to live up to. I would hate for my great-grandfather to see that I'm not living up to his example. I believe that I have many useful years ahead, and I want to put as much into them as I can so that when I leave this world, I leave it a better place.

Take Your Time

Yes, I've had setbacks. Some projects haven't worked out. People have come and gone. But Churchill's words are still there. If England, in its darkest hour, can stand alone against Germany's might without surrender, I can persist in business. I have plenty of role models. Edison, Drake, Bell, or more modern examples, Musk, Bezos, and Jobs. They all had their setbacks. I can weather mine.

That mining company I brought back from the brink, I worked with for 20 years before the wonderful moment it put over a million dollars into my pocket. Most of that was part-time, off and on, a week here, another there. I was getting to know the history, the players, the personalities. Once I focused my energies on that project and formulated my plan, it was a more modest five years. It was five years of concentrated effort, five years of persistence, five years of not "giving in."

I think it was worth it.

What about you? When was the last time you gave up on your dream? Did you quit just three feet from gold? What about next time?

JAMES'S THOUGHT LEADER LESSONS

Personal Development

I am deeply involved in personal development and have been for 25 years. I'm very passionate about it. In fact, it is part of my purpose in life and one of my core values.

I learned personal development from a network marketing company that I joined in the early '90s called The People's Network. The product was personal improvement, and the faculty was Jim Rohn, Brian Tracy, Darren Hardy, and other thought leaders in that space. I jumped in with both feet and invested thousands of dollars on personal development programs.

I went through Mastery University with Tony Robbins. I took away from that his concept CANI, Constant and Never-ending Improvement. I work towards growing and improving everything in every way. I think coaching and mentorship is really important.

One of the coaching courses I took was fundamentally built around helping the student or the coaches identify and uncover the things they may be blind to that are standing in their way. I'm always listening to personal development. It's a challenge to myself to be better and pass on what I know to other people, and help inspire them to be better.

Success

Earl Nightingale defined success as "the progressive realization of a worthy ideal." I think success is a journey to be pursued. Great success is finding something you enjoy and that you are passionate about, and pursuing until you achieve. A lot of people define success as material things. I think the simplest definition is to be able to do what I want when I want, how I want, and with whom I want.

Travel

The bigger the plane, the farther it goes, the better I like it. I loved Venice, Barcelona, and Naples. I love to cruise—my wife and I have been on over two dozen dozen cruises. One of my favorite places, a ranch in West Texas where I grew up, I no longer have access to since exiting the family company. I've been to 45 of the 50 states and every country in North America and Central America, except Nicaragua. There are several places on the bucket list.

Q&A WITH JAMES

What is your favorite movie?

I'm a tech junkie, I love science fiction, and I got my degree in television in film production, so I love movies. My all-time favorite is Stanley Kubrick's 2001: A Space Odyssey. The production was cutting-edge and so far ahead of its time. And, it was written by Arthur C. Clarke, one of my favorite science-fiction writers.

What are a few of your favorite quotes?

"Never give in. Never give in. Never, never, never, never give in—in nothing, great or small, large or petty—never give in, except to convictions of honour and good sense. Never yield to force. Never yield to the apparently overwhelming might of the enemy." – Winston Churchill

"If you don't have time to do it right. When are you gonna have time to do it over?" – John Wooden

Who are your mentors and greatest influences?

Winston Churchill was an amazing man. He suffered from depression, battled alcoholism, and endured terrible failures in a number of situations and leadership roles. He had one of the worst naval disasters in history when he was First Lord of the Admiralty which is comparable to the Secretary of the Navy in the US. But when it came to the salvation of England in World War II, he was the man. With dogged determination and refusal to succumb, he made it happen.

Jim Rohn is a mentor. I've used his philosophies in my life for many, many years. Another mentor is Darren Hardy and also Kyle Wilson.

Steve Jobs. I take from him the fact that he never quit. He was fired from his company and immediately created another company that was profoundly successful. He actually created Pixar so that he could sell the NEXT Machine, so there was a use for the NEXT Machine. Then he came back to Apple and made it the world's most valuable company at the time.

What is something most people don't know about you?

A lot of people know I cook barbecue. I've been sober for 27 years. But I'm addicted to Blue Bell Homemade Vanilla Ice Cream.

I was bullied terribly when I was in grade school. I'm very persistent. And I've never found a microphone I didn't like.

What do you consider your superpower?

You probably can't tell by looking at my office, but I am pretty meticulous about what I do.

I'm not a perfectionist, but I want things done right.

What would you tell your 18-year-old self?

I'm a serial entrepreneur, and I've been in a whole bunch of different businesses. I think that's also one of the biggest mistakes I've made. I think the number one thing I would say is to find something that you're passionate about, that you enjoy, and that interests you, and stick with it. Don't change your direction quickly. Be very deliberate about changing what you're doing. It has been said that the most successful people make decisions quickly and change them slowly.

Also, be very careful who you align yourself with. There are a lot of scumbags out there who come dressed in pretty clothes.

What books do you often recommend?

The Magic of Thinking Big by David J. Schwartz
The Slight Edge by Jeff Olson
Think and Grow Rich by Napoleon Hill
The Science of Getting Rich by Wallace Wattles

Serial entrepreneur James Blakemore is active in oil and gas, real estate investing, M&A, and more. His current project is buying and scaling small businesses and strategically developing a portfolio of real estate investments to provide lower-risk investments with reasonable returns to today's busy non-real estate professionals. Contact him at james@jamesblakemore.com or visit www.ironmountaincapitalgroup.com.

JEANETTE ORTEGA

Fit from the Inside Out

Jeanette Ortega is a health and wellness expert, creator of the Bootoga® method, and WBFF Bikini PRO passionate about helping others transform their mind, body, and soul to achieve balance and joy. As a three-time bestselling author and motivational speaker, Jeanette inspires others to become Wellness Warriors and live their dreams through holistic well-being.

The Void Behind the Victories

Over the years, being in fitness, people have assumed that I have it all together. They witness my work ethic, going strong for many years of owning and operating my gym, competing and winning many titles in the fitness industry, and gracing covers of health and fitness magazines—yet throughout all of this, I felt a deeper feeling of constantly having to prove my worth. It was never enough. There was a void inside, and I was trying to fill it with more and more accomplishments which never left me feeling "whole" the way I dreamed they would.

We all have a "POV" (point of view: our opinion or way of thinking) that we assume at a young age—either from parents, a teacher, something a friend said, deep trauma, etc. My point of view was "I am not enough."

I've learned that this POV originated from being adopted. My adoption was one of the BEST things that happened to me in my life; yet, at a young age, I chose to believe it was because I wasn't enough. We create stories in our heads as children, and they remain with us throughout adulthood and carry into every area of our lives. I didn't give myself time or permission to understand this or love "myself" for exactly who I was. I was too busy running my business and feeding the need to always look and be a certain way for others.

As a consequence, I saw my POV show up not only in my business but also in my personal relationships. It wasn't until I survived a very emotional divorce many years ago, and then a few long relationships that turned out to be some of the hardest lessons of my life, that I decided to dig deep to get to the bottom of my mess and heal my wounded heart.

Finding Who I Am

There I was, frustrated and angry at myself, my gym, my relationship at the time, my finances, and my body. I had no internal peace. I would cry, wondering why everything seemed like it was falling apart all at once. I had worked so hard. I had done everything I could possibly think of, and the worst feeling of all was that I felt like I wasn't enough in all areas of my life.

I was standing in the way of my own greatness. I didn't love myself enough to appreciate my accomplishments or accept people's love, help, and guidance—or even my own inner guidance.

It was time for me to surrender, time to stop resisting love, joy, and happiness for myself and believe that I was enough. I was worthy of self-love. I had to put a stop to these limiting beliefs and figure out the root of it all. My first question, *Where did this POV come from?*

The root was LOVE, or lack thereof. In therapy, I realized how much "my story" of my adoption created the lack of receiving love since I deemed myself "not enough." When there is fear of love, lack of love, no self-love, or hurt, it blocks us from receiving anything greater.

When I was emotionally ready to grasp this, it blew my mind. My thoughts and actions were fear-based, which attracted more fear into my mind, body, soul, and ultimately, my life. The void I was trying to fill was fear of being loved, not enough, and seen just as I am.

We are always creating our own "reality" based either on fear or love. Once this sinks into our spirits, we have the choice to shift our entire thought process. We have the power to make new choices. I had to ask myself, am I willing to live in love or in fear? Are my decisions and actions based upon fear or love?

Once these answers were clear to me, I had to step into the place of the unknown and trust myself enough to do the work in therapy. I had already completed so much personal development work over the years. *How did I miss some of these crucial pieces?* I realized that we are always in a state of constant change, and we don't know what we don't know until the time comes for us to be open for healing to occur.

What did I truly want? Not for others, but for me? It was time to be open, vulnerable, and authentic with myself, my friends, and my family.

I love health and fitness and always will, but to me, fitness means so much more than just the physical. We need to be fit in our minds, bodies, and souls for true health and wellness to occur. I knew I was here to help people heal emotionally, spiritually, and on a soul level, but first, it had to start with me.

Laying Down the Layers

I showed myself some grace, knowing that I had many layers to uncover and peel back, one at a time, until I got to my core. This was my moment to continually surrender to the unknown, the true love of myself, and my gifts and talents. I would remind myself that I was strong enough to get through all the years of emotions that were built up inside of me. It was time to release all of what no longer served me.

I read book upon book about adoption, and this yielded so much insight and clarity. Almost every line that I read, I thought, *This is me, I do that,* and it helped me understand why. There is power in knowledge. This knowledge helps us to identify the triggers in our lives. It shows us where we are reactive versus finding a healthy conscious resolution, despite how much we want to go back to our old ways of being and handling situations. Reading and researching led me to find my birth parents, meet them, and have a beautiful connection, an understanding of my adoption and closing the wound of "I'm not enough."

Healing takes action. My actions provided an uncomfortableness that led to my growth and a healthy, happy completion in my life. It was freeing.

Meditation was also a game-changer for me. It has been one of the constants in my life, and when I fall off track with it, I am always reminded to get back to it. There's no wrong or right way to meditate. The best type is the one that fits your daily routine. You might feel more relaxed straight after meditating, but the ripple effects—including attitudinal and behavioral change—come after making meditation a regular habit. There is clarity and peace in the mind and body which also helps our parasympathetic nervous system while we are healing any traumas.

Journaling became another part of my healing. Writing guides us to release emotions. Writing a letter to someone, whether or not you send it, is so healing. I would "free flow" a lot about whatever came to my mind, and it usually led me to what I needed to release. This brought me peace and a confirmation that I was on the right path.

I believe we often feel that we have done "enough" to let go of our baggage, yet if we don't allow ourselves to feel the challenging emotions of surrender, we still hold on to it. If we stop when the healing becomes challenging, eventually, our baggage starts to build up.

I was patient and stayed the course, yet it took quite some time to heal. It was one of the most challenging couple of years of my life, but I am a completely different woman today versus who I was when this soul-searching journey began. For this, I am so grateful.

Mind, Body, and Soul Fitness

I knew I was here to help guide, heal, and be of service to anyone I encountered. I was to create a program and workshops that incorporated being fit in mind, body, and soul, not just the physical aspect of fitness—the whole meaning of true wellness and fitness. I was to help my clients, family, friends, and eventually, people globally (starting in Belize, my first humanitarian trip), to understand their mind and body connection from the inside out. I would help guide them with true transformation of their mindset, physical body, and spiritual fitness for a lasting change to live the life of their dreams and pass this on to their families and communities.

Hence, my fitness method Bootoga® was born—a fusion of boot camp, yoga, and meditation. This inspired me to create my own workshops, complete my life coach certification, and create programs to serve the community of people looking and longing for an answer from within, a deeper purpose in life, but just not knowing how to access it. My method serves all three aspects for a complete, balanced life centered in self-love, the root of it all.

Building this program and my workshops helped me heal myself, and then it helped heal young ladies in rehab centers recovering from drugs, alcohol, and prostitution. It helped women in prison in Belize and young, underserved Belizean children in a summer program, along with my gym clients, private celebrity clients, and more. We are all in search of true love, but we must first love ourselves. When we get out of our fearful thoughts, our true presence appears. This is our authentic self, the self that is unconditional love.

Today, I am taking this program and creating a platform for women of age who are now encountering the menopause years. We are barely learning to understand this time in a woman's life. I am creating a program to help women reclaim their health, bodies, and minds in joy, peace, clarity, and self-love. Personally, these past four years of menopause have been some of the most insightful and disruptive years of my life. I have gone down the rabbit hole and want to provide information and knowledge to women for an empowered life in these years.

JEANETTE'S THOUGHT LEADER LESSONS

Pickleball and Recovery

I never thought I would enjoy pickleball as much as I do, but I love it. I'm now two years into being a pickleball addict. I've played and won tournaments, yet the best part is the amazing community of people. This sport is great for cardio, keeping active, and strategic thinking. As with any sport, there can be injuries, so it is important to add in rest days, yoga, and mobility to honor your body for the long haul.

I also highly recommend weight strength training. We need to keep building our muscles to protect our joints and bones. This becomes more and more important as we age.

Recovery is essential. On my rest days, I rotate infrared saunas, cold plunges, massages, and acupuncture as recovery aids. There are so many benefits to these, such as weight loss, skin health, circulation, sleep, and pain management, to list a few. I suggest trying them and seeing which work best for your body.

Where to Start with Fitness

Fitness is different for everyone and knowing your "WHY" is important so you stay committed to your health goals.

Accountability then becomes huge for consistency. We can talk about our goals all day long, but if we don't have someone to show up to, we usually don't do it. When we start a new routine, it takes time to create a habit. The first 30 days are crucial, so as a coach, I ask my clients to report to me weekly—same day, same time. At first, accountability may seem challenging, but in my experience, clients end up loving the relationship that has been nurtured.

Daily Rituals

When I get up, one of the first things I do is take a walk with my dog with a gracious cup of coffee. This moves me into the sunshine which helps wake me up, gets my body moving, and starts to regulate my cardiovascular and neurological systems. Sometimes I take my earbuds and listen to a meditation, but most days I want to listen to the birds, be in nature, and get present to gratitude.

After, I refer to my list for the day. I organize my time for work, journaling, errands, workouts, and pickleball. I have to get in my workout. This is a non-negotiable for me and one of the best times of the day. I love the feeling of providing my body with the strength and endurance to carry out any task in my life.

I end the day with warm water with lemon and ginger or peppermint tea for digestion and reflection. Sometimes I'll journal about my day and then maybe what I have the next day, focusing on gratitude.

Q&A WITH JEANETTE

Have you had any past challenges that turned out to be blessings?

The sale of my gym in Los Angeles was a big challenge for me. Two years prior, someone asked if I was interested in selling, and there was no way. My gym was my baby. When the sale was complete, it felt like I lost my identity. I owned my gym for so many years, I didn't know who I was without it. I went through such a shift and came out the other end stronger, knowing who I truly was inside versus what everybody saw me as.

Who are your mentors and greatest influences?

I love Maya Angelou. She speaks to my soul. Her voice would remind me of my great-grandmother, who was the minister and founder of our church. When my great-grandma would speak, you would just listen. It would just resonate with you. I feel this in Maya Angelou. Her wisdom and her presence are powerful yet with kindness and love.

Ambassador Shabazz, Malcolm X's daughter, is one powerful woman. I've traveled with her to Belize quite a few times on humanitarian trips. She is filled with so much wisdom and grace. I always tell people who first meet her to listen when she speaks because this woman drops wisdom constantly. She has had quite a life and she speaks loud for those that are not heard. She is a role model for so many women that power and grace can co-exist.

How do you recharge?

I love to recharge by taking a complete day off either at the pool or, if I'm traveling, by the beach. Reading a book, having a good glass of wine, being with my husband and dog or enjoying time with good friends and having great conversations.

What is your favorite song?

"Strength, Courage & Wisdom" by India Arie. That song inspired my first tattoo. It talks about having the strength, courage, and wisdom to show up and be who you are, to own your voice, your gifts, and your talents.

Jeanette Ortega is a health and wellness expert, writer, three-time bestselling author, fitness model, creator of Bootoga®, celebrity trainer, life coach, speaker, menopause coach, and WBFF Bikini PRO. Contact her at Extremefitchic@gmail.com, JeanetteOrtega.com, Bootoga.com
IG: @extremefitchic @bootogalifestyle
Twitter: @extremefitchic Facebook: Jeanette Ortega

DOMINIC LAGRANGE

Personal Responsibility in Love and Success

Expert advisor and coach of visionary leaders Dominic Lagrange has coached over 8,000 clients into action, both physically and mentally, including over 350 nutrition and sports coaches. Since 2014, he has coached over 200 leaders in their development as super achievers and inspirational leaders.

The Woman of My Life

In 2003, I had my first experience with intuition. I was coming to the end of a difficult relationship, typical of those first loves where our personal identity, values, and limits are not yet clearly defined.

I have no memory of why I went out that night. I was in the middle of preparing for a fitness competition. I was on a very strict diet, and skinny, practically sickly, but I still went out with my cousin.

We were in this bar called Le Phoenix, a tavern in the basement of Au Vieux St-Georges in Quebec. We were packed like sardines. The music was blaring. Everyone was partying, except me! There I was, with my water bottle, really wondering what I was doing at this hour in a packed bar. I thought I was a real idiot because I knew I was going to feel like a dog when I got home, partly because I would not eat. Even back then, I was possessed by an excessive level of commitment. This capacity to be in action would take me on a rollercoaster ride over the next decade and a half, ultimately making me an inspirational leader, and later, a visionary leader.

I was about to leave when I saw this woman walk past me. Time slowed down before my eyes. The music faded away. This woman was a vision, and despite the crowd, all I could see was her. Nudging my cousin with my elbow, I said, "That's the kind of woman I want in my life."

Eight months passed before I saw her again.

I was in a relationship at that time, but my heart wasn't fully in it. A few weeks before my ex and I would permanently part ways, I was in the same bar with friends, and I saw this woman again. My heart recognized her. For the next three weeks, every Thursday, this girl appeared at that bar, and every time, I couldn't stop looking at her. She hypnotized me.

My ex and I broke up on a Sunday, and despite myself, I was excited, because now I had the opportunity to take action.

This vision, this woman, haunted me. I wanted to make a good impression, so I imagined the perfect scenario for approaching her. I could already see us falling in love, getting married, and starting a family.

Our first meeting was actually anything but chivalrous... but in the end, I must have charmed her because Sylvie and I have been together ever since.

Life Is Full of Surprises

Over a decade later, in 2016, I was looking for "the solution." I saw myself as a failure. I couldn't keep a promise I'd made nine years earlier, the one where I said I was going to take my family to the top, where I said that, thanks to my success, our future would be glorious! It all looked perfect from the outside. I was married to Sylvie, an extraordinary woman. We had a beautiful home. I had a provincial bodybuilding champion title, and I had a booming business in a new business model. The truth was quite different.

I'd just come out of the saga of my previous company, where I'd experienced failure, betrayal, and devaluation of my work. At the same time, our family was going through a descent into a miserable daily existence. We were trying to live the best way we could with our oldest child Robin's diagnosis of autism, hyperactivity, and severe dyspraxia, while giving as much time as possible to our baby, Mélodie, who was also suffering. Financially, we struggled to make ends meet. And finally, we were trying to rekindle the love in our relationship and family.

Back in 2012, I had decided to save myself first, to the detriment of my family, when they needed me. At a time when our nest was on fire and it felt like everything was falling down around me, instead of acting responsibly and being a leader for my family, I took refuge where I knew I was good, where I could demonstrate that I wasn't a loser and failure, by resuming my bodybuilding career. Doing this effectively left Sylvie alone with the young children and providing for the family.

Between my business trips that went nowhere, my training, and the four bodybuilding competitions in four years, in 2016, we were in hell.

The Turning Point

Discovering Darren Hardy and his Living Your Best Year Ever program, inspired by his mentor Jim Rohn, marked a major change in my life. The seven years that followed were inspired by a concept: "If you want more, you have to become more...."

This phrase enabled me to gradually emerge from the abyss and become the father, husband, man, and inspirational leader I had always wanted to be. This journey allowed me to define myself in excellence. It helped me understand true success and the process of living like a visionary leader guided by his purpose for existing.

Who I am as a man today and what I do in life as a coach and advisor are the consequences of this two-decade journey and a never-ending quest for success. It's an achievement that developed on a chaotic path, and there's nothing heroic about it.

Today, I am empowered to coach people to create clarity in their goals and to be an example of a happy and healthy success for their family by living in excellence, being in action with a 360-degree approach, and creating a healthy success for myself and my family.

Today, I have a deep respect for the person who means the most to me, a person who allowed me to define myself as an inspiring leader, and who gave me the chance to go where very few men will go or understand. I'm enormously grateful to you, Sylvie, the woman of my life, for keeping the family spirit intact throughout all these years... AND I'm even more grateful that you're in my life today. It's up to me to return the favor and show you that you made the right choice and that this sacrifice will allow us to achieve our full potential, without regret, surrounded by the people we love.

DOMINIC'S THOUGHT LEADER LESSONS

Leadership and Vision

The 100-Year Vision I use in my coaching is not just a plan for an organization or project, it's an extension of a visionary leader's purpose for existing projected and magnified to impact society positively. It's a long-term aspiration that guides leaders in building an impactful legacy, opportunities, education, behavior, wealth, and healthy success.

True Success

One day, the CEO of a multinational company in Canada shared with me his definition of true success in life. He pointed at the luxury car in the parking lot and said, "You know, I've worked my whole life to afford this kind of car, a big house, and multiple properties. But once I acquired them, I realized the actual satisfaction I got from them was minimal. True success is being happy with the people you love."

Since that day, I've understood that success as a father and husband is the legacy I want to leave for society. It's about learning how to be happy and successful in life and in business and learning how to fully realize oneself. For me, educating my children to experience healthy success through my actions and example is the most beautiful legacy I can leave.

Health and Wellness

In the life of a super-achiever, wellness is more than just good health. It's the means to reach an unlimited level of achievement and the means to maintain it.

For me, health is the foundation. Health brings us to full awareness in the present moment. Investing in 360-degree wellness ensures that we are 100% in control of our resources and that we are masters of our time.

The Pursuit of Knowledge

We must make choices that will allow us to demonstrate our worth, be the solution, and create a significant impact in people's lives. In my private coaching group, we appreciate the idea of creating more value for valuable people. At certain moments in our lives, we have the chance to show this value. It is up to you to decide whether luck will lead you to the top or if you choose to become the solution right now. Continuing education and personal development are the keys. As Jim Rohn aptly said, "If you want more, you have to become more."

Relationships and Family

Success is being happy, united with the people we love. My greatest accomplishment is having climbed this mountain with our children and having nurtured a life of love and sharing with my life partner. I realized years ago that to be well and happy, I had to first focus on my family's development and prioritize those relationships. I understood that if my family relationship was healthy, I became limitless; I could fully achieve my goals in my purpose for existing and push my BHAG (big hairy audacious goal) even further. However, the priority must remain the family. For me, I had to start rebuilding this relationship with my family 15 minutes at a time. Today, my family and I are climbing a metaphorical Mount Everest. I couldn't dream of being part of a better team for this adventure.

Spirituality

Even after forgiving certain significant events, feelings of powerlessness and incompetence can persist, leading to impulsive actions and a relentless pursuit of external validation. A leadership workshop powerfully illuminated this reality for me, using the analogy of a punctured Styrofoam cup to represent emotional wounds. The water poured into the cup, symbolizing self-confidence, and would flow out through the holes, illustrating how our past can erode our current confidence.

The workshop facilitator offered a liberating perspective: these holes, these wounds from the past, will never fully disappear, but we can choose to "fill the cup" every day by nourishing our self-confidence. Much like in a garden, this confidence needs to be consistently maintained and watered. This realization was a turning point. I saw not only my personal responsibility in maintaining self-confidence but also the power of gratitude and self-appreciation as tools for personal growth.

Q&A WITH DOMINIC

What is something most people don't know about you?

At the age of 11, I was not able to read and could barely construct written sentences.

What are a few of your favorite quotes?

If you want more you have to become more.
Success is repetition.
True leaders are always responsible. Own it.

What is some of the best advice you've received?

You can change whatever you want in your mind simply by thinking differently.
We can do whatever we want, no matter where we start in life.

Who are your mentors and greatest influences?

I've had several influential mentors in my life: Nelson Ayotte (fitness coach and mentor for 10 years), Darren Hardy, and now Kyle Wilson. But an unexpected mentor has influenced me through his desire, commitment, and lack of limitations in life, and that's my son, Robin. Although I am his father and it's my role to educate him, he has taught me significant and powerful lessons on self-improvement.

Have you had any past challenges that turned out to be blessings?

At one point I lost my business while I was raising a child with autism and another who, from a young age, had significant learning delays and a great need for self-confidence and appreciation. During that time, we created a family dynamic focused on taking small steps and unshakable personal growth. We know that success is achieved through action.

What do you make sure you always do?

Every day I repeat my magic sentence: I love myself, I appreciate myself, thank you life.

What hobbies do you enjoy?

Reading, mountain biking, and ski touring.

What books do you frequently recommend?

The Big Five for Life by John Strelecky
Leading an Inspired Life by Jim Rohn
The Compound Effect by Darren Hardy
Good to Great by Jim Collins
Built to Last by James C. Collins and Jerry I. Porras

What would you tell your 18-year-old self?

1. Eliminate all negative talk from your speech.
2. Appreciate every moment. Say "thank you."
3. Be aware of the impact of your relationships. Are they positive? Do they make you feel bigger or smaller? Deep down, you know.
4. Don't silence that little voice that's constantly speaking to you. It's there to guide you. Learn to listen to it.
5. You attract success by the person you become. So, work harder on yourself than your current job. Become a better person.
6. Never stop learning. Feed your subconscious with inspiring, constructive works.
7. At the same time, eliminate all negative information. You no longer have the right to be influenced in that way. Your calling in life demands it.
8. Don't focus on the how! Look at this image of yourself, love it, and live excellence every day.

What is your image of an ideal world?

I am working to create a world where people can fully realize and fulfill themselves, a world without limits to creating a better world and making an impact. I strive to support and develop inspiring leaders as they achieve their raison d'etre (RDE) within a 100-year vision. In an ideal world, community leaders will have the opportunity to take action and realize their potential in turn as visionary leaders one day.

What has been your greatest lesson?

Never take things for granted.

Super achiever leaders contact Dominic Lagrange for coaching in clearly defining their purpose for existing and to become an example of healthy success for their family and community. Dominic coaches entrepreneurs to lead their businesses in excellence and to build legacies of knowledge sharing, recognition, and self-fulfillment. To join the 100-year vision group and impact society as a visionary leader, contact Dominic at: www.dominiclagrange.com or info@dominiclagrange.com.

 Be part of my list, in the mind of a super achiever.

RON JONES

Learning Curve
Leadership, Relationships, and Wellness

Ron Jones brings a wealth of experience and knowledge as a 40+ year veteran of the insurance and leadership industry, Grant Cardone certified coach and trainer, entrepreneur, author, and speaker who has traveled across the country to meet with sales teams of all sizes.

Dyslexia and Anxiety

When I was nine years old, sitting in Sunday school, I felt my heart race as the teacher announced we would be reading from the Bible. The prospect of reading aloud filled me with dread because I couldn't read. As my turn approached, a wave of nausea hit me. I seized the moment to tell the teacher I didn't want to read, avoiding the humiliation of exposing my inability.

My challenges with reading began early. In the fourth grade, after my mother remarried, we moved to Texas. Despite being nine years old, I was placed back in the third grade because I couldn't read or recite my ABCs. This setback, however, didn't deter me from aspiring to success.

From a young age, I exhibited an entrepreneurial spirit—shining shoes, delivering newspapers, and collecting Coke bottles for deposit to earn lunch money. By high school, I had mastered the art of avoiding reading aloud. In 1975, as a sophomore, I approached a counselor about graduating early. With a plan that included additional classes, a work-study program at McDonald's, and a correspondence course (completed with the help of my girlfriend), I graduated in 1976, skipping my junior and senior years.

Realizing college wasn't immediately feasible, I enlisted in the United States Air Force in June 1976. Although my learning disability quickly surfaced, my strengths as a marksman and runner gained recognition. Classroom tests, however, led to my training instructor questioning my abilities. Determined to prove myself, I persuaded him to give me another chance and enlisted a squad mate's help for tutoring.

Technical training brought new challenges, but with extended test times, I thrived, and I excelled in the dexterity-required tasks that being a dental technician required. After my Air Force service, I continued in the Texas Air National Guard. Even now, reading aloud remains a struggle due to my dyslexia. Despite overcoming the embarrassment, I recognize the discomfort it causes others so I avoid it.

Dyslexia has been a unique challenge, yet it has honed my listening skills and compelled me to develop strong coping mechanisms, like memorization. These experiences have not only shaped my character but also strengthened my leadership abilities, teaching me the value of perseverance and adaptability.

Entrepreneur Roller Coaster

By the time I was 24, my deep-seated entrepreneurial spirit had fully emerged. I started, owned, and operated three dental labs, employing 12 people. After a few successful years, I expanded my ventures into real estate investments, mortgage banking, and construction, becoming a millionaire before the age of 27. However, by the time I was 30, I lost everything.

This was a devastating blow but also a period of immense personal growth and self-discovery. I had to look inward and question how I had ended up in such a situation.

In my 20s, I had become incredibly arrogant. Everything I touched seemed to turn to gold, and I believed it was all because of me. I thought I was smarter than everyone else. I couldn't blame my downfall on my family, friends, associates, business partners, or the economy. It was entirely my doing.

I wish I could say I immediately learned all the lessons I needed to. However, the following years were challenging. I went through a divorce and became a single parent. I tried to be a good father to my two daughters, succeeding in some ways but failing in others. Tragically, I was a poor father to my son, who took his own life before I could build a relationship with him.

It wasn't until I grasped some simple yet profound principles that I was able to rebuild my life. These principles were implemented over time through consistent, rational thoughts and behaviors. Over the past 40 years, I have overcome financial, relational, and emotional destitution. My only regrets are the times I hurt people in my life. Now, I understand that when I am with my children or grandchildren, they are the most important thing.

After Bankruptcy: Leadership and Taking the Leap

In 1987, after my divorce, I found myself with only $270 in my pocket. Though I had a strong desire to continue on my entrepreneurial path, the need to pay bills was pressing. I took whatever jobs I could find, including waiting tables at the Black-Eyed Pea Restaurant.

I was very interested in entering the insurance business. In Texas, you can get a temporary license and then you have 90 days to pass the licensing exam. Each time I took the test, I struggled to read the questions and ultimately failed. This led to a cycle of starting, quitting, and taking W-2 jobs in between.

Determined to find a more stable path, I decided to pursue an associate degree in counseling. Counseling offered an entrepreneurial angle, allowing me to choose my clients, set my rates, and manage my schedule.

While I excelled as a counselor, the emotional toll was significant. I found it difficult to leave my clients' problems at work, and the job became very draining for me.

One day, my brother Harold mentioned that an aviation company was hiring. He was going to drive a truck for them and suggested I check it out. Despite knowing nothing about the aviation industry, I applied and became a ramp agent.

After completing my training, I confidently told Harold, "Give me 90 days. Everyone in that room... I'm going to be their supervisor."

Harold responded, "You know, somehow I believe that." True to my word, I was promoted to lead within 90 days, then to supervisor, and to manager over two airlines within nine months. I knew I could succeed because I understood people, management, and leadership. My business background helped me identify gaps and inefficiencies, and I approached my role by being helpful, avoiding stepping on toes, and giving credit to others whenever possible.

During this time, I met my wife, Diana. We were celebrating my promotion to national trainer for the East Coast when a friend pointed out that a lady across the room kept looking at me and suggested I ask her to dance. After a few drinks, I cheekily said, "She'll ask me." She did ask me to dance, and we married six weeks later. We've now been married for 23 years.

When we got together, Diana was a schoolteacher, and I was working a regular job. In 2004, I told her, "Honey, I'm quitting my job to sell insurance on commission. She had no experience with entrepreneurship and initially begged me not to quit. Eventually, she decided to trust me and adjusted to this new reality. Four years later, thanks to our decision, she retired from teaching and hasn't had to work since 2008.

Wellness Clinic

The COVID-19 pandemic was a turning point for me. With the looming threat of the virus, I decided it was time to get healthy. I began researching, listening to podcasts, and learning about anti-aging and biohacking.

I started a regimen of intravenous (IV) vitamin treatments every two or three weeks and took daily ice baths. I wish I had made these changes earlier! I transformed for the better. I began feeling stronger and looking better than I did more than eight years before. Physically, mentally, and emotionally, I once again felt like I was 45. My initial goal was to get healthy, but soon, I noticed my skin clearing up and wrinkles fading away. This transformation greatly boosted my confidence. This part of me was always there; I just didn't realize it.

I began to think, *Why not start my own wellness company? Even if it doesn't make money, I want to make these life-changing treatments available to others.*

Then, at a treatment, I met the man who was administering my IV, a young paramedic with entrepreneurial aspirations. Together, we decided to create an IV business—a new treatment clinic. This would allow me to mentor and support him while we fostered a meaningful cross-generational bond. I know our friendship was meant to be.

I didn't anticipate starting another business, especially as I approached 65. I just started taking naps for the first time in my life and am loving it. But I don't see myself ever retiring. I knew that whatever I did next, it would be in business, and it would be for myself and those I care about.

I'm excited as I launch my first of many clinics, as I bring the knowledge of how to start, run, and scale a business. This venture is for my partners, future partners, and anyone else who joins us. It is about leaving a legacy for generations to come.

RON'S THOUGHT LEADER LESSONS

Mentorship

I'm at a time in my life where my greatest joy and my greatest pleasure is from being able to mentor.

I'm mentoring the next generation in entrepreneurism. That said, I've learned just as much, or maybe more, from my mentees as I have taught them. I've learned so much from my grandkids. They're not necessarily in the business, but I am involved in their lives and feel like a mentor to them. On Wednesday nights, I meet with a small group of teenage high school boys at my church. It's not about what I can say to them, it's about what they're saying. I listen. I am empathetic and understanding. They're not going to want to listen to me until they know I've heard them. The saying is no one cares until they know you care.

Self-Discipline

It takes discipline to get up at five o'clock in the morning and take a dip in a 37-degree tub of water for three to seven minutes. It takes even more discipline to do that every single morning. I've taken an ice bath every day for the past year, and I'm going to do it every single day as long as I can. First, because they make me feel fantastic and second because of the journey to make it happen.

The discipline I've developed through consistently taking ice baths has given me the confidence to make other health decisions in my life. Knowing that I can commit to something as challenging as an ice bath has empowered me to pursue other healthy habits with the same determination.

The first time I went out of town, I almost missed a day. As it came down to the wire, somebody at the conference walked up to me and said, "Hey, I don't know what you'll think about this, but I've got a bathtub in my hotel room if you want to take an ice bath in there."

And I said, "I don't know you. But yes," and went to buy the ice!

There are things out of your control. But where there is a will, there really is a way. You start getting creative when you are committed to achieving a goal! It has become such a routine for me that I don't even think about how cold it is. Sometimes I even enjoy it.

Q&A WITH RON

What is your favorite quote?

"Condemnation without investigation is the purest form of ignorance."

I've said that for years. That's how I would combat people who didn't want to buy from me if it was a product or service I knew they needed. That's the reason I've been successful in most of my endeavors. When I use that quote, I'm thinking they just don't have enough information yet. They don't know what they don't know.

What has been your greatest lesson?

"Is this really going to matter in one hundred years?" I always thought I understood what that meant. But I now realize, all the worldly things I've worked for, a house, cars, Nike shoes, offices... in a hundred years they're not going to be worth anything.

I build with the understanding that in one hundred years, even my bloodline will probably not even know who I was or anything I accomplished. Instead of trying to make them remember me, I think it's important to value the relationships I have right now. Cherish these moments.

How do you define success?

It sounds morbid, but at the end of the day, success is when I'm being lowered into the ground and people look back and think about the ways I helped them or changed their life. Success is being able to have an impact on other people's lives.

Ron Jones is a life-long entrepreneur and author. Check out *Discover Your Superhero Within*, a deep dive into what it really means to be a superhero and seeing the superhero in those you love and *Breaking Boundaries*, an exploration of intergenerational cooperation in the insurance industry. rjones08@att.net / 817-734-7400

 Connect with Ron

RON WHITE

Two-Time US Memory Champion and Creator of The Afghanistan Memory Wall

Two-time US Memory Champion Ron White is a speaker, author, and trainer. He has been featured on Stan Lee's **Superhumans***, National Geographic's* **Brain Games***, CBS'* **The Morning Show***, and more. Ron is the creator of the Afghanistan Memory Wall, his tribute to fallen soldiers in Afghanistan where he served in the US Navy.*

Paper Boy of the Year

My first job was a paper route at age 14. While the typical kid would sign up one household for the paper per day, I signed up eight to 10. It was the first time I felt good at something. If you got eight sign-ups in three months, you won a season pass to Six Flags. In a weekend, I was getting me, my parents, and my sister a season pass. I was *Mid-Cities Daily News'* carrier of the year. It was a fun time, and it taught me lessons that carry me to this day.

At 18, I worked as a telemarketer for a chimney cleaning service. It was brutal. One day, the man who picked up interrupted my script to say, "Ron, we don't want our chimney cleaned. We're trying to sell our house."

Then I said the words that changed my life: "Sir, don't hang up the phone. If you're trying to sell your house, you're going to need a clean chimney." I was only 18, but I knew how to overcome objections.

Laughing, he asked me, "Do you want a job?" He offered to pay me more than I was making, which was pretty easy to do, and I took the offer.

How My Speaking Career Began

It was July 1991, and I was beyond eager to start my new position. At the time, there was a popular infomercial on TV for Kevin Trudeau's Mega Memory. It seemed like magic to me. Now, I had the chance to work with them.

When I started telemarketing for them, I observed their speakers going out to give presentations and sell, and I knew that's what I wanted to do. The company wasn't interested. I was 18, and they didn't have a speaker under 28. Most of them were closer to 40, and all were established in business.

So, I joined Toastmasters and invited my sales manager to go with me. I wanted him to see me speak. Once he did, he said, "Ron, you need to get a tent and do revivals. You can speak!"

I said, "I don't know if I want to do revivals, but maybe...memory training?"

That's when a speaker, who was bringing in a remarkable $30,000 a month, quit the company. There were two choices—cancel all his speeches or get a new speaker. They had no speakers in training, but they had me. Even if I didn't make any money, they wouldn't come out any worse with me than if they had canceled.

The first year, I was terrible, the worst in the company by far, according to the numbers. With the generous coaching from the president of the company, it took me a year to achieve the company average. Now, I do much more than that. I just had to take that time to learn.

Memory Expert, But No Special Ability

People always want to know when I realized I had special memory ability. The truth is, I don't have a special ability. I learned a system that anybody can learn. People will say, "I remember the face, but I don't remember the name." That's because they look at the face but never see the name.

The mind remembers what it sees, so you have to visualize what you want to remember, whether it's a deck of cards, phone number, poem, quote, or speech. The first step is to turn what you want to remember into a picture. The next step is to place that picture somewhere. This step is a technique called the mind palace, which has been around for 2,500 years. Put simply, in the mind palace technique, you use your house to memorize things.

The majority of people can say with confidence that they can memorize three words. The magic of the memory palace is that you can use this system to memorize three items one hundred items or 7,000 items once you understand how it's done. The trick is to apply the technique to what interests you—a speech, your classmates' names, or knowledge to help you in your job.

Naval Service, Two-Time US Memory Champion

When September 11th happened, I joined the Military as a Navy Reservist at 28 years old.

I served in the United States Navy from 2002 to 2010. In 2007, I was deployed to Afghanistan. I was an Intelligence Specialist. IS1, Petty Officer 1st class.

I did 51 convoys, but I saw no combat action. There is nothing extraordinary about my service or deployment. It was just a regular deployment like many others. But countless men and women were in extraordinary circumstances. Combat veterans and too many others paid the ultimate sacrifice.

When I got back, I decided I wanted to compete in the US Memory Championships. I hired a coach, United States Navy SEAL TC Cummings. He taught me a lot about mindset and discipline. He had me memorizing cards underwater. He had me memorizing cards in noisy bars. He had me changing my diet, getting up early, and training like a Navy SEAL would train for war so that I would be a well-trained brain athlete for the memory tournament.

I won back-to-back years, becoming a two-time USA Memory Champion, and set the record for the fastest to memorize a deck of cards in the United States. That record held until 2011.

The Afghanistan Memory Wall

After winning, I wanted to do something more special with my memory, something I was passionate about. As a Veteran of Afghanistan, I decided to create a tribute for everyone who died there, so they would not be forgotten.

More than 2,400 US Military died in the War in Afghanistan. As a Veteran and an American, this deeply affects me. I've memorized the rank, first name, and last name of each of the fallen. Those 2,400 names were made of over 7,000 words, and I memorized each of them using the mind palace. I travel the USA rewriting each name entirely from memory on an expansive traveling wall to honor their memory and service.

When I was memorizing the wall, for a year, I lived in solitude. I took a book filled with each soldier's name with me everywhere I went. When I was sick, I was memorizing. When I was tired, I was memorizing.

I'm humbled by all who have come to witness this across the country and at major events like NFL games, NASCAR races, MLB games, Independence Day at the National Mall in Washington, DC, and on Veteran's Day. I have countless stories of how The Afghanistan Memory Wall has made an impact on friends and family of fallen soldiers that shake me to my core.

Every time I set up the wall, I brief my helpers beforehand, because I know what is coming. "I don't know when it will happen today, but it will. Someone is going to walk by this wall and ask what it is. In an instant, their eyes are going to fill with tears, and they will be barely able to contain themselves. Then they will give us a name and ask us if it's on the wall. I will take them to that name, and they will stand in silence with tears running down their face."

When I began the process, I didn't know any of them personally. Now I feel like I know all of them. Not just their names, I feel like I know them. Honoring and giving respect to others has given me purpose and a mission that I would not trade.

My Day Job

Since 1992, I've been a full-time speaker and trainer on the topic of memory. Companies and organizations have me come and speak at their conventions and to their teams.

I make memory entertaining. It is something I love doing. I also have multiple courses on memory, including Black Belt Memory.

I love what I do because it impacts others, adults and children alike! I do not have a special memory, and anyone can learn to do what I have done, whether it's setting the world record for the fastest to memorize a deck of cards, winning and defending the US Memory Championship, or memorizing the names of 2,400 fallen soldiers. That is what I love to teach.

RON'S THOUGHT LEADER LESSONS

Following Your Passion

I've learned that when I'm training for something, whether it is a memory tournament or The Afghanistan Memory Wall, that's when I'm at my best. There are times I think I need to focus more on my business, but the truth is, when I follow my passion and I have a big project or goal that will serve others, that is the very thing that helps grow me and my business. To paraphrase Jim Rohn, the true reward is the journey and what you become in the process.

Stoicism and Personal Responsibility

Marcus Aurelius said you have control over your mind, not outside events. Realize this, and you will find strength. A lot of stoicism has to do with not trying to control the uncontrollable. Just try to control your mind. That quote sums that up for me. I aim to just worry about myself, my mind, and my thoughts.

Q&A WITH RON

What is your favorite movie?

My all-time favorite movies that have impacted my life are *The Adventures of Indiana Jones* trilogy. He always was standing up for something that was right, and I love the adventure of it. He was an adventurous guy and traveled, and that's something that has been part of my life. He loved history. I've always been a collector of historic things, especially old presidential autographs and memorabilia.

Who is your favorite sports team?

The Texas Rangers. I'm a long-time season ticket holder. I went to my first game as a kid and just fell in love with the team.

How do you recharge?

Two ways help slow my mind down. I like to go for walks. I enjoy doing that out in nature. I also do jujitsu because, when you're there, if you are thinking about anything but jujitsu, you will lose or even get hurt.

Who are your mentors and greatest influences?

There are two great influences on my life. The first was my mom, and I didn't exactly realize how much she influenced me until she died. I know now she did, and the impact she had on my life was tremendous. I admired her strength. She lived her life under tremendous grief for decades, and she handled it with such grace. That is such an inspiration to me. I wish I could have five seconds with her just to tell her that.

The second is Kyle Wilson. I met him 20 years ago, and he believed in me and my product. When I was in a tough situation, getting ready to get kicked out of the Navy for $40,000 in debt to the IRS, he gave me a loan and started selling my memory course. Within six months, I had repaid him through the sales proceeds. He wasn't just a mentor of mine, because he has been a tremendous friend, and a mentor in how to market myself.

Have you had any past challenges that turned out to be blessings?

I think some of my biggest disappointments have blessings. I won the 2009 and 2010 USA Memory Championship, and in 2011 I was defeated. It was crushing. When you win the championship, the media surrounds you. You're on *Good Morning America*, *The Martha Stewart Show*, and *The Dr. Oz Show*. The next day, your phone is ringing off the hook. But when I lost in 2011, I found myself walking around New York City. My phone wasn't ringing, and I thought to myself, *How do I stay relevant?*

If I had won, I would have had to start training to defend my title. Losing was the greatest gift to me because it freed me up to no longer focus on the USA Memory Championship. I shifted to The Afghanistan Memory Wall, which became 1,000 times more important, more grand, more everything.

What is some of the best advice you've received?

My mom would say to just be kind. Be kind to people regardless of how they treat you. If they're treating you bad, you don't have to stay there in the situation and let them treat you bad. Just walk away.

What is something most people don't know about you?

I'm an introvert and need solitude and alone time.

What would you tell your 18-year-old self?

Get a good CPA. It would have saved me 10 years of mistakes.

How do you define success?

Success is contentment.

The two-time US Memory Champion and professional speaker Ron White can be found at www.blackbeltmemory.com, YouTube, Facebook, and Instagram.
Email: ron@ronwhitetraining.com Podcast: www.americasmemory.com

STEFAN WHITWELL

The Curious Connection Between a Famous Zen Master, BJJ, Modern Investing, and Tax Strategy!

Stefan Whitwell is the founder of Whitwell & Co., LLC, advising clients on health, wealth, and purpose. With expertise in tax planning, non-traditional investing, and mergers and acquisitions, he helps business owners from early growth strategy to sale preparation. He is passionate about venture philanthropy and legacy planning. Stefan is a father of four, martial artist, and violinist.

Rebellious Teenage Business Aspirations

My parents were academics (my father earned a doctorate and was a lifelong university professor and author of 60 books at last count) and since the opposite of academics are "businessmen," that's what I wanted to be. Through hard work and even more luck, I was admitted to The Wharton School at the University of Pennsylvania, which was life-changing. In retrospect, I learned as much from my peers as I did from my professors. They forced me to up my game for which I remain deeply grateful.

Living and Learning Big in New York City and Tokyo

After finishing my sophomore year at Wharton, I took leave for a one-year adventure in Japan. I wanted to study martial arts and Eastern philosophy and, through fate, was invited by an old, famous Zen master to apprentice in his monastery atop a beautiful mountain south of Tokyo. I was the second foreigner to ever be invited to do so in that monastery's 600-year history.

After graduating, I was hired by the global mergers and acquisitions powerhouse James D. Wolfensohn, Inc., where I worked for banking heavyweights James D. Wolfensohn and Paul Volcker, among others. There, I learned how to tear apart corporate financial statements and gained insight into mergers and acquisitions' inner workings. I was frequently in meetings with Fortune 500 CEOs. It was an extraordinary opportunity to learn by listening to the private thoughts of senior executives running America's biggest and most influential companies.

Wall Street was also exciting because I was being paid to learn! On finishing my two-year analyst program, I accepted an invitation to interview at Goldman Sachs, and 53 interviews later, I landed a job on their highly respected equity derivatives desk on the trading floor at the headquarters in New York City. Goldman was an extraordinary place and taught me what a strong culture can do for a business.

While at Goldman, I was asked to fill a position on their Tokyo equity derivatives team, and while living in Tokyo, I began traveling throughout Asia. By the time I left Tokyo, seven years later, I was fluent in Japanese.

After years of living abroad, I felt the urge to come back home, especially since I then had one kid and another on the way. I wanted my kids to get to know their grandparents. After considering various cities across the US, we chose to make Austin, Texas, our new home.

Major Real Estate Business and Major Crisis

Moving back to the US also enabled me to continue building my real estate investment business more earnestly. I had started acquiring properties in the US several years prior, while residing in Tokyo. Although I had learned and made a lot working for several global and prestigious banks, I felt the tug to be my own boss, in part because it would give me more control over my schedule, which was something I had admired about my dad. Although he worked a lot, much of that was at home, and whenever I had a question or wanted time with him, all I had to do was walk to the living room—he unfailingly made time for me. I followed my heart and built up a significant real estate investment business and owned $50 million worth of real estate.

In 2009, I faced an existential crisis. As several commercial loans were coming up for routine renewals, my bank (a large, money center bank) was struggling to survive and refused to renew my loans. Their message: if you can prove that you don't need the loan, we'll renew it. I felt angry that they would not work with me despite years of working together with a perfect track record.

I had too much real estate debt to "friend and family" my way out of it—even though the loans were a small percentage of the total value of the underlying real estate. Nobody was lending at that time, and I was in trouble. This turned out to be one of the most difficult chapters of my life. I lost my entire net worth and was forced to place several of my investment entities into Chapter 11 and Chapter 7 bankruptcy.

This was humiliating and pushed me to my limits emotionally, mentally, and financially. I learned a lot about how the world really works, which diverged significantly from the Ivy League textbook case studies I had read years earlier.

I lost everything, including my marriage.

Three things helped me get through this chapter and rebuild even stronger. First, were my family and friends. My dad treated me to a weekly lunch during those dark days and his unfailing belief in me meant more than words can express. My kids, too, were a source of inspiration. I loved them and wanted to be a source of security for them once again. My kids and my parents taught me to follow my heart, and all good things have come from that.

Second, my training in Brazilian jujutsu (BJJ) was my therapy, with the side benefit of getting a total kicker of a workout. BJJ taught me to breathe through difficult situations (such as when a bigger guy is pinning you down) and reverse them using technique, not strength, speed, or size, and that the reversal is often right there, you just have to be alert to it, move, and explore a new angle. Often a great reversal can be found in counterintuitive directions, which is why I believe curiosity and listening are key to success in BJJ, life, and business.

Finally, I owe a lot to a mentor. The simple question he asked me after I emerged from bankruptcy shocked me: "Have you ever thought about going into wealth management?" I was incredulous but desperate for a way to put this difficult chapter to good use. I had successfully repaid the banks every dollar and avoided being sued by keeping my co-investors truthfully updated on a regular basis, but I was struggling to figure out how to move forward.

What my mentor said next changed my life: "Stefan, I would much rather have a guy like you as my financial advisor BECAUSE you have had to walk through fire." Boom!

That was what I needed to move forward.

With that, I joined a multi-billion-dollar wealth management firm and helped them open their Austin office before starting my own firm several years later.

Lessons From Wealth Management

Seven years into building Whitwell & Co., LLC, I love what I do! I work hard to protect our clients so they never have to face what I did. I am glad that I followed my heart in choosing to build another firm. It's the best thing I ever did.

I am living proof that you can rebuild. You can go through a painful, difficult life chapter and emerge stronger and more compassionate on the other end.

Yes, I have worked hard to earn the trust of the high-net-worth clients we serve and to beat out competitors from small regional firms to Goldman Sachs or UBS. But it was not just hard work: it was also built on faith and teamwork.

When I started rebuilding, I vowed to be heart-led in my personal and business life. You have to believe in what you are doing. To make the impact we strive for in the lives of our clients, the work has to be team-built and team-delivered. The way we serve clients is team-oriented through and through, which is rare in our industry.

Today, I work primarily with business owners and senior executives. I frequently run into owners who have made the same mistake I did—being too focused on investing all of their wealth in their business instead of diversifying or being too bullheaded to consider anything other than their own success. If I'd had a strong wealth advisor to help me diversify earlier and protect those assets, when things did get crazy, I would have had a much better set of choices. Every owner can benefit from having an objective team watching their back.

When it came to rebuilding, I needed to do so quickly. One big "aha" was that for roughly 20 years, I thought my CPA had been doing tax planning for me only to realize he was focused on "tax compliance" and minor deductions. Worse, he was an economic historian—always focused on last year—whereas tax planning is forward-looking. I became curious about tax planning because everyone I met had an opinion on the right kind of entity to use or whether a ROTH conversion was really as good as some said it was, but nobody would quantify things. That drove me crazy. I needed to know whether this technique would move the needle for me, and if not, I had no interest. Ultimately, I was forced to build my own spreadsheets. The benefits were so big that after my first spreadsheet, I figured I had made a mistake. I rebuilt the spreadsheet only to get the same result. Out of an abundance of caution, I rebuilt the spreadsheet a third time and compared my numbers to a sample calculation done by one of the few competitors—only to find that mine were more conservative. I was hooked.

Not only is this making a big difference in my life, we also started doing tax planning for clients while partnering with their CPA to do the return. With tax rates likely to go up, tax planning is only going to become more important. Helping minimize my clients' and my own taxes is a mission I'm passionate about!

STEFAN'S THOUGHT LEADER LESSONS

Five "Life Hacks" for Building, Enjoying, and Sharing Wealth

Building Wealth | Life Hack #1 (Tax Strategy):

When we are young, most of our cash flow is generated from our time and effort. With rare exceptions, as we achieve a greater level of wealth, more and more of our cash flow is generated by our investment capital (not our labor). Mastering this shift requires smart tax planning because taxes are the single biggest drag on cash flow when living entirely off one's capital income.

Make sure you get a tax plan in place so you can keep more of what you make and protect yourself against the likelihood of future tax rate increases.

Building Wealth | Life Hack #2 (Non-Traditional Investing):

About 30 years ago, stocks, bonds, mutual funds, and ETFs were the only game in town. But over the last several decades, the private investment sector has grown in size and stature and today serves as an important component of the investment landscape for both institutions and individual investors.

Failing to harness the benefits of non-traditional investing is like going to fine restaurants but limiting yourself to the left side of the menu. That would be a flawed strategy for ordering food. Only using traditional investments in your portfolio is equally limiting.

Building Wealth | Life Hack #3 (Quality of Life):

Building wealth is not just about growing your financial assets. It is equally about raising the bar on the quality of your life. One of the smartest things you can do is to intentionally use a portion of your growing wealth to invest in you! Ask yourself, for example, how much you have budgeted this year to invest in your health. How much do you have budgeted for experiences that create life-long memories? It is critically important to have some fun along the way! Life is short and it is too easy to let years fly by without making these investments.

Enjoying Wealth | Life Hack #4 (The Big Shift):

You sold your business or left your executive role, sold your stock, and now have a sizable nest egg. What's next? After a longer-than-usual vacation, you might be tempted to start a new business. But this is a colossal mistake!

Do nothing. Take some time off to let yourself decompress (this is often "new territory" for the hard-charging exec and can even feel uncomfortable at first).

Keeping in mind that merely having wealth is no guarantee of happiness, now is the time to ask yourself deeper questions about the shift that often accompanies the achievement of a major professional goal and financial windfall: the shift from success to significance. In our younger years, we often chase "success." But once we've attained that, in time, we often become aware of this nagging question inside of ourselves: *What is my legacy? What is my life purpose? How would I like to be remembered once I'm gone? How can I make a lasting difference in this world?* The more one explores this, the more one tends to focus on the experiences, relationships, and activities that generate deeper value for you, whether that is spending more time with family and friends, on hobbies, or on giving back, such as through mentoring up-and-comers in your industry, philanthropy, or perhaps by writing a book to organize some of your amazing stories.

While wrestling with questions of significance is no easy task, in working with our clients, I have found that it is immensely rewarding.

Sharing Wealth | Life Hack #5 (What and How to Give):

Clients often ask me questions like, "How much should I leave my children? I want to give them a head start but I do not want to rob them of incentive to achieve their potential. Should we put it in a trust? When should we give them control? Should we use a trustee?"

Are the logistics important? Yes! But there's something more important.

What values around money and wealth are most important for you? What values would you like your children to inherit? What experiences can you curate that will help them learn these values and how to manage the wealth they inherit? Children who inherit substantial assets will need skills and values to do that well, even if they hire a first-class wealth management firm to handle the day-to-day.

Q&A WITH STEFAN

How do you recharge?

Reading. Training in Jujutsu (exhausting but, weirdly, it recharges me). Playing violin. Spending "slow time" in nature (walking on a gentle path or sitting on the beach).

What is some of the best advice you've received?

First, be present. Second, focus exclusively on the things you can control. Do not invest your emotion and time in the things that you can't. Both are much easier said than done but both pay big dividends.

What do you consider your superpower?

I feel my superpower lives at the nexus of listening, creating, and leading. People feel comfortable sharing deep stuff with me—which in part I attribute to the value I place on listening. I love to create solutions—paths by which my friends and clients can get what they seek. I am passionate about giving people the encouragement they need to go for it—to get after their dreams and summon the courage to take that next big step.

Professionally, one of my superpowers is simplification. I'm exceptionally good at taking complex financial and corporate situations and solving and talking about them in a plain and easy-to-grasp way.

How do you define success?

Living at the intersection of health (emotional, physical, and mental), wealth, and purpose, where your dreams benefit others, too—not just yourself.

Take the next step towards securing your financial future and achieving your life goals. As the founder of Whitwell & Co., LLC, Stefan Whitwell combines his expertise in tax planning, non-traditional investing, and mergers and acquisitions to guide business owners from strategic growth to successful exit. Connect with Stefan at stefan@whitwelladvisors.com or visit www.whitwelladvisors.com.

 Schedule a complimentary Discovery Visit with Stefan Whitwell, CFA.

LESLIE VERA

Roots in the Amazon
A Journey of Rediscovery

Leslie Vera, founder of Casa Kallpa LA and a retreat center in Peru, is a healing practitioner dedicated to guiding others on their spiritual journeys. Born in the Peruvian Amazon and shaped by challenges of migration and trauma, Leslie has turned her resilience into a mission: helping others heal, grow, and reconnect with their true selves.

I was born in Peru, a place that shaped the earliest parts of me. My childhood was simple and rooted, but it carried an innocence I couldn't fully appreciate at the time. At nine years old, everything changed. My family uprooted our lives, moving to the United States in search of better opportunities. It was a decision made with love, but for me, it felt like the ground beneath my feet had been stolen.

Suddenly, I was in a new country, struggling to navigate a world that didn't understand me—and one I didn't understand either. I couldn't speak the language. I couldn't read the social cues. At school, I was the odd one out. No one said it outright, but I felt it in the glances, the way others talked around me instead of to me. For the first time, I realized I was different, and that realization grew into shame.

I began to change myself. I didn't want to stand out; I wanted to blend in. I dropped the parts of me that didn't fit into this new culture—the language, the traditions, the pride in where I came from. I became someone else entirely, someone who could pass unnoticed in the hallways of school and later in the rooms of adulthood. It worked, but only on the surface. Beneath the mask, I felt hollow, as though I'd abandoned something vital.

By my 20s, that hollowness became impossible to ignore. On paper, my life looked fine—maybe even good. But inside, I was lost. I began experiencing what some call a "dark night of the soul," a period where every part of my being felt weighed down. No distraction or achievement could fill the emptiness.

The hardest part of this period wasn't the pain itself; it was the memories that started to surface. Traumas I had long buried, moments of deep hurt from my past, came rushing back. I realized how much I had ignored, how much I had tried to bury not just my heritage but my pain, too. I could no longer avoid the truth: I had to confront everything I had been running from.

Healing wasn't immediate. It began in small, hesitant steps. I turned to practices that helped me reconnect with myself. I started journaling, writing out the things I couldn't say aloud. I explored yoga and breathwork, which helped me feel safe in my own body again. Sound healing became a source of comfort, something that reminded me joy was still possible. And, perhaps most importantly, I sought help—from therapists, healers, and those who understood the messy, non-linear process of healing from trauma.

Through this journey, I began to rediscover myself. I reconnected with the girl I had left behind when I tried to become someone else. I allowed myself to grieve for her, for the experiences I had lost, and for the parts of me that had been silenced. Slowly, I started to see my heritage not as something to hide but as a source of strength. I began to understand that the pain I carried wasn't just something to overcome; it was something to honor as part of my story.

Returning to my roots, both metaphorically and physically, became a turning point. I revisited my homeland, reconnecting with the culture and traditions I had cast aside. The act of returning felt like reclaiming a piece of myself I thought I'd lost forever. It wasn't just about going back to a place—it was about embracing the person I had always been beneath the mask.

Now, I live a life that feels authentic. I've built a career and a calling that centers on healing, not just for myself but for others who are navigating their own journeys through Casa Kallpa Healing Center, a meditation studio in Los Angeles and Retreat Center in Peru. I've come to understand that belonging isn't about fitting in; it's about being true to who you are. And while my past still echoes in my life, I no longer fear it. Those echoes remind me of where I've been, but they don't define where I'm going.

Healing isn't a destination. It's a continual process, one that requires courage and patience. But it's also a gift—the chance to become whole again, to reclaim every part of yourself, and to live in a way that feels true. That's the life I'm building now, one step at a time.

LESLIE'S THOUGHT LEADER LESSONS

The World as a Mirror: Lessons from Spirituality and Travel

Traveling has been one of the greatest teachers of my life. Each journey—whether it took me to a bustling city, a remote village, or a sacred natural site—has given me more than just sights to remember. It's allowed me to meet myself in ways I never could have imagined, peeling back layers of who I thought I was and revealing truths that only experience could show.

Over the years, I've visited more than 20 countries. Each one left an indelible mark, not just because of its beauty or culture but because of the people I met and the lessons they offered me. At first, I traveled out of curiosity, a pull I couldn't explain but knew I had to follow. Over time, I realized that every journey was also an inner one, guiding me closer to my own essence.

Following Your Curiosity

Curiosity is a divine compass. It has taken me down winding streets in Greece, into hidden temples in Thailand, and deep into the Peruvian Amazon, where I reconnected with my roots. Following that spark—without overanalyzing or needing a clear reason—has always led me to exactly where I needed to be.

For instance, in Thailand, I felt drawn to do a yoga certification course. Something about the invitation of stillness spoke to me. There, I met a stranger who shared her story of healing from grief. Her vulnerability unlocked something in me, inspiring me to confront the lingering sadness I hadn't yet acknowledged. I left Thailand not just with memories but with a lighter heart.

Curiosity reminds us that the unknown isn't something to fear but to embrace. It's in that space of exploration—of leaning into what calls to you—that you find what your soul is truly seeking.

Listening to Your Intuition

Travel taught me to trust my intuition, the quiet voice that speaks when logic has no answer. There were moments when plans fell apart—a canceled train, a wrong turn—but those "mistakes" often led to the most magical experiences.

This past summer, I missed my return flight to LA from Spain. Instead of stressing over my missed flight, I embraced the redirection the universe was offering me. It led me to explore five more cities in Spain that were not planned but had a significant impact in my journey. This adventure wasn't on any map or itinerary, but it fed my soul in ways no guidebook could.

Intuition is our guide through the unknown. It's the voice that nudges us towards growth, even when we don't understand the why. The more I trusted it, the more I realized that it was leading me not just through the world but towards myself.

The Power of Play

In the seriousness of healing and self-discovery, I've learned that play is just as essential as reflection. Travel taught me how to laugh again—at myself, at the unexpected, and at life's quirks. Whether it was dancing barefoot under the stars in Costa Rica or attempting to learn how to make pasta in Italy, those moments reminded me that joy is a form of connection.

Play allows us to shed the layers of adulthood that can weigh us down. It reminds us that life isn't meant to be a rigid path but a dynamic, ever-changing dance. Through play, I've learned to approach life with lightness, even in moments of challenge.

Seeing Everyone as a Teacher

Perhaps the greatest lesson I've learned is that everyone we meet is a reflection of us—a teacher disguised in the form of a stranger, friend, or fleeting encounter.

In Japan, I met a woman who ran a small tea house. She didn't speak much English, but her kindness transcended language. She served tea with such reverence that it felt like a sacred ritual. Watching her, I realized that presence and gratitude could elevate even the simplest acts into something profound.

In Bali, a young boy selling crickets on the street taught me about resilience. Despite his struggles, his laughter was infectious, and his joy seemed unshakable. He reminded me that the human spirit is stronger than circumstance.

These experiences taught me that every person who crosses our path reflects something back to us—our fears, our strengths, our potential, or the parts of us that need healing.

Expanding the Mind and Soul

Travel strips away the familiar, pushing you out of your comfort zone and into a space where growth happens. It shows you how small your problems are in the grand scheme of things and how interconnected we all are.

Standing before the vast expanse of the Egyptian Pyramids or the towering peaks of the Andes, I felt humbled. These places reminded me that life is both infinitely larger and more beautifully intricate than I often realize.

But the real expansion didn't come from the landscapes—it came from within. Travel helped me see the patterns of my own thoughts, the fears I needed to release, and the truths I needed to embrace. It taught me that home isn't a place; it's a state of being, one you carry with you when you're aligned with your true self.

Insights to Carry Forward

1. Trust the Journey: Not every step will make sense in the moment, but every step matters. Trust where your curiosity and intuition lead you.
2. Embrace the Unexpected: Some of the most profound lessons and adventures come from unplanned detours.
3. Find Joy in Simplicity: Play, laugh, and savor the small moments—they're the threads that weave a meaningful life.
4. Honor the Teachers Around You: See every person and experience as a mirror, reflecting back where you need to grow.
5. Stay Open: The world has an infinite capacity to teach and heal us, but only if we're willing to listen.

Through travel, I've learned that life is the ultimate adventure. And the more I explore, the more I understand that the journey is never about the destination—it's about coming home to yourself.

Q&A WITH LESLIE

How do you recharge?

Spending time alone allows me to reconnect with myself. Whether it's meditating, journaling, or simply being still, solitude is where I find clarity and peace.

Have you had any past challenges that turned out to be blessings?

Moving to the US was one of the hardest transitions of my life. But it gave me the opportunity to dream big, overcome adversity, and create a life that reflects my truest self.

What would you tell your 18-year-old self?

To start. Start whether you're scared, unprepared, or unsure if it will work out. Trust that you'll figure it out along the way.

What is your image of an ideal world?

An ideal world is one where people are deeply self-aware and actively healing themselves to return to their true essence. I've dedicated my life to creating safe spaces for others to heal, like Casa Kallpa which is a wellness studio in LA and retreat center in Peru. Through Casa Kallpa, I help create this reality by offering tools, spaces, and practices for healing, including plant medicine and nervous system work. By sharing my knowledge and experiences, I guide others on their path back to themselves.

Leslie Vera's journey—from the Peruvian Amazon to creating Casa Kallpa—reflects the power of resilience, healing, and transformation. Her mission is to guide others back to their true selves through holistic practices and plant medicine. Ready to begin your own healing journey? Contact Leslie at CasaKallpa.com or connect on Instagram @CasaKallpa.LA

 Casa Kallpa Healing Center Classes & Retreats

ROY SMOOTHE
Mastering Your Brand Journey

*Author, publisher, speaker, and branding genius Roy Smoothe is the founder of **So Smoothe Records** the world's #1 motivation music label reaching over 500 million streams across major music and media platforms. His unique company combines cool branding strategies and cutting-edge song tracks to create world-class projects and high-impact initiatives for brand and business development.*

Branding Out from the Crowd

From a young age, I was captivated by the world of fashion and personal style. My earliest memory of this goes back to watching my father, impeccably dressed in his tailored suits. He had an undeniable presence, and it wasn't just the suits—it was the confidence and the way he carried himself. That left a lasting impression on me. From then on, I found joy in buying, wearing, and even redesigning clothes, which eventually led me into the men's clothing industry. Sadly, my father, who introduced me to the world of style and branding, passed away a few years ago. But the legacy of his **"live your life in style with a smile"** mindset lives on in everything I do.

My fashion career started humbly but quickly escalated as I became a director at a major fashion retail company within nine months. I ran 57 menswear concessions across England, Ireland, Scotland, Wales, and Jersey, with a turnover of £5.9 million annually. The thrill of running a successful operation drove me to pursue even more ambitious goals, leading to the ownership of my own chain of fashion boutiques. Interestingly, my first shop was a ladies' fashion boutique. This venture was born out of necessity when my late wife, Jane, who was then my fiancée, struggled to find a dress for our engagement party. I decided to fill that gap, and the boutique became extremely popular, not just for the clothes but also for the connections and friendships it fostered.

A pivotal moment in my career came when I started developing and hosting stylish, entertaining, and engaging fashion shows with a twist. Unlike traditional shows, I took the shows to the audience instead of expecting them to come to me. We hosted events in high-end fitness clubs, business centers, wine bars, and restaurants—places where no one else was doing fashion shows at the time. These events were branded as The Smooth Operator Fashion Show, inspired by Sade's iconic song "Smooth Operator." It was during this period that I became known as the smooth guy, which led to the birth of my personal brand, Mr. Smoothe.

Life in the fashion industry wasn't always smooth. When the recession hit, I witnessed firsthand the devastating impact it had on business owners. That was a wake-up call for me. I realized the importance of creating a strong personal brand that could adapt and pivot with life's changes. To solidify my knowledge, I went to Oxford University Business School and the University of Nottingham where I earned a postgraduate degree in marketing.

Armed with new insights, I developed the concept of a Smoothe Card, a lifestyle brand embodied in a contactless card that doubled as a loyalty card for fashion shops, bars, clubs, fitness centers—essentially all lifestyle venues. Despite stiff competition from a well-funded startup with a $20 million marketing budget, I managed to secure a major contract that they were vying for. This experience taught me a valuable lesson: **it's not the smartest who get ahead; it's the boldest.**

Jet-Setting and Big Life Challenges

While launching the Smoothe Card, I also took on consultancy work for a software company. My expertise in brand development proved invaluable, and I eventually became the president of international business development. In this role, I managed sales, collaborations, and marketing with major Fortune 500 and FTSE 100 companies.

This marked the beginning of my international jet-setting lifestyle. My personal brand, Mr. Smoothe, played a significant role in my success. It opened doors, built instant rapport, and secured major contracts, including one with Microsoft in Vancouver, where a senior director notably remarked that I looked "like a million dollars." **Yet, even with the demands of global business, I remained committed to maintaining a strong and secure family life.**

Unfortunately, life took a difficult turn when Jane, my adorable, loving, and spiritual wife, was diagnosed with breast cancer. I made the tough decision to become her full-time caregiver while also raising our six-year-old son, Josef.

This period of my life led me to a new calling as a motivational speaker. I began speaking at schools, universities, and business events, and once again, my personal brand, Mr. Smoothe, accelerated my entry into this new space. Unlike most speakers who are talked about after they leave the room, my brand ensured I was talked about as I entered. And that continues to happen to this day.

So Smoothe Record Label

A unique twist to my speaking career came when I decided to put my recorded motivational speeches to music. Initially, this was a fun way to teach my son about life, business, and spirituality. But it quickly dawned on me that this could be my future: creating music-cool concepts and services and turning them into motivational song tracks under the Smoothe Mixx genre. The first album I created was a personal message about my amazing relationship with Jane. Josef loved listening to each track, and the music subliminally cemented the messages in his mind.

Once Kyle Wilson, founder of Jim Rohn International, heard the sample tracks I created using Jim Rohn's messages, he commissioned me to create an album of Jim Rohn's materials.

Today, with over **500 million streams across major music and social media platforms** and collaborations with legendary icons, millionaire and billionaire business owners, thought leaders like Denis Waitley, Les Brown, Brian Tracy, Dr. Greg Reid, and world-famous sports celebrities, the Smoothe brand continues to thrive. We've had over 14 Amazon Music #1 bestselling albums and singles. But the real bonus is that Josef has grown into an amazing young man—wise, honorable, and emotionally intelligent beyond his years.

Looking to the future, I'm excited about the growth of the So Smoothe Record label. We have a vision to build our client base of successful authors, renowned thought leaders, executives and global business leaders, sports celebrities, and professional speakers, using the power of music to generate additional revenue streams and increase their brand visibility.

We're currently working on a global vision to release **The World's Greatest Motivational Album Collection**, a project that will be featured in the book of *Guinness World Records*.

Through this journey, I've learned that the secret to mastering your business brand is about making strategic connections, providing massive value, and creating big wins for clients. And from experience, I have proved that the best way to get your message out to the world is through the universal language of music.

ROY'S THOUGHT LEADER LESSONS

Brand Leadership

To lead others effectively, you need to have a clear vision for yourself as well as for your company. This vision must be something you can embody and share effectively with others. While you can communicate a vision in writing, your personal brand will always shout louder than your written words.

Personal branding in terms of your leadership vision is not about creating a false image or pretending to be someone you're not. Instead, it's about strategically and accurately communicating your values and vision. It's about standing out from the crowd, being known for your expertise, and creating a lasting impression that opens opportunities for others to join and share your vision.

Through my journey, I have learned several invaluable lessons that have shaped my approach to leadership and personal branding:

1. Identify the uniqueness and strengths of your personal brand and consistently showcase them.
2. Be willing to evolve your brand as your industry changes.
3. Maintain authenticity to build trust with your audience.
4. Share your brand across different platforms to reach a wider audience.
5. Use your expertise and influence to make a positive impact.

Business Philosophy

In today's interconnected world, I believe that a personal business philosophy must embrace the expansive reach of the digital revolution. No longer confined to the traditional boundaries of colleagues, professional reputation now has a global platform. I am committed to leveraging the internet and social media to communicate effectively, connect meaningfully, and conduct business with a broader audience.

Fashion and Style

Personal style is more than just clothing; it is a powerful statement of identity and a unique calling card. To truly make an impact, one must be bold and daring, willing to branch out from the crowd and embrace individuality.

In a world where first impressions are often lasting, the way you present yourself can create tremendous value. If your style doesn't grab attention, it holds little significance. Fashion is an opportunity to tell your story without words, to make a memorable mark that resonates long after you've left the room.

Q&A WITH ROY

How do you recharge?

By taking advantage of my beautiful natural surroundings and engaging in physical activities. Whether it's walking along the beach, exploring the cliff tops, biking through the New Forest, or working out in the gym, these activities not only enhance my physical health and mental well-being but also strengthen my personal brand by showcasing my commitment to a balanced and fulfilling lifestyle.

What are a few of your favorite quotes?

Jim Rohn's wisdom has deeply influenced my approach to personal and professional growth, especially in the realm of personal branding. Here are a few of his quotes that resonate with me the most:

"If you work on your job, you make a living. If you work on yourself, you make a fortune."
"Profits are better than wages."
"For things to change, you have to change."
"It's not the blowing of the wind that determines your direction; it's the setting of the sail."

These quotes by Jim Rohn encapsulate essential principles for personal branding: the importance of self-investment, the entrepreneurial mindset, the necessity of personal change, and the power of intentionality. They serve as daily reminders to continually work on myself, embrace an entrepreneurial approach, adapt to changes, and be intentional in my actions. By embodying these principles, I strive to create a personal brand that is authentic, resilient, and influential.

Have you had any past challenges that turned out to be blessings?

Losing a kind, loving, spiritual, and physically beautiful wife was an incredibly challenging and painful experience for me. I suddenly found myself as the sole parent to our then-seven-year-old son. Navigating the complexities of grief while ensuring he had a stable, loving environment was no small feat. Yet, this profound loss turned out to be a catalyst for immense personal and professional growth.

What is some of the best advice you've received?

"It's not the smart that gets ahead—it's the bold!"

What do you consider your superpower?

My superpower is a combination of my smile, confidence, and calm demeanor. These qualities are integral parts of my personal brand and have consistently opened doors to friendships, relationships, and new opportunities in both life and business. They communicate the inner joy and peace I maintain, even in circumstances where others might crumble or falter.

What would you tell your 18-year-old self?

Focus on developing a personal brand that embodies tremendous value for the people you work with or engage with. A strong personal brand can open doors to building meaningful relationships, gaining access to influential networks, and joining groups that will enhance your personal development.

A personal brand is not just about self-promotion; it's about authentically showcasing your strengths, values, and passions. It's about consistently delivering value to others and making a positive impact. This authenticity and value will naturally attract opportunities and relationships that align with your goals and aspirations.

What do you consider your greatest achievements to date?

One of my greatest achievements to date is the creation of Smoothe Mixx, a new motivational music genre that has transformed people's lives in business, work, and mindset. This genre blends uplifting lyrics with inspiring melodies designed to empower and motivate listeners to achieve their goals and overcome challenges. The impact of Smoothe Mixx has been profound, reaching over 500,000 streams across various music and social media platforms. At the same time, I partnered with a client to help achieve a staggering 25 billion views on their YouTube channel.

How do you define success?

I define success as the ability to have the freedom to work in a field you love alongside people you enjoy collaborating with and traveling to places you wish to explore. Ultimately, success is about living the life you dream of and achieving the goals you set to make it happen.

If you would like to take your brand to the next level on a global scale, achieve a Guinness World Record and feature in Roy Smoothe's *World's Greatest Motivation* album, get in touch: smoothemedia@gmail.com or @roysmoothe on LinkedIn and Facebook.

MORKOS AZIZ

You Can Have It All!

Morkos Aziz succeeded in earning a multimillion-dollar status in only a few years. On the road to financial independence, real estate has become one of his greatest passions. He has a background in corporate finance, private equity, and asset management with a bachelor's in economics from Cairo University. He is originally from Egypt and moved to the US in 2011.

"For I know the plans I have for you," declares the LORD, "plans to prosper you and not to harm you, plans to give you hope and a future."

– Jeremiah 29:11

Capacity Is a State of Mind!

While relaxing on the pristine sands of Jumeirah Beach in Dubai, I reminisced about the last decade since I moved to the US and was deeply moved by an overwhelming feeling of joy and gratitude! It has been a long journey with so many setbacks that have humbled me. Through all of these experiences, I have emerged as a new person. As I look back, I feel glad that I've chosen to commit and give my best!

With the grace of God, I've achieved great success in Egypt by working my way up from the very bottom. I attended one of the top-tier economics schools, landed a highly-desirable job in a big investment bank, and then earned scholarships to pursue the most prestigious credentials on Wall Street. In the US, while looking for an investment analyst job, I worked as a cashier in a Manhattan liquor store for minimum wage. Eventually, through unwavering tenacity and determination, I secured my first analyst job, and while climbing the corporate ladder, I realized that I couldn't live the American dream as an employee. That's where real estate investing came in. Capitalizing on my expertise to identify and revitalize underperforming assets, I started acquiring distressed properties and turning them into well-oiled cashflow machines, ultimately building a substantial real estate portfolio within a short period of time.

My life has been about testing my limits and using my God-given gifts to make a meaningful impact! My world experiences never matched my age! The way my mother was pushing me was like no other! Her love has been the steadying and motivating factor that gave me the foundation for life!

Proverbs 12:24 says, "Diligent hands will rule, but laziness ends in forced labor." This verse has been a constant source of inspiration and guidance for me. I always trust the fact that if I did my part behind closed doors, winning is inevitable!

I believe with every inch of my soul that character contributes more to one's success than superior intelligence and that persistence beats talent every single time! The ability to persevere on a given path despite adversity and unexpected events is the key to achieving the desired results. What I've found to be true is that our potential is directly proportional to what we believe we deserve and that human capacity is usually never the problem! It is the work we did a long time ago—when it seemed that we weren't making any progress—that can make all the difference!

In many ways, it was a blessing to learn at a young age that rejection is better than regret, emotions have to be measured, and vulnerability is the only way to build deep and meaningful connections! In any negotiation, I believe it has to be a "win-win." I always strive for mutually beneficial relationships.

I learned that being a good listener is extremely valuable and that a team of smart people talking openly can effectively address any challenge. When I seek clarity, I gather more information. That could mean reading dozens of books or grabbing coffee with someone halfway across the world!

Starting from scratch served me well. It gave me the drive to want it all, and the wisdom to trust the process! I've made a number of unwise decisions and a few good ones. All of them have taught me the lessons that I treasure today!

The Grind May Go Unnoticed, But the Results Won't!

I was always inspired to do something big with my life. I thought at one time that I had to be so smart to win, until I read this quote by Warren Buffet: "We don't have to be smarter than the rest; we have to be more disciplined than the rest." Big dreams and ambitious goals stretch across lifetimes. The key is not to overestimate what we can accomplish in a year or underestimate what we can accomplish in a decade and not to let the expectations of how life should be become an obsession!

Fortune favors the bold who defy the status quo and embrace their unique path, even if it means going against the grain and becoming different! I choose not to let the pressure to conform to societal norms hold me back. Bold moves also require bold asks, and we usually adhere to this principle, particularly while we are acquiring assets, "If you are not embarrassed by your offer, you are probably offering too much." I am always prepared to endure months of emotional risk in exchange for the life lessons and the joy that comes with winning.

Reality can be rewritten and now my reality is that I travel the world and connect with world-class heavy hitters and leverage their wisdom. The conversations usually take on a whole new depth. To my amazement, these connections have led me to lifelong friendships, remarkable experiences, and extraordinary deals! When I go to New York, London, Montreal, or even any smaller city, there's always a group of people I can bond with and exchange ideas.

From Johannesburg to Hawaii, I've made friends in more than 40 countries. Sometimes, I could be soaking up history in Egypt, touring the Alps in Switzerland, exploring the dark mysteries of Italy, jogging on the beach in Greece, eating paella in Spain, lounging by an infinity pool on the Dead Sea in Jordan, riding a cable car in Brazil, sailing the Caribbean with a catamaran in the Dominican Republic, resting under a palm tree in Mexico, and swimming on a private island in Colombia! In short, I've uncovered a path to do work that I am passionate about while still nurturing a wide range of diverse relationships with people from all walks of life.

Action Mitigates Fear

Fear, not laziness, is the primary reason that holds most of us back from reaching our full potential. It is the most costly of all human emotions. The fear of not being loved and the fear of not being enough—all other fears are rooted in these two fears. Our actions are often guided more by the desire to avoid fear than by the pursuit of success. Napoleon Hill asserts in his book *Think and Grow Rich*:

Fear paralyzes the faculty of reason, destroys the faculty of imagination, kills off self-reliance, undermines enthusiasm, discourages initiative, leads to uncertainty of purpose, encourages procrastination, wipes out enthusiasm, and makes self-control an impossibility. It takes the charm from one's personality, destroys the possibility of accurate thinking, diverts concentration of effort; it masters persistence, turns the will-power into nothingness, destroys ambition, beclouds the memory, and invites failure in every conceivable form; it kills love and assassinates the finer emotions of the heart, discourages friendship and invites disaster in a hundred forms, leads to sleeplessness, misery, and unhappiness.

While fear could be an inherent aspect of personal growth and it can manifest itself as we push our boundaries, it should not influence our choices. As Philippians 4:6 says, "Be anxious for nothing, but in everything by prayer and supplication, with thanksgiving, present your requests to God."

We can overcome fear by going out and doing it. That sometimes requires allowing small bad things to happen. We tend to burden ourselves with unnecessary stress by seeking perfection. Making meaningful progress is the goal. Massive imperfect action cures fear and feeds confidence.

I made it a habit to challenge my fears every day: from contacting renowned thought leaders for advice to networking with prominent business people who are world-class at what they do. Nothing inspires me more than being surrounded by people who have done more than me. The key is to have burning desire backed by faith to push through fear and limiting beliefs!

Money Is a Great Servant But a Bad Master

I have pondered the morality of pursuing financial independence for so many years. I was confused about the true value of money. Then, I read something Jim Rohn wrote, that really hit me:

> Once you get money out of the way, you can't believe the other dimensions of your life you can work on. Once you solve the money problems, now you have the time, more time to work on certain other areas in your life that will really start to grow and expand. It is not the amount that counts, it is the extent of your reach that counts.... If you could do better, should you?

In thinking about the relative importance of unique experiences and money, I found that I could happily exchange money for true value. I have always been much more drawn to the experience. In his book *Man's Search for Meaning*, Viktor Frankl had it right when he said what you experience, no power on Earth can take it from you!

True wealth is not merely about the possession of material things. Money is just a way of keeping score and is one measure of success. I do things because I enjoy what I do. Making money was an incidental consequence of that and sometimes translates into more money than I would have made if I just went after the money!

There's a lot of debate over whether or not money can really buy happiness, but from experience, we know that money can solve problems, expand options, and enable a life of contribution, and certainly, all of these can bring happiness! Margaret Thatcher famously said: "No one would remember the Good Samaritan if he'd only had good intentions; he had money, too."

I strongly believe that wealth is consistent with Biblical teachings. In fact, Solomon was the richest man who ever lived and Abraham was blessed with abundant riches. If material things were insignificant, God would not have created us in a physical form, which is inherently material!

One of the greatest joys in life is doing the best with what we have and continuously exploring how far we can go. However, pursuing financial success at the expense of other important values will ultimately lead to loss, not gain! As highlighted by the wise Zig Ziglar in his book *See You at the Top*, "...we must not make money or anything else our god because when we do, we will never be happy—regardless of how much we have."

He Is God of Abundance

The belief that abundance is out of reach has been sold to many. I don't buy that! Stress, selfishness, jealousy, and envy stem from a scarcity mindset. I know I always wanted more and I always wanted better. Who doesn't want more quality time with loved ones, increased productivity, more peak memories, better finances, more peace, more gratitude, more love, and more contribution to humankind?

To experience abundance, it's important to embrace giving. It is the most tangible way that we put God first! It helps program our minds to recognize that there is more than enough for everyone, thus increasing our awareness and enhancing our capacity to hold more of the next experience! Sharing our wealth, time, or energy brings an incredible feeling often more rewarding than the numbers in a bank account. We have two hands, one to pull ourselves up and the other to pull someone else behind us.

Faith in God helps instill an abundance mentality in us and allows us to realize that we live in a world of overabundance of everything our heart could desire! In John 10:10, Jesus declared, "I have come that they may have life and that they may have it more abundantly." A prosperous and abundant life awaits us all. God's provision is infinite and His grace endures forever for every single one of us!

Morkos Aziz is an economist, investment banker, and real estate developer. Follow him for inspiration and learn how to achieve financial independence on his Facebook page https://www.facebook.com/morkos.aziz. Morkos can also be reached at morkos.aziz@gmail.com

 Scan to contact Morkos Aziz

HOWARD PIERPONT
There Is Always a Solution, If You Listen

Howard Pierpont is a solutionist for the Institute for Preparedness and Resilience—the educational arm of DERA, a 501(c)3. Howard retired from the Intel Corporation with responsibility for business continuity and preparedness. He worked in the FEMA Long-Term Community Recovery Office. He speaks on resiliency, media, and government during disasters.

Learning Adaptability Then Faith

I was fortunate to be born into a warm, considerate family. There was a sense of faith: faith in oneself, each other, and our extended family. I knew I could depend on my relatives as well as a circle of friends. I learned that you worked on issues as they arose and built trust in relationships.

My mother and father came from vastly different backgrounds, both with large families. Both had careers that, due to setbacks, involved the need for agility. After she finished college, my mother became a schoolteacher and later worked as a substitute. After my dad came home from World War II, he went to school to be a weather observer and then worked in several other jobs. Neither ever ran for office, but they were both influencers who worked in the background to assist in community decisions.

I learned from my parents that striving toward a predetermined goal often does not yield the desired result. They never pushed me in a career direction but encouraged me to explore the possibilities.

I went off to college and made a series of decisions that were not the best. I started a family and left college to keep things going. The jobs I found were low on the pay scale. While I struggled to make ends meet, I became further concerned that I was not headed toward my dreams.

Over time, I would rebuild my faith in myself. The more personal faith I had, the further I progressed. I made company moves from Connecticut to California and then to Oregon. I went from having a "job" to retiring after almost 27 years in the same company.

Today, as a solutionist who has found my own faith, I get to meet and talk to many people. It doesn't matter where they are from or what religion they may have, they are people—people with issues and unresolved needs. Many times, the issues and needs are derived from some earlier misunderstanding or lack of personal knowledge. With just a little bit of ongoing attention, everyone can continue to grow and have faith in themselves.

But, as I worked through my career, I often found that people only wanted me to work on outcomes, even if the outcome would not be effective. I held a series of jobs where I would be given an assignment to deliver a particular product or process. Often the product (or process) did not meet the needs of the end-user or was outdated before it was delivered. Often the end user and I were not pleased with the final product. Although I tried hard, I was not very successful.

Seeing All Sides

As part of a new job, I had to work with the dreaded corporate audit team. No one had ever had any success dealing with them. They were seen as work drivers, not solution creators.

Rather than work toward a specific result, I looked around the entire landscape to see all sides of the issues. I removed the predetermined outcome and the idea of the adversarial relationship between their department and the others. When one takes out the melodrama and the "I must be right and win," a reasonable solution can be found.

Eventually, with my background in corporate knowledge, persuasion, and consensus building, I was asked to join the audit team! I had never been an auditor, but that wouldn't hold me back. I was asked to change things. I soon became the subject matter expert on business continuity.

In the spring of 2002, I assumed a position in the corporate business continuity office. I had been enjoying the audit job and had traveled to Russia, Malaysia, China, Mexico, Ireland, and across the States. I worked to hone my listening and solution skills.

Over the next 18 months, I was making a significant impact on the individuals in the company and making the business run more smoothly as a whole. Every situation needed to be handled differently, but I was always working for positive outcomes. Sometimes those outcomes would be nothing I expected.

Called to Disaster Relief

There were occasionally people who were hard to work with. One of my biggest obstructionists went on vacation to Miami and encountered the remnants of a hurricane: no electricity or air conditioning for a week. When she returned, she never wanted anyone to go through anything like that again! She asked how she could move the continuity plans I was teaching forward! I was struck by how the conditions in Miami inspired her change of heart, and I felt pulled to become more involved in disaster relief.

I decided to join FEMA as a reservist in the long-term recovery group. Many people think a disaster will never happen to them. My job involved working with survivors, small businesses, not-for-profits, and governments in recovering toward a new normal. Disasters are real, and disasters are personal.

While it is satisfying to assist people, they need to make their own decisions. They are in control of their recovery.

In 2012, I was assigned to support Waterbury, Vermont, as part of the long-term recovery team after Tropical Storm Irene.

Flooding from the storm had damaged hundreds of roads and bridges and thousands of homes and businesses statewide and caused long-term power outages. Waterbury, home to Green Mountain Coffee Roasters, Ben & Jerry's Ice Cream, and the Vermont State Hospital, was uniquely impacted. Flooding at the Waterbury State Office Complex displaced approximately 1,500 state employees, seriously jeopardizing the community's economic sustainability.

In the aftermath of the disaster, the Waterbury community began developing a long-term recovery plan with a series of public meetings and workshops at the start of January, I was assigned to assist.

Of the many recovery project ideas, the community needed to agree on which to pursue. A project champion requested the creation of a performing arts center.

There was already a visual art center in place that had not been disrupted by flooding. A disagreement arose on whether there was a need for a separate center.

The performing arts center was still a dream, but national stage and television performer and local resident Monica Callan, moved forward after she and I exchanged ideas about the creation of a not-for-profit. What the community perceived as an even bigger issue was the potential cost of constructing a performance location. Where would the money come from?

One phone call would change the velocity of things. The members of the National Grange of the Order of Patrons of Husbandry were getting older, and the membership numbers were decreasing. The Grange had been around for years, and their building was showing its age. That call led to a conversation and the Grange members selling their hall to a new not-for-profit Across Roads Center for the Arts, and the new Grange Hall Cultural Center came into being.

Because all parties remained flexible throughout the solution-creation process, Waterbury has a wonderful new landmark. Grange Hall Cultural Center has become a highly popular family-friendly destination. Using a solutionist method allowed for the flexibility necessary to bring everyone to a happy agreement.

Here, again, I was able to listen to their setbacks and have an open dialog on potential courses of action. A solutionist method allowed space for several creative solutions that I didn't even expect.

Let Others Have Their Success

I spend most of my time now listening to people talk about what they think are their issues. Then we discuss what the genuine issues are and potential solutions. Finally, I assist with creating a roadmap and by checking in to see the progress they have made.

I have found that too many groups have had someone come in, think they know the organization's problem, and then create a final action plan. These groups feel that their investment was not optimized with a pre-determined consultant output.

Look at what you have done before, even if it wasn't the right solution at the time, then look around and see what has worked or not worked for others. Build on the best of everything and be willing to be flexible.

HOWARD'S THOUGHT LEADER LESSONS

Investing

I grew up in a family where my parents invested in long-term stocks. They had electric, water, telephone, and natural gas companies. They bought enough stock so the dividends paid the taxes and our household electricity, phone, gas for heating, and water bills every quarter.

This reduced the need for additional cash to pay the bills and allowed for some stock to be sold off later if there was a need.

Relationships

In a business situation, you need to understand the relationship your proposed partner has with other businesses in the industry as well as the individuals. Do their core values complement your own?

In personal relationships, one needs to pay close attention—not only to the individual but also to those around them and their situations. Are they similar to you or are they different enough that the issues that arise may not be resolvable? If one is always planning and the other spontaneous, can things be worked out? Money is another significant area. One might be a spender and the other might be putting money away to ensure bills are paid, and the future is secure. Are there other outside influences that are driving the situation that you may not be aware of?

Philanthropy and Giving

Know who you are supporting and ensure that they map to your philosophies, do it in a financially prudent manner. I enjoy supporting music, live music, and public music radio stations.

Business Philosophy

One needs a plan with milestones and targets. There may be times when the timing of the milestone needs to be reconsidered. If you force a solution, you may never reach your goal. Sometimes, when you wait, the final product is better than anticipated.

Q&A WITH HOWARD

What is your favorite song?

"Forever Young" written by Bob Dylan. The Rod Stewart version was played at the recessional at my son's high school graduation. Just listen to the words.

"You're Gonna Miss This" by Trace Adkins. Words of wisdom. I wish I had heard this years ago.

Any Donna Summer song when driving 70 miles an hour at 2:00 a.m. with the windows down.

Who are your mentors and greatest influences?

Life is a mentor. If you pay attention to the people and things around you, you can see what works and doesn't work. If I witness someone fail by doing something the way I would have done it, I can learn from that and not have to fail that way.

What would you tell your 18-year-old self?

People that have things, worked for them. Those things don't magically appear. You have to work for them, and they are expensive.

If you have more stuff than will fit in a VW Microbus, you have too much.

How do you define success?

My definition of success depends on the situation. If the situation completes and meets the needs, that is success.

Success for me is having someone wake up in the middle of the night and say, "I heard somewhere…. What if we do this?" and they are successful—all based on something I said, or something we talked about.

A group of solutions will make determining your decisions easier. Howard Pierpont is a solutionist for the Institute for Preparedness and Resilience—the educational arm of the Disaster Emergency Preparedness and Response Association (DERA), a 501(c)3 organization.
www.Preparedness.org
Howard.Pierpont@Preparedness.Org
www.Howard.Solutions
Twitter: solution_howard
970-397-5526

SUZY PENDERGRAFT

Through the Storm, Toward the Light

Suzy Pendergraft, a Realtor with 25 years of experience, is known for delivering exceptional service in Denver, Colorado. Continuing her mother's 50-year legacy as a Realtor, Suzy leads a thriving team, which includes her sister and 22-year-old daughter (three generations!), and grows their business through client referrals and nationwide Realtor partnerships.

The Greatest Storm

I believe that gratitude, attitude, and courage to do the hard things are critical in the pursuit of success, happiness, and fulfillment in life.

The past three years have been the most difficult of my life. In 2022, I made the decision to leave my husband of 24 years. I can pinpoint the exact moment I realized that my marriage was falling off a cliff. I was devastated! I was petrified! I was so scared and so sad. We have two kids and I knew this would crush them. My kids are the center of my universe, and I never wanted to do anything to hurt them.

From June of 2022 to July of 2023, when my divorce was final, I felt like I was living through the greatest storm of my life. I grieved so hard. I could NOT believe that this was happening… what we were going to lose. It absolutely broke my heart.

I learned a lot over those 13 months though. The first lesson was thanks to my dear friend Heather. It was Thanksgiving morning 2022, and I was bawling my eyes out as we talked on the phone. Heather had recently gone through a divorce, so she knew what I was going through, and it was as if she said, "Suzy, pull yourself together," (or at least that's how I remember it) when she gave me this advice.

She said "Suzy, you HAVE TO DO THE WORK! You have to spend time journaling, reading, listening, thinking, and grieving as you go THROUGH this. You have to do the work."

Do the Work

Over the next year, I did the work. I allowed myself to grieve, A LOT, and it was often at inconvenient times and with people I'd prefer to not share these sad emotions with (like clients), but I tried very hard to just be authentic and real, and let the emotions flow. I learned that walking was therapy for me, and I would often journal on my phone while walking. I listened to podcasts on divorce, love, health, and survival, and I loved hearing stories about how others had overcome life's challenges and come out the other side whole and happy.

I spent lots of time thinking, and I leaned heavily on my family. I don't believe I could have survived this without the support and love of my family. I also leaned into my friends, and as someone who doesn't like to ask for help, I learned to ask for and be okay with their help and support. I sought out the help of a psychologist and I found his insight to be brilliant and incredibly helpful.

I came to realize that there was no way around this storm, that I had to go right through it and deal with all the emotions, heartbreaks, and fears in order to be good on the other side.

A New Mountain

Once I survived 2023, I was a whole new person. I was happy, and I was okay. I survived! I thought that 2023 was my hardest year and that 2024 was my comeback year.

In January 2023, I remember telling my business coach, Buffini and Company's Kelli Snyder, that I knew 2023 was going to be a hard year, but it was going to be a good year. I didn't want to wallow in the drama. I wanted to put my head down and focus on getting through it while also having a REALLY good year in my business. I told her that 2023 was going to be good (and it was—it turned out to be my second-best year ever in my real estate business), but 2024 was going to be GREAT.

My focus now turned to 2024 which was going to be MY year, the year that I would rebuild. The divorce had devastated me financially, but I was committed to making lots of progress this year. I was going to have my best year ever selling real estate and get back on my feet financially.

With all the confidence in the world, believing that my life was on the up and up and that everything always works out for me, in December of 2023, I decided to build a new home, in my dream neighborhood, where I had wanted to live for years. The builder was offering some nice incentives to try to move some inventory before the end of the year, and I was able to negotiate a great deal, so I went under contract and my new home would soon be underway.

With talk about the interest rates adjusting down several times in the coming year, this was perfect. By the time I was ready to sell my current home, it would be the best selling season and I'd sell it for top dollar. Based on the sales in my neighborhood and our desirable lot, it made sense to remodel before selling. The comps were very strong, and I knew I'd easily see the return on my investment. So, from January to May, my son Josh and I lived in a construction zone. It was really hard, but he was such a champ. My daughter Lexi was off at college and we sent her periodic photo updates as the transformation took place. She was so supportive and excited about it too.

By early May, it was done and it turned out beautifully. I put the home on the market in the second week of May, and I had no concerns that it would sell quickly.

Unfortunately, the Denver market took an abrupt turn in early May. I ended up selling my home for about $80,000 less than my bottom line—the number that made moving to the new home make sense. I had to choose to either walk away from the $55,000 that I had put down on construction of the new home or cut my losses, sell my home for less than my bottom line, and make this move. I decided to be courageous, sell my home and move. I did not expect this second financial blow in 2024. But with that chapter closed, I chose to move on.

Learning Forward

I believe that our greatest challenges in life offer us the greatest opportunity for growth. I also believe surviving the trials of life puts us in a better position to help others as they struggle through their own life challenges.

I have always had a passion for helping others, whether it's helping them overcome their fears and doubts, guiding them through challenges, or helping them achieve a goal.

I once heard on a podcast by Ed Mylett that we are most equipped to help the person we used to be. I knew that after surviving this storm and getting through this divorce, and after all that others had done to support me, that I would use this experience to pay it forward. I would be there to help others who were going through the same thing. I wanted to be there for people who were going through a divorce, to guide them and counsel them, to provide support, and to let them know that the ONLY way to happiness and peace on the other side is to go straight through the storm. There's no way around it.

I also wanted to set an example for my children, and for others, of what life on the other side of divorce can look like. I believe that my former husband, my children, and I will always be a family and that we can choose how we treat one another as we go through the rest of our lives. We chose to be kind and compassionate towards each other, and we still gather, all four of us, for holidays, birthdays, and my son's soccer games. My family even recently threw a 60th birthday party for my former husband.

Crossroads and Lessons

As I look back on my life of 50+ years, the hardest things I ever went through were the making of me. My life has been filled with many of these moments, crossroads where I have a choice—a choice to be bitter, discouraged, hopeless, and frustrated with the cards that I've been dealt or to have an optimistic outlook, and a determination to get through it and be better for it. Over the past 30 years of my adult life, I've recognized a pattern of how I've dealt with adversity and challenges. I believe that gratitude, attitude, and courage to do the hard things are critical in the pursuit of success and happiness in life.

After my parents went through a divorce when I was eight years old, I went through a really dark time. We moved twice in two years, and when I started fifth grade in a new school where I knew no one, I started hanging out with the wrong kids, using drugs, and getting into trouble at school and with the law. I was also physically abused by a teacher. Thank God, I decided at age 12 to break away from that group of kids and turn my energy towards sports. I played competitive soccer, and with the help of some exceptional coaches and great teammates, I went on to win two state championships with my high school team. I survived!

I got into college by a slim margin but I matured a lot and had great success, graduating with a degree in psychology. After college, it seemed like every dream I chased, I was able to achieve, even though each pursuit had its challenges. I had developed an attitude of "do whatever it takes," and I just would not quit until I accomplished my goal.

After college, I spent 10 years as a ski instructor, even though I was initially almost not hired. I worked as an Outward Bound instructor for five years, despite being told I lacked the necessary technical skills and experience. I achieved my dream of completing an Ironman for my 40th birthday, despite warnings that I might not finish and that it could jeopardize my marriage or even put my life at risk.

When I was pregnant with my daughter, I was told in a job interview that they would be hiring a man to fill the position because of the high price point of the product they were selling. I was clearly being discriminated against for my gender and the fact that I was pregnant. I made a choice to pivot with a career change shortly after this happened, which is how I ended up in real estate.

I've learned to ignore the doubters and believe in myself. I've learned that all of the hard things I've overcome serve as the greatest opportunities for growth for me and possibly inspiration for others. I realize that my life story is still being written and I have total faith and confidence that the next chapter will be amazing. Second half, BETTER HALF. It's a good life!

SUZY'S THOUGHT LEADER LESSONS

Some of my core beliefs:
- Always be kind to others – you never know what others might be going through.
- Everyone deserves a second chance and everyone has their story—even those who are at the top of their game, or appear to be… they, too, have their story.
- Everyone who has achieved great success in life, or sports, or business, has inevitably made great sacrifices and worked very hard to get where they are.
- Don't let anyone tell you that you can't do something—even those who love you most. If you want something, go get it. NO EXCUSES!
- When one door closes, another door opens. ATTITUDE IS EVERYTHING!
- Attitude, gratitude, and courage to do what needs to be done (Do the hard thing, as Darren Hardy says) are the fundamental keys to success in business and to living a life of abundance, happiness, and fulfillment.
- I made a list of what I'm looking for in my next life partner. I believe that to attract this man, I must become or have all of these traits and characteristics as well. I've been working very hard on being the VERY best version of myself in order to attract this "perfect" man.
- NO REGRETS!

Q&A WITH SUZY

What is your favorite movie?

One of my favorite movies is *The Pursuit of Happyness*. My favorite scene is when Chris Gardner is playing basketball with his son. His son has a dream to be a professional basketball player, and Chris crushes his dream by telling him that it will never happen. Then Chris realizes what he's done and delivers THE BEST advice you could ever give a young person: "Don't ever let somebody tell you you can't do something, not even me. You got a dream, you gotta protect it. People can't do something themselves, they want to tell you that you can't do it. You want something, go get it. Period." Whenever I watched this movie with my kids I'd always stop at this scene and repeat these words to them. It drove them crazy but I didn't care.

What are a few of your favorite quotes?

- "Good timber doesn't grow with ease, the stronger the wind, the stronger the trees" – Douglas Malloch
- "Courage is not having the strength to go on, it is going on when you don't have the strength" – Theodore Roosevelt

Who are your mentors and greatest influences?

Brian Buffini – He taught me the importance of life balance and systems to be successful in business and in life.

Darren Hardy – He's one of my favorite mentors in the area of leadership and business.

The community of people I've met through my involvement with Brian and Darren – I have a network of friends across the country. These aren't just friends, they are like family, and we love and support each other as we go through life together. They inspire me to be the very best version of myself and to aim for goals and dreams that are sometimes beyond my imagination.

My mom – She has worked 50+ years as a Realtor and is still going strong at 80 years old. She is strong as a bull and one of the kindest and most generous people I've ever known.

My kids – Josh and Lexi have made me a better human and a better mom. They call me out on things, challenge me, love me unconditionally, and treat me with respect. I am so immensely proud of the good humans they are becoming. They are still my WHY even as they have grown into young adults.

My brother and my sister – They have sacrificed so much over the past few years to support and love me through this difficult season of my life. We are always there for each other. I'm very blessed to have an amazing family.

My dad – After a very tough upbringing and an abusive father, he is the most loving, supportive, and kind father.

How do you define success?

To me, the most significant part of success in life is around relationships. I may not be changing the world, but I know that I can make a difference in the lives of the people in my world, and this is what I try to do each day.

Suzy Pendergraft hopes to inspire others to live with gratitude, embrace hope, and understand that life happens for them, not to them. She is passionate about helping people navigate life's challenges, especially in parenting or divorce, and is always available to assist with real estate needs in the Denver area. Reach out at 720-363-2409, suzypendergraft@gmail.com, or visit her website www.suzypendergrafthomes.com

BOBBY ADKINS

Entrepreneurship and Growth
A Texas Tale of Oil, Gas, and Tech

Bobby Adkins is a husband, father, grandfather, entrepreneur, and philanthropist. As a business-building strategist, he specializes in driving hyper-growth residuals across industries including oil & gas and technology. Through his venture capital firm, Bobby has developed innovative software solutions for high-profile clients like Match.com, Hotels. com, and American Airlines.

Texas: Sweetwater to Dallas – My Journey in Business, Family, and Life

I grew up in Sweetwater, a small town in West Texas, with a population of about 12,000 people. Though it was a quiet place, it was a perfect environment for me to develop the values that have shaped my life. I was raised in a family steeped in entrepreneurial spirit. My father worked in the oil business and was also a cattle rancher—the very picture of the stereotypical Texan. Whether we were driving cattle across vast ranches, drilling for oil and gas, or helping at the oil and gas supply stores, which were akin to 24/7 hardware stores, I learned early the importance of hard work, dedication, and taking initiative. These were not just values we talked about—they were values we lived by.

In Texas, sports are more than just games; they are a way of life. I played football at Sweetwater High School, and in the fall of 1985, our team pulled off an incredible feat by winning the 4A High School State Championship. We were always the underdog, often considered too small and too slow to compete against larger schools like Austin Westlake and Houston Tomball. But what we lacked in physical attributes, we made up for in heart, hustle, and a relentless work ethic. The grueling offseason training, modeled after the Odessa Panthers of *Friday Night Lights*, gave us a mental and physical edge that carried us to victory. The lessons I learned on the field—about teamwork, determination, and overcoming adversity—have stayed with me throughout my life.

After high school, Texas Tech University football offered me an invited walk-on kicker position. The "business" of Division I football was formative. Pursuing a business degree in what is now the Rawls School of Business also deepened my excitement for business. College was a time of personal growth and leadership development.

At Texas Tech, opportunities to thrive were fresh and invigorating. I joined Sigma Phi Epsilon (Sig Ep) fraternity and was able to serve as treasurer of our 150 men. This set the course for managing Sig Ep capital and cash flow as well as becoming part of the executive team leading our vision. We later were recognized as a top Sig Ep Chapter in the United States with the coveted Buchanan Award. As a junior, I served the entire interfraternity system as the scholastic leader of over 23 fraternities, deepening the value of education I held. That same year, a wonderful group of friends and I started our own business fraternity, Phi Sigma Beta. It was an honor serving as the vice president and leader of business education. Texas Tech University and the relationships from college were vital to my growth and development.

During my college years, I also met a mentor who would have a profound influence on my life: Walter Hailey. Walter was an older successful Sig Ep, and I will always look up to him with a deep appreciation as a mentor. He introduced me to the principles of sales, scale, replication, personalities, and customer service. His insight, coupled with my lifelong admiration for Zig Ziglar, inspired my personal development and entrepreneurial mindset.

After graduation, I joined Procter & Gamble, where sales training was paramount. While I appreciated the experience, it became clear to me that my true calling was entrepreneurship.

Soon after, my father gave me an offer I could not refuse; to work together and help grow his business, either in Midland, Sweetwater, or Dallas, Texas. As a young, single guy just starting out, Dallas seemed like the perfect choice. My father's offer was simple—$2,000 a month, a company vehicle, no expense account and a commission structure. Though the expenses were on me, I saw this as a chance to make my own mark.

It did not take long before I was applying my entrepreneurial instincts to the oil and gas sector. By 1993, it was time to start putting together oil and gas deals. At the same time, I was starting Adobe Oil & Gas for acquiring oil and gas mineral royalties. It was a challenge to find sellers. Once someone has "mailbox money," they rarely sell. Fortunately, sellers could be found, as the hunt for buying quality, long-life, generational income was a difficult task, but fun and challenging.

In 1998, the internet was an unknown technology touting a bright future. It seemed like there was enormous upside and adventure. I created Teton Investment Capital while the internet boom was in its infancy. Seemingly loose and crazy software ideas were funded and growing. We were able to start providing subcontracted IT services with code writers. Soon after, friends and clients began bringing us software development and investment deals. Over the years, we gradually grew into venture capital, focused on solving real-world problems.

The family in which you grow up and are loved makes such a difference when viewing the world. My parents certainly had us growing up traditionally, instilling in us the importance of hard work, integrity, and perseverance. Good or bad choices can change the course of each life. The best choice for me was the sweetheart I married. Nicole and I have been married for 29 years, and together, we have raised three wonderful sons. My sweetheart is the bright spot in everyone's day and makes my life worth living. My parents, still happily married after 57 years, continue to be an incredible source of inspiration. And as a family, we have always found strength in our faith. For us, the answers to life's most difficult questions can be found in the Bible, if we are open to seeking them. We are grateful.

Solving Problems: What Drives Me

One of the things that excites me is solving problems—especially those that have a lasting impact on business, leadership, and the community. I find purpose in addressing challenges head-on, whether they relate to strategy, human development, or even large-scale problems that benefit society. The way I see it, the more you serve others, the more you grow yourself—a philosophy that aligns perfectly with Zig Ziglar's famous words: "You can have everything in life you want, if first you will just help enough other people get what they want."

In leadership, I know the target for our team is to always keep top of mind the alignment between strategic vision and tactical execution to achieve the mission.

A key element included in calculating our future outcome of the target is time. Time is also one of the most overlooked factors in success. When it comes to achieving goals, we do not just set arbitrary "goals;" we set **targets**—specific, measurable objectives with time deadlines. We train our team to embrace this mindset, with the understanding that timing matters. A common statement is "What we measure, we can manage, and what we manage, we can improve." Constant improvement is key, and we always strive to be just a little better than our "yesterday selves." A family saying exemplifying this action as well as in our companies is, "The difference between ordinary and extraordinary is the little, "extra!"

Investment Philosophy: Building for the Future

My investment philosophy revolves around Zig's philosophy, while understanding risk and knowing when to take it and when to avoid it. We find lower risk investments relative to potentially high returns. One of our pinnacle principles is to have a strong, experienced management. We also prefer to be actively involved. The adage of "inspect what you expect" is true. This helps with creating a great management team. A management team which has key performance indicators such as high margins and residual income is a critical component to building a sustainable portfolio. Residual income—cash flow that keeps coming in long after the initial work is done—has been a key factor in ensuring long-term growth and revenue.

Additionally, always looking for opportunities that have the potential for scalability. The goal is to build something with rapid scalability, a company that does not just grow—it explodes with growth and turns into hypergrowth! It's so easy to think too small. When studying a market, we quiz ourselves, asking, "How much can this company grow? What is the potential for long-term cash flow? What is the potential for generating returns that last and while scaling rapidly? Can it achieve hypergrowth?"

Mindset: The Foundation of Everything

One of the most important lessons I have learned in life and business is that without the right mindset, achieving anything of significance is incredibly difficult. Life and business are full of obstacles, but the ability to maintain a positive attitude, step out in faith, and believe in your ability to achieve great things makes all the difference. Personal development—whether spiritual, physical, or professional—is the foundation of any successful venture. Our mindset shapes who we are, how we approach challenges, and how we interact with the world.

At the end of the day, my journey reflects the principles I live by: faith in Jesus Christ, hard work, service to others, and a relentless commitment to solving problems. Whether in business, family, or life, we have a responsibility in America to our following generations. I hope that the legacy I leave behind is one of love, care, dedication, perseverance, and a commitment to helping our family and others achieve their dreams.

Q&A WITH BOBBY

What is your favorite movie?

It's a Wonderful Life has always been my favorite. Jimmy Stewart's portrayal of George Bailey really resonates with me. George discovers the incredible impact one life can have on a community and how even small actions can leave a lasting mark on others. It is a timeless reminder that the way we live our lives has far more influence than we often realize.

Another movie that stands out is *Rudy*. Rudy Ruettiger's story is the ultimate underdog tale. Despite being told he was too small to play for Notre Dame, his passion and determination led him to achieve his dream. It is proof that no matter the obstacles, persistence and heart can turn dreams into reality.

How do you recharge?

Sunday is my day to rest and reset. We go to church, and then I try to spend the rest of the day at home with our family, taking it easy. Of course, not every Sunday is perfect, as life often calls for travel or other personal commitments, but we really try to prioritize rest and reflection with a Sabbath day.

I draw inspiration from how David (...of David and Goliath) in the Bible would recharge. Even in battle, he would take time to reconnect with God. It is a powerful reminder that we need moments of stillness when life gets hectic to gather strength for the next challenge. During the week, I like to begin each day in prayer, thanking God for another day and asking Him to grant me wisdom and guide my steps. After submitting my day to the Lord, I trust no matter what happens, it is in His will.

I also find peace in nature. I love taking walks outside and enjoying the simplicity of the natural world—it is one of the best ways for me to clear my mind and recharge.

What is something most people do not know about you?

I strum an acoustic guitar. Also, my wife and I enjoy art and other museums. We appreciate and admire the efforts of those before us. We enjoy taking our children to science museums. What a fun and amazing way to educate and pass down humanity's achievements to our next generation.

What books do you often recommend?

One book I always recommend is *How to Win Friends and Influence People* by Dale Carnegie. It teaches timeless principles about how to connect with others, build relationships, and lead with influence. I have found the lessons in that book to be incredibly valuable throughout my career and personal life. This has been one book I buy in bulk to hand out to young people just starting out in the business world and life.

Bobby Adkins is the CEO of Teton Investment Capital, LLC. He is the founder of numerous fintech and technology companies. He is also a Texas Oil and Gas producer, O&G mineral/royalty buyer, and O&G services provider. To book a consultation, podcast, or speaking engagement, please email Bobby@TetonCapital.com or call 817.461.4690 (office).
LinkedIn: Bobby Adkins www.linkedin.com/in/bobby-adkins-a606ab24

Adkins Companies: Technology / Oil & Gas YPO-Lonestar Chapter

TIM COLE

Bringing Honor and Healing to Veterans

Colonel Tim Cole is a retired 31-year Marine leader, author, speaker, and enthusiastic advocate for military Veterans and their families. His passion is helping families and friends understand their Veterans' service and honor their military heritage.

Blue-Collar Kid

I'm a blue-collar kid who grew up in the shadows of industrial steel mills of Northwest Indiana. My grandparents were sharecroppers in Missouri, laboring in exchange for living on the owner's land. After Dad served in the Army during the Korean War, he married Mom, and they moved north where he found work in the steel mill. They escaped a life of poverty and became successful in the eyes of their family.

I grew up in an uncertain family environment created by alcoholism, which meant life as a kid was chaotic and confusing. These formative childhood years came with embarrassment, shame, and guilt, impacting self-confidence and self-esteem.

School sports helped pull me out of that home environment. I was not a great athlete, but I chose to show up, suit up, and get in the game. That was my attitude—get in there and do the very best I could. Sure enough, I began to have success in athletics. I made the freshmen basketball team and played four years of high school football. Although I was not a big guy, I was strong and quick and played with aggression. Our team was not expected to do well my senior year, but we won our district and went to the state playoffs.

My friend's father, Mr. Wilson, became a mentor to me. He was confident I could play college football. My parents didn't have high school diplomas, so they felt a high school diploma was a great achievement. Mr. Wilson showed me how to write letters to college coaches and then drove me to visit colleges. With his help, I'm the first in my family to earn a college degree.

The Front Office

After graduating with a business degree, I moved to Kansas City where I found a job at a small, family-owned, metal fabricating plant. I had grown up pouring concrete, moving brick and mortar, patching roads, and dumping garbage, so I understood how to do blue-collar labor. I didn't know what my business degree could do for me, so I went with what I knew, working in the plant as a machine operator. A few weeks into my new job, the owner came over to me and asked, "Do I understand you have a business degree from Graceland College? I want to give you a job in my front office." It turned out he was also a Graceland graduate.

That year I learned how a business operates. The owner was a one-man show. I was fortunate to witness and learn everything from purchasing materials and equipment to ensuring delivery and customer service from right outside his office.

The Realization

A year later, I was hired by a Fortune 500 company. Things around me began to change. People were getting married, buying homes, and having families. When I witnessed a coworker die from a heart attack at the office, something inside me encouraged me to live more fully. I needed to get away from the corporate world for a while and challenge myself.

So, I went to the Marine Recruiters that afternoon and enlisted in the Marine Corps at age 24.

I was looking for a challenge, something that would test me. Nothing would test me like becoming a Marine. I knew I could always go back to an office job.

A Patriot

In my 31 years of military service and in my corporate world, I've traveled all over the world. And yes, I've seen some desperate places that do not have the advantages we have in the USA, places that remind us that people at the poverty level in the USA are amazingly among the wealthiest people in the world.

Our history is far from perfect, yet an amazing heritage of opportunity fuels my patriotism.

After a full career of active military duty, service members are honored with a formal retirement ceremony and celebration. Fellow military servicemen and families attend. A military award is presented to the Veteran, flowers and gifts are presented to the family, and all the medals earned during the Veteran's service are honorably displayed in an award case.

On active duty, I saw and conducted a number of these memorable and edifying ceremonies.

I once asked my dad where his military awards were. He noted he received one award and didn't know where it was. So, I wrote to find out about my dad's awards, and I was intrigued by what I found. I wanted to honor my father's military service, so I assembled a medals display made with Dad's medals. His was the first medal awards display I created.

Because of my military service, I knew exactly what the medals were and what it took to earn them. I gave the award display to Dad at Christmas in front of our family, who did not understand what these awards meant. As I explained each of the medals' service requirements and recognition, I witnessed my dad get choked up. Nobody had ever talked about him and his military service in a way that was so honoring. It helped our family understand what he had accomplished.

After Dad got misty-eyed, I asked him why. He said, "The military helped change my life. It pulled me out of backwoods Missouri. I began to have confidence that I could do things others could do."

Having witnessed that, I began doing the same research and honoring for family members and friends in the early 1990s. Now, I have held a couple hundred of these ceremonies to honor men and women who have served our country.

TIM'S THOUGHT LEADER LESSONS

Fitness

Staying healthy and active has served me well throughout my life. It helped me get to college via sports, into the Marine Corps, and connected with my family and grandkids. To me, fitness is foundational. If you don't have your health, what good is all the wealth in the world? I can't buy health, so I focus on my fitness, health, and wellness first.

There's even more that I feel like I can be doing and should be doing. That said, not only do I want to live a long, healthy life, I want to live a good life.

I stopped drinking alcohol 30-plus years ago. Ultimately, that was for my mental and emotional health, and that decision allowed me to make many better choices. That also allowed time. Phil Collen of Def Leppard talks about how when he finally put away the drugs and alcohol, he found that he had all this extra time in his day. That's when he started getting into fitness, mixed martial arts, and boxing. I learned he's only a year younger than me, and he's in phenomenal shape.

The other thing is consistency. As I get older, it can be challenging to get in a 30-minute run in 90+ degree heat, but I always get that endorphin rush that says, *Man, I'm glad I got it done, no matter how slow I was*. Besides, I want to have that positive influence on my kids, grandkids, and friends.

Passion for Honoring Veterans

In the USA, we're in this environment of freedom, liberty, and opportunity, and that doesn't happen by accident.

More than 200 years ago, brave men and women in England's American colonies said, "Taxation without representation is not right," and England responded by sending the world's strongest army to America to enforce taxation, igniting the American Revolution.

I've been fortunate to spend time with US World War II Veterans. Evil was prevalent, powerful, and moving through the world. I would not want to think about living under Nazi Germany control or extremist Japanese rule. It was evil what the Axis powers did at that time. Yet, Allied people stood up and said "We can't tolerate this. There are God-given rights, and we need to protect them," and heavy sacrifices were made. America lost 400,000 in World War II, and Russia and England lost millions to help protect our liberty.

We need law and order to provide us the opportunity to do the things we love and to take care of the people we love. Unfortunately, there are forces that want to take those opportunities away and believe it's appropriate to murder innocent people. 9/11 would be an example of that.

Who protects that opportunity today? Our nation's military—our servicemen and women—around the globe. And law enforcement has the home game. People die to protect our opportunity. Ron White does the Afghanistan Wall, writing 5,000-plus names that he memorized of men and women who served and gave their lives in Afghanistan so we can be here today. That's the foundation for why I value the military.

In my 31 years of Marine Corps service, I've been both enlisted and an officer on active duty; on Active Reserve duty; and mobilized Active Duty after 9/11 including combat zone tours during the Global War on Terror.

The military has a team mindset. Most Veterans of the military are not "me, me, me," and I've found in my years of honoring Veterans that many of them have never really been recognized.

Families may ask questions, but Veterans are hesitant to talk and tell all, resulting in many thinking it's because they saw bad things. That may have been the case for some Veterans, but also it's a philosophy that's about the team, the unit, fellow warfighters—it's not all about "me."

Veterans love America, democracy, and their families. But the reality is, under incoming fire, you're fighting for the guy and gal next to you. Military uniforms and their ribbons and patches tell that Veteran's military story if you know how to read them.

I learned years ago that I can effectively tell a Veteran's story. Especially when I have the privilege of doing this in front of family, the family is many times awestruck because they had no idea who Dad, Grandpa, Mom, or Grandma were in their military service. And, occasionally, we learn that there was genuine heroism. Telling their story is healing and emotionally impactful.

Personal Development

I feel like I was late to the game. The very last semester of college the light finally came on. Learning is lifelong. I am always learning for personal development and for growth.

When I got into a business career, I learned the value of education. So I started a master's program then enlisted in the Marine Corps.

In the business world, I did a lot of reading, books like *The 7 Habits of Highly Effective People*, and was introduced to network marketing. And that was the world of real personal development: Jim Rohn, Zig Ziglar, Brian Tracy, and Darren Hardy. In network marketing, everybody's trying to grow themselves. Like Jim Rohn said, I started working harder on me than I was working for somebody else. That was a big catalyst for change for me, and it has paid dividends many, many times over in my professional and even more so my military career.

Ultimately, it led me to Kyle Wilson and his Inner Circle community. I come from very humble beginnings. Getting a college degree was a big deal in my family. I knew how to work and how to work hard. But Kyle Wilson's Inner Circle mastermind group has been a real transition for me to learn how to become entrepreneurial.

Mentors

There are two key Wilsons in my life: Mr. Wilson from my childhood and, of course, Kyle Wilson.

Mr. Wilson was the father of our high school quarterback. I grew up in a town where we all went to school together, so by the time you're playing high school football alongside these guys, it's personal.

These are your dearest friends. Mr. Wilson was a true mentor to me. Mr. Wilson is the guy who said, "Tim, you may be 5'11" and 190 pounds and all the coaches are saying you're too small to play college football, but don't believe them. You can play small college football." And as it turned out, he was absolutely right. I lettered for four years and was a starter for two years on a small college team with three winning seasons, a conference championship and a bowl game appearance.

Kyle is a dear, dear friend. I'm grateful for him. While we are very much alike, both from humble beginnings, we're always growing and changing and have lived very different lives.

Q&A WITH TIM

What is your favorite movie?

Secondhand Lions – Because of the "What Every Boy Needs to Know About Being a Man" speech. Among seemingly irrelevant elders are genuine, true-life heroes capable of influencing and improving the lives of younger generations.

Rudy – Overcoming immense adversity with grit, persistence, passion, and sacrifice both inspires and affects others around you… even those with great gifts.

Saving Private Ryan – Today's generations are fortunate beneficiaries of the Greatest Generation heroes who fought to protect and preserve the freedoms we enjoy today. Our personal and individual call is to "earn this" and make our own impact for good in this world.

What are a few of your favorite quotes?

- 5 P's – Prior Planning Prevents Poor Performance.
- Lead, follow, or get out of the way, but do something (action over inaction).
- A person of integrity expects to be believed, but if they're not, they simply let time prove them right (actions over words).

What philanthropic causes do you support?

Quest of the Keys – 501(c)(3) organization – a character development program for middle school to early high school-aged students applied via a fan fiction adventure story. I've served on the board for several years and have witnessed its positive impact.

What would you tell your 18-year-old self?

You have absolutely no idea of the life that is ahead of you…. far above and beyond what you can now comprehend and understand. Suspend your doubt and trepidation. Live life fully. Remain a lifelong learner. Apply the multitude of gifts, skills, and talents you have now and will acquire ahead. Live your best life, living fully and gratefully, building relationships, and inspiring and encouraging others. Show Up, Suit Up, and Get in the Game of your own life! You will not regret it!

To learn more about how to honor the Veterans in your life, reach out to 31-year Marine Colonel, speaker, and Veteran advocate Tim Cole at
Email: jtcole50@gmail.com
Social Media: www.facebook.com/tim.cole.940
linkedin.com/in/james-tim-cole-382b8914
Website: www.coloneltimcole.com

GARY PINKERTON

Achieving Agency
Turning Poverty into Abundance by Following God and Betting on Yourself

Gary Pinkerton improves the lives of his clients as a wealth strategist specializing in family banking, tax efficiency, and legacy and estate planning. He employs 30 years of ethical leadership gained at the US Naval Academy and honed as a nuclear attack submarine Commander as an experienced business owner, motivational speaker, and real estate investor.

Poverty Is a Great Motivator

I grew up dairy farming in southern Illinois. My father would be milking the cows at three o'clock in the morning and then again in the afternoon, rain, snow, or shine.

In high school, I was driving an embarrassing old car and wearing hand-me-down clothes. The high inflation of the early 1980s meant food, shelter, and clothing cost more than most people I knew made. In 1984, we had 18% variable interest rate loans on our farm, and soon the bank foreclosed, and we were broke, living in a borrowed trailer on my uncle's land. My father's health had failed and I found myself working odd jobs every moment I was not in school to put food on the table. I resented that life and dreamed of a life with a safe, secure W-2 job.

As an adult, for 20 years, all I was thinking about was monetary wealth and keeping my kids from living the way I had. Now though, I recognize that in comparison my children are far more disadvantaged.

My background created a chip on my shoulder. I had a burning desire to change my situation, and I worked as hard as I could to get straight A's then to get accepted to the Naval Academy, selected into submarines, and finally, commanding my own ship and retiring as a Navy Captain.

Nuclear Submarine Commander

I commanded the USS Tucson, a Los Angeles-class attack boat. Submarining is certainly a unique lifestyle. Being underwater without opening the hatch for 70 days is common. We produced our water and air onboard and had over 30 years of nuclear fuel. We had spare parts and the ability to make more. With the exception of food or a very unique part, we could operate indefinitely.

In command of a submarine, you have a team of 150 people. It's an amazing group, the best of the best in the military. While their enthusiasm may wane after long weeks at sea, they are patriotic, extremely smart, American heroes. It was truly an honor to serve and lead these wonderful people.

When I took over, the ship had just completed an almost two-year overhaul. It was fitted with the newest state-of-the-art systems. But the crew had to re-learn how to go to sea all over again and we failed many times. We eventually succeeded and deployed for six months to Asia. It was just incredible—a very difficult challenge at the beginning with a tremendous result at the end. It's something I'll never forget. I'm truly humbled and honored to have been given that opportunity, and fully acknowledge there was never a clearer example of God's hand guiding my life than in safely navigating the dozens of harrowing crises we encountered in that harsh deployed environment.

Refocusing Patriotism

As I finished that tour that brought many accolades and a path to making Admiral, my personal life was crumbling. I was married to a wonderful lady, who had understandably grown weary of this life, and was a dad to two wonderful young boys who barely knew me. I saw the difference between wealth and legacy. Wealth is what you leave to someone. Far more important, legacy is what you leave inside them. Reflecting on all I learned from my dad in those long hours on the farm, the legacy of experiences and lessons he'd left me, I realized how fortunate I'd been. I needed to be around my kids much more and could not achieve that while climbing the ranks within the military.

I spent most of my last years as a Navy Captain in the Washington, DC area working in big government, leading a division for the Chairman of the Joint Chiefs in the Pentagon. It was another incredibly rewarding opportunity to work with the best of the best, and this time, across all the military services. This experience also taught me something very important about myself: Senior military roles and big government life were not for me.

I realized that my love for America was not about nationalism, but rather our founding father's ideas embodied in the constitution, its enduring focus on protecting the rights of individuals and their life, liberty, and property. I wanted to help sustain this 250-year-old experiment—a vision, unique across the globe in the 1700s, that an individual owns their body, their property, and the results of their efforts in creating goods and services. That experiment was wildly successful and spread prosperity and hope around the world. But it is always at risk, never guaranteed, and I realized patriotism to me meant protecting the ideals and freedoms of our republic.

I shifted my focus to helping business owners and entrepreneurs prosper by improving their finances and sharing their unique genius with the world. These were practices I saw and loved when I was a kid on the farm. Back then, there was no Amazon.com. Things we needed were made locally. Someone just started making it, and often, a thriving business was born. My dad and I made apple crates for orchards for a few years because they needed them, and we had trees and a sawmill, and we were paid well to solve that challenge. I love that about America.

But DC taught me that when government grows, it takes on the traits of a living being—its goals become survival and to get bigger, not service to the people. That results in ever-increasing taxes that crush the small business owner and steal agency and freedom from the very people who elected the government.

Funding a Personal Economy, A Foundation to Wealth

Protecting our Republic and the American dream comes down to people having the ability to, first, focus on what they're uniquely good at or interested in and, second, prosper from that. That is agency, and strengthening the financial position of American families and their businesses keeps the power with them, not the government; elected officials work for the people by providing the rule of law to support them, not control them. What does my business of high cash-value life insurance have to do with that?

I help people build a personal economy where they've got control over how they use their resources and what they choose to do in life. A personal economy lays a foundation that enables you to invest in yourself and your business, which is far more important than investing in your 401K. To be successful long-term, you need reserves in a place that is protected and private, and you need to offset risks that typically cause many families and small businesses to fail, like inflation and high taxes.

I use insurance-based financial strategies and services to build a foundation for wealth. At the core, my team educates on the use of an insurance policy as a vehicle where you store emergency money, reserves for your businesses or properties, and cash for upcoming major expenses and investments, where it's protected and can grow three or four times as fast as it would in a savings account, and without the impact of taxes.

This financial foundation, the life insurance benefit, privacy, protection, and tax-free wealth available through this strategy is amazing. And it is the best foundational savings vehicle I've found in my two decades in the financial industry for enabling agency and growing permanent wealth.

GARY'S THOUGHT LEADER LESSONS

Building a Family Legacy

*Wealth is what you leave **to** others. Legacy is what you leave **inside** them.*

All living things have a basic instinct to survive and teach their young the skills needed to ensure survival. However, to humans, God adds a powerful and unique drive to prosper. This quality is the initiative to optimize and innovate far beyond mere survival, to "advance the football" with each generation leaving the world a better place than they found it.

The challenge is that many entrepreneurs and business owners spend so much time building their businesses and amassing their fortunes and then reach the end of their lives without having taken the time to pass on the lessons that made them successful. That was me a decade ago—in 20 short years, I'd gone from a negative net worth and not knowing what the military was to leading at some of the highest levels in the Navy and at the Pentagon with one hundred times the wealth my father achieved. My father taught me the work ethic and business skills of success, yet at that point, I had not done that for my boys. It was a wake-up call, and I changed.

There are no shortcuts to passing on a legacy. You have to thoughtfully put on paper what you're about and put in the time to demonstrate and teach those values to the next generation. If both parents work two jobs to make financial ends meet and don't often spend time with each other or the children, then a legacy is nearly impossible to achieve. So, establishing agency, having the financial resources to live life on your terms, is a prerequisite to building a legacy.

I help clients first establish the foundation of savings and protection, then we move into assets that you directly control like your own career, business, and real estate. The strategy is called building a Hierarchy of Wealth and is essential for creating lasting agency and generational wealth. Speculative stock market investments, where I had all my money in 2010 and most Americans still do today, have a very small role on this more certain path; it is taking lessons from wealthy families that have operated this way for centuries.

Trusting that God Is by Your Side

The greatest lesson I've learned is to recognize the presence of God's guiding hand in every challenge, setback, and success I experience. At a young age, I was wired to take credit for the wins. As I matured, I started taking credit for the losses too. Then, after many experiences of bad judgment and trying to do it alone, I realized this short time on Earth is all in God's hands and playing out as He intended. I'm simply a character in His movie and when I listen to His intent and take His path, I excel, and when I decide I know best and will do it with brute force, we fail. Perhaps that is what surrendering to God means—having the wisdom to realize you are not personally making this all happen, so start asking for guidance and listening.

Q&A WITH GARY

What would you tell your 18-year-old self?

My greatest advice to my 18-year-old self is simply to recognize I'm not alone. Acknowledge God's presence and pay attention to the clues. I first got a glimpse of this when I was 16 and didn't understand the message of a near-death accident. Driving a tractor on a major highway one Saturday morning, I was hit by a commercial van. The driver never saw me and didn't hit his brakes. The police estimated he was traveling over 70 miles per hour. I was going 15 miles per hour. The impact put him through the van's windshield, caused the tractor's front wheels to come five feet off the ground, and destroyed both vehicles.

My tractor had no seatbelt, seatback, or cab. Yet, I walked away without a scratch. I considered myself incredibly lucky and concocted a handful of coincidences to explain how that must have happened. As a proud scientist and engineer, I've explained away God's hand in my life many times in that same way. If you do the same, I'd encourage you to acknowledge God's will and your minority role in this movie of life. You will gain immediate peace, joy, and success.

Contact wealth strategist, entrepreneur, motivational speaker, and real estate professional Gary Pinkerton to learn more about insurance-based financial strategies, reducing taxes, real estate, private banking, and alternative investments for guaranteeing a better future at garypinkerton.com or directly at gary@garypinkerton.com.

 Connect with Gary at garypinkerton.com

SOPHIA STAVRON

Alchemy of Philotimo
Ancient Greek Lifestyle for the Modern Day

Sophia Stavron is the authority on the ancient Greek, Philotimo Lifestyle™ and an intuitive spiritual advisor, #1 bestselling author, executive producer of Emmy award-winning films, facilitator of global retreats, music producer, and transformational speaker. She's also on the advisory board of the Boys & Girls Club.

Lessons From Loss

I never anticipated that my greatest transformation would come from the deepest sorrow. When my father passed away in 2021, it felt like a part of me had died with him. For years, he had been my guiding light, my rock, and my greatest teacher. In return, I spent half my life caring for him as his life-enhancer when he experienced mini-strokes after an emergency back surgery that changed his life in 1998. His passing left a void I didn't know how to fill, a silence that seemed to echo through every corner of my life. Yet, amid this profound loss, I found myself being pulled toward something deeper, something that had always been there, that I always practiced, and that was now demanding my full attention... Philotimo.

Philotimo is an ancient Greek word that is untranslatable, yet its essence is profound. In English, the translation comes from another ancient Greek word, *philotimi*, love and honor. It's about living with honor, integrity, and a deep sense of purpose. It's about recognizing the interconnectedness of all life and understanding that our actions affect not just ourselves, but also the world around us. Growing up, I watched my Greek immigrant father live by these principles. He was a man of quiet, kind strength and unwavering values, always choosing what was right over what was easy. He taught me that the true measure of a person's worth is not in what they achieve, but in how they live their life and the impact they have on others.

As I grappled with the loss of my father, I realized that his greatest gift to me was this understanding of Philotimo. It was the compass he used to navigate his life, and it had become the foundation of mine. For over 25 years, I had built a professional career teaching others about this ancient Greek philosophy, using it to help people find purpose and clarity, create wealth, heal, and unlock their full human potential. Yet, in the wake of his death, I felt called to go even deeper, to explore what it truly meant to live a life of Philotimo.

I decided to take a step back from re-engaging a social life to give myself the space to mourn, reflect, and reconnect with myself. I rented a small cottage on the island of Paros, Greece, a place that I wanted to explore when my father was alive. There, I allowed myself to be still, to listen, to deeply feel. Then I returned to the city of Nafplio, Greece, and walked along the ancient paths, letting the wisdom of the land seep into my bones. I spent hours by the sea which held many special memories, watching the waves crash against the shore, feeling the rhythm of the universe, connecting to the spirit of my father.

It was during one of these quiet moments that I realized the true alchemy of Philotimo. It wasn't just about living with honor or integrity; it was about transformation. It was about taking the raw materials of life... the joy, the pain, the love, the loss... and turning them into something beautiful and meaningful. It was about finding strength in vulnerability, courage in fear, and wisdom in every experience, no matter how challenging. This realization was a turning point for me. I knew that if I was to truly honor my father's legacy, I needed to embody these principles in a deeper, more authentic way. I needed to live Philotimo out loud, not just teach it. I returned home with a renewed sense of purpose and a deep commitment to integrating these values into every aspect of my life.

Applying Philotimo

I started by reevaluating my business. For years, I had focused on growth and expansion, and now I wanted to focus on depth and impact. I wanted to create a space where people could learn about Philotimo and experience it, live it, and embody it in their own lives. I launched a new reimagined initiative, "Living Philotimo," a series of workshops and retreats designed to take people on a journey of self-discovery and transformation. These weren't just seminars; they were immersive experiences that blended ancient wisdom with modern practices, integrating meditation, mindful breathing, and transformational storytelling.

The response was incredible! People came from all over the world, drawn by the promise of learning, and of transformation. I watched as they arrived with excited yet heavy hearts, weighed down by their grief, doubts, and insecurities. And I watched as they left, lighter, more empowered, ready to embrace their potential and live with purpose and a new sense of forward-moving energy. It was a powerful reminder of the transformative power of Philotimo, of the magic that happens when we live in alignment with our true selves.

The true alchemy of Philotimo, alongside the transformations I witnessed in others, was in the transformation I experienced within myself. As I continued to lead these workshops, I found myself becoming more open, more vulnerable, even more authentic (there's always more soul expansion to experience). I was no longer a teacher; I was a participant in my own journey of self-discovery. I began to see my father's death instead of as a loss, as a magnificent catalyst for my own newer level of awakening.

I started to write about my experiences, sharing my journey in a way I never had before. I wrote about the sleepless nights, the moments of doubt, the overwhelming healing of my past caregiver Self. I wrote about the times I felt like giving up, and the moments of clarity that kept me going. There were so many God whispers along the path that helped shift my perspective in moments of darkness. I wrote about my father, about the lessons he taught me, about the love that still guided me every day. My writing became a way to process my emotions, to make sense of my experiences, to find meaning in my pain.

I found my words resonated with others way more than I anticipated. People reached out to me, sharing their own stories of loss, of searching for purpose, of finding themselves amid their own struggles. I have a famous quote I share with my clients: simple creates tsunami results. I realized that in simply sharing my story, I was helping others navigate their own, which in many cases, created tsunami results. I wasn't just teaching Philotimo anymore; I was on a whole other level of living it, embodying it, and inspiring others to do the same.

This journey of self-discovery and transformation has been the most challenging and rewarding of my life. Three years into my transition into my new self, once again, living Philotimo has proven to be more than just a set of principles to live by; it is truly a way of being... a way of seeing the world. I've had to honor my own journey by saying many more noes so I can easily say yes to myself. I've experienced a deeper essence of living with integrity, with courage, with compassion. The greatest gift to ourselves is about choosing to align with our highest values, about being true to ourselves, about honoring the interconnectedness of all life.

The true alchemy of Philotimo lies in its ability to transform us from the inside out. Living Philotimo is about the adventurous path of finding the courage to face our fears, to embrace our vulnerability, to serve others, and to live our truth. It is about recognizing that we are all part of something greater than ourselves, that our actions truly have the power to create ripples of change, to inspire, to uplift, to transform.

As I continue this journey with no destination, I am deeply grateful and blessed for the opportunity to have the greatest mentor of Philotimo in my life for as long as I did. My father's final transition indeed was a profound loss, and it was also the beginning of a new glorious chapter, one that I am writing with intention, love, and a deep commitment to the values that have shaped my life and business. And I know, with every breath, that he is with me, guiding me, encouraging me to keep going. He's my biggest fan!

I am no longer the woman I was before. I am even more aware, more connected, more alive! I am living Philotimo, every day, in every way, and I am inviting others to do the same. When we live with purpose, we awaken to the truth of who we are, we find the courage to live our highest potential, and we create a life that is beyond meaningful and incredibly beautiful. That, I believe, is the greatest gift you can give to yourself and the world. Enjoy the journey!

SOPHIA'S THOUGHT LEADER LESSONS

Problem Solving

In third grade, I learned an important lesson from my father which has been one of the most valuable in life. This lesson is in my daily practice, is the lesson most taught to my clients, and the lesson most profitable to me in business.

One evening, I simply asked my father to help me with a homework problem. Then, I felt the sadness in his heart and saw the look of despair in his eyes.

With a gentle, kind, and loving voice, he said, "I don't know the answer. I will do anything to get you the help you need. I didn't finish school, and I really wish I could help you now."

I felt my heart expand exponentially with a rush of conflicting feelings. I felt his deep unconditional love for me along with the hurt and sorrow in his spirit. Truly, this whirlwind of emotions felt visceral in my body and rang of the most powerful human need, which is being seen.

My expertise in teaching Philotimo, healing techniques, connecting to your intuition, spiritual guidance, and fundraising for nonprofits was either birthed or affirmed in this courageous moment. Moving forward as an innate solution provider, I teach this mantra, "I honor the solution that may be unclear at the moment." Science has proven its power! Thanks, Dad!

Honoring your journey is a continuous life lesson, a way to instantly heal your past, a practice to connect deeper to your divine essence, and a path to courage and service to others.

Q&A WITH SOPHIA

My formula for life and business:

Entrepreneurs, Visionaries, Change Agents, etc. + Massive Possible Impact On Humanity + FUN! = Sophia's ALL IN!

What do you make sure you always do?

I start my mornings with gratitude, prayer, meditation, stretching, breathing, and visualization techniques… no matter what!

What do you consider your greatest achievements to date?

I was an Alzheimer's Impact Movement member and influential speaker on Capitol Hill to senators who passed a bill for a $400-million increase to fiscal year 2017.

I halted my father's vascular dementia, and the neurologist had no words other than, "What you've done is not in the medical books!"

What is something most people don't know about you?

- Most people have no knowledge of how I shrunk my sister's cancer tumors before she started an altered chemotherapy treatment per my firm request to her John Hopkins-trained Dallas oncologist.
- I co-created the Gianni Versace 1999 retail fashion show in Dallas, Texas.

- I was owner/director of Sophia's Creative Learning Center, Inc., a non-profit daycare licensed for 80 children at age 25.
- I started teaching meditation to my sister when I was age 6.
- I became a Godmother at age 12, a goal I set at age 10.

What are some favorite places you've traveled to?

The summer I was turning three years old was my first memory of experiencing my level of consciousness and connectedness to energetic patterns on my travels to Greece.

What do you consider your superpower?

Seeing and translating perspective to others.

What hobbies do you enjoy?

- I was born with a passion for music, playing sports, and spending time exploring nature… I love creating!
- I was a first-chair violinist starting when I began orchestra in the seventh grade.
- As a vocal soloist at church, chandeliers are known to vibrate!
- At age two, I played with the Lawrence Welk band from my living room with homemade instruments.

Connect with Sophia Stavron on unlocking, developing, or elevating your intuition and living a Philotimo Lifestyle or engage her for speaking by visiting www.sophiastavron.com.
Email questions to sophia@sophiastavron.com.
Find free resources and retreat info at LivingPhilotimo.com
Creating a massive positive impact on humanity? Sophia's all in!

 Scan to discover your deeper essence at sophiastavron.com.

TOM ZIGLAR

Growing Up Ziglar

Tom Ziglar is a speaker, a trainer, and the CEO of Zig Ziglar Corporation, as well as the author of 10 Leadership Virtues for Disruptive Times *and* Choose to Win.

Joining the Family Business

Even having Zig Ziglar as a dad, I didn't really feel the pressure of growing up with a famous dad. I'm just not wired that way. It was such an incredible experience having him as my father.

Dad traveled a lot, and while we were in school, he was gone up to three nights a week, 40 weeks a year. But when he was home, he would change his schedule so he could take me to school and play golf with me. For me, that was normal.

Dad was intentional and when he was with us, there weren't any distractions. He was different from most people. He wasn't afraid to say no to people, which took a lot of burden off his shoulders and allowed him to make us a priority. This is a really powerful leadership concept.

When I came into the Ziglar company, I had to work my way up. I was 30 when I became the president and CEO. It wasn't until 15 years ago that I started speaking and training. I'd never wanted to. Why would I go out there to speak when we already had the best in the world? Some of that was based on my personality, some of it was fear. I finally got talked into speaking for the first time and liked it, but it wasn't fun while I was getting ready for it. It was nerve-wracking, and my stomach would do somersaults.

I spoke several more times, and then I finally had to have a "sit down with myself in the corner" talk and ask, *What's my worry? What am I anxious about?* I realized I had burdened myself with the idea that people wanted me to be Zig Ziglar on stage. I had to step out of myself and ask, *Do people really want you to be like Zig Ziglar on stage?*

The answer was no. They wanted me to have the same principles and values but to be the best version of *myself*. When I am not myself, it comes across as fake, as wearing a mask. That understanding put the pressure in the right place, developing myself and understanding what people needed. I realized it wasn't about me or the opportunity I had to speak. It was about every person in the room.

I decided to engage Poll Moussoulides, a speaker trainer who coaches Fortune 100 CEOs in Europe and voice coaches movie stars. I flew to Dublin, Ireland and spent two days with him. I needed somebody who knew of Zig Ziglar but wasn't in the fan club. Sometimes you run across people who are such fans that they won't tell you what you need to hear. I needed somebody to shoot straight.

Working with Poll, I realized that while I could be myself, I could not ever wing one of my speeches. The top in any profession never wing it. They have diligent intentionality about perfecting their skills. Poll's input massively influenced me and gave me the confidence to be myself on stage.

What You Feed Your Mind Determines Your Appetite

One of my favorite quotes from my dad is, "You can change what you are and where you are by changing what goes into your mind." It's really simple. Who do you want to become? What do you have a burning desire and a passion for? Feed your mind that.

The number one lesson I learned from my dad was, control your input. Be intentional about your input. There's no action that happens without someone first thinking about it. When we intentionally choose the right input—what we read, what we listen to, and who we associate with—that changes our thinking.

Our thinking changes our beliefs. Our beliefs also change our thinking. It's a loop. In turn, your thinking changes the actions you take, and the actions you take affect your results. Your input determines your outlook, your outlook determines your output, and your output determines your outcome. Input, outlook, output, outcome. It all starts with what we choose to put into our minds.

Years ago I was in Nashville having dinner with the late Dan Miller, a great friend who wrote *48 Days to the Work You Love*, and his 25-year-old grandson Caleb Miller. My book *Choose to Win* is about habits. The fastest way to success is to replace a bad habit with a good habit. Caleb said, "How do you know if you have a bad habit?"

It's astonishing how awesome a question that is. Most people may feel it is obvious what is or isn't a bad habit. Not necessarily. I said, "If your goal is to get lung cancer, then smoking is a great habit. Here's the problem, most people don't have clearly defined goals or a purpose, something they want to achieve in their life. To test if you have a good or a bad habit, ask yourself if what you are doing is taking you closer to or further from your goal."

Grow Yourself — Grow Your Team

A 2022 survey of 2,000 people by JobSage discovered that 28% of people quit their jobs in the previous two years because of mental health reasons. When asked about the major contributing factors:

- 55% said Stress and Burnout
- 38% said Depression
- 37% said Lack of Motivation

Do you relate to any of these factors? Here is how to deal with them—focus on the solution, not the problem. The solution to stress and burnout is quality of life. If you are rocking it in your mental, spiritual, physical, family, financial, and personal lives, then stress and burnout will not cause you to quit your job.

A powerful solution to Depression is Purpose. If your work has a higher good, cause, or purpose that aligns with your personal Why and Purpose, then Depression will not be a reason you quit work. A powerful solution to Lack of Motivation is Growth. If you are growing and learning every day, then motivation automatically shows up. Think about this, if you are growing towards your purpose and living a balanced, quality life, would you quit your job?

If you lead a team of people and they know you are helping them grow towards their purpose and you are protecting their quality of life, would they quit? I think not!

What Inspires Me

I got a six-minute video from a lady whose brother had been really struggling. He had made a lot of bad life choices. He even tried to commit suicide. She said she had given him tough love. In the hospital with COVID-19, finally, he realized he had to make a change. And she said she would help him.

He arrived home, and when a Ziglar book showed up, he asked if he could read it. He read it three times in a week, with all the notes. Stories like that inspire me. I am grateful for every single time I am able to share a life-changing message and then see the ripples it creates.

TOM'S THOUGHT LEADER LESSONS

Thriving in Disruption

Disruption doesn't create problems, it creates opportunity. That's a very slight yet powerful mindset shift. The people who do best in Black Swan events like the pandemic are those who quickly recognize it's never going to be the same and embrace what is.

Coach leaders focus on growth more than results. If I have an organization that's growth-focused, then the more disruption there is, the more we're going separate from the pack. As a learning, growing organization, we're not anchored into old ways and don't get frustrated when things change. In fact, we love it when things change because change brings more people to serve and more problems to solve. I'm not saying ignore results, but if you're constantly focused on growth, the results will come.

With the rise of artificial intelligence, disruption is only going to increase in intensity and frequency. Love the growth, love the change, love the disruption, and figure out how many problems you can solve in the world because the world loves problem solvers.

How to Show Up Prepared – The Mental Model

The other habit I really like is what I call The Mental Model. Brain science backs this up. If I have an important business meeting, a meeting with somebody on my team, a speech, a training, or a podcast, I write it down on my calendar. Then, that morning, I spend one minute in my mind envisioning the answers to a few questions: *Who's the audience? What's their biggest need? What are the drivers of the people there? What are they worried about? What would be a win for them?* I start playing in my mind how the event might go. If I'm going to sell something, then I think as a salesperson. *What are the objections they might have? What are they going to hear from the competition? Who are the influencers in the group who might have a say in this decision?* What I'm really doing is creating slots in my mind for when we actually have the conversation. It could go exactly the direction I want or it could veer a little bit, but it doesn't matter. Either way, I'm prepared in advance for what could happen. That makes me more productive and makes for a much better outcome in general. Allowing the subconscious to work on the situation before you get there prepares you.

Q&A WITH TOM

What is your favorite movie?

Hands down *The Greatest Showman*. I've seen it seven or eight times. I love it because it's what we do. The story behind the story is the misfits who don't fit in. All of a sudden, PT Barnum comes along and says, "You can be great. You deserve the stage." And he creates a stage. In the end, we're all misfits. We all feel like we're less than or don't belong, and we need somebody to come into our life, see the potential, and say, "You're a great one. You can do that." And I believe that's why I do what I do.

How do you recharge?

The Perfect Start, which is my two to three-hour routine for starting my day. I get up at five and read, do my gratitude journal, do my goals for the day, and read Proverbs. I'm also doing something fun. Every morning I will use ChatGPT and continue to grow in knowledge. I will then get a workout in, with at least 30 minutes of intentional movement.

What are a few of your favorite quotes?

My lifetime favorite quote is from Dad: you are what you are and where you are because of what's gone into your mind, and you can change what you are and where you are by changing what goes into your mind.

My favorite quote for now also came from my dad, a year before he passed away. Dad was struggling with Alzheimer's, so as he tried to say this well-known quote, he added something to it. He said to me, "Son, God, don't make no junk. And, thanks to your mother, neither do I."

How do you define success?

Dad said that success is the maximum utilization of the abilities that you have. So, my personal mission statement that drives everything is to create the atmosphere that allows you to become the person God created you to become. So, for me, success would be that wherever I am, there's an atmosphere that allows whoever I'm with to become the person God created them to become.

Tom Ziglar is the CEO of the Zig Ziglar Corporation and Ziglar.com and the author of *10 Leadership Virtues for Disruptive Times* and *Choose to Win*. Order his books at www.ziglar.com. To book speaking engagements, please email tom@ziglar.com

RAVIN S. PAPIAH

A Mentor Is the Bridge

Ravin S. Papiah is highly decorated in the industries of professional speaking and network marketing. He is a certified speaking professional (CSP), a founder-partner, certified coach, speaker, trainer, and executive director of the Maxwell Leadership Certified Team, and a two-time distinguished toastmaster (DTM).

Living Beyond My Dreams

This will be my seventh book with Kyle Wilson! Kyle has called me the Jim Rohn of my country, Mauritius. If, 25 years back, someone would have told me that I would be co-authoring multiple #1 bestselling books with the marketing genius behind the great American philosopher Jim Rohn's roaring success, I would have roared with laughter.

How can someone who was born and raised in a third-world country, who was condemned to a short life, who was bullied at every level in school, and who was a super-ultra timid guy, become an Amazon #1 bestselling author? Good question!

My life was a bag of problems starting when I was a child. If you read my first three co-authored books published by Kyle—*Life-Defining Moments from Bold Thought Leaders*; *Don't Quit, Stories of Persistence, Courage and Faith*; and *Success Habits of Super Achievers*—you will understand my challenges and how I solved them along the way and turned the problems into possibilities, the adversity into diversity of opportunities, and the challenges into sweet lozenges.

Early Teachers and Lessons

My teacher, Chantal, introduced me to reading, but I don't believe she imagined that she was inculcating the notion of giving in me. Giving back became a mantra for me at a very young age. Being sick and bullied is not a gift, but what I got from my family and my teachers was more than a gift. In fact, it was a real blessing. I entered the magical world of reading and met superheroes doing super things to help people. My inner self got attracted and even addicted to this. I could see how my teachers and my siblings were also my superheroes, protecting me from the bullies and providing me with a sense of belief that I was valuable too and that I could also help and support others.

It all started for me when I was 11 years old and just entering college. Some of my parents' friends called and asked if I could help their kids in primary school by giving them private tutoring. I was a scholarship winner at my primary school final exams despite my frailties. The answer was a quick YES. I wanted to help these kids, not because I was smart (I didn't believe that yet!), but because, like my teachers, especially Miss Chantal, and like my siblings, I now wanted to help others, other kids like me, who were timid, a bit late in their studies, and looking for that helping hand.

The results were amazing, and very soon, I was flooded with tutoring requests from more parents for their kids. It went on for a couple of amazing years, indeed. I helped the kids by sharing what I knew, and more importantly, how I studied. At that time, there was no electricity at home, and I had to study till late while burning the midnight oil, in the real sense. I didn't understand at that time that I was adding value, but I was.

Solving my continuous series of challenges created a new mindset within me. If there are always people present to help me, and if I have been helped all throughout my life, then I should also be available to help others.

Turning Problems into Value

Turning problems into value does not just happen. Three vital things are necessary to solve problems and produce value for the world and leave a legacy:

1. The awareness that problems are NOT there to punish us but to test our resolve.

2. The presence of people (teachers, mentors, coaches) to enlighten us of that awareness and provide us wisdom and tools to fight the odds and continue our march towards our purpose.

3. The attitude of a student—to listen, learn, respect, apply, observe, and record results and to continue to build upon past results, good or bad.

I am very blessed to have a mother who fought for my survival beyond everyone's beliefs, siblings who supported me all the way through, and a father who spoke little but imbued me with values, including always keeping my hands open to give, for there is no bigger pleasure than giving. He told me, "The whole world awaits getting, but only the chosen few are givers. BE one of them, Ravin." But beyond my close family, there have been exceptional beings who have marched alongside me through a particularly difficult life—my teachers and my mentors.

The tree can be filled with excellent fruits, but if there is no one to pluck them and share them with others, the fruits just rot. So is value.

Les Brown tells us to not die with the music within us. He asks us to die empty, having poured out our gifts to the world. The world is waiting for our voice and our gifts. This is why mentors are important.

Mentors are the ones who discover, or I should say uncover, our gifts, make us aware of them, and teach us how to share them with the world, in the process, creating our legacy. Our legacy is that which we leave for the benefit of others, just like we are benefiting from the legacies left by others, such as Jim Rohn. The mentor who took me by the soul, made me see my value and my gifts, and crafted the way I can share them with the world, creating my legacy in the process, is none other than the great marketing genius, Kyle Wilson. Kyle is my friend and my mentor!

The Trip Across the World

In May of 2017, I was at the door of Kyle's house. I had butterflies flapping in my belly, for I was going to be face to face with the MAN who had been mentoring me virtually for more than 19 years! After 36 hours of flying and transits from the little island of Mauritius, I arrived at Kyle's house for a meeting of his mentorship group. It was unreal. It was a dream and a magical reality. That day I met incredible people—Bob Helms, Ron White, Tom Ziglar, Robert Helms, Tim Cole, Kelli Calabrese, and so many more. It was a day that completely changed my life, but I would soon have a better day, a full day with Kyle one-on-one—a gift from the MAN for my dedication to being present, traveling the world to be the only foreigner in the house on that day.

That day, as Jim Rohn would say, turned my life around. While I was complaining and bemoaning my broken life, Kyle listened to me studiously, without interrupting, taking copious notes and giving me that mentor's look that calms you down and gives you that space for a breather. Then, he started showing me how my broken life had pieces of genius that could help the lives of so many people around the world.

You see, I was only looking at the challenges that were falling on me. I didn't focus on the fact that I conquered those challenges and kept advancing through my path, which led me to meet Kyle 16,820 kilometers away from my home. While I worked hard to be able to take that first trip to meet with my mentor, I was not realizing the feat. Yes, it was a feat, especially for someone who was saying his life was in tatters, to work hard and save money to do the kilometers to finally meet with his mentor! That was an achievement in itself.

Discovering My Value

Kyle showed me that my life and its turn-around was a piece of art that should be shared with the world. I would tell my story so the many others who would STAY at the moaning and complaining stage could take inspiration and move to the next level of conquering their demons.

Kyle showed me the way and identified the point where I was stuck. I was afraid to take action. I did not have the courage to ACT on my decisions, which was stalling me in my endeavors. I had come a long way. I was very near my breakthrough, but I lacked the courage to take the actions necessary to liberate myself to fulfill my purpose.

That was a revelation for me because I believed I was courageous. Yes, I was courageous, but it was physical courage, while Kyle was talking about INNER courage—the courage of the heart, the courage of will, the courage to believe in your purpose and go for the actions needed without worrying about other people's opinions and comments. Inner courage—that's what I needed.

Seven years later, I authored a chapter in my seventh book, hosted an international radio program with the International Business Growth Radio Network for three seasons, launched a podcast, *Building You to Build Your Business*, and hosted more than 500 episodes of *The Ravin Papiah Show* on Facebook, while many more great things are unfolding.

You may be good. You may be very good. You may be a star, but you may not be aware of it. As I say, "If you are not aware, you are nowhere!" It takes a genuine mentor to uncover your potential and unleash it to the world. For me, I will be leaving my legacy in books, radio shows, podcasts, and many other forms, thanks to my mentor, Kyle Wilson.

Who will you choose to mentor you to solve your problems, bring value to the world, and leave a legacy that will act as a benchmark for the benefit of future generations?

RAVIN'S THOUGHT LEADER LESSONS

Mentors

Early in my career, when I was navigating the challenging world of sales, a mentor taught me the importance of listening and building relationships. This experience was transformative and showed me that effective mentorship goes beyond teaching skills; it involves instilling confidence and fostering growth. This belief is encapsulated in my philosophy: "If you are not aware, you are nowhere," which emphasizes the importance of self-awareness and growth in mentorship.

Personal Development

My commitment to personal development became a driving force when I transitioned from banking to sales. During this time, I dedicated myself to learning everything I could about sales and leadership, attending workshops, and reading. This relentless pursuit of knowledge not only helped me excel in my career but also equipped me to mentor others effectively. It reinforced my belief that growth is a lifelong journey that requires dedication, awareness, and the willingness to adapt and learn.

Leadership

During a challenging period when my sales numbers were down, I had to choose between giving up or rallying my team around a new vision. I chose the latter, and through shared goals and determination, we turned things around. This experience taught me that leadership isn't about being the loudest voice in the room; it's about fostering a shared sense of purpose and guiding others toward achieving collective success. My journey has shown me that a true leader is someone who can inspire others to see beyond their current circumstances and realize their full potential.

Business and Entrepreneurship

Bringing value in business goes beyond profit; it's about building meaningful relationships and creating sustainable impact. When I transitioned into entrepreneurship, I realized the importance of understanding my clients' needs and delivering solutions that truly made a difference. Successful entrepreneurship involves prioritizing long-term relationships and ethical practices, rather than focusing solely on immediate gains.

Giving

Whether it's through mentoring young professionals or supporting local causes, I've found that the act of giving is one of the most rewarding aspects of my life.

I've learned that giving, whether through time, resources, or knowledge, reinforces the values you stand for and inspires others to do the same.

Q&A WITH RAVIN

Have you had any past challenges that turned out to be blessings?

Absolutely. My early struggles with health and financial difficulties were initially daunting, but they taught me resilience and the importance of perseverance. Those challenges pushed me to seek out mentors, invest in my personal growth, and eventually become a mentor myself. These experiences were blessings in disguise, shaping me into who I am today. They also reinforced my belief in the importance of awareness; by becoming aware of my strengths and limitations, I was able to navigate my way through adversity.

What do you consider your superpower?

My superpower is my ability to connect with people and inspire them to see the potential within themselves. I've always believed in the power of storytelling and sharing personal experiences to motivate and empower others. This ability to connect deeply with people has been a driving force in my career as a mentor and coach. It's rooted in the principle that "If you are not aware, you are nowhere." By helping others become aware of their potential, I help them unlock their true capabilities.

What books do you often recommend?

The four books that have truly inspired me and that I always recommend are:

- *Think and Grow Rich* by Napoleon Hill, which teaches the power of mindset and the principles of success;
- *How to Win Friends and Influence People* by Dale Carnegie, which offers timeless advice on building meaningful relationships and effective communication;
- *Leading an Inspired Life* by Jim Rohn, which provides insights on living a purposeful and fulfilling life; and
- *The Richest Man in Babylon* by George S. Clason, which shares fundamental lessons on wealth creation and financial wisdom.

These books have profoundly impacted my life, guiding my personal and professional growth, and reinforcing my belief in the importance of awareness, discipline, and relationship-building.

How do you define success?

I define success as the ability to make a positive impact on others while living a fulfilling and balanced life. It's not just about achieving personal goals or financial milestones but about contributing to the growth and well-being of others.

Success, to me, is when you can look back and see that you've made a meaningful difference in the lives of those around you. This aligns with my belief that awareness is critical to success; if you are not aware of what truly matters to you and the impact you want to make, you can't achieve genuine fulfillment.

Connect with Ravin S. Papiah, professional speaker, trainer, and certified speaking professional (CSP) on Facebook, LinkedIn, via his website at https://www.johncmaxwellgroup.com/ravinsouvendrapapiah, or by email at ravinpapiahleadership@gmail.com.

 Scan to visit Ravin Papiah's website

CHERI PERRY

Serve Others and Persist to Find Your Purpose

Cheri Perry, the owner of a national credit card processing company, author, trainer, speaker, and business coach, has built her legacy through massive action, success principles, and BIG thinking. She inspires clients to push boundaries, lead by example, and prioritize bringing value to others first. Throughout her career, she has demonstrated a deep commitment to personal growth and helping others find their purpose.

I Learned Early: It's the PEOPLE!

Before starting a business, various work experiences shaped my journey, helping me find something I wanted to pour my heart into. My first job was as a certified nursing assistant (CNA) at a nursing home. I hated almost every part of that job except talking to the residents. The connection with people was the only aspect I enjoyed, highlighting the importance of human interaction in my work.

In the fast food industry, I quickly realized that when your heart isn't in a job, it's easy to clash with policies and procedures. Fast food service wasn't my calling. Later, I worked as a nanny, which initially felt like a dream job. I loved the children, but over time, I began to feel judgmental about how they were parented. It was one of the toughest decisions I've made, but I knew I wasn't in the right place.

Through these jobs, I discovered that I loved serving people. This realization sparked a hunger for knowledge. I read every book I could find on self-development, joined Toastmasters, and attended events led by top motivational figures. Meeting and developing a relationship with Zig Ziglar helped me identify and cultivate my passion for people.

Eventually, I owned several businesses, some successful and others teaching me the lessons needed to become a strong leader. Today, as a business coach, speaker, and owner of Total Merchant Concepts (TMC), a national credit card processing company, I'm blessed to make a difference in the lives of those we touch. My experiences shaped the way I work with my team and our clients. Hard work, varied experiences, and a desire to help business owners led to early success with TMC, growing steadily over 18 years.

Crisis of Destiny

Approaching 20 years in business, I was worn out. Staffing issues arose, and I began questioning my future. I decided to become a Certified Ziglar Legacy Trainer & Coach, feeling it was a natural transition given my love of business and people. Then, a pivotal moment occurred.

While helping train the second class of Ziglar Certified Trainers, Bob Beaudine, author of *The Power of WHO*, posed a life-changing question: "What are you doing with the people God gave you?" This question reignited my passion. Over the next five years, I focused on adding value to the lives of our team members. Our team fell in love with their work and clients, transforming into a close-knit work family. We were recognized by *Inc. Magazine* as one of the Top 400 Workplace Environments in 2019, became the #1 company to work for in Washington in 2020, and witnessed the emergence of many leaders within our company.

You Are Where You Are Supposed to Be

Looking back, I see the importance of grace in life's journey. Regret and second-guessing don't honor the fact that we're where we're meant to be. Adding value and making a difference doesn't require a special degree or a trouble-free past. It does require the courage to fail forward, the tenacity to keep trying, and the attention to recognize clues pointing to your passion. Living with a value-adding mindset allows you to reap the rewards.

Being lukewarm about anything doesn't lead to desirable results. To make a real difference, we must find our purpose and commit fully. If you're unsure about your destiny or passion, keep experimenting until you find it. If you're blessed to know your purpose, go all in. People are waiting for you and your gifts.

CHERI'S THOUGHT LEADER LESSONS

Leadership and Vision

Leadership isn't about position; it's about influence. Everyone has influence, regardless of their title. Our vision for the future determines how we apply that influence. Seeing bright possibilities allows us to lead effectively.

Team Building

Building a great team starts with self-improvement. By being the best version of yourself, you attract like-minded individuals who contribute to a cohesive, high-functioning team.

Philanthropy and Giving

Giving is a mindset, not just about money. Creating a culture of giving leads to better business outcomes and a richer work experience. Businesses that embrace giving tend to perform better financially, and their team members find their work more rewarding.

Continuous Education

I love continuous education and people who are hungry to learn. Zig Ziglar said that increasing your knowledge also increases the power of the knowledge you already have. Continuous learning should be woven into every role within a company. It's crucial to hire individuals who value knowledge and seek growth, regardless of whether they have a formal education.

Family and Parenting

Growing up in a family business taught me the importance of a strong work ethic. As a mother, I wanted to pass on this work ethic to my son while ensuring he knew he was more important than the business. Balancing work and family is challenging, but at the end of the day, our businesses exist to support the life we want to live.

Spirituality

Life comes with challenges, and sometimes we need divine intervention to navigate tough times. My relationship with my Creator has guided me through difficult decisions and provided strength when leadership felt overwhelming. It's essential for teams to know they have a leader who is being led by a higher purpose.

Business Philosophy

My responsibility is to do the most with the people God gives me. This involves creating a dynamic business with systems that help people succeed, delivering products and services with passion and integrity, and developing leaders within the team.

Business Culture

Culture is what we do every day, not just what we aspire to. A strong culture, driven by daily actions, makes overcoming business challenges not only possible but enjoyable. Poor cultures ruin opportunities, while strong cultures build resilience and foster success.

Q&A WITH CHERI

Favorite Movie

What About Bob? – A lighthearted comedy that offers valuable life lessons such as getting outside your comfort zone, appreciating the little things, and understanding the power of baby steps.

Favorite Quotes

"You can have everything in life you want if you will just help enough other people get what they want." – Zig Ziglar

"Suck it up, buttercup."

"Comparison is the thief of joy."

"When you fight for your limitations, you get to keep them."

Mentors and Influences

Zig Ziglar taught me the importance of a healthy self-image and humility. My father taught me life lessons, and Howard Partridge taught me not to give up on my dreams and to enjoy the journey.

Past Challenges

Losing my daughter was a tremendous challenge, but it shaped the mother I became and made me treasure my son even more.

Something Most People Don't Know

I've completed two Seattle to Portland bike rides (non-motorized).

Books I Recommend

2 Chairs by Bob Beaudine

He Chose the Nails by Max Lucado

See You at the Top by Zig Ziglar

Greatest Achievements

My greatest achievement is being Tyler Perry's mother and raising a good man of character. Another is creating a nationally recognized workplace culture where people grow and thrive.

Greatest Lesson

When life deals you a devastating blow, pick yourself up, surround yourself with supportive people, and get back to work.

Connect with author, trainer, speaker, and business coach Cheri Perry for business development and leadership training or inspirational keynote presentations. Her authentic, uplifting delivery inspires teams and their leadership to develop rich and productive cultures that deliver results. Training@CheriPerry.com, 360-980-0392

 Scan to visit cheriperry.com

HOWARD PARTRIDGE

From a Welfare, Throw-Away Kid to International Business Coach

Howard Partridge is an international business coach and a bestselling author of 13 books with coaching members in over 100 industries in 20 countries. He is also the founder of Phenomenal Business Coaching, the exclusive small business coaching company for the legendary Zig Ziglar Corporation.

Starting Out with 25 Cents

I'm originally from LA (Lower Alabama). I grew up on welfare in Mobile. There were seven kids crammed into a 600-square-foot shack. The roof was so bad that we had to get out the pots and pans to catch the leaks. My mother fed us on $100 a month from the welfare department. As a rebellious 18-year-old, I got in a fight with my stepdad and got kicked out of the house. I deserved it. My friend helped me scrape up $39.95 for a Greyhound bus ticket to Houston, Texas to live with my real father who left when I was only a year old.

By the time I was 18, I had only met him twice in my whole life. He had become successful in Houston, so I decided to move in with him and his new wife. When I stepped off that bus, I literally had 25 cents in my pocket.

I lived with my dad for a couple of years and worked a few odd jobs. Then I became a professional waiter and worked in some of Houston's top restaurants. I wore a tuxedo to work and learned how to do tableside cooking. I made dishes like steak Diane, bananas foster, and cherries jubilee. Setting stuff on fire inside at that age was pretty cool, but I always wanted my own business. But I only made enough money to pay the rent at that time.

Then I met my wife. Denise Concetta Antionette Pennella. Now that's Italian. And she was from New Jersey. As it turns out, when you marry into an Italian family, you don't get wedding presents, you get CASH! The tradition is to have a little purse that is made to match the dress that is perfectly sized for envelopes. After the wedding, we spread the envelopes out on the bed and counted $3,000.00! That was more money than we ever had at one time.

2 Life-Changing Secrets

There was a friend of my wife's family at the wedding who was the same age as me, 23 at the time, who was tooling around in a little red Mercedes convertible. I wanted to know what that guy did and if it was legal! As it turns out, he was a business owner. As soon as Denise and I got back to Houston after the wedding, I spent the entire $3,000 starting my first business out of the trunk of my car. Denise was concerned, to say the least.

Over the next 13 years, I became a slave to my business. I worked 24/7. I was no longer running my business. My business was running me! Then, in 1997, I learned two secrets that changed my life forever.

My mentor, the wisest man I know, used to come by my office. As he observed the chaos around me, he said, "Howard, you need to read The E-Myth by Michael E. Gerber." The book taught me that I needed to have systems in my business. And, it said I could transform my business into a predictable, profitable, turnkey operation. In other words, I could have a business that ran without me.

The first secret I learned is that the one and only reason my business existed was to help me achieve my life goals. The second was that I needed to have systems in my business so it could be more predictable and profitable.

After reading the book, I took a trip to Destin, Florida, my favorite place in the entire world. I bought a stack of spiral notebooks and took them down to the beach, next to the crystal clear, emerald water, and dug my toes into the sand. I began to dream about what my business and my life might look like. I filled those spiral notebooks up with ideas and a new vision.

Then, I came back to Houston and began working on the business and transformed that same business into a predictable, profitable, multi-million dollar, turnkey business. It makes money for me without me even having to be there. And my clients and my team members are all super happy.

Building that turnkey business wasn't easy. In fact, I experienced a great deal of frustration building that first business. Systems were one thing, but becoming a better leader, getting it profitable, and building a phenomenal dream team took some work. But we did it!

Sharing the Secrets...

Other business owners wanted to know how I was doing what I was doing, so I began training and coaching others on my methods. Along the way, I became friends with Michael E. Gerber, and we have shared the stage many times. My company became the exclusive small business coach for the Zig Ziglar Corporation and I have had the pleasure of being endorsed and mentored by such greats as John Maxwell, Brian Tracy (thanks to Kyle Wilson), Dave Ramsey (thanks to Tom Ziglar), and my company helps small business owners all over the world have phenomenal success.

Almost every day I get messages from clients that tell me how our work has helped them have a smoother, more profitable business and more freedom in their life.

I hope this story inspires you, that you learn the simple systems of success, and that you find the right coaching community to help you become the person you were created to be, so you can do the things you are called to do and have the life you were created to have.

HOWARD'S THOUGHT LEADER LESSONS

Keys to a Great Business

I started my first business out of the trunk of my car and built it into a multi-million dollar business because I was able to build systems. I learned about systems from Michael Gerber. I still own that business today. The two key things that you need to have to make a business work are great people and great processes in place. I'm fortunate to have both.

But you're not going to attract and keep the right people if you're not a good leader. And people aren't going to use those systems if you don't have people who are engaged and willing. So, you need to become a stronger leader to build a phenomenal dream team.

When you start thinking about your business, especially when you learn that the one and only reason your business exists is to be a vehicle to help you achieve your life goals, then you go to work every day on yourself to build a great business.

Become a student of business. If you want to be successful in anything, you have to become a student! And you have to work hard. You have to apply what you learn. I wrote a book called FTI Failure to Implement: The 10 Principles of Phenomenal Performance. The number one reason people don't reach their biggest dreams and goals is not because they don't know what to do or how to do it, it's just because they don't do it.

Mentors and Teachers

The greatest life lesson that I've ever learned is to get around people who have already done what you want to do and have a plan for you to follow. This is why everybody should be in coaching. You want to be mentored by someone who's already traveled the road.

Accountability

There's an ugly side to success. When you can do what you want, when you want, with who you want, and how you want, you can make bad choices. You can decide not to do the things that you really should do. Or you can decide that you're going to believe your own press and that you know what's best or you can cut corners. We need accountability to prevent that from happening.

Q&A WITH HOWARD

What is your favorite song?

"Sweet Home Alabama" by Lynyrd Skynyrd

What are a few of your favorite quotes?

"You can have everything in life you want, if you'll just help enough other people get what it is that they want." – Zig Ziglar

"Once you get a taste of significance, success will never satisfy." – John Maxwell

Have you had any past challenges that turned out to be blessings?

Getting in debt. That hurt so much that it's a blessing because I will never go there again.

What do you consider your superpower?

Building winning relationships.

What books do you often recommend?

The E-Myth by Michael E. Gerber
The 21 Irrefutable Laws of Leadership by John C. Maxwell
See You at the Top by Zig Ziglar
All of my own books, of course!

What do you consider your greatest achievements to date?

Keeping a phenomenal, smart, Italian woman married to me for 40 years.

What has been your greatest lesson?

Love never fails.

How do you define success?

Success is becoming the person that you're created to be. When you become that person, you will do the things you need to do in order to have the life and business you deserve to have.

Go to HowardPartridge.com and get his book, *The 5 Secrets of a Phenomenal Business*, for free.

RANDY HUBBS

Harmonizing Life
Insights on Passion, Purpose, and Legacy

*Randy Hubbs is a real estate broker/owner, investor, and fund manager. He and his wife, Jana, have 81 years of experience in education and 90 years in real estate investing together. As co-founders of LegacyInvestors.US, they use their unique skill sets to help others with their mission to **solve the special needs housing crisis in the US**.*

Following My Predestined Path and Discovering My Why

I grew up in Richland, Washington, part of the Tri-Cities and home to the Hanford nuclear project, which began in 1943 as part of "The Manhattan Project." The area's demographic included scientists, technicians, engineers, and skilled tradespeople, so as kids, science and engineering were emphasized in school.

My love for music showed up early. I followed the traditional route through school music band programs until high school, quitting after sophomore year due to an unmotivating band director. Fortunately, I discovered my natural gift as a musician with the Columbians Drum and Bugle Corps. After earning the drum major position, I found a love for teaching music. This was also where I met Jana, my wife of 43 years.

Though I loved music, I also excelled in math and science and planned to become an engineer to work on the Hanford project and earn a good salary. Entering my senior year, I was one of six students accepted into a new Inquiry to Science and Engineering internship program at the Hanford site. This became a part-time position, allowing me to work while attending Columbia Basin College (CBC). I planned to transfer to the university recommended for mechanical engineering the following year, but after my visit, I was disappointed with the department and campus to the point that I started to doubt my career choice. Afterward, I was venting my frustration to my girlfriend, and she interrupted me, saying, "You don't seem excited about engineering. Why don't you change your major to music because that's what you love?"

That became a life-changing, pivotal moment for me. The following week, I visited Central Washington University (CWU) and changed my major to music education. My poor high school band experience inspired me to become a great band director, determined never to discourage anyone from pursuing music.

Pursuing My Career but with a Long-Term Exit Strategy

After graduating from CWU, I returned home to work as a substitute music teacher. My friend, Warren, decided to buy his aunt's house, fix it, and sell it for a profit. He invited me to help, and I eagerly moved out of my parent's house to join him.

I wasn't unfamiliar with real estate. My grandmother, parents, and future father-in-law all owned rental properties, which laid the foundation for our real estate education.

At age 22, I landed my first full-time teaching job at Pasco High School, and Jana began her teaching career the following year. We were serious about our relationship and didn't want to retire on a teacher's salary. After starting my job, I asked her father, a Realtor®, to find me a house to flip. Within a month, I closed on a small two-bedroom home needing significant work. I focused on teaching that year and remodeled the house with Jana during the summer.

Unaware of the national housing decline, we saw the crash catch up to the Tri-Cities, witnessing people we admired get crushed. This lesson shaped our future investment philosophy.

Life Transitions

Jana and I married in June of 1981 and lived in that house for two years. We then bought a larger home, keeping the first as a rental and realizing the benefit of extra cash flow. Over the next few years, we purchased two more rental homes.

We were passionate about our careers. Jana taught life skills at Kennewick High School, helping special needs students transition to independent living. Little did we know, this planted the seeds that became our legacy project. Jana's success led to an administrative role and eventually the Director of Special Education for the Pasco School District.

I taught high school for eight years and accepted the Instrumental Music Director and Associate Professor of Music position at Columbia Basin College (CBC) in 1987. This welcome change allowed us to focus on starting our family.

Ramping Up Our Financial Future

In 1997, we began focusing on acquiring more property. We found a home that needed work, and I bought a book on flipping houses. This became another pivotal moment for us. That book taught us how much we didn't know about real estate investing, and after making a substantial profit on the house, it was time to start learning more.

The next book I found was Robert Kiyosaki's *Rich Dad Poor Dad*. Like so many others, it changed our lives. We decided buy-and-hold was smarter than flipping, using flipping profits to invest in our first multi-unit property. In 2001, we bought a five-duplex portfolio. By 2003, I was out of the rat race. Thank you, Robert!

Surviving Our Second Crash

We had seen many real estate market cycles and learned to pay attention. In 2007, when we reached the maximum number of properties we could acquire through conventional financing, we noticed the market frenzy and moved to the sidelines to learn about commercial multifamily investing.

On September 15, 2008, we saw the Lehman Brothers collapse on CNN, signaling the Great Recession. We agreed an excellent buying opportunity was coming.

We attended a boot camp by Anthony Chara of *Apartment Mentors*. Within six months, we closed on a 32-unit apartment complex in Texas, followed by more apartments in different markets.

Abundance Mindset and the Power of "The Tribe"

The next live event I attended was a Dallas real estate market field trip by The Real Estate Guys™, leading to more trips, including their first syndication event in 2011. Seeking bigger deals, syndication was our next step. This event preceded their annual Summit at Sea. After our class, we were invited to a cocktail reception held for the summiteers before boarding their ship the following day. We were surrounded by many successful real estate investors, entrepreneurs, and mentors—all with abundant mindsets. Jana and I were disappointed to fly home instead of joining the week-long summit but promised to attend the following year, and we have every year since.

After the 2012 Summit, I told my friend Bill McKay, Dean of Arts and Humanities at CBC, about my desire to transition to full-time real estate. He arranged a sabbatical for me the following year to develop an online jazz history course.

The following year, I went part-time, teaching online, and Jana retired to work full-time in our real estate business. I retired the following year after 28 years at CBC.

Reestablishing My Identity as a Real Estate Professional

I was known as the music guy, and Jana and I seldom mentioned our real estate investing. Through participation with the Real Estate Guys Syndication Mentoring Club Inner Circle, I got my real estate license and branded myself as an investment housing broker.

Jana and I continue with this group, raising millions for multifamily and luxury resort properties. I was also honored when Anthony Chara offered me a "Gold Coach" position for Apartment Mentors. I am back to teaching but with an entirely different subject!

Creating a Legacy

People ask how we like retirement. The reality is, yes, we are retired in that we live on our terms and can do what we want, when we want, living a life of abundance and adventure, but our destiny does not end there.

After more than five years of research and implementation and two years of content creation, we're thrilled to have launched our groundbreaking online course, **"Solving the Special Needs Housing Crisis in the US."**

The crisis is that individuals with developmental or physical disabilities are struggling to secure housing on their own. Traditional efforts to address this issue have relied mainly on nonprofit organizations, but the limited availability of funds has resulted in long waiting lists across every city and state. In some cases, individuals have had to wait for **15 to 20 years** if they ever receive placement.

Our solution is a "for-profit" approach that has proven to outperform traditional rental models and other models, including most short-term rentals. This socially responsible cause presents an unprecedented opportunity for real estate investors to achieve greater profits and for dedicated parents/guardians to provide housing for their loved ones and relieve worries over what will happen once they can no longer care for them.

Our 45 years of real estate investing, teaching backgrounds, and Jana's special education knowledge uniquely qualify us to guide this process.

We followed our "why" from the start, teaching to make a positive impact, and are now helping others learn how to leave a lasting legacy that will continue to live long after we're gone.

RANDY'S THOUGHT LEADER LESSONS

Leadership

I'm passionate about leadership. Growing up in the local drum corps, we competed fiercely with a group out of Spokane, Washington, but never beat them. Later, I joined a National Championship group from Anaheim, California, where, similarly, a drum corps from Santa Ana had their sights on beating us. Because our staff taught us to focus positively on ourselves and team culture, seeking ways to improve on each attempt, we had no rivals and soared to incredible new heights.

I applied these leadership principles to my bands, emphasizing self-improvement over competition. I taught students to celebrate their best efforts and respect any group that outperformed them. The ultimate reward was seeing their personal growth surpassing their expectations and often winning first place, even when we weren't expecting it.

This approach with my high school and college groups led to many achievements. Whether it was a rehearsal, performance, or competition, it constantly yielded feelings of success with my students, and many of them still remind me of that today.

Daily Habits and Rituals

Habits are crucial in my life. Darren Hardy and the Brian Tracy 3-Day Event produced by Kyle Wilson greatly influenced me. I implement Darren's focused "jam sessions" regularly, which has made a significant difference. Much of our success can be attributed to the concepts taught in Brian's book, *Goals*.

Self-Education

Self-education is far more critical than institutional learning. Just because someone has a degree or certificate does not necessarily make them successful in their field. I saw this firsthand in the public school system. Many of the best teachers at our college did not have degrees in education but were passionate about their field and were hired based on their skills and prior accomplishments.

Today, many of my mentors don't have college degrees, but they're amazingly qualified teachers who have achieved high levels of success.

Q&A WITH RANDY

What is your favorite song or who is your favorite musical artist?

As a former music teacher and performer, people often ask about this. I have no favorite; I enjoy all music genres. Historically, music, art, and theater have influenced society's behavior and fashion. When pressed, I mention ZZ Top, which surprises people and sparks conversation.

What is some of the best advice you've received?

The best advice I've received includes my mother's wisdom: "Don't stress over things you can't control, everything in moderation, and don't fight imaginary battles." Bob Helms, The Godfather of Real Estate, urged me to get my real estate license, which elevated me from music guy to "professional real estate investor status" and reduced our tax liability.

What hobbies do you enjoy?

Jana and I have always loved travel and adventure. Since our 20s, we've owned RVs and boats and enjoyed camping. We attend educational events to sharpen our business skills and love vacationing in beautiful destinations.

I'm an action and adventure sports enthusiast. Besides fishing and hunting, I grew up snow and water skiing, riding motorcycles, white water kayaking, and scuba diving. Skydiving is my top passion; I started at 18, paused to raise our family, and resumed in 2016. It's the ultimate adrenaline rush. These activities keep me focused and motivated, despite no longer having a Monday-to-Friday routine.

What books do you often recommend?

I often recommend Michael Hyatt's *Free to Focus* and have a top 20 book list I share with interested people.

What do you consider your greatest achievements to date?

Jana and I have many career achievements, but our greatest is developing and launching our course: **"Solving the Special Needs Housing Crisis in the US."** I love being a multifamily coach and will continue syndicating apartments.

How do you define success?

Success comes in different shapes and sizes and only sometimes involves money. Anyone striving to achieve their goals, dreams, or purpose in life and is happy with their results is successful.

With their extensive backgrounds in real estate investing and teaching, Randy Hubbs and his wife Jana help others become financially free through real estate. To learn more about their online course and get a free copy of their eBook, **"Solving the Special Needs Housing Crisis in the US,"** contact info@legacyinvestors.us or visit www.legacyinvestors.us.

 Download the Ebook on Special Needs Housing

PATRICK GRIMES

Alternative Investing Mastery
How the Wealthy Thrive in Downturns

Patrick Grimes, a former high-tech machine design and robotics engineer, is an alternative assets investor in real estate acquisitions, commercial debt, oil and gas, litigation funding, and more. He is an avid traveler, mountaineer, and adventure sports enthusiast. Originally from California, Patrick lives with his wife and son in Honolulu, Hawaii.

My Turning Point

Every year, my brothers and I travel to Mammoth Mountain Ski Resort in the Sierra Nevadas. It's one of my favorite trips.

Some years back, after sacrificing countless hours over the holidays designing an automated assembly line for a new disruptive medical device—I was excited to share my success with them. This project would bring in six figures of practically passive income for my family for years to come.

While in the car with my brothers on our way up the mountain, I received a call from the son of the company owner I was contracting with. He wanted to discuss the project with the customer directly.

We called the customer, and to my shock, the company owner's son said all the wrong things. Despite having a signed purchase order and contracts finalized, the customer, also shocked, retracted the order due to the inexperience of the owner's son.

In that moment which had promised to be so joyous minutes before, I was devastated. I realized how little control I had over my financial future.

Why Many Successful Professionals Work Until They Die

By most all accounts, I was a high-paid successful professional. I came from a middle-class family of educators and pastors and grew up in a mountain town near Yosemite National Park. I developed an affinity for technology and went on to earn a bachelor's and master's in engineering and an MBA. I had worked my way up the corporate ladder at Gallo, the world's largest winery, became intimately familiar with Toyota's Japanese work ethic while doing engineering at their manufacturing plant, which is now Tesla's, and won an engineering design competition for my invention, "The Grill-O-Mation," which automated perfectly grilling a steak.

After a gap year traveling through Europe, I chose a challenging career path, custom machine design, automation, and robotics. I was successful and began seeking opportunities to invest my bonuses. Like most Americans starting out, my investments were limited to my employer-sponsored 401(k), which I had maxed out but saw the slow growth that would have me working with virtually no end in sight. Then I met with a financial planner whose suggested plan would have me create an IRA and diversify into REITs, which, despite being real estate investments, are traded like stocks and subject to the same market fluctuations and volatility.

The Advice That Changed Everything

I sought the counsel of my current firm's owner. He said his only regret was not investing more in real estate sooner. I was stunned. He was a titan in the technology industry who had access to the latest technology investments, and he explained that more millionaires are created through real estate than any other investment. "Make your money in high-tech but spend it in real estate."

My Real Estate Crash Course

Not a procrastinator by nature, I immediately dove into a pre-development project that had the potential to rapidly double or triple my returns.

The financial collapse in 2008 sent the project spiraling, I lost everything. My investment was tied to recourse loans, and the banks threatened to come after my personal assets as well. My attorney helped negotiate a settlement, but the foreclosure left my credit in tatters.

I learned the hard way that growing true wealth requires patience, a far more risk-averse approach, and a careful balance of allocations into non-correlated alternative investments, ones that don't rise and fall on the same market cycles.

The DIY Landlord Grind – When Success Leads to Burnout

After finding a new sense of self and purpose through a dual master's program and a year-long spiritual journey through the Middle East and Asia, I found myself back as a high-paid professional seeking where to invest.

Following the breadcrumbs of the wealthy led me back to real estate, but this time in cash-flowing rental properties in recession-resilient cities. I was very successful, but being a landlord was a grueling business that I couldn't scale, especially with a demanding day job. And, it yielded limited profitability unless I constantly bought, improved, sold, and repeated.... I found myself burned out in the single-family rental trap.

Unexpectedly, my priorities shifted when I met my soon-to-be wife, and I wanted my nights and weekends back. After closing the refinance on my last single-family deal, I pressed pause on real estate and we got married.

Learning to Scale Through Partnering

When I was ready to pick up real estate again, I knew rental homes weren't the sustainable growth vehicle I was looking for. A podcast by a fellow engineer-turned-real estate investor laid out a different approach—that involved partnering with experienced investment sponsors to acquire large assets and raising the capital needed from passive investors. The appeal of this strategy was tremendous as it allowed me to share the workload with various sponsors, not just myself, and obtain diversified exposure to numerous cities and investment types. It also allowed me to invest through my self-directed retirement accounts, a challenge for rental properties.

My wife and I began exploring different markets, meeting brokers, and building a team. We found ourselves in a time of tremendous growth. We analyzed hundreds of deals and settled on buying cash-flowing large apartment complexes. I eventually made the difficult decision to strike out from my tech firm and set up shop as my own S-Corp, doing similar work off-site as a consultant to obtain the availability I needed to succeed in the investing world.

During the COVID quarantine, my wife expressed her desire to live in Hawaii, and within weeks, we were watching the sunrise from our lanai in Lanikai, Oahu. We learned about larger investments, I learned to overcome my hesitancy to trust, and I learned how to partner until, two and a half years later, we closed on our first apartment community—86 units in South Carolina from a distressed owner. Since then, we have expanded our portfolio to nearly 5,000 multifamily apartments along with retail centers and industrial buildings across seven states.

Expanding Beyond Real Estate

As we scaled our real estate portfolio, I realized I was facing a common challenge: When I became very good at something, I got comfortable and ended up over-concentrated in that one area, exposing me to greater risk. I realized the fear of taking a risk on something new was the very thing driving risk in my portfolio.

I learned that Morgan Stanley suggests allocating at least 25% of one's portfolio to alternative investments for higher returns and lower risk, and studies by Wolff further show that the wealthy allocate 49% of their portfolio to alternative investments to achieve portfolio resilience in market downturns.

I realized, to be truly recession resilient, the wealthy know they need to allocate their wealth into alternative investments—those that won't rise and fall and that are non-correlated to the cycles of stock market and real estate investments. Taking decisive action on this helped stabilize my portfolio by spreading risk across different asset classes and reducing dependence on market fluctuations.

I first targeted energy investments, an initiative that was well-received by investors seeking diversification. This began my new venture into alternatives.

The Vision Behind Passive Investing Mastery

While Invest On Main Street was successful, it became clear that a company solely focused on real estate wasn't enough. This realization led me to create Passive Investing Mastery, a platform that better serves the investor community through education and sponsoring various alternative investments.

On this platform, I produce a weekly Wealth Accelerator Series educating investors on achieving mastery in passive investing. I also host a bi-weekly Alternative Investing Mastery Series, featuring panelists discussing unique asset classes and market trends. This approach introduces our investors to a broad range of strategies, including real estate, energy, litigation funding, and more.

Embracing Lesser-Known Investments

As investors become more sophisticated, they realize that a well-balanced portfolio requires diversification beyond the well-known investments—stock market, real estate, and oil and gas—and into sectors like healthcare, education, and legal services that offer stable growth, even in recessions.

We established the Diversified Litigation Portfolio to provide access to the legal industry—an asset class offering investors stability and high returns without the volatility of the rest of their portfolios. The strategy finances attorneys litigating late-stage cases, near settlement, enabling them to represent thousands of individuals harmed by corporate misconduct.

Embracing Opportunity: The Upside of Downturns

As I expanded Passive Investing Mastery, I adapted our strategies to evolving market dynamics, particularly in real estate. Post-COVID, we began to see many performing properties with good fundamentals but with owners in dire financial distress, often due to rising interest rates, decreasing property valuations, rent delinquencies, and short-term loans coming due. Learning from past downturns, we turned this challenge into an opportunity by creating opportunistic funds where our investors can win by becoming the source of relief to these operators.

The Acquisitions Fund enables our investors to take advantage of the best buying opportunity in commercial real estate of our lifetime and capture high-yield returns by acquiring properties in cash at steep discounts when owners want or have to sell.

The Income Fund, a real estate asset-backed debt portfolio, provides a vehicle for investors to beat inflation and pocket high, immediate monthly cash flow by being the source of relief for operators who need access to gap or bridge debt at a time when interest rates are high and the country's banking system is distressed.

Building Wealth with Purpose

As a busy professional, I'm passionate about guiding other high performers, like me, who are disillusioned with the risks of startups, volatile stocks, and heavily taxed retirement plans. They fear market crashes, inflation spikes, and recessions.

Through Passive Investing Mastery, I am able to educate investors on alternative investments that provide true financial security and abundance, allowing them to contribute to the causes they care about most. My goal is to help others avoid the slower paths I took and become the heroes of their own financial success stories.

PATRICK'S THOUGHT LEADER LESSONS

Simplifying the Complex

We created a process of "simplifying the complex" when we realized we were confusing many investors with too much investment jargon. This was counter to our value of complete transparency. Whenever someone uses jargon, we now stop and break it down into simple words.

This practice helps us maintain clarity and ensures that the information we share about investments is understood by all.

Purposeful Beginnings

It would have been easy to fall back into the routine of daily life, but I stayed motivated toward my financial goals. I labeled my 6:00 a.m. iPhone alarm "Complacency & Comfort = Same Life." This reminds me to take intentional steps every day to make progress.

Every morning since college, no matter where I am, I start my day with a run. During these runs, I engage with thoughtful TED Talks, podcasts, and audiobooks on leadership and investing. This keeps me updated on market insights and new strategies.

Investing with Impact

While our primary goal is to deliver high returns, we also focus on investments with a positive social impact. Our apartment investments provide a cleaner, safer, and improved living experience for our residents. Our Litigation Funding investments provide access to justice for those harmed individuals who otherwise wouldn't be able to afford it, improving their lives while holding large institutions accountable for major misconduct.

Supporting the Causes That Matter Most

The pursuit of investing goals isn't just about financial freedom; it should focus on achieving financial security and abundance. This requires a resilient, diversified portfolio that thrives in downturns.

That's when investors can truly reach the second part of our mission at Passive Investing Mastery: Providing abundant financial resources to help you surpass your economic needs, allowing you to support your family, friends, hobbies, and the causes you care about most.

Q&A WITH PATRICK

What fears did you have to overcome along the way?

Well into my real estate journey, I was still operating like a typical engineer—keeping my nose to the grindstone, focusing on getting the work done, and keeping my successes close to the vest. With 2,000 apartment units under my belt, I still hadn't shared my story with most of my friends, colleagues, or even family. When I attended a conference on how to win funds and influence people, I connected with a mentor who helped me realize that my reluctance wasn't just about downplaying my successes. I was fearful of exposing past failures and alienating others close to me with my successes.

He emphasized that our stories—both victories and setbacks—have the power to inspire and guide others. He connected me with his publisher who coached me through my fears to co-author Amazon #1 bestseller *Persistence, Pivots, and Game Changers* where I shared my story for the first time.

Articulating my thoughts in writing was one thing, but transitioning to live interviews and public speaking was another. The fear I felt before my first podcast was overwhelming, but I pushed through. Since then, I have been invited on over 100 podcasts and have spoken on dozens of stages across the country. I continued writing, co-authoring *Pivotal Leadership*, a Barnes & Noble #1 and International Bestseller.

This journey was not just about overcoming fear; it was about embracing the responsibility to help others by sharing my story.

What do you consider your greatest achievements to date?

Becoming a father to my wonderful 18-month-old son has made me realize the greatest reward of my success is the time and location freedom I now have. I can spend time with him throughout the day and adjust my schedule to do all the things he loves. I often look back and realize that if I had stayed in the engineering world, I would have missed so many precious moments.

Chapter co-authored by Patrick Grimes and Sheri Grimes.

Patrick Grimes guides each investor to be the hero of their story, family, and legacy through diversifying into alternative investments. Rather than worrying about market volatility, start allocating your wealth to recession-resilient non-correlated investments and achieve true diversification at PassiveInvestingMastery.com.
Patrick@PassiveInvestingMastery.com | (209) 403-6096

Ready to master the art of passive investing? Scan to schedule an introductory call with Patrick today.

DENIS WAITLEY

Cultivating the Seeds of Greatness

Denis Waitley is a world-renowned speaker. He has written 16 bestselling classics, including Seeds of Greatness *and* The New Psychology of Winning. *His audio album* The Psychology of Winning *is the all-time bestselling program on self-mastery. Denis is the former chairman of psychology for the US Olympic Committee's Sports Medicine Council and is in the National Speakers Association Speaker Hall of Fame.*

The *Seeds of Greatness* Planted in Grandmother's Garden

Growing up, I would go to Grandma's house because Grandma was the positive one in my family. I rode my bike 10 miles every Saturday, mowed her lawn, and got my reward: "Oh, you're such a good boy. You mow such a good lawn. I think we deserve a piece of apple pie a la mode or a lemon tart." She just kept teaching me with positive reinforcement.

But, the most important thing was the subject of my bestselling book, *Seeds of Greatness*. We planted a victory garden together during World War II. We had little packets of seeds with a picture of the fruit or vegetable. Holding the cucumber seeds, I said, "Grandma, how do you know this little seed is going to turn into that?"

She said, "Because the seeds of greatness are already planted within the DNA of the cell, and if you cultivate it, water it, and care for it, you'll get out what you put in."

"But be careful. Weeds don't need watering. They blow in on the wind. They come in every day, and we have to pull the weeds out, being mindful of the flowers. The weeds are going to come. Carefully, pull them out, but don't focus on them. Instead of the weeds of failure, we want the seeds of greatness."

I said, "Will we lose the war?"

She said, "No, what goes around, comes around. You harvest what you sow. Here's what you do. Model yourself after people who've been great in their service to others, and you'll be successful and happy."

My grandmother, in addition to my children and grandchildren, has had the most incredible influence on my life.

Values Are More Likely Caught Than Taught

I have four children, many grandchildren, and now great-grandchildren, one of whom is already a teenager. I've learned to be a role model, not a critic. If they shouldn't be doing it, neither should you. Be someone worth emulating to your children. Set the example in your life. By preaching, I never got anywhere. I'm a highly sought-after professional speaker, I give a good lecture, but still, they watched me more than they listened to me talk. It's much better to walk your talk.

I have made every mistake you can make as a husband, father, son, friend, brother, you name it. I've lectured throughout the world and all over China, where a young Chinese woman said to me, "You are so perfect. Everything you say is perfect. I'm a failure because my husband divorced me because we had a little girl instead of a boy."

I said to her, "No. Your marriage failed, but you're not a failure. That's an event. I have failed in marriage. I am not married now, but I am not 'divorced.' I'm a single man. I don't continue to be divorced because it is finalized. I'm a flawed person who's not impressed with myself. I made that mistake, but I'm not going to keep living in it."

The older I get, the more I realize the importance of the few we love, our handful of friends, and helping young people by passing on everything we've learned. Knowledge is just like money. It does you no good when you have it, only when you employ it. If you die with it, it does you no good, so you'd better pass it on while you're alive. What you leave your children in values is much more precious than the valuables you leave them in your estate. They will cherish the time you spent with them much more than the money you spent on them.

Chase Your Passion, Not Your Pension

For me, a widow with a rose garden is as important as a politician, rock star, or superstar athlete. Let's say that you're not interested in entering your roses in the local flower show and the blue ribbon is not important for you, but you love taking care of flowers. The sheer exhilaration of doing something excellent for its own merit—not to prove it to others, not to get the money, and not to get accolades—is its own reward. We all want to be experts in something. We all want to be competitive and beat somebody to make us feel a little better. We all want material things. But the two greatest motivators of all are the sheer exhilaration of doing something excellent, that feels good, and doing it independently without somebody telling us to do it. Those two motivators drive more people to accomplish great things than all the money in the world.

Every success I've ever known has not been a success because he or she wanted to be rich. It was because each had something inside of them that had to be said or done. Success was then a byproduct because they were filling a need or solving a problem. I have talked to Bill Gates, Steven Spielberg, Jonas Salk, and others. They never really thought they were going to be rich or famous. It happened because what they did was magnificent and solved a problem or filled a need.

Don't let the financial expediency of your first job, paying off your student loans, or starting a family make your life decisions. Many young Gen Zs and Millennials are changing paths more often because they've learned what I learned. Chase your passion, not your pension. If you chase your passion, you're likely to get a bigger pension because you're doing something you love.

Don't let your first job determine your career. Keep learning everything you can. Dust off your childhood. Think of the things you did after school and that you loved to do in school. Think of the things you like to do on weekends. Hidden there are latent talents that you can bring out. Maybe your true passions are in an avocation or an after-work activity. Maybe you have a natural gift that will make you more money than your job. Your job does not have to be the major source of your income. Your present job may not be the source of your inspiration either. That may come from a hobby, an avocation. Make sure you're doing things that you love and don't just get caught up in the grind. Don't follow the crowd. Follow your core values. Follow your internal compass. Follow your heart. Live in the moment, not for the moment.

Resilience and Finding Your Will in a Crisis

My early life consisted of a series of roller coaster events, many of which were negative. My most noteworthy work, *The Psychology of Winning*, was written while I was losing in nearly every aspect of my life.

However, it wasn't until 2018 that the demand for authentic resiliency paid me a sudden visit. I returned from a speaking tour throughout Asia, Europe, and the Middle East, and a health checkup revealed that I had inherited a heart valve condition from my mother. In my mid-80s, feeling good, I opted for a new valve so I could happily reach my goal of 100 golden years. Unfortunately, a surgical error severed my femoral artery, and I nearly died on the operating table.

During recovery, I contracted a life-threatening infection and spent three months in isolated skilled nursing care. Just when I felt better, I noticed a chronic sore throat, which was diagnosed as acid reflux. Nearly a year later, a biopsy revealed I actually faced advanced-stage throat cancer requiring immediate, massive radiation and chemotherapy.

I rarely speak about my own pain and suffering, preferring to dwell on desired outcomes. Suffice it to say, it has been the most brutal, indescribable experience. Internal and external radiation burns. COVID lockdowns in skilled nursing facilities. Cognitive challenges from chemotherapy.

I'm 91 now and see it as a privilege to be old. What is my prognosis? Well, I am a happy, grateful father, grandfather, and great-grandfather to a loving inner circle. I am on a permanent, liquid diet, with no taste or desire to eat. But I can smell the fragrance of beautiful lilacs and roses, and my memory is filled with exquisite senses. I know there are many keys to a life well lived and one size does not fit all.

Resilience has become one of the most important things in my life. To be resilient, you have to be optimistic that you can handle anything God throws at you. Resilience is the thing that keeps me going.

Targets are important, especially targets that are just out of reach but not out of sight. Victor Frankl said that a purpose behind the purpose, something that drives you toward where you want to be, is the key. Always have something you're reaching for. There's something more for me, and as long as I'm allowed the privilege of living, I'm going to make sure that I'm making the world better for my having lived.

DENIS'S THOUGHT LEADER LESSONS

Prime Time Is YOUR Time

Prime time is 6:00 p.m. to 11:00 p.m. EST. That's when everyone is watching their favorite programs on TV. What are they watching? Other people making money and having fun. Wait a minute. Sure, TV watching gets you out of your mundane daily grind. Okay. Maybe an hour, that's enough. Live in prime time, don't watch it. It's the greatest lesson I learned in my early life. I fell into the routine of coming home after my day in the Navy, relaxing, and watching TV. When I decided to write a book, I had to write it at night and on weekends. That break in my routine allowed me to become involved in my life. I learned that my family and I could play instead of watching other people play. Instead of watching professional athletes, we could play softball or Frisbee, and instead of watching a beach, I could go to the beach. So, I got out of my chair and got into life rather than watching it. I don't want to be a spectator.

The Importance of Nature

I wish I would've moved to a natural retreat in my 60s. I said to all my friends and colleagues that I would walk off stage and out of the arena. They said I never could, that I needed the applause. I finally realized that's not what I wanted at all. It never was, but I chased it for a while.

Now, on the family compound, we have deer, fish, bobcats, coyotes, and every kind of tree: walnut, almond, macadamia, peach, plum, apricot, orange, grapefruit, pine, palm, pepper, and even redwood trees. I get to walk around, smell the roses, and notice every butterfly and bird that passes. I still do yard work whenever I can. It's great to have something that you want to do, that you enjoy, rather than having to do it or feeding your ego. But I am not retired and never will be. I am engaged in teaching succeeding generations via distance learning. I don't need the money or the social media following. I need to exercise my brain, which like the body, "If you don't use it, you are bound to lose it."

From age nine, I've been interested in wildlife. The most amazing experiences in my life have been taking my family almost every year to the middle of Africa on safaris. In fact, I wrote one of my better books, *Safari to the Soul*, on these trips. It wasn't a bestseller because I wrote it for my family. Sitting in the wild, you're close to your maker. Struck with the awesome creation of the world, I would sit for hours and hours. I'm not trying to record it to show others I was there, I'm engaged in it. We kept going back to Africa year after year. I regret not making those pilgrimages earlier in life and feel more at home there than in any other setting.

Along the way, I got caught up, like we all do, in trying to perform and arrive "there." But there's no there. Living successfully is a process, not a status.

Q&A WITH DENIS

What is your favorite movie?

Fantasy: *The Wizard of Oz*
Movie with a Message: *To Kill a Mockingbird* and *Citizen Kane*
Musical: *The Sound of Music*
Spiritual: *The Robe* and *The Ten Commandments*
Based on a True Story: *The Boys in the Boat*

How do you recharge?

I recharge by praying a lot more than I used to, being thankful a lot more than I used to, and going out into God's natural beauty, breathing deeply, and being so thankful. Also by hanging around younger people, especially children.

What do you consider your superpower?

My greatest superpower is to believe that I'm as good as the best but no better than the rest. Always being humble and never having any hubris about what I've done. Always treating people the way they need to be treated to have all good feelings about themselves. I always give compliments and aim to never be overly critical.

What are a few of your favorite quotes?

The most important meeting you'll ever have is the one you have with yourself.

"Live as if you were to die tomorrow, learn as if you were to live forever."
– Mahatma Gandhi

To learn more about Denis Waitley and his speaking, courses, and teachings, please visit www.deniswaitley.com.

DR. EBERHARD SAMLOWSKI

Former Board-Certified Surgeon Leaving a Generational Legacy

Eberhard Samlowski passionately teaches people how to create financial freedom by using a little-known concept called infinite banking. A former board-certified surgeon, he has a 30-year history of investing in real estate and the market and has used the infinite banking concept for over 12 years to help himself and others achieve financial freedom.

Money

I grew up in a middle-class neighborhood. My father was a physician. My parents left Germany with the clothes on their backs. Instead of buying a big, fancy house, they spent their money traveling the world. Starting at an early age, they took us four boys all over the world on incredible adventures that had a profound effect on my worldview. I saw extreme poverty and extreme wealth.

My parents scrimped and saved to pay cash for college for us four and then medical school for three of us four. For the rest of their lives, they lived frugally, some would say cheap. They bought their clothes at thrift stores. And when they died, they left a substantial inheritance for each of us. Their only expectation was that we "pass it forward" by doing the same for our kids and grandkids.

Growing up, I saw that our wealthiest friends owned real estate. One friend didn't have enough money to pay for school and had a mentor pay his way through pharmacy school. Later, he began buying real estate and became a hugely successful developer of shopping malls. He became my wealthiest friend. Through him, I learned individuals could own skyscrapers. Before he died, he left Ohio State College of Medicine the largest donation it had ever received.

I ended up being a physician and surgeon. I spent 34 years of my life being educated, from homeschooling before kindergarten through surgical residency. I trained at Baylor, at the time known as the most brutal surgical residency in the country. My first rotation at Baylor was with a world-famous heart surgeon. But what got my attention wasn't his fame. It was that he owned thousands of acres in the greater Houston area. He also owned oil and gas wells, a cement factory, and other enterprises. He told me, "Oil and gas is a boom and bust economy. It is far better to own the land and the minerals than the drilling company." In the subsequent years, I saw two boom and bust cycles myself.

Living for the Future

I was single when I got out of residency. Other than splurging on a fire-red Nissan 300 ZX Twin Turbo, all my money went into investments and real estate. I bought everything from raw land and a 300-acre ranch to commercial real estate.

I bought most on mortgages of 10 years or less, some as little as four years. Money was extremely tight. There was no room for hiccups. When I got married in 1994, all my money was tied up in investments. We bought a double-wide and placed it on 82 acres I owned overlooking our town lake. If there was an error in my plans, it was that I always planned 20-30 years into the future, not living for the present.

During those years, we increased our tithe every year. At our peak, we were giving over 50% of my pre-tax income. During that same time, the beginning of HMO insurance, my per-procedure reimbursement was cut by 75%. There was no way I could make up for those losses by working harder or longer.

Things remained extremely tight financially. Most of my investments were growing on paper but were not cash-flowing.

The Fault of Altruism

I wasn't your typical surgeon. I was a skilled surgeon, but I had a captive audience in the operating room of scrub nurses, scrub techs, anesthesiologists, and nurse anesthetists, so I would teach personal development and entrepreneurship. I played hours and hours of tapes of Jim Rohn, Denis Waitley, Zig Ziglar, Brian Tracy, and so many others.

One day, a nurse handed me a book, *Becoming Your Own Banker* by R. Nelson Nash and asked what I thought about the concept. I rapidly read it and dismissed the idea. I scoffed, "It involves whole life insurance, and everyone knows that is the worst place to put your money."

For years, it had been drilled into me: "Buy term and invest the rest. Never, ever buy whole life." I asked the nurse if she wanted her book back, but she said she had no use for it, so I put it on my bookshelf.

I didn't plan on my hips going bad—standing on concrete operating room floors for 10-14 hours a day, plus years of skydiving, snow skiing, running, and biking took their toll. In 2009, I had my first hip replacement. While on the table, my left ulnar nerve, which is responsible for sensation in the fourth and fifth fingers and some motor function, was injured. I was told it would most likely recover in three to four months. It never has.

For a surgeon, lack of sensation and motor function in the hand is not good. My surgery career was OVER.

The Missed Concept

During my recovery, I was a voracious reader. I happened to see R. Nelson Nash's book on my bookshelf and decided to reread it. The second time, it was like being hit over the head with a two-by-four. I thought to myself, *You fool! You missed the entire concept.*

From the picture on the book, I knew Nelson had to be up in years, if even still alive. *Is he still teaching?* I got online, and a God thing happened. Nelson would be lecturing half an hour from where I lived in two weeks. I immediately signed up.

I was blown away by what he was teaching and called my wife from the meeting to tell her she needed to be there. One month later, Nelson was speaking in Waco, Texas. She joined me and was also blown away. We started implementing his concepts in a big way.

The Most Powerful Tool

Nelson and I became friends. For the next 12 years, I read and reread Nelson's book at least two dozen times. Each time, I picked up another kernel of wisdom. During those years, I was able to hear Nelson speak at least 25 times. I also was able to pick his brain.

How infinite banking works and how it saved me financially is for a future book. It is the most powerful concept and tool that I have come across.

In the late 1960s, The Who released the song, "I'm Free." The lyrics are, "If I told you what it takes to reach the highest highs, you'd laugh and say nothing is that simple…" That is the way it is with infinite banking.

Infinite Banking

The concept involves dividend-paying whole life insurance, banking, and taking out personal loans. For a moment, keep an open mind and forget what Dave Ramsey, Gary North, Suzy Orman, and others say about life insurance. We are not talking about your typical whole life insurance policy that is structured for the highest death benefit for the least amount of money.

Nelson came up with the idea of structuring a policy with the largest immediate cash value with the least death benefit. It sounds counter-intuitive, but by doing so, your death benefit will later be much greater than it would in a traditional policy. You do this by adding just enough short-term, term insurance. That term insurance drops off in five to seven years, before it becomes a financial drag on the policy. What many experts don't tell you is that less than one percent of term insurance ever pays and most people drop their policies in their 60s and 70s when it becomes prohibitively expensive. This shortchanges their family's financial needs.

I took this to heart and bought huge policies on myself, my wife, and my children. I was able to put over $200,000 into these policies, but I wasn't obligated to do so. Why would I do so?

Because of the next step—the "banking process." Nelson told me over and over that infinite banking was not a product but a process and a total paradigm shift. It requires imagination, reason, logic, and prophecy.

The System that Created My Family Legacy

Nelson's next big revelation was that everything we purchase in life involves finance. We either borrow money, pay money to someone else, or pay cash, giving up any future interest that money could have earned. Over time, I used Nelson's framework to create wealth for myself and my family by taking over my outstanding debt and paying myself interest instead of creditors.

Nelson further taught, if you ever borrow from a policy, you need to pay it back at the same or greater interest rate an institution would charge or an interest rate you could make on an investment. A portion of that interest would pay the interest the insurance company charges. The remainder would buy additional "paid up" insurance, greatly increasing the velocity of your policy growth.

This was what I did. Over a 10-year period, I used the policies to finance our lifestyle as well as pay down debt. We liquidated most of our properties, including our homestead, and dissolved many of our joint venture agreements.

I still own several million dollars of property. When they sell, a portion of the proceeds will go to paying off policy loans, and the remainder I will use in 1031 exchanges to buy income-producing properties. In this way, there will be over two million dollars available (tax-free) for my retirement, that is still growing tax-free at four to six percent.

I will leave an inheritance of over eight million dollars. Part of that money will go into an insurance trust set up for banking for future generations. The remainder will go to pay off policy loans on my children's policies which I will gift them (tax-free) when they can demonstrate that they understand the infinite banking concept.

As my parents did for me and my siblings, I have created this legacy for my family. There were obstacles, and if it weren't for this amazing wealth storage system, I may not have been this successful. I am compelled to share what I have learned with others who yearn to create their own financial freedom and generational legacy.

EBERHARD'S THOUGHT LEADER LESSONS

Crap Happens! Lessons Learned from a Bitter Divorce

Little did I know, as I was writing my chapter for the book *Bringing Value, Solving Problems, Leaving a Legacy*, my wife was planning her exit strategy from our marriage.

The Lessons Learned:

1. Before divorce is filed, there can be signs that your partner wants out, like a lack of meaningful conversations.
2. If you have a joint bank account, after divorce is filed, have the court freeze it immediately. The court will split the account equitably.
3. If you receive a paycheck by direct deposit, have it deposited into a new personal account.
4. This is huge. Consult your local state attorney. If either spouse fully owns an asset prior to marriage, keep and maintain it as separate property. In many states, even joint ownership states, if you can prove ownership of an asset prior to marriage, it may remain yours even without a prenuptial agreement.

5. In case of an inheritance, receive those assets into a separate personal bank account. If those assets are put into a joint account, even if you can prove where those assets came from, 50% belongs to your spouse.

6. Be careful putting assets you personally own into an LLC for estate planning purposes. Again, consult an attorney. The LLC may not need to be set up 48%/48% general partners and 1%/1% limited partners. Once in an LLC, the judge can force the liquidation of assets at wholesale prices. In my case, the judge forced the sale of over 50 rental properties, farms, and investment properties at wholesale prices.

7. Try to remain on good terms with your children if you have them. They see and hear more than you think. Try not to disparage your ex-spouse. Bitterness will only destroy your own happiness. Money is a thing that can be replaced, but relationships can't. The divorce cost my children financially, too, more than me. However, because of what I learned from Nelson Nash, I kept all the life insurance policies I owned. Thus, my children will still end up with a substantial financial legacy.

Generational Wealth: A Simple Solution That Works

I believe that I have one of the simplest ways to create generational wealth. It goes against all conventional wisdom and teaching. I have to give full credit to my friend and mentor, Nelson Nash, whose brain I got to pick for 12 years. My criteria for creating this system were that it had to require little effort and be simple, reproducible from generation to generation, judgment-proof, and most importantly, tax-free in most circumstances. How is this possible?

I have very large whole life insurance policies on myself and my children. Insurance companies don't care who makes the premium payments, but I do, and so will you. Because I am the owner of the policies, I am able to take out policy loans to pay for college tuition, room and board, medical and dental expenses, vehicles, and anything else. Over the last 14 years, their policies have grown tremendously in death benefit and cash value.

When I think they are mature enough and understand the simple concepts, I can transfer ownership to them as a tax-free event.

For future generations yet to be born, ideally, my children would call their agent on the day of birth and start policies on them. Because, as a grandparent, I have an insurable interest, as does my ex-wife, we would start policies at the same time. Thus, the cycle becomes perpetual.

This can all be done without any fancy trusts or legal documents. Hopefully, someday in the future, some offspring will say, "That Eberhard must have been some cool, smart, interesting dude."

To get into contact with Eberhard Samlowski about how to implement the "Infinite Banking" concept, send an email to ebsamlowski@hotmail.com. His only requirement is that you have read Nelson Nash's book *Becoming Your Own Banker*.

DALE YOUNG

From "Just a Job" to a Divine Calling
My Journey of Eternal Purpose

Dale Young inspires entrepreneurs and business owners to embrace their unique calling. Sometimes called Divine Design, this creates peace, direction, fulfillment, and joy. Through a unique system, he helps them accept and adopt their identity, community, and calling. Dale is an author and speaker. Step Into Your Calling and craft your legacy.

"What is the difference between an inheritance and a legacy?
One word of two characters.
An inheritance is what you leave **TO** someone.
A legacy is what you leave **IN** someone."
– Dale Young, 2023

My Unique Greater Purpose

I graduated college with a degree in computer science in 1975. I worked for cutting-edge IT companies until 1980 when I started working for E-Systems, a government defense contractor. I worked for them for almost 14 years, including 10 years in Australia. During this time, there were large benefits for employees overseas.

In 1992, while in Australia, our office announced that the government was going to start taxing the housing and utilities benefits we had been enjoying. A group of us were sitting around the lunch table griping about this, when out of my mouth came: "This is JUST a job, not a career." At that moment, I realized I wanted something bigger. This was the start of a 30-year journey.

Years later, I had a successful career: vice-president of a startup company that was #10 on *Entrepreneur Magazine's* Hot 100 companies, selling a contract worth a million dollars a year, building the team that delivered that contract for more than 10 years. But I realized that a career wasn't enough. What I really wanted was a calling. A God-given, God-sized, God-inspired, God-energized purpose.

In 2011, I found that calling. Through a series of God-incidences, I discovered Christian Life Coaching, started becoming a life coach, and got my first paying client. I had dreams and plans to eventually make this my full-time career.

The future was bright. My marriage was comfortable. We had chosen to not have children. I had committed my life to Christ in 1998 and since then had been growing, serving, and learning about my faith. And I had a solid career in information technology (IT) on an upward trajectory in salary, responsibility, and leadership.

Little did I know, in 2012, I would enter a downturn that would last a decade.

The First Incident

The long downhill slide began on Sunday, May 20, 2012. I remember a light startle as I became fully awake. I was sitting on the side of the bed, fully dressed for church. The bed was made. It was as if I had sat down to do something and had one of those micro-naps. But I had no memory of what was prior to that. I checked the time, said out loud, "It's time to head to church," stood up, and started calling out for my wife.

Our two-story house was quiet, and I didn't find her on the first floor. I checked the garage, and her car was there, so I assumed she was upstairs and not hearing me. I sent her a text: "Where are you?"

She immediately called. Over the next few minutes, I learned that she'd been with her family in Tennessee for the last week. She was heading to the airport later that day to return home, and I had talked with her less than 30 minutes before to confirm that I was picking her up. I had no memory of any of this, and we were both scared.

She called a neighbor to take me to the emergency room where I was admitted and observed for several hours. After lots of tests, they found… nothing. They labeled it TGA—transient global amnesia—and sent me home.

An incident like that shakes you to the core of your being. Fortunately, I was part of the church, believed that God would take care of us, and still had my passion for helping people grow and live their best lives.

The Descent

Later that year, my wife started talking about moving to Tennessee without me. She wanted a divorce. I was shocked. Despite counseling, the gap between us widened. In 2014, she filed for divorce, but I continued to hope. However, our separations became longer and more frequent.

This stress was compounded by changes in my IT job. The company I worked for had been looking for management that would take them to the next level, which meant that I had a succession of new bosses… at least six over five years. The company was changing directions, and my role was being minimized.

Friday, September 11, 2015, was the day I knew the marriage was over. I invited her on a date to see the movie War Room. I knew it was a Christian movie, but I didn't know that the plot involved a struggling couple who were brought back together through the power of prayer. As the movie unfolded, I was praying that this might be the turning point that would bring us back together.

After the movie, we went to a coffee shop and talked. She broke the news that she was leaving for Tennessee the next day. I was crushed. It took six months to legalize the divorce, but in my mind, that day was the end.

Winston Churchill: "When You're Going Through Hell, KEEP GOING."

Around this time, someone shared a quote with me: "You can get bitter, or you can get better—and the choice is yours." I chose to get better. I leaned into God instead of running away. I didn't understand the road He had me on, but I chose to keep walking.

Two weeks after the divorce was final, out of the blue, my boss asked me to go part-time.

I wish I could say it was an easy road. It wasn't. On my path to building a successful coaching business, there were years of losing money, struggle, and doubt.

After some false starts, in late 2018, I was coached through my CliftonStrengths. Two things stood out. First, was the uniqueness of this Gallup assessment. Each of us has unique fingerprints, and our strength profiles are just as unique. Second was my non-strengths. When I looked at my struggles in building a coaching business and looked at the things where I'm not as strong, there was a perfect correlation. I saw how this process could help others and provide some of the missing pieces for my business, and worked to achieve a certification in this process.

Several business leaders who have since been through this process with me have totally transformed their businesses to give them more freedom, income, and impact. For instance, one business owner, Sam, started her new business after going through the process with me. Five years later, she now has 30+ clients nationwide, and 15+ contractors, and is looking to take her business to the next level.

Restoration

In 2021, I felt like my worst decade was finally over in a big way.

I met someone, Kayla, online. A few days later, we met in person, and through several God-incidences, we knew we were right for each other. I loved her church and her family. She had a passion for helping others in a way that was compatible with mine and yet unique to her. We were married four months later and moved into a new house. Her friendship and support have encouraged me to pursue my dreams and my coaching business. She brought her three kids and four grandkids into my life, and I'm enjoying discovering what it's like to be a parent and grandparent.

In the last three years, a new level of clarity about my calling has developed through multiple God-incidences. God blessed me with a framework (see Personal Development below) that I use to lead people to discover, confirm, and begin to follow their calling in a lot less time than it took me. God opens doors to get the calling message out to the world through stories like this, podcast interviews, and speaking opportunities.

My calling is to inspire calling in many others.

DALE'S THOUGHT LEADER LESSONS

Team Building

I wrote a book in 2020, The Identity Key, an overview of several dozen assessments, how they are similar or different, where they are best used, and more.

For working with teams, the absolute best assessment I've seen is The Working Genius, invented by Patrick Lencioni and the Table Group because:

1. It's 20% personality, 80% productivity.
2. People grasp its simplicity and start to use it in minutes.
3. It's applied to the art of getting things done.
4. It's focused on the lens of joy, fulfillment, and energy.
5. It gives you a language to clarify where you are in the process of work, which avoids misunderstandings.

Spirituality

As Christians, we all have a shared *general identity*: we are children of God, we are redeemed, we have a home in Heaven, we have the Holy Spirit in us, we are new creations, and more. We also have shared *general calling*: the great commandment ("love God and love your neighbor as yourself") and the great commission ("make disciples... teach them to obey").

However, we also have unique assignments — 1 Corinthians 12:18 says that each of us is just a part in the overall body of believers. We each have a *specific identity* that is unique as well as a *specific calling* that we are uniquely equipped and destined to be and do in this world.

Romans 11:29 says that our gifts (specific identity) and calling (specific calling) are irrevocable. This means we have it, and God is not going to take it away. But that doesn't mean most of us find it without work and effort.

When you do find your specific calling and start following it, you'll have more peace, direction, joy, and impact.

Personal Development

Personal development starts with understanding WHO you are—your **identity**. You are unique and special. Understanding your uniqueness is essential: how you're created, what you like, what you can do easily, and what gives you energy.

The second step in personal development is understanding WHERE you hang out, where you spend your time, and who you are spending your time with—your **community**. Humans are relational beings; even the most introverted of us need other people.

The third step is understanding WHY you are here—your **calling**. Your WHY gives your WHAT more impact.

The clarity people get through this identity, community, and calling process has prompted them to change careers, improve relationships, and save marriages. They have more direction in their lives and can stay on the path easily.

Q&A WITH DALE

What is your favorite movie?
By the number of times I saw it in the theater (nine times in the theater and likely a dozen times on video), the original 1977 *Star Wars*.

How do you recharge?
Travel, Christian concerts, or sitting on the side of a body of water and watching a sunset, preferably with an adult beverage.

What are a few of your favorite quotes?
"What would happen if we studied what is right with people instead of focusing on what is wrong with them?" – Don Clifton

"You don't get paid for the hour. You get paid for the value you bring to the hour." – Jim Rohn

"Don't ask yourself what the world needs. Ask yourself, 'What makes me come alive?' Because what the world—a wife, a child—needs is men who have come alive.'" – John Eldredge

"Not finance. Not strategy. Not technology. It is teamwork that remains the ultimate competitive advantage, both because it is so powerful and so rare." – Patrick Lencioni

Have you had any past challenges that turned out to be blessings?
My divorce—it freed me to be an entrepreneur, pursue my dream, and meet the woman I was destined to marry.

What are three books you often recommend?
The Holy Bible
The Prayer Powered Entrepreneur by Kim Avery
The Other Half of Church by Jim Wilder and Michel Henderson
The Six Types of Working Genius by Patrick Lencioni

How do you define success?
At the end of the day, do I feel like God is smiling at me?

To find out more about Dale's Step Into Your Calling program, the results that have been achieved, and whether it might be right for you, send an email to dale@coachdale.com and mention Step Into Your Calling. Website is https://CoachDale.com. Follow Dale on https://LinkedIn.com/in/CoachDale or https://Facebook.com/CoachDaleYoung.

 Scan to take The First Steps to Aligning Your Faith & Business

DAN MCCARTHY

Your Crowning Achievement in the Entertainment Industry

Dan McCarthy, musician, singer-songwriter, actor, and co-CEO of Coronate Productions, has written, played, and promoted music his whole life. He believes the entertainment industry should be a balance of art, talent, and marketing equally distributed to move product. Dan shares his 30 years of experience with promising artists who should not have to die for their genius and influence to be recognized.

Music Training, Early Years

I started taking guitar lessons at age eight and continued for a number of years. In my earliest lessons on the guitar, I started with "Mary Had a Little Lamb," much to my disappointment, as I would have rather been playing Metallica at that time. One day, I brought in a Metallica record to my lesson. My guitar teacher played a track, listened, and then shredded the solo on an old jazz guitar, leaving me speechless. Then he proceeded to tell me that learning the basics was an integral part of becoming unstoppable on guitar. He told me, "If you put your mind to it and practice, you'll be teaching the guitar player in Metallica a thing or two." I never forgot that valuable lesson, and to this day, I'm still amazed, as he was in his 60s at that time.

When I returned to music in my teens, I started vocal training with two separate instructors. This taught me so much about my voice and capabilities I didn't know I had. Singing all different styles helped me to appreciate music in a whole new way. I began experimenting with my voice and all the sounds around me, turning kitchen utensils, birds, trees, work tools, and more into instruments to bring symphonic orchestras I composed in my head into reality.

Bands and Live Experience

My first experience with producing and performing live shows of original music was Programmed Response—a solo project that soon turned into a full-fledged live band. After many successful gigs as well as record label interest, the band split into different projects. These projects would include A Brief Interruption, Jeff Gaynor Band, Shoemania, and Incomplete Denial. A Brief Interruption was a short-lived band as expected, hence the moniker. Shoemania was the next in line and would eventually turn into Incomplete Denial which is currently ongoing but on hold for now.

Then came the Dan Exactly era, which had great success, including playing the 4&20 Festival in Weed, California, run by the great Sylvia Massy. Sylvia Massy is best known for working with the hard rock/heavy metal band Tool and for her association with the super producer Rick Rubin. Dan Exactly was conceived as a pop project under the guise of a steampunk world traveler creating pop music with a machine-like quality. I had the idea for this character but did not have a name for the project. That's when my producer and co-writer at the time, the amazing Mark Radice (of Aerosmith, Barbra Streisand, *Sesame Street*, and a great solo artist under his own name) came up with the idea of Dan Exactly. Apparently, at the time, I used the word exactly enough to become Exactly myself.

It was an honor when Dan Exactly's first single "Two Left Feet" won an award for best new music video. It was presented by soap opera star Michael Damian (of the cover hit "Rock On"), a successful music artist himself, and his brother Larry Weir, a very successful music producer himself.

Learning from a Difficult Reality

With success came disappointments. Dan Exactly would go on to record a full-length record featuring amazing musicians from all over as well as the great Andre Betts (producer of Madonna, Swing Out Sister, Living Colour, and so many more) producing. However, it was too big of an undertaking at the time, and due to a lack of funding to market it properly, I had to put the release on hold indefinitely. After that difficult decision, I took a long break from music to reorganize my thoughts.

Eventually, that led to the creation of something outside of myself to be known as Coronate Productions. During this time, I had the pleasure of flying out to California to be mentored by the great Darren Hardy at his High Performance Forum and Business Master Class (HPF/BMC) twice, the second time as a VIP, as well as enrolling in his Insane Productivity course and so much more. Learning from Darren was awesome as it gave me a clear direction regarding where I needed to go with my business. I am so grateful to him as well as others who helped me to grow to where I am today.

Birth of Coronate

Coronate Productions was formed alongside my partner, co-CEO Nike Raymond, as a roadmap for creatives and artists to learn the business and grow exponentially as independent contractors, not just artists. We help to set up and provide funding for promoters, studios, musicians, and fellow creatives to help in their creative development.

Coronate was born as a way to help artists navigate a direct path to breakthrough. The goal is to knock down as many of the barricades that artists-in-the-making encounter as possible.

Coronate is expecting multiple new projects to hit the marketplace in 2025. As a production company, we are always interested in and looking for upcoming talent in art, music, film, theater, and more who we can help on their journey forward. After all, we are still creatives and artists ourselves and are still breaking through obstacles! Artists shouldn't have to go through it alone. Coronate was created to be a creative's GPS guide along the artistic journey.

DAN'S THOUGHT LEADER LESSONS

The Creative Process

When an artist is discovered, they are noticed for their creativity and craft. Shortly after they are discovered, they are picked apart and told what to change about themselves to become a product. This is very limiting. It limits their vision and takes away from an artist's full potential. Essentially, it's clipping their wings before they can take flight. I believe that taking what's great about the artist and building upon that is the way to go. Let them soar and build their greatness without restricting that greatness.

The Business of Music

So many artists are not equipped to understand the complex nuances of the music and entertainment industry. As an artist, I have experienced this journey firsthand and am still navigating it to this day. Knowledge is so important and is a must for any pursuing this as a career. If you don't know the business, you can be taken advantage of, and without knowledge, the regrets will outweigh the results.

Q&A WITH DAN

What is your favorite movie?

I have always been a fan of avant-garde and experimental films, theater, and music artists who challenge themselves to create something truly unique. Two films that stand out: *Freaks* (1932) by Tod Browning and *Poor Things* (2023) by Yorgos Lanthimos. Both appeal to me because of how the underdogs in the film bond together despite overwhelming odds.

What are your favorite quotes?

Quotes to live by:

- "Work harder on yourself than you do your job." – Jim Rohn
- "Your past does not define you, it prepares you." – Darren Hardy
- "If you don't see us as one, you don't see us at all." – Coronate Productions

Where did you grow up?

I grew up in a small town in Bergen County, New Jersey, called Dumont. After kindergarten, my parents sent me to private Catholic schools outside Dumont, so other than the friends I knew from kindergarten and a few others, I did not know too many people in my town.

From a young age, entertaining was in my blood. My dad was an artist who loved to draw but hid his talent because he never wanted to draw attention to himself. He could sing as well but he would sing only around the house, never for a crowd. My mom on the other hand was always singing. She even had some success singing with her sisters in a girl group when she was younger. Even when I had thoughts of giving up, I looked to them for inspiration.

What is your favorite song or who is your favorite musical artist?

My musical influences range from Frank Zappa to Jimi Hendrix, Marvin Gaye, The Beatles, Prince, Tom Waits, Thelonious Monk, Miles Davis, Wayne Shorter, Herbie Hancock, Handel, Bach, Beethoven, Mozart, and so many more, as they were always ahead of the game with their craft.

Coronate Productions, run by co-CEOs Dan McCarthy and Nike Raymond, is summed up by the mission statement "Your crowning achievement is our crowning achievement." Coronate knows that adding value to others and making them feel valuable is the most important thing they do. Coronate works alongside artists to build a partnership and work towards achieving all of our common goals. For more information about Coronate: danexactly02@gmail.com | nikesonline@gmail.com

CHRISTINA RENDON

Embracing Becoming
The Path to Inner Alignment

Christina Rendon is a therapist, meditation guide, author, and speaker committed to empowering individuals and groups through mindset and personal growth. With extensive experience in holistic wellness, she holds a degree in religious studies and a master's in clinical psychology.

Throughout our lives, a deep calling often arises—a whisper that urges us to seek more, to understand ourselves on deeper levels, to connect with something greater, and ultimately, to grow. This calling awakens a desire to turn inward, to question the patterns we've lived by, to explore the unknown depths of our hearts and minds, and to uncover the potential we have yet to see. For me, this journey began with a simple yet profound intention: to understand myself more fully and to create a life that resonated with my true self.

This inner calling quickly transformed into a yearning for something deeper—a desire for a more meaningful experience of life. I wanted to realign myself with this new intention, to feel truly alive, to engage deeply with every aspect of my being, and to discover purpose in both what I did and how I lived.

My journey has had its ebbs and flows, with challenges that ultimately became opportunities for growth. Looking back, I realize it was the moments that prompted me to ask deeper questions that pushed me to develop emotional insight and a curiosity about how to find true fulfillment in life. Like many of us, I found that we aren't always supported at the depths needed to fully explore our emotions or inner discovery. However, the journey began with an intention and a series of questions about life. During this time, I started exploring self-development tools focused on mindset, energy, and meditation, which helped me navigate uncertainty and connect more deeply with myself. These early experiences became pivotal, laying the foundation for a lifelong journey of healing and personal growth.

As I continued on this path, I felt drawn to explore the many facets of human potential and holistic wellness. I came to realize that at the heart of our experience is our relationship with ourselves, others, and life itself—a dynamic interplay that shapes everything we know and feel. This curiosity led me to UCLA and various training programs, where I immersed myself in an integrative approach, blending psychology, culture, communication, philosophy, meditation, and spirituality. These studies deepened my understanding that our inner worlds profoundly influence the realities we create.

Meditation became a profound love—not just as a practice of stillness, but because of how deeply it benefited me as a transformative tool for healing and guidance. The more I shared these teachings, the more I saw how people longed for connection and growth. Sharing meditation workshops became a passion, leading me to guide others in settings ranging from festivals and business events to retreats. I taught in meditation studios, inside a galactic dome at Burning Man, and in the peaceful surroundings of Guatemala. Each opportunity flowed naturally, reaffirming my belief that when we listen to our inner calling, our path unfolds.

Still, I soon realized I wanted to support people in a deeper way. When others sought my guidance for life's greater challenges, I felt drawn to help them beyond our moments of meditation. I became more interested in helping them move through the deeper layers of their experiences, guiding them past the blocks that held them back, and supporting them in creating lives fully aligned with their true selves.

This shift became even clearer after facing one of the greatest challenges of my life: the sudden loss of my mom. Her passing brought profound changes to many areas of my life, leaving a heartbeat that impacted me deeply. Yet, through this deep loss, I found an unexpected gift. In her transition, I gained a deeper sense of presence and love—something that now influences so much of what I do.

I began to understand that wholeness and healing are possible through every phase, even in the midst of profound grief. Though I still wish she were here, her transition has taught me to live more fully, cherish each moment, and connect with others with as much presence as possible. I've come to see that even in our deepest grief, there can be quiet blessings—a deepening of our ability to love, grow, and appreciate the beauty in life.

Our life experiences can clarify our path. I realized that my work wasn't just about teaching or writing; it was about being fully present in the complexities of life. I wanted to help people navigate their own journeys and guide them back toward their inner light. In essence, my work was about embracing the process of becoming—aligning with my true self and helping others do the same.

This realization led me to focus more specifically on mental wellness by becoming trained as a therapist, with the intention of incorporating my previous work in holistic wellness. I wanted to support individuals, couples, and groups as they worked through emotional, mental, and energetic patterns, helping them move toward their authentic potential. I became deeply committed to assisting people in navigating their unknowns and creating lives that felt meaningful and true to who they are. I believe that life isn't just about the journey but about the becoming, through the intentional co-creation of our lives.

As my journey unfolded, I realized my path was about weaving together everything I had learned, from my studies to real-life experiences. This led me to create meditation content for various platforms and speak at events alongside some of my inspirations. Whether facilitating therapy sessions, leading meditations, or speaking, I blended mindset work, meditation, and therapeutic approaches to support individuals and larger groups in achieving meaningful growth and transformation.

I believe each of us has a beautiful journey waiting to unfold. Mine has been about facing challenges, seeing them as teachers, and building a life rooted in authenticity and connection. I've learned that vulnerability is a powerful path to healing, both for myself and others. As a therapist, my deepest intention is to guide people back to themselves, helping them clear away whatever blocks them from their healed selves and authentic potential.

With each step I've taken, I've learned to recognize my progress and practice self-compassion, which has been vital to my growth and central to my work. Every quiet hour of reflection, every intentional choice, has fueled my transformation.

I hope to share the insights and tools that have guided me and others toward healing. By cultivating self-awareness, gratitude, and holistic health, I believe we align with our true potential and create lives of greater fulfillment. While I feel aligned with my path, I know that I am still in the process of becoming. I remain committed to growth and creating spaces where transformation can thrive. My journey is ongoing, and I am excited to see where it leads, knowing there are always new horizons to discover.

CHRISTINA'S THOUGHT LEADER LESSONS

Embodiment: Living in Alignment with Our True Selves

Embodiment is about fully living in alignment with our true selves, integrating our heart, mind, and body to create a more connected and authentic experience of life. It involves embracing both the joy and the pain, the light and the shadow, and finding strength in our vulnerability. This process isn't about perfection but about honesty—acknowledging where we are and making choices that reflect our deepest values and desires. For me, this means nurturing my mental, spiritual, and physical well-being through practices like mindfulness, meditation, and movement, which help me feel whole and balanced. I've learned that many people struggle because of a disconnection from one or more of these aspects, and by bridging these gaps, we find our path to true wellness.

Living in alignment with our true selves requires tuning into our inner experiences, listening to what our body, mind, and emotions are telling us, and allowing these insights to guide us. The deeper we connect with ourselves, the more clarity, purpose, and intention we bring to our lives. It is a deeply personal and evolving journey, one that invites us to stay open to all our experiences, trusting that each challenge offers an opportunity for growth and greater understanding. When we commit to this path, we cultivate a richer, more meaningful life.

Relationships: Navigating Growth

Relationships have been central to my journey and one of the reasons I became a therapist. I believe that relationships are foundational in our experience of life and shape who we are—whether it's the relationship with ourselves, with others, or with life itself. The strength of these relationships influences our sense of inner alignment, which in turn affects how we show up in our work, creativity, and the things that inspire us.

Relationships can be a source of great joy or immense pain. They can bring about heartbreak, grief, and loss, or they can elevate us through mentorship and connection. I've learned that relationships thrive on integrity, values, and the courage to stay true to ourselves. Not all relationships are meant to be permanent or positive, but every relationship offers an opportunity to learn. Some of my greatest lessons have come from navigating difficult dynamics and learning to trust myself more deeply in the process.

I've realized that healthy relationships are built on mutual respect and a shared commitment to growth. They empower us, help us heal, and support us in becoming more of who we are. Knowing how to cultivate meaningful relationships—those that are nourishing and supportive—can be one of our greatest tools for expansion and personal growth.

Transformation: Trusting and Knowing Ourselves

Transformation is not a one-time event; it's a continuous journey of growth and self-discovery. It involves looking inward, confronting fears, and embracing change with openness and courage. True transformation begins with self-trust—knowing ourselves so deeply that we can navigate life's challenges with clarity and confidence.

Through my journey, I've learned that transformation often comes from moments of discomfort. It's in those moments that we confront our fears and doubts, realizing that they are gateways to growth. Trusting ourselves means believing in our ability to change, to choose what aligns with our true selves, and to navigate life's uncertainties with grace. Transformation is not always easy, but it is a process of letting go, evolving, and stepping into our potential.

Q&A WITH CHRISTINA

What are some favorite places you've traveled to?

While I've loved many places I've traveled to, the place that resonates most deeply with me is Colombia. Being from a mixed background, connecting with the culture of my family has been incredibly transformative in my life.

What hobbies do you enjoy?

I spend a lot of time engaging in practices that nurture my body, mind, and spirit. I enjoy working out, going on nature hikes, meditating, and spending time with friends in beautiful environments. I also enjoy consistently learning and taking classes that expand my understanding of topics I'm passionate about.

What would you tell your 18-year-old self?

I would tell my 18-year-old self to believe in herself above all else. To trust her inner wisdom and not seek validation from outside sources. To pursue her passions wholeheartedly, even in the face of doubt or challenge. And most importantly, to recognize that she is enough, just as she is.

Therapist, meditation guide, author, and speaker Christina Rendon is dedicated to guiding others on their journey toward transformation and helping them create a life that is most aligned for them. Christina combines therapeutic techniques, meditation, and mindset work to support personal growth and healing.
Connect with her at: Christinarendon.com
Instagram: https://www.instagram.com/christinarendon_

EARL ENDRICH

Developing Positive Habits
The Path to Referral Excellence

Earl Endrich is a real estate professional with 20+ years helping buy and sell homes in Pennsylvania, Delaware, and Maryland. Focused on exceptional client experiences and built on referrals, Team Endrich is among the top 1% of Berkshire Hathaway worldwide. Earl loves travel, golf, fitness, his wife, Krista, and their two fur babies, Nalu and Magnus.

Choosing "The Easy Route"

Since I was 18, my mom wanted me to get into real estate. She had built a successful business as an agent while raising me and my siblings as a single mom. After I graduated from high school, I didn't have any real direction. I was going to school part-time, doing construction with my uncle, working at a vitamin shop, and doing bodybuilding competitions. And when I wasn't doing that, I was going out and partying. I had a lot of friends, but in the back of my mind, I thought this might not be the best lifestyle choice for me long-term.

When I was 24, I decided I'd "go the easy route" and get my real estate license. My thought was, *This is going to be easy. My mom has an established business. She'll give me all her leads, and I'll be rich.* I figured I would focus on bodybuilding while I unlocked some doors and collected checks.

Well, I joined my mom at Berkshire Hathaway, and... it wasn't as easy as I thought it would be. I got my license in 2007, and by 2008, the market took a massive turn, and we were in a global financial crisis. Very few people saw this coming and even fewer were prepared. My mom's business went from very successful to almost nothing. She told me she couldn't give me any of her clients. But, if I brought in a deal, she would help me close it.

Looking back, this bad timing was a very valuable opportunity for me. My mom taught me all the old ways of drumming up business, including lots of door-knocking and cold calls. Money was tight, but with her help, I did a good number of transactions in my first 100 days. Anytime I had a deal, Mom would help with the closing and take a bit over half of the commission. I'd just make sure I was in the room watching and learning. My mom taught me not to look at the commission, but to help the client, and then the commission would come as a byproduct of the service I provided.

Transforming with Brian Buffini

In those first hundred days after I got my license, I gained a lot of perspective. While I had some limited success, I also realized I had no idea what I was doing. I didn't really know how to get and keep business, and I really didn't like cold calling—so much so that I seriously thought about leaving the business.

Fortunately, my manager at my office, Gail, was doing a program called 100 Days to Greatness by the Brian Buffini Company, and I started using the program. Gail was a big supporter in my office and a cheerleader for everyone.

With the Buffini program, I started doing better and better. The cold calls became a memory and, instead, my day-to-day became about building relationships.

As a part of the Buffini program, I had to call every person I knew. At first, I fumbled my words all the time. So, I put a little "easy button" at the corner of my desk, and after I'd hung up, I'd just smack that easy button. It was an affirmation: "That was easy!"

Gail would always say, "Do another one!" I got a kick out of her getting a kick out of it. I kept doing it, and I got better.

Soon, I could call each of my friends and chat naturally. Eventually, they'd ask, "How's real estate?"

And I'd say, "Man, we're doing okay. It's a little tough out there, but… actually, do me a favor. If you come across someone looking to buy a house, let me know, man. I'd love to help them."

And they'd say, "Oh, yeah! Of course."

The first day it actually went smoothly, I was like, *Nice, how do I do that again? I've got to do that again!*

From Rotating Credit Cards to Budgeting and Growth

While I was persevering through the challenges of starting a new career in a recession, I was still young, single, and having a lot of fun with my friends. And, I had credit cards. I was spending all the money I was earning.

My rule was to make sure I never carried a credit card balance for more than two months. I would revolve my debt around who I could hold off paying without impacting my credit too much. Sometimes I'd use one card to pay off another.

In 2009, there was a lot of money available for agents who facilitated transactions with first-time home buyers. First-time home buyers were the majority of my clientele, so I did very well. By the end of June, I made the most I had ever made, about $40,000. This was awesome!

The beaches in Delaware were about an hour and a half drive away, and in the summertime, people went down there for the weekends. And, on the weekends, that's where you could find me. I'd get a hotel room, go to a restaurant or club, and buy rounds of drinks for me and my friends. There was this group of five restaurants that offered a rewards card, and if you spent $200, you'd get $20 free. I'd go hang out at happy hour, and have people put their tabs on my card. People thought I was obsessed with this one restaurant and their "really good nachos" because I always wanted to go, but I was obsessed with the "savings."

A mortgage officer in our office started teaching me about personal finances. She told me to put my credit card on ice. I asked her if that was figurative. She said, "No, put your credit card in a container, fill it with water, and then freeze it. If you need to use it, you'll have to thaw it out."

I did that, and it helped. But, by the end of the summer, I had $800 of that $40,000 left in my account. On top of that, my sales were down because I wasn't doing any of my proactive work to bring in business.

That's when, in 2010, I went to a Buffini event and signed up for coaching. At that point, I only had a couple hundred bucks in my account, so hiring a coach was scary.

My coach, Misty, got me in line. She taught me how to put my budget together. Actually, it wasn't a budget; it was a spending plan! Still, it was time to buckle down. For a while, I stopped going out. Misty knew how to talk to me, and I didn't want to disappoint her. That next year, my production went up by 40%!

Building Positive Habits

I stayed with Misty for eight years. It took maybe six of those years (she'd probably say two) for her to break me down a little bit—really it was about me breaking old, bad habits. Then, we started building new habits.

At first, even though I heard about how good meditation was for stress, I was completely against trying it. Eventually, I did try it, but I didn't like it.

Then, I heard someone within the Brian Buffini community say, "That's what I do in the morning." *Well, maybe I'll try again.*

Now, every day, I do about 10 minutes of meditation, maybe more, no matter what. And that habit has created a massive shift in the way I feel.

Then it became about stacking on more good habits. Misty suggested I try to read four books a year. I tried that, then progressed to a book a month.

The biggest habit shift was around events. I'd always just drive to a couple of events a year in Philadelphia to listen to the great content and then drive home. I wouldn't talk to any other Realtors. I thought, *Why would I want to talk to a bunch of Realtors?*

One day, Misty said, "Why don't you drive to this event in Richmond?" I had a small team at the time.

I went, and it was incredibly worthwhile. Now, I'm engulfed in the community. I'm meeting people for breakfast or lunch any day of the week, and from every person I'm learning so many skills and tactics that are completely applicable to what I'm doing.

Then I met my friend Angie who told me about a mastermind. I was skeptical, but three years later, I was flying to meet more Realtors. Another friend got me into Brian Buffini's The Peak Experience, and I became a conference junkie.

In 2022, I was evaluating my business. A lot of our business was coming from client referrals, but I also saw that 20% of new business was coming from agent-to-agent referrals from across the country.

At the time, I had a goal of going to four conferences a year. In 2021, I attended six conferences. Since 20% of my business was a result of attending conferences, for 2023, I decided to double down and go to as many as I could and see what happened.

I went to 13 conferences—almost all the Berkshire and Buffini conventions, then I started going to Tom Ferry and Darren Hardy. And, my referrals more than doubled! This means going to conferences more than pays for itself.

What I really love so much about conferences is the community—the friends you have dinner with after that you learn so much from. Plus, the conferences themselves have great content.

Success

Learning a system that's based on relationships changed me and my business. I just talk to my friend. I let them know I want to do such a good job for them, or whoever they refer to me, because that's the only way I'm going to get business. So, yes, the selfish reason is that I want to stay in business, but the benefit to them is I have to do a great job. I want my client so excited by the end of this transaction, and for them to have such a great experience, that they want to tell two or three of their friends. Learning that, you can do this business with such integrity and still grow.

If I had stayed just with my mom without learning that program, I'd probably be inactive. It was tough trying to get the business, and I pushed through and found out that I had perseverance I didn't even know I had, but that way just wasn't for me. I'm glad I stayed in. I know I had drive, but I was a rebellious child. Which direction would that drive have gone, I don't know for sure.

I ended up growing my business larger than my mom's was at her peak. Once I got to that level, we joined together and built the team. I was actually wanting to build a team to help her retire. As a single mother, she worked so hard. Well, now, she never wants to retire because she loves our team and what she does. She's been able to step back though and take some more time for herself.

Now, we're doing the work to put back into the people on our team. Growing the agents and helping them is something I enjoy. We want to help them grow. My current aspiration is to have a hundred million-dollar-plus team. I also want to be to a point where I don't always have to be here if I don't need to and the business still runs.

I began investing in real estate in 2020, and I want to build passive income so I can scale back at work and spend more time with my family. I love vacations—going somewhere warm with a view of the water, whether it is a lake or an ocean, and spending time with family and friends. We go to the Caribbean Islands, and we're looking forward to one day visiting Europe.

EARL'S THOUGHT LEADER LESSONS

Mentorship

In this industry, since I started, no one wanted to share their success secrets. Even people in our office were standoffish at first. It's no longer like that here. In our office, we share our success strategies. Now, I tell everybody everything.

One of my colleagues asked me why I would always tell people exactly what I did; didn't it worry me? The truth is, it doesn't worry me at all. First of all, even when you tell people what to do, most people aren't going to do it. Second, if they do it, and they get better, I will have to get better to keep up with them. Either way, it's a positive outcome.

You can build an office where everybody is doing very well, then you have to elevate to try to keep up. I feel if you're the smartest in the room, you've got to find a different room.

Q&A WITH EARL

What hobbies do you enjoy?

I'm not really good at golf, but I enjoy playing. I also like to stay in shape, so while I'm not doing body-building anymore, I ride my Peloton every morning.

Earl Endrich's success is built on referrals and delivering exceptional client experiences. Whether you're buying or selling, Earl is ready to guide you every step of the way. Reach out at earl.endrich@foxroach.com or visit https://www.foxroach.com/bio/earlendrich. Follow @earlendrich_realtor for the latest real estate insights.

SEAN G. MURPHY

Dreams on Trial
How to Win Over the Silent Jury Within That Keeps Us Stuck

Sean G. Murphy helps individuals navigate personal growth and self-mastery. Drawing from his experiences, he focuses on the patterns that keep us stuck and how to overcome them. Sean offers practical strategies for transformation, believing that lasting change begins by reshaping the stories we tell ourselves.

I Took Care of Me

It has been a 50-year journey. The moments when I felt I was not in control of the events in my life have been many. I remember at age five when I thought the world had ended because one of my dogs was hit by a car in front of the house. I remember the time I was 14 and my family was shattered with a story of what seemed like tragedy. How was I able to get through these moments? What has helped you or hurt you? We've all struggled—here is how I took care of me.

We are, every one of us, doing our best to live up to the expectations of other people. In psychology, it's called approval addiction. It's that emotion that keeps us stuck, keeps us from advancing, because at some level we really do care what others think.

Have you not asked someone out on a date or not asked someone for help because you were pretty sure they would say NO? We fool ourselves into thinking avoiding fear is being successful—it's not. That's the fear of rejection. I bet you are like me, and you are addicted to doing almost anything to avoid rejection. These are addictions that were wired into us from our childhood. We have become so used to these addictions. We call that a functional addiction.

Wait, it gets even more interesting. Have you ever set a goal and missed the target date or, maybe even worse, told yourself that it's not important anymore? Even more tragic is forgetting about the goal altogether. That is the addiction to sameness.

Have you ever avoided something because of how it was going to make you feel? Knowing full well that if you achieved the request, the ask, the goal, your life could dramatically improve? I would imagine you have to say yes to that! I know I do.

That's why I want to share with you some profound, simple steps you can take to begin to take back control of who you really are.

Mental Habits

The culprit is dopamine! When you hear a sound, see a picture, taste some food, or smell something, especially if it's a habit, how much thought did it take to do that habit? The brain loves patterns, and it's when you break those patterns, which is producing new chemicals in the brain, that you have to decide, on this, the new, or to keep doing the old.

If all our interactions, memories, thoughts are some form of chemical cocktail in the brain, then we should want to know the ingredients for success and the ingredients for failure, right? After all, we have been studying the secrets of success for hundreds of years. We should at least have a basic ingredient list, right? Wrong.

Our cocktail for success is rarely ever created by ourselves. It's been the opinion of others. I call them the jury of our minds!

We have on average 70,000+ (more than seventy thousand) thoughts a day! Science reveals to us that about 90% of those thoughts are repetitive! What's even scarier is that of the ones that we repeat, about 80% of those are NOT in our favor!

That means that the goals you are setting today to overcome, to change, to grow yourself, have to compete with years of previous thoughts and conditions that have made you who you are. Dr. Joe Dispenza says, "Your personal reality makes up your personality."

Are you at a place where you want to change or know you have to change? If it's the latter, then there is some stress, and the brain has a Default Mode Network and it defaults back to old patterns, quickly!

Six Areas for Major Change

Let's look at six key areas you can focus on today to help you make some serious changes. It is time for you to have the leverage you want and need and to silence the jury, those negative voices in your mind that have been keeping you stuck for so long. Take a moment and really dive into these six areas. Doing so can transform your life.

1. **Personal Motivation** – What's keeping your motivation low? Is it stress, a poor relationship, or your job that's not going so well? These challenges can keep you from "getting motivated."
2. **Personal Ability** – You have the ability to change what you need to in order to get started right now. Recognize the thoughts you have when you say, "I'm going to, I have the ability to get started." If you fail to start, it is most likely the jury, those thoughts of past programming stopping you.
3. **Social Motivation** – What groups and activities are keeping you stuck? You know what I'm talking about. What groups could you get out of or into that would help move you toward your goals?
4. **Social Ability** – There are groups that would be of great help for you, be they Facebook groups or all of the social connections available. Find someplace to harness your personal motivation that allows you to be in support or service and move it forward.
5. **Structural Motivation** – This includes current habits you have, what you do, and how you are programmed to deal with your environment. Become aware of how much your reality is dictating how you should feel or act, these are environments you need to review.
6. **Structural Ability** – What about your environment can you improve for your benefit? That means the people you hang out with, the online chat groups you frequent, or the cable news channels you yell at because you get mad at the stories!

SEAN'S THOUGHT LEADER LESSONS

Personal Development

If you are like me, you know you are better. You know you can do more and have more.

I've spent most of my life searching for the reasons 90% or more still struggle month to month or paycheck to paycheck. The simple answer is most people have a shaky foundation.

I get asked often, "How long till I get it, till I have a solid foundation?" and I answer—UNTIL— which is one of the favorite words of Jim Rohn—until you get to your core values, chip away what society has labeled you, rip away any negative programming your parents wired you with, and deal with the childhood traumas that are locked inside, then and ONLY then will you develop into the person you have envisioned. Remember you have been programmed with some pretty amazing qualities as well. We sometimes forget that.

Time Management

Fact: You cannot manage time. You can't add one more second to a year, or take one away. Time management is an illusion. What's not an illusion is getting clear on what you will do with your time, down to the day, hour, and even the minute. So, you can manage time if you are willing to manage your energy.

My life consists of three things:
1. The things I do.
2. The stories I tell myself and that others tell about me.
3. The way those stories make me feel.

If you are like me, you have apps or tools that when you get serious about your success, you pull them out or make a commitment: I'm going to do those things that have worked before, right?

I do my best to remember what Jim Rohn said about becoming successful: Don't start your day till it's down on paper.

Sometimes we let the "to-do" interfere with the "doing" of life and we miss so much. Some even use perfection as a tool for procrastination, avoiding their life altogether.

If you want to manage your time, manage your energy in the time you have so you don't wind up on your deathbed, saying "I wish I did." Die with memories, not dreams.

Mentors

In the world of growth, I've found three kinds of instructors:
1. Teachers – They will give you guidance and opportunities to learn a new skill that is necessary for your growth. We are taught good manners, reading, driving a car, flying a plane, or playing an instrument.
2. Coaches – These are folks you seek out to guide you in how to get better at something you know and want to excel at while compressing the time it takes to do that.
3. Mentors – You can't hire a REAL mentor. First, you must know, they seek you out. Second, their entire role is to help you do things you didn't know you could do!

I didn't become a mentor until I really learned the fine art of dynamic listening—listening to understand what my mentees were saying and what they were not saying and looking to understand where that came from.

If your desire is to be a mentor, you must be aware of the absolute joy you receive from being a witness. You must also be prepared for people to come up short, time and time again, in their efforts. It's not because you didn't give them the best. It's that their identity is not ready for their best!

Learn the most valuable skill of teaching, and you will understand what it means to truly bring value to valuable people. Not everyone can be a mentor, yet everyone can benefit from committing to start the journey.

Leadership

They don't care how smart you think you are!

Nature has a way of taking you back to basics, and I love that. It would be comical for me to walk into the barnyard and announce my credentials to all the livestock, thinking that would have any influence over their decision-making.

You and I are the same way. Do your teachings succeed or fail based on the number of followers you have, books you've written, or stages you've stood on? Not so much. The animals know if you are there to help or hurt, so I live by that adage. People do business with people they know, they like, and they trust!

Q&A WITH SEAN

What is your favorite movie?

Young Frankenstein. From the opening scene, it's a take on life.

Igor: "Dr. Frankenstein?

Frankenstein: "It's pronounced *Fronkonsteen.* You must be Igor."

Igor: "No. It's pronounced I-GOR...."

This goes back to Dale Carnegie: the most beautiful sound to someone is their name, and the biggest topic they love is themselves. Not to mention, it's a gut-busting, laugh-out-loud movie.

How do you recharge?

I became "LambPa." I go and sit with our newest members of the herd, Bunny, Apollo, and Astrid, our baby lambs, who are growing by the minute. I sit and let them remind me of the gift I have to give, love—and lots of scratches and head nuzzles. Those who make it to The Ranch for an event can see what I mean.

What is some of the best advice you've received?

From the father of professional public speaking, Bill Gove: Be responsible to them, NOT for them!

Mark Victor Hansen told me, Give them everything you got. Don't hold back. Because to make it work, they need you!

From Kyle Wilson: Get them on the wheel, find an audience, talk to them, and give them a chance to raise their hands!

From Bob Proctor: Do the thing until you don't have to do the thing!

What do you consider your superpower?

To unravel and undo the trauma someone has experienced in less than 45 minutes, without them needing to tell me anything about the trauma! It's a gift I never take for granted.

What books do you often recommend?

* *Excuse Me, Your Life is Waiting* by Lynn Grabhorn
* *Fearless Living* by Rhonda Britton
* *The Magic of Believing* by Claude M. Bristol

How do you define success?

Did you make enough of a positive impact to be remembered for the life you lived after you are gone? There are two times we die: the day they put us in the ground and the last time our name is mentioned! Live a life of success so others can benefit.

To experience The Ranch, one-on-one or at a live event, connect with Sean G. Murphy. For over 40 years, Sean has been at the forefront of personal accountability coaching and mentoring. His clients include CEOs who want to maximize their mindsets as well as entrepreneurs who want to leverage every drop of talent from their souls. To learn more, visit www.seangmurphy.com.

KELLY CORT

From Transactional to Relational Sales
Investing in Relationships Always Wins

Kelly Cort is a nationwide loan officer and the team leader of The CORT Team, powered by Guild Mortgage — Your Home CORT Advantage. Kelly has been a leader in residential lending solutions since 1999, specializing in matching buyers and investors with competitive rates to achieve their homeownership goals and grow their net worth.

Latchkey

I grew up in Petaluma, California, a sweet little farmer town in Sonoma County wine country.

As the only child of a single mom, I would take the bus to ballet and gymnastics which kept me out of trouble until my mom could pick me up after work. My dad lived close by, but we didn't build a real relationship until I was about 20 years old. I may have been an only child, but I was never lonely—I would always bring my friends together. Every weekend it was a "party at Cort's!"

When I moved to Sacramento for college with my lifelong friends as roommates, I wanted to take it easy and work as a grocery bagger at Lucky Grocery, but when two of my roommates became tellers at a bank, and they had great benefits and decent pay, I followed them, and that decision changed my life.

The Big Box

I worked my way up the corporate ladder. After eight years of promotions and growth, I found myself beating out a great talent pool to manage what was at that time the bank's third-largest depository in the US. My office was in downtown Palo Alto, the heart of Silicon Valley, in the middle of the dot-com boom.

One side effect of the glamor of Silicon Valley was that customers frequently recruited my team away, creating a revolving door of employees. As a manager, I became frustrated.

One night, as we were closing the vault door, my in-house mortgage lender partner said, "You work too hard and too many hours for too little pay, Kelly. You should consider coming into mortgage lending." He was right!

In July 1999, I took the plunge into mortgage lending and never looked back. But, I was still under the thumb of the big bank.

In January 2006, I finally worked up the courage and took a leap of faith in myself. I left the big bank and became an independent mortgage loan officer. I was now an individual contributor, completely responsible for my own production. The market was rip-roaring hot, and homes were flying off the shelves at breakneck speeds. But what I didn't see coming was the largest mortgage and real estate meltdown in recorded history, The Great Recession.

The confidence I had in leaving the big bank turned out to be false confidence. I had believed my value would be appreciated by my past clients and the wonderful real estate professionals in my hometown. I quickly found out that my fundamentals in working a business by referral were weak, and my past client relationships which had helped give me my confidence were not necessarily *my* relationships at all.

Don't get me wrong, my clients liked me and enjoyed working with me, and I felt the same, but they came to me through the big bank, and ultimately, many of them decided to stay with the bank. This was a blow to my ego, but it gave me crystal-clear insight into my lack of focus on relationship building.

In August of 2008, after two and a half years of being beat up by the mortgage meltdown and massive financial duress, I decided that the structure and rigidity of the big bank was the perfect foundation for me to work on my fundamentals of working by referral, building relationships with clients and referral partners by providing an exceptional client experience. This opened a steady stream of mortgage business handed to me by the bank. I called this "low-hanging fruit."

From Transactional Loan Officer to Relational Loan Advisor

Leveraging the "low-hanging fruit" meant reinventing myself and showing up as a true professional and guide, advisor, and friend. I started taking a genuine interest in my client's personal lives and asking lots of questions to deepen our relationships and then offering insights where appropriate.

The Great Recession in 2008 was a rough season. Although market constraints required meeting with approximately 12 applicants before I could successfully serve just one family, this climate was rich with opportunities to grow my servant heart and truly care for these families as they faced economic conditions unparalleled by any other recession. Many of these folks faced short sales and foreclosures, and holding their hands while they were suffering these tremendous losses grew my empathy and compassion deeper than ever before.

I learned that to feel appreciated, people need to be seen, heard, and understood. People want to know three things before doing business with you:

1. Can I trust you?
2. Are you good at what you do?
3. Do you care about me?

"Do you care about me?" was where I had failed in the past. I hadn't shown authentic interest in my clients' lives. They were a loan transaction to me. Now they had become family in need of a roof over their heads and a place to call home. I had learned to serve the person and not just facilitate the transaction.

I also decided to focus on the ever-present market of home buyers versus riding the unpredictable waves of interest rate fluctuations that either created or dried up loan refinance demand. This helped me take control of my loan volume production, take ownership of my success, and change my business to a sustainable source of revenue, creating a robust career.

I began to consistently show up to real estate events in my local community and across the country, building relationships with the best real estate professionals through my coaching affiliation with Buffini & Company. This led to opportunities to serve alongside agents locally and nationwide. Branding myself as the Nationwide Lender of Choice, I became an expert at serving clients relocating across the country and also connected real estate professionals together to develop reciprocal relationships and grow their networks inside the Buffini Community. I became known as "The Connector."

In 2022, I took a major leap of faith and went out on my own again. I said goodbye one last time to the big bank and joined a small retail mortgage bank primed for growth when the market once again turned south, seemingly overnight. Mortgage interest rates nearly doubled in a matter of a few months and again, I was faced with a nationwide economic shift in the middle of a company change. But this time was different. This time I had been faithful and constant in developing and investing in relationships for 14 years.

Prior, I believed real estate agents only came to me because I was at the big bank. In fact, being at the bank kept people away from me. Once I left, I could really see the magnetic pull of my relationships inside the Buffini Community. Real estate agents today still say, "I always wanted to work with you, but I couldn't while you were there." The mortgage industry fluctuations caused me to move companies three times within 12 months, yet I kept hearing from my agent partners, "It doesn't matter where you are, I just want to work with you."

Through coaching and training as a client of Buffini & Company and Darren Hardy LLC, I have built a 100% referral-based business fed by top-producing real estate professionals and business leaders across the country with servant hearts and a focus on life-long client relationships.

The Connector

To this day, I love to throw parties, just like when I was a kid. I like to create an environment for like-minded people to mingle, connect, and deepen relationships. Real estate conference schedules run tight leaving little time during breaks to locate people and have a meaningful conversation. To combat this, I make it a habit to host after-event mixers at convenient locations so people can catch up with old friends and develop new relationships.

I like to ask mixer attendees about their biggest pain points or gaps in their business where they need support, then introduce them to another attendee who has mastered this area or a service provider or training program I know can help. Knowing I have offered guidance toward solutions and potentially left an impression on their lives brings me great joy and fulfillment. People often tell me stories about connections made many years ago that have generated millions of dollars of revenue.

Looking Toward the Next Thing

Mortgage lending is helping me build relationships with growth-minded people who are looking to tap into their potential and fully realize their intentions.

Over the years, I have worked with my team and trusted consultants in my industry to perfect a carefully crafted framework for lending industry success. In the future, I plan to expand my team through leveraging this incredibly robust system, which ensures an exceptional client experience from the moment of client introduction to long after they buy their home. This client experience benefits not only homebuyers but also their real estate agents and the agents representing the sellers. This system, the Diamond Standard of Excellence, is so comprehensive that expanding it will allow me to devote my time to coaching, training, and mentoring my team and agents.

Success is knowing I made a difference in someone's life and helped them move closer to their goals, all while supporting my family, being a kind and attentive daughter, partner, and friend, and leading my team to stretch, grow, and learn from each other.

KELLY'S THOUGHT LEADER LESSONS

Marketing

For me, marketing is helping people get the most out of themselves because then they value our exchanges and crave more of them.

When you lead with a servant heart and truly give without the expectation of a return, people will ask how they can give back. Don't blow them off. Get specific and tell them how they can help you. When people ask, they really want to help.

Building a Team

I surround myself with people who have high expectations of themselves and everyone around them—not perfection but excellence as a minimum standard.

But, if something goes wrong on my team, it's my fault. If something went wrong, it's because I, the leader, didn't have a system to catch it. If something went decently, we, the team, did it. If something went really well, the team member did it. Giving credit where credit is due helps the team to have a vested interest and feel appreciated.

People don't leave businesses, they leave leaders. You should always be your team's best option. If you're not appreciating people every day, they will find somebody who does. I'm perfecting this and have a lot of room to grow.

Relationships

Listen for an unspoken need, then deliver.

For example, a friend of mine heard me say "I love doing puzzles," then sent me one. Little things really warm the heart. Even if you don't have money to buy a puzzle, when you see a pretty puzzle, take a picture and text them: "I was just thinking about you. I saw this beautiful puzzle and thought you might enjoy it."

When you provide somebody an opportunity to live out something they're passionate about, you let them know you're thinking about them, and that you *heard* them, *see* them, and *understand* them. This is a foundational building block to deep and lasting relationships.

Q&A WITH KELLY

What is your favorite song or who is your favorite musical artist?

Queen. I love Prince and Elton John as well, but Queen is my favorite. My favorite song is "Don't Stop Me Now" because it removes all limits. That song helped me leave my big corporate job. It inspires an unstoppable force of love and encouragement.

How do you recharge?

I love live music. Without fans, a musician's dreams don't come true. As a fan, I'm part of the reason they can live their dream, and I feel vested in their goals, life, and passion. When I'm there, I feel like the muse. I'm part of the music, part of the experience. It's visceral in every nerve in my body.

Who are your mentors and greatest influences?

Brian Buffini has impacted my life by curating a community of growth-minded individuals making it very easy to find my tribe. These are the people I'm doing life with, my best friends.

Darren Hardy has influenced me to continuously level up. He has helped me refine my systems to create an exceptional experience for my team and my clients.

Everything I do with Darren compounds. As I've applied the principles I'm learning, I've become more attractive to the people in my industry. People see me performing at a higher level, are attracted to that energy, and want to do business with me and learn alongside me.

What is some of the best advice you've received?

From Darren Hardy as a guest speaker at a Buffini & Company conference, "You get in life what you tolerate."

Be careful tolerating behaviors and circumstances because they're not going to change if you continue to tolerate them. This message was the turning point that gave me the fuel and confidence to end my unhealthy relationship with a huge corporation and many self-limiting beliefs that working there created. This has since translated into improvements in every aspect of my life.

What books do you often recommend?

The Noticer by Andy Andrews is my all-time favorite to support a shift in perspective.

The 5 Love Languages by Gary Chapman – Show appreciation and love in a way that speaks to the receiver.

The Compound Effect by Darren Hardy – Helps people understand that a life of extreme success is all about discipline, consistency, and changing one habit at a time.

Kelly Cort has been a servant leader in the nationwide real estate community, specializing in residential and relocation lending solutions, since 1999. She is moved to connect people with resources to live out their most intentional lives.

https://www.linkedin.com/in/kelly-cort-homecortadvantage/

To learn more about joining Kelly's team and the Diamond Standard of Excellence, email kcort@guildmortgage.net

 The Cort Team - Guild Mortgage

SIMON T. BAILEY

Giving Value in Service

Simon T. Bailey is an international keynote speaker, success coach, author of ten books, television host, and philanthropist. His purpose in life is to help you discover your brilliance. In his 30 years of experience, he's worked with over 2,000 companies in 50 different countries and helped countless people find their spark.

Becoming a Speaker

Sophomore year of high school, I met my English teacher, Ms. Rita. She said to me, "Young man, I want you to write a speech and give it before the entire school." She saw something in me that I didn't see in myself, and I am forever grateful. That moment was the seed of my successful, 30-year coaching and speaking career.

I finished high school, and Mom and Dad dropped me off at Morehouse College in Atlanta, Georgia, where Dr. Martin Luther King, Samuel L. Jackson, and Spike Lee attended school. I enrolled as a mass communications major.

At the end of my freshman year, Mom and Dad called and said, "We don't have the money to send you back to Morehouse, nor do we have money to bring you back home, but we do love you."

I dropped out and moved into a drug-infested community in southwest Atlanta. I only had a mattress on the bright green carpet from the '70s and a black and white TV, with a hanger hanging out of the back, set on top of a couple of milk crates turned over. It was one of the lowest points in my life.

I transferred my credits to Georgia State University. I was working during the day and going to school at night. I got a job at the front desk of the Days Inn Hotel making a whopping $5.10 an hour.

Lost as a goose in a blizzard, I was trying to find my way. It would take me about 10 years to finish my undergrad degree. It was during this rough time that I stumbled into reading. One of the books that really impacted me was *Think and Grow Rich* by Napoleon Hill. When I got a hold of that book at 19 years of age, I was like, *Whoa, this is incredible.*

Shortly after, I went and saw Les Brown. I was mesmerized by his craftsmanship, his confidence, his positivity. It became a template. I thought, *Wow, I think I can do that one day.* I ended up joining The National Speakers Association. I was still working, but I was now moonlighting as a speaker.

Then I had a chance to meet Zig Ziglar. Tom Ziglar invited me to have a private lunch. I was mesmerized. I had just started my speaking career, and I said to Zig, "What is it that I should tell people going forward?"

Zig said, "Always remember, if you help enough people get what they want, enough people will help you get what you want." It was a fingerprint on the canvas of my soul.

Disney, Thinking Big, and Finding the Path

Disney started recruiting me in 1994. After a two-year period, 10 interviews, and a 10-page psychological analysis from Gallup, finally, they hired me. I had four different jobs while I was there from 1996 to 2003. One of the cool things I got a chance to do was go over to Disneyland Paris for a few weeks and work with a client out of London.

Leaving Disney sent me in a new direction, where I was meant to be. Meeting Zig and Les and seeing what I could become... sometimes a person gets a snapshot of their future before they walk into it.

Speaking is a tough business. It took me about 18 months to really get it off the ground. I left Disney when the country was going to war with Iraq for the second time. Corporations were laying off personnel by the thousands. And there I was, putting out a shingle saying, *I'm a speaker! I'm a coach!*

I cashed in my entire 401k with significant Disney stock. I had about a three-year runway, and there was no plan B. My wife, the mother of my children, didn't work outside the home. I had Pampers to buy and a mortgage to pay. It was real.

Ten Books in 18 Years

The first book came out in 2003. I went to the National Speakers Association annual meeting, and they said every speaker needs a book. I realized a book is a marketing tool that will reach people you may never meet and go places you may never go.

I needed some help. As a perfectionist, sometimes I can get in my own way.

I would use the articles I was sending out via the newsletter. If I were sending out one article a month, that was 12 chapters that could go in a book. Over two to three years, I had 24 or 36 articles that I could cherry-pick stories, points, and how-to's from. We went on to write 10 books in the next 18 years.

I tried to keep on that schedule, but then it felt forced. I want a relationship with readers.

I'll never forget this. One of my mentors, may he rest in peace, a wonderful human being and phenomenal speaker, Keith Harrell, introduced me to literary agent Jan Miller (Dupree Miller & Associates). At the meeting, Joe Tessitore, a senior VP of HarperCollins, asked, "Do you want to be a bestselling author?"

I said, "No, I want to be an effective author, and if I'm effective, I'll be bestselling." That's what I've stayed true to. I want to be an effective author. I'm not just writing to write it.

Ignite the Power of Women in Your Life

Ignite the Power of Women in Your Life: A Guide for Men was prompted for every person who has gone through divorce and doesn't believe they can bounce back. It's for those who have been drowning in debt. It's for those who have doubts about whether they will ever find love again. And it's for those asking, how do I continue to show up and be relevant in my career in years 40 through 50?

It took me three years to write. And I wasn't going to release it. It was too personal, too vulnerable.

I wrote the book after being married for 25 years. My then-wife had said to me, "You give everybody the best of you, but you give us the rest of you, and I don't want the leftovers anymore."

I had built a house, but I'd lost a home. I was chasing money but had no meaning. I was pursuing power but had no purpose. I wrote from that place of going to therapy and doing the work.

One day, my wife Jodi said, "I really think you should bring this book to the world because it can help people."

Since we released it, corporations have asked us to create an e-course called How Do You Ignite the Power of Women in Business? based on the book. It's created a lot of dialogue, helping men and women think about how we can ignite our potential.

I've heard from women all over the world who said, "I have read the book and could not put it down."

I heard from Dr. Jean Watson, a scholar in caring science at the University of Colorado, Boulder. Of course, I had incorporated some of her scientific research into the book. She said, "I read your book in one sitting. I could not put it down." To hear that from somebody who I have admired is like whoa!

Mentors and Mindset

I wake up every single day to hug people with my words. I intentionally look for ways to connect, not just communicate. When I'm with an audience, they sometimes will feel that they're in a room of one because I talk directly to you. I discovered that a paycheck is given to people who show up, but opportunities are given to people who think and work beyond what they're paid to do. So, we are willing to do what others won't do.

I realized a decade ago, I'm not paid to speak. I'm paid to think.

Then, I discovered that corporations and businesses don't really care about your speech. They want to know if you can listen to their problem, then create solutions that solve their problem. And they want to hear it in a fresh, new way. When I had that epiphany, I was like, *Oh my goodness, that's it. Stop speaking and start connecting. I am not paid to speak. I am paid to think.*

I'm a student. I don't work, I learn every day.

SIMON'S THOUGHT LEADER LESSONS

Leadership and Vision

I believe we're at a critical point in history. David Brooks wrote a piece in *The New York Times* entitled "The Rising Tide of Global Sadness," and at the end, he says that the emotional health of the world is shattering. A 50-year study showed that people are doing worse off now than they were before. That means people are showing up to work hurting and struggling.

I invite leaders to think about what I have coined Velcro leadership. Velcro leadership is first, how do we connect, care, and coach when we connect to the humanity in a person. When we care about that person, we are doubling down on putting purpose before profit, thus becoming more profitable.

The days of command and control are gone. I think CEOs are waking up to leading differently, with a generational perspective. Gen Z is now one-fourth of the workforce, and they need leaders who believe in them and will validate them. Millennials want strategic thinkers who will mentor them. Gen Xers know where the bodies are buried and where the landmines are. They're the latchkey generation and want their leaders to stay out of their way. Boomers who are in the workforce specifically want to be respected for their time in and knowing how to get things done.

And, many leaders are waking up to the power of vulnerability. They understand they don't have to be Superman or Superwoman. They can be honest about their challenges. That vulnerability allows people a window into their journey.

Culture in the Workplace

I did some work for the amazing folks at Chick-fil-A, and what I began to understand about Chick-fil-A is that aside from their religious beliefs, from a business standpoint, what they do is care for humanity. They double down on treating their people well so that their people treat their customers well.

So, here's the framework. Leaders create the experience for employees. Employees create the experience for customers. Customers drive revenue. Reverse-engineered: Revenue comes from employees who took care of their customers who have been engaged by an employee who works for a leader who has created a subculture that people have bought into. What's in that subculture? Trust, emotional honesty, consistency, and feedback. Those are the things that build culture.

Culture doesn't happen overnight. It happens over time and when no one is looking. Culture is the thing that people do because their character has been developed in such a way that they want to do right by the organization. When leaders transfer psychological ownership to those individuals closest to the customer, those team members feel like they own the company. That's the way it's supposed to be.

Resilience at Work, How to Coach Yourself into a Thriving Future

I wrote a book for individuals who in business and life have been knocked off their surfboard and find themself in the ocean. It's their resilience that gets them back on the board, and it's their brilliance that allows them to catch the next wave.

We recently did a national study asking working Americans how they define resilience. We gave them 17 choices, and the top three choices were perseverance, grit, and problem-solving.

When an individual, in business or in life, has this ability to problem-solve, when they find their grit, their resilience, they're getting back on the surfboard. Resilience is not just sticking to it, it's being better. It's bending, not breaking.

Personal Development, Habits, and Daily Rituals

My father would often say, the best hand to feed you is the one at the end of your wrist. So, I recognized no cavalry was coming to help me, I had to develop myself. That required me, on a daily basis, to take my meds. MEDS is meditation, exercise, diet, and sleep every day—especially those days, I don't feel like doing it. Since I started this routine and developed this habit, I have seen my confidence increase. I've lost weight and I have more clarity.

Mike Murdoch said, you don't decide the future, you decide your habits, and your habits decide the future. So, in my personal development, I've developed a habit of reading at least an hour or two in the morning and writing in my journal.

Philanthropy: The Helper's High

I came across research from Emory University that says, when you help someone else, the reward centers in your brain begin to light up almost as if you have been on the receiving end of the help. They call it the helper's high. So I'm trying to get high every day.

Behind the scenes, over the last few years, we've given to a non-profit in our local community that feeds the homeless. There are a lot of people with food insecurity. Recently, they called me to thank me for giving for the last 22 years. I had totally forgotten how many years it had been. Then, they gave me a rock painted by some children who had been at the shelter as a thank you. That was so kind, and I cherish it!

We've also provided scholarships to students around the world. Our dollars can go a long way outside of the United States.

Q&A WITH SIMON

What is your favorite movie?

I love *The Shawshank Redemption*. I've probably seen it a dozen times. And every time I watch, it's as if I'm watching it for the first time. I think it's the story of resilience, perseverance, smarts, and just doing something that's different.

Who is your favorite musical artist?

My wife and I recently went to see Earth, Wind & Fire on tour with Lionel Richie. It was the best ever. Both EWF and Lionel Richie have been performing for over 50 years. In front of 20,000 people, at 74, Lionel Richie was effortless. Philip Bailey and all of EWF were unbelievable. I did some research to find out what has allowed them to last for 50 years, and Philip Bailey said it best: humility, always being a student, and always giving the fans more than what they ask for.

Have you had any past challenges that turned out to be blessings?

My book *Release Your Brilliance* was rejected 13 times by New York and California publishers when I was just starting out almost 20 years ago. That rejection became a blessing because I self-published the book, sold 17,000 copies in 18 months out of my trunk, and then was introduced to Jan Miller and Shannon Marvin who took me to New York and put me in front of five publishers. Within 72 hours, we had three offers for the rights to the book. That's when I learned the power of a literary agent who carries a big stick.

What do you consider your superpower?

I think my superpower is to be present in the moment, synthesize a lot of information, and spit it back out in the simplest, easiest way possible. I can take it in, and I've got it locked in and can explain it like it is.

How do you define success?

Success is understanding that when you give, it's not about you but about everyone connected to you. What you discover is you move from success to significance and that significance is success.

Find speaker, author, and coach Simon T. Bailey on LinkedIn and Instagram. If you haven't yet, make sure to pick up and read a copy of *Shift Your Brilliance*. Visit IgnitethePowerofWomen.com to access a six-week course and a one-year, free, impact plan on how to really operationalize the book in your life. SimonTBailey.com

DAVID KAFKA

From Mistakes to Legacy
A Firefighter's Path to Entrepreneurship and Real Estate Wealth

David Kafka is an honest real estate agent and broker in Belize. He educates people on moving to Belize, buying property, syndications, development, and starting a business in one of the fastest-growing Caribbean countries. David volunteers with animals, the Placencia Village Fire Department, and Better in Belize.

The Wrong Crowd

My German mother was brought to the US by my father who was in the Army. He left her in Columbia, South Carolina, and she became a single mother of two who knew no English.

I grew up poor and started working at 13 with some friends. I wore K-Mart clothes and hand-me-downs. I wanted to have what others had. In high school, I drove a '72 Oldsmobile Delta 88. "Yellow Submarine" I called it. Others had nice BMWs or Ford Mustangs.

Around that time, video games were getting big. I started hanging around with some kids who worked at Walmart like myself, and we stole and sold video games. We made a lot of money doing it. Then we started taking radios, speakers, etc. My part was to hold the stuff in my car. One day, one of the group got caught and turned us all in. Then, the authorities ran a sting and caught us all. All this because I wanted what I couldn't afford and didn't earn it. I was 17.

Volunteer Firefighter

Since it was my first offense for a nonviolent crime, I was given a second chance. I had to tour a prison, was banned from that Wal-Mart, and was made to pay restitution. One of the worst things was telling my mom. She was devastated. Finally, I had something like 250 hours of community service. If I did all of this, my record would be erased like it never happened.

I moved away in June of 1989 to Charleston, South Carolina. By this time, I had graduated high school and went into electrical work. I can't recall why but I chose to do my community service at the Ashley River Fire Department (ARFD).

The chief at the time was Larry Hall, a good friend to this day. Their station was in front of the Charleston division of Bosch, a German company, and my mom had been working there. The guys at ARFD made fun of me for the amount of community service hours I had. It was the record for a long time. I would go in a few times a week and wash the trucks, Chief Hall's car, equipment, the fire hose, and the station, and anything else they needed, I was their guy.

I noticed these guys had a comradery like I had never seen before and they were happy. When my community service time was done, I didn't want it to be over. I wanted to be a part of this group. They had open volunteer and paid positions, and I applied for the volunteer firefighter position. I GOT IT. I am friends to this day with so many of them, and they all mean a lot to me! They helped me train, educated me, and sent me to the three classes you had to go to at the time to be a firefighter. I was having such a great time and the adrenalin from fighting fire was intense and awesome.

From all of this, I learned that if you hang around the wrong people, you will pick up their habits, good or bad. I learned I never wanted to give my mother the headache and heartache of the day I told her I was arrested. I learned what you put into something you will get out. Work hard and never take what is not yours. I knew this growing up in a Christian faith, but it was not in my heart. The best thing in my life was getting caught. That set me on the path to get to where I am now.

I loved the brotherhood and sisterhood I saw at the fire department. I talked to Chief Hall and told him I wanted to do this full-time. He told me what I needed to do and then to apply at one of the fire departments. I chose the Mount Pleasant Fire Department in Mount Pleasant, South Carolina. They had three stations, and I interviewed with the assistant chief at the time, Chief Tetor and the head Chief Pye. Chief Tetor gave me so much opportunity and went on to become chief. He passed away on October 22, 2023. He dedicated his life to the people of Mount Pleasant.

Engineer

For my age at the time, I was making okay money with pension and health benefits. Plus, we had a lot of time off. So, I worked part-time at Ashley River Fire Department (ARFD), too. I couldn't get enough. In my time at ARFD, I had the privilege, with others, of successfully reviving a heart attack patient who happened to be part of the board for the department and received a Lifesaver award that I still have as a treasured memory to this day. I enjoyed the job, the brotherhood, and fighting fire. I liked the adrenaline rush.

I worked hard, took classes, and eventually became an engineer, which is someone who drives the trucks. I was a South Carolina Fire Academy instructor and taught a couple of classes. Then, I went for Lieutenant. Due to seniority and staffing issues, I didn't get the position, but I did get to spend a lot of time as acting lieutenant and then got to go back to fighting fires. I had the best of both worlds. I didn't have the politics of a lieutenant and got to do the job I loved, fighting the fire. Mount Pleasant grew fast from three stations to five.

Freedom

By this time, I wanted to make a little more money, so I stopped working for ARFD part-time and started a lawn cutting service on my days off. I made flyers and did it in the areas around the station where I was based. One job led to another and another. I did a yard, I put fliers at each house along the street. I put the same effort and work ethic into building this business as I did everything else. Eventually, I built a full-service landscape and maintenance company and was working on beautiful houses that were second and third houses to people in resort areas. I built the company to a decent size and eventually sold it and moved to Belize debt-free. I was broke and starting over but debt-free.

In Belize, I started at the bottom and put my work ethic to work. Within three years, I was a top agent in the Caribbean and owner of the franchise. I met my first mentor by going to a conference. Then I was introduced to Darren Hardy and the Darren Daily. I heard about the purple book from Robert Kiyosaki. Not *Rich Dad Poor Dad*—but *Cashflow Quadrant* is what hit me. Then, I met my second and third mentors, and I saw all these people doing great things. I wanted to be a part of it.

I learned that being rich is not about the amount of money in your bank account. It's the freedom you have. I can have whatever I want if I help enough people get what they want. I like to serve, so this hit home for me. I learned that I could make good money selling real estate, but I could become wealthy if I become my own best client. I learned that what you think, you can achieve; I learned about limiting beliefs. I learned the only difference between me and great ones, like Richard Branson, is what I do with my time. We all have the same amount of time in a day. It's how you use your time. I learned about goals, and they WORK! I learned about relationships; I always enter a relationship like it is for life. I learned about inflation and how saving money is no good. I learned about cash flow, gold and silver, crypto, and much more.

I have met some of the wealthiest and most famous people, and they are just like you and me. If they can do it, and if I can do it, you can do it. To my fellow brothers and sisters on the front lines: If you want to do something, believe it, put in the effort, get a mentor and take small step after small step. As they compound, you will achieve your goal. You can build a free life for yourself, a life of choice, one where you give yourself to the job because you want to, not because you have to pay the bills.

I now own three houses in two countries, a mountain lot with a beach view in Nicaragua, and over 155 acres spread throughout every district in Belize. My partners and I own 34 units at the first branded hotel in Ambergris Caye Belize, Mahogany Bay Resort and Beach Club a Curio by Hilton, I own a six-unit beach view resort in Hopkins called Palma D'oro, a 17-unit beach resort in Placencia Belize called Mariposa Beach Resort, 515-acre cacao and hardwood tree farm, and plan to help my investors even more through education and by being a great steward of their funds.

DAVID'S THOUGHT LEADER LESSONS

True Wealth

Can you think of a time when you were doing what you love because you loved it, NOT for the money? When I was in the fire service, I needed the money, but I loved what I did. I wonder how much better it would have been if I'd had passive income that surpassed my bills.

What is freedom? What is wealth? Here is my definition from the school of hard knocks. If I can save several people from making the same mistakes I did on my journey to becoming free and wealthy, then I will keep mentoring and helping frontline workers and anyone who will listen.

Even after I learned my lesson the hard way the first time, I wanted what others had and what I couldn't afford, so I bought it by living above my means and on credit. I wanted to keep up with the Joneses. Was that freedom? Was that wealth? I worked my butt off to pay for all that I had. I sacrificed a marriage. If I had an emergency, I was one step away from bankruptcy. On the outside, I was living awesomely. On the inside, I was struggling to survive.

It was not until I got a mentor and hung around truly free and wealthy people that I learned mindset. It is still a work in progress, but now, if I don't have the cash to buy "it" I don't. I use credit cards, but they get paid off every month.

Now, I work for a different purpose. It's for my family—to leave them with a legacy and to teach my children so they don't make the mistakes I made. It's to give back and teach others. Robert Kiyosaki says that wealth is the amount of TIME you can live comfortably to your standard if you stopped working today. How long could you survive?

My friend Kenny McElroy says you are who you hang around with. What I learned is everyone is too busy to worry about you, so don't worry about keeping up with the Joneses. Surround yourself with people who you can learn from and who uplift you. Make wise investments, live below your means, do what you want to do in life, and enjoy doing it because you can be free.

Q&A WITH DAVID

Who is your favorite sports team?
Dallas Cowboys

Where did you grow up?
Charleston, South Carolina

What are your pet peeves?
All forms of politics and not putting things back where you got them.

How do you recharge?

Being at meetups wears me down but also recharges me, if that makes sense, and being in my boat on a caye, and fishing.

What is your favorite quote?

Staci Gray told me, "If it's not on the calendar it doesn't exist," and now I saw that often.

Who are your mentors and greatest influences?

Robert and Russell with The Real Estate Guys – They opened my world in so many ways and have become good friends and confidants. They opened my mind to investments, macro and microeconomics, and other opportunities outside of the stock market, most importantly, syndication.

Kyle Wilson – His group is some real estate but primarily entrepreneurship and mindset. He is a marketing guru and introduced me to greats like Jim Rohn.

Darren Hardy – I've followed him on Darren Daily and through his classes. He was one of a few who helped me pivot during the COVID-19 shutdowns.

What is some of the best advice you've received?

Your mindset is what will manifest.

What is something most people don't know about you?

I'm a big introvert.

What philanthropic causes do you support?

Autism awareness, Fire Department and Medical in Belize, and humane societies in Belize.

What books do you often recommend?

1) *Cashflow Quadrant* by Robert Kiyosaki
2) *Buy Back Your Time* by Dan Martell
3) *Equity Happens* by Robert Helms and Russell Gray

What do you consider your greatest achievements to date?

First, my children. Second, being a recipient of a Lifesaver Award during my time in the fire department; and, I am proud I have built all I have since 2010 when I was starting over.

Let David Kafka shorten your learning curve by sharing his knowledge and, as his mentors say, giving you education so you can take effective action. Reach out to David Kafka by emailing him at book@caribbeancapitalgroup.com. He is on all social media channels.

 CaribbeanCapitalGroup.com

OLENKA CULLINAN

Starting Is as Important as Success

Olenka Cullinan is CEO of iStartFirst and a C-suite global consultant and business development expert, speaker, and community advocate. Olenka has 15+ years in business scale, operations, business development, and education and has worked with many top businesses—including three of her own—nationwide and globally, helping them execute lean growth plans and two profitable exits.

Permission by Example

She rushed towards me from the back of the room and, eyes filled with tears, gave me the biggest hug, saying, "Thank you! If you can do it, I can do it too! Thank you for giving me permission!"

This was the day I spoke in front of a room of women and the day I met Sara Maria, who has now been a client and a friend for over six years, a woman who has grown, built her business, and continued to change her life.

I have since heard many variations of that exact statement from hundreds of women globally. I call it "the permission to start" because my message to leaders and clients for over a decade has not changed: "Whatever you want to change in the world, your community, or your own life—just start. Because starting is just as important as success!"

Reverse Princess Syndrome

At age 20, after a drawn-out and devastating divorce between my parents, I defied the expectation my mother had for me to take over her CEO position in the factory she built and moved to the US with $450 in my pocket. While I grew up in a fairly well-to-do family, by 16 I went through a "reversed princess syndrome." I was a daddy's girl until I was 12 when my dad started drinking heavily and sold most of our belongings for booze.

I have been passionate about education and growth since I was five. I still remember playing school with my dolls and assigning school roles to all family members. I loved my Grandpa the most, so he was the principal. Professionally, we had no counselors or coaches in my family. We definitely had entrepreneurs.

Watching my mother, a die-hard entrepreneur, go out on a limb every day of her existence taught me that anything could be made possible if one just starts. Since I was little, she would say, "Whatever you will, happens." I always wondered if borrowing $450 from my uncle and moving to another country was willful enough by her standards.

Rise to Wisdom

In the US, I had no support system and no family, so that was really hard. I worked two jobs to put myself through college, spent seven years teaching at the university, community college, and high school levels, and then went on to build my first business—Rising Tycoons. My goal was to impact the maximum number of teens and teach them "success skills" for life. We were not calculating profits. Instead, the goal became the purpose: to put 500 teens through the program, then 1,000. That's how Rising Tycoons became the "startup on steroids," impacting over 9,000 teens and 1,500 educators in three and a half years.

Being a part of the book *Passionistas*, which became an Amazon bestseller, changed things for me. Meeting incredible women from all over the world living out their passion and purpose made me face how much I missed female connection. That's how my #iStartFirst brand was born, —from one hashtag (#istartfirst) to show women that if you want to pursue your passion and purpose—you have to start first. #iStartFirst helps women overcome their fears, expand on their passion, and gain accountability from other women —the "Sparkle Tribe." Coming from humble beginnings, I have lived through nearly every "I-can-never-be-successful-because" excuse a human can make. I lead by example and teach women to stop preparing for the perfect moment and start *doing* instead.

I'm just a woman who believes in people more than they believe in themselves and who isn't afraid to fail. I genuinely believe that every start has failures, which I call lessons. These are a part of the journey. I've had my fair share of lessons in my life: from my parents' dramatic divorce to moving to a new country at the age of 16 without having a clue, almost losing my first business, going through a business bankruptcy with my ex-husband, severely stifling the growth of my first venture Rising Tycoons because of my ego—stating I "got this" instead of seeking mentors and accepting help, and thousands of "NOs" to offset all the "YESs."

I do have a certain fear of failure, but I'm most proud of the impact I get to create in people's lives via my businesses. For me, it's never about the spotlight and always about the impact. I have always said that even if I only change one life forever, I will be happy. I'm the author of two bestselling books, was named one of the top 10 coaches to watch by *Yahoo News*, and have done two TEDx talks to date, but my biggest accomplishment, without a doubt, is the women who have left my iStartFirst Mastermind or coaching and said, "Now, I start first!"

It took me a few years to realize that the best leaders surround themselves with the best teams and mentors to move faster. I also realized that leaders always start or re-start. They treat most experiences in their lives with the humble approach of being new to that experience whether it's a business, hobby, or relationship.

I often had to start first. Having grown up in a patriarchal society and later being surrounded by a male-dominant corporate culture, for a long time, I fed into the dogma that, as a woman, I could not have any balance. I could not possibly be a good mother and have a successful business and personal relationship. To speak about this candidly, I certainly accept my role in my divorce. With a lot of personal self-discovery, I came to realize that I had a subconscious block—a belief that as a woman business owner I could not have time and space in my life for a successful relationship (and what a bunch of old-fashioned, limited beliefs bologna that is!).

We are so hung up on these old beliefs that we forget that balance does not mean that you are always 100% in all areas. Balance adds up to showing up at a total of 100% across the board. So yes, it's perfectly normal to be 60% in your business some days, and only 40% at parenting, as you will have other days where your parenting and relationships will be at 95% and business will only take 5%.

The Power of Borrowed Belief

iStartFirst was born out of necessity. I needed events and coaching programs like the ones I was creating in my life while building and growing up in my business. My mother was one of my big role models. When I was 14, she bought me my first postcard in English, which read, "Always play by your own rules." I still have the card and never stopped following her advice. She believed in me more than I did at the time. This has become one of the biggest trademarks of my coaching success, the phenomenon of "borrowed belief." Many times, while working with my clients, I realize that they don't see my (and their own) visions at first, nor do they have the ability to execute them. This is where I come in with "borrowed belief." I visualize the outcomes with them, I cheer them on, and I create a futuristic vision of winning. After all, you don't have to see it to believe it—you actually DO need to believe it first.

Focusing on what makes life balanced and joyful, I love helping women build life on their own terms. Since 2014, I have been working with female executives as my private clients, along with C-suites of some of the prominent companies globally, learning that all of them lacked one significant belief: you can have a balance of living an extraordinary life and enjoying your success. A high-profile career does not have to come at the price of high-level stress, losing relationships with your kids, and missing connections with your partners. I simply help them to start.

OLENKA'S THOUGHT LEADER LESSONS

Mindset

"Your mind is not your friend!" I remember the face of the monk in an Ashram in India who said this line to me. I was working on meditation—not the 10-minutes-in-bed kind but the grueling, sitting-on-the-mat-for-hours and no-longer-feel-my-extremities kind. I was frustrated, hot, and uncomfortable, and I could not stop my mind's chatter. I remember going to my room that night thinking of how many times in my life I fed into my mind's stories. Of how many times a day we all do that. Stories that are nothing more than projections of our limiting beliefs, past traumas, and made-up attachments. We allow these narratives to dictate everything from how we treat other people to business decisions. Your mind is designed to protect you and pull you back to safety, also known as "the comfort zone." The goal is to stay rooted in reality and not your mind's stories.

Leadership

"Go for no" is not a new concept. Where I like to shift the narrative with my leaders is, the goal is not a "no," the goal is "who do you have to be to change it into a 'yes.'" Whether we like it or not, people judge us before we ever open our mouths. So my mentor always asks me—who do you need to be that day/at that meeting/during that moment for them to say yes? We place so many standards and expectations on other people while we are the ones holding the power of "yes."

Q&A WITH OLENKA

What is some of the best advice you've received?

I recently was given this statement as advice: "I'm not perfect, I'm practiced." I related to it so much. I've put a lot of work into embracing disappointment and failure as a part of my journey. I truly see it as a stepping stone and a part of success. I don't believe in mistakes; I believe in lessons learned. I always try to look at how I can grow from a difficult situation, and that's what keeps me going.

What is something most people don't know about you?

- I used to speak fluent German.
- I'm terrified of insects. (Yup, I don't even like butterflies).
- I'm dyslexic in math, but it doesn't prevent me from working with money!

What do you consider your superpower?

I believe in other people's potential more than they believe in themselves. Almost to a fault. I cheer them on, empathize with them, and empower them to succeed.

How do you define success?

Success is what happiness looks like for you. For some it's being a stay-at-home parent, for others it's travel. For me, it's living a life of impact while building a lifestyle and freedom with people I love.

As an up-and-coming speaker, educator, author, and entrepreneur, I was having difficulty finding a direct path to scaling my business and life early on. It was through my trials and errors that I created a roadmap for other women to equip them with the tools to succeed and start living.

iStartFirst has impacted thousands of female leaders since its inception. From the very first in-person iStartFirst Boot Camp in Phoenix, Arizona, to the weekly virtual calls that span across the globe, #iStartFirst programs have helped women—from Realtors to attorneys, pet services, doctors, clothing lines and stay-at-home moms seeking to rediscover their identity—gain confidence and build purpose around their goals.

In addition to helping women achieve business success, iStartFirst coaching helps women overcome personal and professional insecurities they struggle with and provides the unwavering support of the Sparkle Tribe. #iStartFirst firmly believes women are not meant to do things alone.

Connect with the global executive consultant/coach, speaker, and author Olenka Cullinan for C-suite individual and teams' business coaching or her all-women's business Mastermind and receive Power Hour training FREE — https://istartfirst.com/inner-circle-membership-ph
Follow her for inspiration on Instagram: olenkacullinan and connect at olenka@olenkacullinan.com

 Olenka Cullinan's Live for Livin Women's Mastermind

LISA HAISHA

Actress Turned Philanthropic SoulBlazer

Lisa Haisha is an experienced life coach and founder of The SoulBlazing™ Institute and the non-profit foundation Whispers from Children's Hearts. Lisa teaches women, men, and couples how to "show up" in their lives with her fearless expression as a globally sought-after life counselor, life coach, and mentor.

I Always Wanted to Be an Actress

I moved to Hollywood when I was 22 years old. I'd wanted to be a star since I was 10 when my maternal grandmother shared with me and my four sisters how an intuitive told her that our mom (a Southern belle) would marry a foreigner (which she did), that she'd have five kids, and that one of them would be a star and very rich. I claimed it on the spot and started reading autobiographies about Liz Taylor and Audrey Hepburn. That moment never left me. I just didn't know how that would work. Having an Iraqi father who was very strict, we weren't even allowed to move out of the house until we were married.

My parents ended up divorcing when I was 19 years old, which now gave us more flexibility, but I chose to live with my father, which included his rules. It was tough not being able to go out except for one night a week but doable because of my bigger goal of being an actress in Hollywood. I channeled all my energy into studying the biographies of the great actresses of the day and the past as well as saving money. I was obsessed with the sacrifices the top actresses made to create their dreams.

Meeting Madonna and Travel

One day, a friend told me Madonna was coming to our school, San Diego State University, to perform her first live concert, The Virgin Tour. I was ecstatic. Madonna was my hero. Her father was very strict and Italian, but she'd broken through and expressed herself in a way that was groundbreaking at the time. She was self-actualized while I was still stuck in my cocoon, dying to burst free and fly.

I went to the concert, and afterward, my friend and I found out where the band was staying and decided to go to their hotel. We sat waiting at the bar, and an hour later, the band showed up, but Madonna was not with them. They headed for the elevator. We quickly approached them and told them how much we'd enjoyed the concert, and they invited us up to their room. Score.

We had a great time being in this rare situation. We felt like groupies... really living life. It was a big deal for two small-town girls with no real life experience. At around 10:00 p.m., the party was starting to get a bit wild with more groupies and friends packing the suite. The alcohol started flowing. I was having a good time chatting with Madonna's keyboard player, so we exchanged phone numbers before I left to meet my curfew.

Over the next three months, we kept in touch with late-night calls. He invited me to concerts all over the country, but my father reminded me that I wasn't allowed to spend the night away from home, even though I was 20 years old. Finally, I decided to rebel and meet them in New York for the five-day tour finale. I felt it was my destiny and I couldn't pass it up. I started saving money and then decided (since I may not be able to leave my house again) to add a two-week European vacation to the trip.

When the time came to leave, I left a note for my father explaining that I had to go, and quickly left while he was at work. When I arrived at JFK airport, my "boyfriend" picked me up, and we went straight to a gathering where I got to meet Madonna. It was the moment I had been waiting for. She was rude at first, outright ignoring me, while flirting with my boyfriend, but after a few days, she warmed up.

I was confused by her behavior. We had such similar conservative upbringings, but she was so liberated!

When I got my chance to have a conversation with her, one of my first questions was, "How did you self-actualize into Madonna from being one of seven children in a patriarchal family?" We spoke for about 15 minutes, and here's a paraphrase of what she said:

It's hard when, as a child, you didn't have the freedom to think the way you want or to experience life freely. But the advice I would give you is to travel. And travel alone, so you can make all the decisions yourself, be brave and meet people, and explore ideas and activities with no judgment from your family or friends. We're so brainwashed from birth and indoctrinated into our parents' viewpoint on life. You have to dig deep and learn who you are—what your soul came here to express.

I took her advice seriously, and that's what I did. I went straight to Europe for an exploration of my new ideas. I went with my best friend, which was a good start, creating the travel bug in me. Since then, I've been to over 60 countries, and in 50 or so, I traveled alone or partially alone. Some of my adventures include: meditating in an ashram in Nepal and hiking part of the Himalayas, studying with the Sufis in Cappadocia in Turkey, taking in San Pedro in Peru with Shamans, studying with aborigines in Australia, modeling in Japan, and voyaging to Iraq to meet Saddam Hussein. I immersed myself fully into these experiences that were presented to me, just like Madonna advised me to do.

I was told to trust my intuition and expect miracles because they are everywhere. I was told that everything has already happened and we just need to claim it. I took that to heart. I felt it meant if you want something, ask for it because if it's a strong desire, it is fate. But be careful what you wish for.

Moving to California to Become an Actress

After I returned from my whirlwind vacation, I moved to Los Angeles to become an actress fueled by a memory of my grandma's prediction that I would be a star. I ended up meeting an agent on the train ride up from San Diego. I felt that it was meant to be. She got me work right away. I was booking small jobs and then bigger ones, earning good money. However, I was an ingénue, and everyone wanted me to do nudity or something compromising. I had several #MeToo moments. I was way too conservative for that and had to quit. Not being able to take great roles because of the R ratings and producers wanting favors on the side was depressing.

When I realized acting wasn't for me, I met with the owner of my favorite 24/7 restaurant and the hottest new hangout in Hollywood, Gorky's Café and Russian Brewery, and suggested we start an open mic night called Hollywood Underground. He got on board. They already had the first microbrewery and bands playing each night. The open mic would be from 1:00 a.m. to 4:00 a.m., Thursday through Saturday, when business was slow. Almost immediately, we welcomed stars like Chaka Khan, The Brat Pack, and Iggy Pop, since the restaurant was already a hot spot for celebrities. Watching these stars create material each week to perform and test inspired me to write. So I wrote my first screenplay with the help of a book called *How to Write a Movie in 21 Days* by Viki King.

Getting My First Movie Made

As funds were getting low, I got invited to go to Japan for a three-month modeling gig. I took it and pitched the idea of investing in a Hollywood movie to everyone I met. I ended up raising a million dollars. That led to me producing, writing, directing, and acting in a small part in my independent feature film called *Psycho Sushi*. It wasn't the best film ever made, but the experience was invaluable.

After making the movie, I realized that we do all have a destiny to a certain extent, but achieving our desires is about whether you take the torch and follow through with it, whether you're able to see the miracles presented to you, and whether your mind is free from chatter enough to hear the whispers of your higher Self guiding you toward your dream. You have to be brave and believe in yourself. You don't have to know how you'll get there, but you do need to follow the breadcrumbs.

Discovering My Iraqi Heritage

When the film project was finished, I had a lot of questions about my Iraqi heritage, which I felt had held me back my whole life, especially in decision-making, people-pleasing, and relationships.

My childhood was still affecting my life, as it does for most people. I felt I was still rebelling or conforming, and nothing was from my soul. So, I read self-help books and attended workshops, but it seemed like going to Iraq and learning about my father's culture would be most beneficial—so that's what I did.

The year was 1998. I booked a ticket to Jordan because, at the time, there were no flights into Iraq because of the Gulf War "no-fly zones." I made my connection in New York. At the airport, I met a woman who was also going to Iraq. She was an emigration attorney from Michigan a few years younger than me, and we connected right away. We both were looking for an adventure and to be inspired. We knew we were heading into danger, and it didn't really matter to us what happened.

I asked why she was going, and she said, "I want to die but can't commit suicide because it'll hurt my family."

And I said, "I want to get kidnapped so I can escape and write a tell-all book about the experience." We both laughed. She wasn't really suicidal, and neither was I, but we were unhappy since we weren't tapped into our life's purpose.

Though we were both somewhat successful and high-functioning, we were both broken in other ways, feeling depleted and dead inside. We wanted to see action, to put ourselves in a situation that would wake us up. At heart, we were both funny, alive, and adventurous people, not so much depressed as wanting to feel alive again. We could even laugh at our horrible states of mind, and yet it was serious enough to cause us to set out for Iraq alone—until we found each other.

We landed safely in Amman, Jordan and we were prepared with our fake cubic zirconia to flash to the guards that checked our visas and other paperwork. We heard from the news that from Amman to Baghdad there were five stops where people were often robbed or kidnapped, especially Americans. We wanted to make sure we were the Americans that got kidnapped. Whenever the bus stopped, everyone was quiet, but we made an extra effort to start a conversation with the Generals checking our bags for paraphernalia or anything not allowed. We would say things like, "Oh, let me find my passport and visa. It must be in my Gucci wallet" and we'd allow the cubic zirconia to spill out a bit. We were trying to let them know we had money, and we'd be great candidates to kidnap. But they couldn't be nicer—all five stops. We made it safe and sound to the Rasheed Hotel, where all the journalists and media stayed because it was in the Green Zone in the center of Baghdad. Now we just had to figure out how to meet Saddam Hussein.

My dad and my new friend were both born in Tel Keppe, an Assyrian town in northern Iraq (the same town where Saddam was born). When we visited, all they had were caves connected to each other where people lived, a school, an ice cream truck, a liquor store, a church, and an orphanage.

We went into the orphanage and started talking to the kids. They asked us, "Why does the world hate us? Why doesn't anyone love us? Why do they let us hurt like this?" I fell in love with these kids. I saw myself in them. I had felt the same way. I wanted to give them a voice and memorialize their words.

Then, I visited more orphanages in Jordan and Israel and talked to the children there too.

Whispers from Children's Hearts

Over the next five years, I went to 15 countries to visit orphanages and asked the children the same three questions: Is God fair? If you had one wish, what would it be? Who in the world would you want to meet and why? That ended up becoming a book, *Whispers from Children's Hearts*. That book launched my speaking career. I spoke in schools and gatherings across the globe, sharing the words of the unheard children.

I continued traveling the world and aiding SOS orphanages, which are in 135 countries. Soon, other people became interested in getting involved. My trips soon turned into a non-profit. I didn't charge money, but rather, everyone who joined had to bring a suitcase of supplies and help. We'd visit orphanages or knock on poor people's homes near the orphanages to ask them what they needed. If they needed a new roof, we'd hire a local roofer, so every penny spent went to the community and the kids.

Adopting and Raising My Daughter

After doing that work for years, I decided to adopt a daughter. It was a magical experience and helped me heal in more ways than I could ever have expected. I got to put my energy into giving to someone else and focus less on me. She was so full of joy and love and made me laugh so much, and still does!

However, I couldn't travel as much now that I had a child, so I transitioned to using my reputation to highlight other people who were doing amazing work on a grassroots level locally in the US. I put on an annual Legacy Gala with over 200 guests, raised $20,000 for their non-profit, and gave them a lot of publicity with over 30 media outlets present.

When I did travel, I brought my daughter to do social work, helping build and repair schools and playing with the kids in various orphanages. We often joined another non-profit Women of Global Change to create magic globally. Watching my daughter make friends with kids in different countries has been incredible. I want to pass the torch to her so she can continue to live her life with an open heart, be aware of the diversity in the world, and not be threatened by other cultures.

This part of my personal journey has helped me let go of my "shoulds" and helped me put the spotlight on others. Now it's more about what I can give back. Once you make that switch, your whole life changes.

The SoulBlazing Process

Today, I teach clients a process I call SoulBlazing. We talk about the seven Impostors who live on the stage of your brain, wreaking havoc in your life, and about your Authentic Soul, who lives on that very same stage. We have to train the Imposters and put a leash on them. Our Authentic Souls know who we are and our mission on this Earth. Once you can understand how your personality is here to assist your soul's journey, magic happens. Once you discover this, you get grounded. Then, through meditation, you can stay focused.

I delve into this on *SoulBlazing with Lisa Haisha*, my Amazon Prime show. I interviewed thought leaders, trailblazers, and Guinness World Record holders. It's about the baby steps they took, how they showed up for themselves, and how other people showed up for them.

Your success is determined by what you believe you can do and whether you step into opportunities. Success is about not having fear of the unknown, not having fear of people, not feeling that you're less than. It doesn't matter where you are in life, it's who you are.

To learn more about having Lisa speak for your organization or about her SoulBlazing method go to Lisahaisha.com | IG: @LisaHaisha

 Lisa Haisha Monthly Immersive Workshop

BRIAN TRACY

You Can Change Your Life

Brian Tracy is the top-selling author of over 70 books, has written and produced more than 300 audio and video learning programs, and has spoken, trained, and traveled in over 107 countries on six continents. Brian speaks four languages and is happily married with four children.

Early Years and Learning to Be an Entrepreneur

I grew up in Edmonton, Canada. It's not the North Pole, but they say you can see it from up there. It's really cold, 35 degrees below zero Fahrenheit in the wintertime.

I began my entrepreneur journey early, at the age of 10. Because of my family situation, I had to earn my own money, so I went out and did jobs in the neighborhood to buy my clothes and school supplies.

So, for me, to go out and work, to start something and make it work, is as natural as breathing. I've started and built 22 businesses in different enterprises including hiring, recruiting, training, producing, selling, and marketing.

When I was 32, I saw an ad in the paper for an executive MBA at the University of Alberta. So, I applied, got in, and spent two years and $4,000 to get an MBA.

Getting Paid to Speak

After university, I put together the content for what eventually became *The Psychology of Achievement.* Even from early on, when people went through the course, the feedback was fantastic. People thought it was great, and they began to tell their friends.

The first seminar I gave, I had seven people, and six of them were family members. The seventh was a paid customer for $295. My next seminar was 12 people, and my next was 15 people in Canada. I then hired a guy for three months to sell for me full-time. Business grew and grew. Soon, I was speaking to 100, 200, and then 500 people. And then, people started to invite me to speak to their audiences.

The Power of Our Thoughts

In my seminars, I talk about the superconscious mind and understanding how you can activate the incredible mental power that you already have. You can turn on this switch and start to attract into your life everything that you want: opportunities, ideas, people, resources, and more, simply by using the power that you already have within your brain.

Every single great accomplishment in history has been an accomplishment of superconscious thinking where people have learned how to turn on this switch.

Imagine that you're making an average living and that you live in a nice home. And in your home, there is a garage, but you've never been into the garage. Then, one day, you go into the garage and turn on the light. And to your great surprise, there's this massive supercomputer there that is capable of answering any question you come up with. You just turn on this supercomputer, and suddenly you're producing 5, 10, 20, 50, 100 times more.

Perhaps you say, "I want to be wealthy, successful, and highly respected. Maybe I don't have a university degree, and I don't have any money right now, but I do have my brain and my ability to ***work***. And that's what I'm going to do," If you actually do the work, you set up a force field of energy in the universe that conspires to get you what you want.

Take Action

One idea can change your life—if you take action on it. One of the most important things I teach over and over again is action. Action! It's not enough to have good ideas or the best information. There are a lot of average people who are self-made millionaires. I have a great hour-long program called The 21 Success Secrets of Self-Made Millionaires. I spent two months preparing before recording it. I buried myself in research on self-made millionaires. What I found is that they had characteristics and qualities that made it inevitable that they'd be successful. And if you simply practice the same things they practice, you become the same people they are. And action is one of the main traits of self-made millionaires.

We Make Our Living by Contributing Value to Other People

Today, we have this big thing in politics about inequality. It's not inequality of money. It's inequality of contribution. We make our living in a free country. We make our living by contributing value to other people. Sometimes I ask my audience how many people work on straight commission, and maybe 10% will raise their hands.

I then say, "Well, that's interesting. Maybe I didn't phrase the question properly. Let me ask it again. How many people here work on straight commission?" And then there's a pause, and it's wonderful, the light goes off! Absolutely everybody works on commission.

Everybody works for themselves. And each person creates value. You get a piece of the value that you create. So if you want to earn more money, create more value. Make a greater contribution. Do more.

A great line from Napoleon Hill still brings tears to my eyes decades later: "Always do more than you're paid for. Always go the extra mile. There is never a traffic jam on the extra mile." The one thing nobody can stop you from doing is doing more than you're paid for.

Earl Nightingale said that if you want to earn more than you're earning, contribute more than you're contributing, and an increase in earnings is automatic.

If you're not happy with your income, go to the nearest mirror and negotiate with your boss, because you are your own boss. You make your own contribution. You make your own decision. If you don't like your income, earn more.

Never Complain, Never Explain

The happiest people in the world are those who feel absolutely terrific about themselves, and this is the natural outgrowth of accepting total responsibility for every part of their life. They make a habit of manufacturing their own positive expectations in advance of each event.

Resist the temptation to defend yourself or make excuses.

Develop an attitude of gratitude and give thanks for everything that happens to you, knowing that every step forward is a step toward achieving something bigger and better than your current situation.

BRIAN'S THOUGHT LEADER LESSONS

The Power of Goal Setting

You build your whole life around your goals. There is a wonderful quote from a dear friend of mine, Vic Conant: "Success is goals, and all else is commentary." Wherever I've been able to persuade a person of that, their life changes.

I now have thousands of self-made millionaires and three self-made billionaires who have told me personally, "You made me rich. I was struggling. I was going nowhere. And after I learned about goals, here I am."

I've learned that you can achieve extraordinary things, and you already have, by setting goals. When you set a very clear, specific goal for yourself and write it down, it triggers what is called a psycho-neuro-motor activity, which means that it programs into your subconscious mind and your subconscious mind then conveys it to your superconscious mind. Your superconscious mind is so incredibly powerful. It's amazing how few people understand this. But once it goes into your superconscious mind a whole series of things start to happen.

Get a spiral notebook, write "goals" at the top, and then write down 10 goals in the present tense. When you write them down, you activate this psycho-neuro-motor activity, it programs into your brain, and then it goes to work 24 hours a day to bring you everything you need, exactly when you need it, especially in the form of ideas.

Keep doing it every single day for the rest of your life. Goals will change, the description will change, the order will change, the emphasis will change, but just keep writing down 10 goals and see what happens.

The Magic Wand Technique

Imagine that you have a magic wand and could wave it and achieve any one goal in your life! Which one goal would have the greatest positive effect on your life? Write it down. Imagine what one great thing you would dare to dream if you knew you could not fail and write it down. Then ask yourself, what one skill if you developed and did it over and over again would help you the most to achieve that goal? Write that down. Then, what you do is you think about the goal all the time and work on developing that skill.

The Formula for Success

I have a formula that I used to teach to my coaches and clients. There are only four ways to change your life, and you can apply them to everything you're doing.

1) What do I need to do more of?

In business, that's almost always revenue generation. Lack of revenue generation is the main reason for business failure.

2) What should you be doing less of?

You should be doing less of those things that are of low value or no value. You've got to discipline yourself. Just say no to low-value activities.

3) What should you start doing that you're not doing?

You know what it is, but it's the hardest thing of all because of the comfort zone. Sir Isaac Newton called it the law of inertia. A body at rest tends to remain at rest unless acted upon by an outside force. In other words, for you to be successful, you've got to move. You've got to take action.

4) What do you need to stop doing altogether?

This one is really important, and you identify this by applying the zero-based thinking, which I teach.

Zero-Based Thinking

Every time I do a strategic planning program worldwide, we start off with an exercise called zero-based thinking. In zero-based thinking, wherever you are in life, you draw a line under your life to this date.

Then, you imagine that you're starting over and ask yourself:

- Is there anything that you are doing that, knowing what you now know, you would not start up again today?
- Is there any investment that you have that you would not make again today?
- If you had to do it over, is there any relationship that you would not get into?
- Is there any person that you would not hire?

You keep going through each area of your life, and you keep asking. If the answer is "No, I would not get into this again," then the next question is, "How do I get out?" and then, "How fast can I get out?" Once you've reached the point where you have that intuitive feeling that you would not get into this again, you cannot save it.

I often say to my friends to ask themselves that question: "Is there anything you're doing in your life that, knowing what you now know, you wouldn't get into?"

If the answer is yes, get out and get out now.

Q&A WITH BRIAN

What is your most important value in life?

Your values are the axle around which your whole life turns. People who are successful are very clear about their values, and they don't compromise them. People who are unsuccessful are fuzzy about their values, and they'll compromise them or give them up with the slightest temptation.

My highest value is freedom. Freedom means having enough money to do what you want.

How do you recharge?

I love to read. I also love to travel with my wife Barbara and our family, including the kids and grandkids. I'm past the age of 80, so I'm now asking myself this question: If you were going to die in one year, how would you spend your time and money? I want to spend my time and my money with my family, because that's the most important thing in life. If I'm on my deathbed, the only thing I'll regret is not having spent more time with my family.

What is your superpower?

I am unstoppable. I will never ever quit. And that's the very best quality you can develop. How do you develop the quality of becoming unstoppable? You say "I am unstoppable" to yourself over and over again. Whenever you think that you may fail, that people may disapprove of you, or that you may lose your money or something, you say, "Wait a minute, I'm unstoppable. So, no matter what, I will bounce back. I will never stop. I will keep coming."

How do you define success?

Success is being free to be the very best person you can be and to do the things that you want to do. The reason we want to be financially successful is because that liberates us so we can be and do the things we want to be and do, including going where we want. It's a great thing to have enough money so that you don't have to worry about money.

To learn more about Brian Tracy's book and audio programs, go to BrianTracy.com.

BOOK EDITOR AND WRITING COACH

Takara Sights is the editor of *Lessons From Thought Leaders*. She has been publishing inspirational and motivational books with Kyle Wilson since 2015. As an editor and writing coach, Takara is all about developing clear and impactful language that connects readers with wisdom from new voices. She loves working one-on-one with authors as they develop and share their stories. She currently lives with her wife and dog in Los Angeles, California.

PUBLISHER

Kyle Wilson is the founder of Jim Rohn International and KyleWilson.com. Kyle has filled huge seminar rooms, launched and published multiple personal development publications, and produced/published over 100+ hours of programs. Kyle has published and sold over 1,000,000 books including titles by Jim Rohn and Denis Waitley as well as his own books including *Success Habits of Super Achievers* with Brian Tracy, Les Brown, Darren Hardy, Denis Waitley, Mark Victor Hansen, *Persistence, Pivots and Game Changers*, and *Bringing Value, Solving Problems and Leaving a Legacy*. Kyle is the host of the *Success Habits of Super Achievers* podcast and the Kyle Wilson Inner Circle Mastermind.

Made in the USA
Las Vegas, NV
11 December 2024

13774301R10190